GOLD UNDER THE FURZE

CAOIMHÍN Ó DANACHAIR
KEVIN DANAHER

Gold Under the Furze

Studies in Folk Tradition

PRESENTED TO CAOIMHÍN Ó DANACHAIR

EDITED BY ALAN GAILEY AND DÁITHÍ Ó hÓGÁIN

THE GLENDALE PRESS
17 Brighton Square, Dublin 6.

ISBN 0 907606 06 7

Published by
The Glendale Press
17 Brighton Square, Dublin 6.

Contents

Contributors

Bo Almqvist, Department of Irish Folklore, University College, Dublin.

Anne-Berit Ø . Borchgrevink, Institutt for Folkelivsgransking, Universitetet i Oslo.

James G. Delaney, Department of Irish Folklore, University College, Dublin.

A. Fenton, National Museum of Antiquities of Scotland, Edinburgh.

Alan Gailey, Ulster Folk and Transport Museum, Co. Down.

Edith Hörandner, Institut für Volkskunde der Universität Wien.

T. Jones Hughes, Department of Geography, University College, Dublin.

A.T. Lucas, former Director of the National Museum of Ireland, Dublin.

Patricia Lysaght, Department of Irish Folklore, University College, Dublin.

Bríd Mahon, Department of Irish Folklore, University College, Dublin.

Åsa Nyman, Dialekt och folkminnesarkivet, Uppsala.

Séamas Ó Catháin, Department of Irish Folklore, University College, Dublin.

Anne O'Dowd, National Museum of Ireland, Dublin.

Dáithí Ó hÓgáin, Department of Irish Folklore, University College, Dublin.

Tim O'Neill, Carysfort Training College, Co. Dublin.

Seán C. Ó Súilleabháin, National Museum of Ireland, Dublin.

Trefor M. Owen, Welsh Folk Museum, Cardiff.

Etienne Rynne, Department of Archaeology, University College, Galway.

G.B. Thompson, Ulster Folk and Transport Museum, Co. Down.

Bruce Walker, Jordanstone College of Art, Dundee.

Aistí ar ghnéithe den bhéaloideas in ómós don mhórscoláire Caoimhín Ó Danachair, arna scríobh ag a chairde agus a chomhleacaithe.

Gold under the furze
Silver under the bracken

Acknowledgements

The organising committee wishes to thank all those who gave financial assistance to this publication, especially the following bodies:

Shannon Free Airport Development Company
Irish Sugar Company
Trustees of Muckross House Museum, Killarney
Ulster Folk and Transport Museum
An Cumann le Béaloideas Éireann
Comhairle Bhéaloideas Éireann
Irish Life Assurance Company
An Bord Iascaigh Mhara
Bank of Ireland
Conradh na Gaeilge
An Bord Bainne

We would also like to thank Brendan Doyle and Catherine Tracey, of the National Museum of Ireland, for their help, and we are grateful for the interest and assistance of many others, too numerous to mention individually. Finally, our thanks to The Glendale Press for the time and care they took in publishing this volume.

The authors sincerely thank the following sources for providing material to illustrate their papers: G.B. Thompson — Bunratty Folk Park, Figs. 1 and 3, The Ulster Folk and Transport Museum, Figs. 2 and 4; Trefor M. Owen — National Library of Wales, Fig. 1; Miss M. Wight, Welsh Folk Museum, Fig. 2; Tim O'Neill — National Museum of Ireland, Figs. 2, 3, 4, 9 and 10; Bord Fáilte, Figs. 6 and 7; James G. Delaney — Anne O'Dowd, Figs. 1 to 8; Alan Gailey — Figs. 1 and 2 are based on Andrews, J. H., *A Paper Landscape* (Oxford, 1975); E. Hörandner — Michael Hess, Vienna, Figs. 1 to 4, Elfriede Hanak, Vienna, Fig. 7; S. Ó Súilleabháin — National Museum of Ireland, Fig. 1. The frontispiece is by George Mc Clafferty.

Introduction

It was in the autumn of 1952 as a second-year student in the University of Uppsala that I first met Caoimhín Ó Danachair. I had enrolled for a course in the Irish language and the teacher was Caoimhín, who was also teaching a course in Irish ethnology there at that time. One fact which stands out in my mind may sound somewhat curious, but it does have its own significance and is worth stating here: Caoimhín Ó Danachair was the first Irishman I ever saw.

He was a splendid teacher. His enthusiasm was contagious, and without very much effort a student could become engrossed in the subject he was teaching. Appropriately the class was using the novel *Séadna*, a literary version by Canon Peadar Ó Laoire of the international folktale AT 330. Caoimhín's reading of portions of that work ring in my mind still — who could have hoped for more in a classroom than such colourful syntax being read by a teacher with such colourful style! I also distinctly remember how Caoimhín could lay bare the very soul of the Irish language in his teaching. One point of his stands out especially clearly. Caoimhín used to say, if you want to express the idea 'you will grow old soon enough' in Irish, it would be the equivalent of 'not small will you consider the speed with which old age will come upon you!' I thought that a very good introduction to Irish syntax. But, in fact, the burden of that phrase is not at all appropriate in talking of the man himself. For one of the most striking of all the attributes of Caoimhín Ó Danachair is that very special faculty of his by which time hardly seems to pass at all — at least, not in the negative sense. The boundless energy which has always inspired his students, the kindness and humour with which he invariably wins them to his heart, clearly stem from this sense of youth in the man himself. It is now thirty years since I first met him in Uppsala, and in all that time there has been no diminution in the enthusiasm, no change in the spirit. This has brought immense pleasure and given great encouragement to all his colleagues in the Department of Irish Folklore, not least to myself. One cannot meet Caoimhín — even for a short time — without being struck by the great *joie de vivre*, the *Lebenslust* which emanates from him and inspires all those in his company.

It is quite easy to illustrate this aspect of his personality. The phrase one always hears him saying is 'there are so many things to do!' Others too may use this phrase, but Caoimhín is one of the very few to whom it has a complete meaning. He says it as something that he really appreciates — it is in fact a subconscious and impersonal way of stating the strength of his conviction to the development of folk studies. And he has put that conviction into practice in his own indefatigable way. The list of his published works included in this volume gives some idea of how wide his researches have been, as also does the selection from the photographic archive he has built up over the years. Of major significance also is the contribution he has made — both in Ireland and abroad — to ethnological mapping. Nor should the large number of sound recordings which he made be forgotten. These have preserved for posterity much of that which would otherwise be lost of oral history, narrative style, dialectology, music and song. A good example of this is the material recorded by him on the Isle of Man in the late 'forties from the last surviving native speakers of Manx, thus ensuring that a permanent record exists of this language. All this work, with its variety and specialty, but always with its comprehensive design, reflects in a special way the character of the man from whom it springs. Caoimhín's approach to his material has always been characterised by the quality of inclusiveness. His wide scholarship in differing fields gives rise to a certain universality in approach, but this is accompanied by an insistence that everything is ultimately a unit and should be approached as such. This belief — along with his insistence on the absolute subservience of theory to data — is not one shared by all researchers and scholars, but the fruits of his labours testify that there is much to be said for this holistic method.

Again this quality is reflected in, and is a reflection of, the man himself and his natural qualities. Those who accompany him on field-trips always notice that he doesn't see things, or rather doesn't look at things, in the same way as other people tend to. He has a keen way of surveying material, a penetrating eye which takes in the basic relevance of the data without being partial or selective. In fact, he has the unique ability to perceive everything at a glance. His zest for inclusiveness means that he can see at once the total picture — he picks out of a landscape myriads of things that others wouldn't be aware of at all. This is one of his great gifts, and it underlines all of his scholarly achievements. It gives his published work in particular a certain panoramic sense, which is paradoxically also telescopic in its effect. And this quality of his is expressed in yet another way: in the remarkable manner in which he in his research has stayed with so many of his original interests. It almost seems to be a reflection of the man's own integrity. The way in which he has developed these original interests, deepening them and also extending their limits, is an indication of his intellectual range and tenacity.

It can be said that in many ways vernacular architecture stands at the centre of his scholarship. His fascination with house-types, with describing and mapping them, with probing their effect on the rest of the environment — both physical and cultural — is a constant throughout his career. This again reflects an aspect of his own character — his homeliness and ease in company. It is no exaggeration to say that one could not find a more entertaining man than Caoimhín Ó Danachair. And he is himself a raconteur of the first order. In fact, his whole background is rich in the oral tradition. Caoimhín is a countryman, and that is a very important factor in this context. He is steeped in the visual aspects and lore of his native county Limerick landscape where he started scholarly collecting at a very early age. This strong sense of locale is complimented and brought to fruition by his international outlook on the whole study. The years he spent in Germany and Scandinavia, his lecturing and research tours throughout much of the world, the contacts he keeps up with colleagues everywhere — all this has had a great impact, not just on himself as a scholar, but also on the advances made in ethnological studies in our time. Typically, he sees his field closely from his own experience and also in the long range from the international perspective at one and the same time.

One of Caoimhín's most significant and long-lasting contributions to scholarship can only be measured in the future. This is the establishment of an undergraduate course in folk-life studies in the Department of Irish Folklore here at University College Dublin. From its inception in 1973, he has put his great energy and zeal into the course, and thanks to that, this country now has people trained in all aspects of folk-life research. This is a very important point to stress when introducing this volume, for much of the fruits of the course can be seen here. The members of the committee who planned this book, Patricia Lysaght, George McClafferty, Anne O'Connor, Anne O'Dowd and Bairbre Ní Fhloinn are all students or former students of his. Along with these, many of his old friends and colleagues have joined in a tribute to a man who has now become a father-figure of Irish folk-life studies. The main editors of *Gold under the Furze* are, very aptly, Alan Gailey of the Ulster Folk and Transport Museum, a fellow-worker in the field of Irish ethnology and one of Caoimhín's oldest friends, and Dáithí Ó hÓgáin, his colleague in the Department of Irish Folklore. The former has been responsible for the editing of the material in English, the latter for the material in Irish. The result is this collection of research papers which demonstrate the depth and the variety for which Caoimhín himself has long been acclaimed. It only remains for me to express my thanks to the members of the organising committee and the editors for their devoted work, and to Caoimhín himself for all he has meant and means to our subject, our Department and to me personally. *Go gcúití Dia saothar na n-údar leo, agus go dtuga Sé saol fada folláin do Chaoimhín Ó Danachair agus dá bhean chéile Áine.*

Bo Almqvist
Professor
Department of Irish Folklore
University College Dublin

Caoimhín Ó Danachair and his Published Work

PATRICIA LYSAGHT

For almost fifty years Caoimhín Ó Danachair has been actively engaged in Irish ethnological studies and it is to honour his long and distinguished career in this field of scholarship that this volume of essays is presented to him. The contributors are his former students and colleagues in Irish and European ethnological studies.

Caoimhín's active interest in Irish rural life and its traditions goes back to his student days at University College, Dublin in the nineteen-thirties. During his Christmas holidays in 1934 he was collecting the oral tradition of his native Athea, County Limerick, for the Irish Folklore Institute which immediately preceded the better known Irish Folklore Commission. In this period his inquiry into Irish rural architecture also began. In 1935 while still an undergraduate student of Archaeology at University College Dublin, he accompanied Åke Campbell, the distinguished Swedish ethnologist who was on his second visit to Ireland, on his field trips to Galway and Mayo, at the suggestion of Adolf Mahr, of the National Museum of Ireland. It was this experience in particular which started Caoimhín on the path he has followed throughout most of his professional life.

Having graduated from University College Dublin in 1937, Caoimhín continued his studies in folk life as a Humboldt Scholar at the Universities of Berlin and Leipzig until 1939. In Berlin he was fortunate in being able to study under Professor Adolf Spamer and he regards this period also as having a formative influence on his subsequent career. Unfortunately his studies in Germany were interrupted by the outbreak of World War II, and he has written sensitively of his student days there (*Sinsear* 1979) when whispers of the coming conflict gave way to the rolling tanks of war.

Back in Ireland he joined the staff of the Irish Folklore Commission in 1940. But the war in Europe was again to affect his work. In May of that same year he was called to service with the Irish Defence Forces and until 1945, when he left the army with the rank of captain to resume work with the Commission, he was instructor in the artillery school, Kildare. It was during this period that he also wrote his Master of Arts thesis on Irish house types.

In 1948 he was in the Isle of Man on behalf of the Commission redeeming the promise made a year earlier by the then Taoiseach, Éamonn de Valera to have the speech of some of the last Manx speakers preserved on records. Turning his attention to the Irish scene once again, he travelled extensively in Ireland for the next four years as time permitted. During this short period he made about 280 hours of disc recordings of singers, musicians and storytellers of all kinds.

In 1952-53 Caoimhín was in Sweden as a guest lecturer in Irish language, literature and tradition at the University of Uppsala. While there he also took part in Dag Strömbäck's Scandinavian and comparative folk-life seminars with Åke Campbell and Oskar Loorits.

On his return to Ireland he resumed his research into Irish rural life. He was responsible for many of the questionnaires on various aspects of folk tradition which were circulated by the Commission and the fruits of one such inquiry forms the basis of an essay in this collection (cf. O'Dowd, pp. 165-184). It was at this time too that he began to build a splendid pictorial archive. The legacy from his keen eye and steady hand on the camera is a magnificent assortment of photographs of the visible aspects of tradition. The collection also contains numerous plans, diagrams and sketches of traditional items. It has been much drawn on over the years for exhibitions and book illustrations and we get a glimpse of its variety and importance from the small selection of Caoimhín's photographs included in this volume.

He also continued to bring the fruits of his research to a wide public, through his lectures, his television programmes, his association with bodies concerned with the national heritage and landscape and especially through his writings. By 1971 he had delivered over five hundred lectures on traditional and historical subjects to university seminars, summer schools, learned and local societies and other bodies both in Ireland and elsewhere. His series of five television programmes in January-February 1967 called 'The Hearth and Stool and All' presented an authentic picture of the Irish countryside, its landscape, farms, dwellings and its people about their everyday tasks, as all these would have appeared at the turn of the century. He was for a number of years a member of the National Monuments Advisory Council and he was also a member of An Foras Forbartha's Nature and Amenity, Conservation and Development Committee (1968). He is presently a member of *Comhairle Bhéaloideas Éireann* (The Folklore of Ireland Council). He devised Bunratty Folk Park, County Clare and still nurtures its development. He is also adviser to the Trustees of Muckross House Museum and he has always been interested in the progress and development of the Ulster Folk and Transport Museum at Cultra, County Down.

But it is in his writings that we see the full range of his inquiry into Irish traditional life and in recognition of his pioneering work in this field the Degree of Doctor of Literature was conferred on him by the National University of Ireland in 1974. He was general editor of the 'Irish Life and Culture' series of the Cultural Relations Committee of the Department of Foreign Affairs from 1965 to 1980 and the bibliography of his writings which follows shows his capacity for ranging widely in time and subject matter. His works, both scholarly and popular, are widely known and read at home and abroad. He is master of the clear concise statement and will not accept involved verbosity as evidence of deep thought. He has never allowed the moon to rise upon his own subordinate clauses! He has always demanded meticulous definition and is intolerant of terminology for its own sake. He wrote also with students in mind and this bore him rich dividends when the Irish Folklore Commission was transferred to University College Dublin in 1971 and became the Department of Irish Folklore. Folklore was now an academic discipline in Ireland and this development marked a new phase in

Caoimhín's professional career, a phase for which the knowledge and experience he had accumulated over the years made him admirably suitable. He was appointed Lecturer in Irish Folklore and he revelled in the challenge of teaching.

It is in his role of teacher and as company on the road — informative and entertaining — during field trips that those of us who are privileged to have been his students best remember him. He gave, and still gives, unstintingly of his time and energy to his students, encouraging, cajoling or good-humouredly threatening them as occasion demands! Tolerant of interruptions, he has always been ready to share his vast store of knowledge with his students, colleagues and with members of the public.

Caoimhín Ó Danachair has never been provincial or insular in outlook, always realising that Ireland is part of the north-west European culture zone. He has always been equally ready to deliver a paper in Istanbul or Nova Scotia as in Dublin or in any other part of Ireland. His long involvement with, and present presidency of the Society for Folk life Studies and his membership of the working group of the European Ethnological Atlas are evidence of his broad vision and his contribution to the furthering and development of folk-life studies generally.

It is fitting, therefore, that distinguished scholars from outside Ireland have contributed to this volume. It is also appropriate that the contributions as a whole deal largely with areas of special interest to Caoimhín down the years as we can see from the list of his publications which follows — settlement and dwelling, livelihood and household support, folk custom and belief, social history, folk narrative and research methods.

So, to salute Caoimhín Ó Danachair on his seventieth birthday, January 30, 1983, this volume of essays is presented to him by his students, past and present, his colleagues and friends, with gratitude and affection.

Only Caoimhín Ó Danachair's writings on folk tradition are included in the following bibliography. He was also for eleven years (1960-71) editor of *The Irish Sword*, the Journal of the Military History Society of Ireland of which he is currently President. But it would be inappropriate to include his writings on military historiography, which appear mainly in *The Irish Sword*, in this present volume.

Both his popular and scholarly works are included and they are arranged in chronological sequence. Condensed versions of articles in *The Irish Digest* from *Biatas, Ireland of the Welcomes*, and other journals are not again included here. Every effort has been made to include as many reviews as possible. In preparing this bibliography I have had at my disposal Dr. Ó Danachair's *Bibliography of Irish Ethnology and Folk Tradition* (1978) and as always, his personal assistance with regard to recent and forthcoming publications and in tracking down reveiws. Any omissions or errors which the list may contain are, of course, mine.

1935

'Old Houses at Rathnew, Co. Wicklow', *Béaloideas*, vol. 5, 211-12.

1938

'Old House Types in Oighreacht Uí Chonchubhair', *Journal of the Royal Society of Antiquaries of Ireland*, vol. 68, Part 2, 226-40.

1944

'Some Beliefs and Customs of the 17th Century', *Béaloideas*, vol. 14, 287-8.
Review of *The Welsh House, A Study in Folk Culture* by Iorwerth C. Peate [second (revised) edition, Liverpool, 1944] in *Béaloideas*, vol. 14, 292-4.

1945

'Primitive Structures used as Dwellings', *Journal of the Royal Society of Antiquaries of Ireland*, vol. 75, Part 4, 204-12.
'Folk Museums', *Journal of the Royal Society of Antiquaries of Ireland*, vol. 75, Part 4, 254-6 (with Patrick O'Toole).
'Traces of Buaile in the Galtee Mountains', *Journal of the Royal Society of Antiquaries of Ireland*, vol. 75, Part 5, 248-52.
'The Questionnaire System', *Béaloideas*, vol. 15, 203-17.

1946

'Hearth and Chimney in the Irish House', *Béaloideas*, vol. 16, 91-104.

1946-48

'Traditional Houses of Co. Limerick', *North Munster Antiquarian Journal*, vol. 5, no. 1, 18-32.

1947

'Lough Gur Excavations, site J, Knockadoon', *Journal of the Royal Society of Antiquaries of Ireland*, vol. 77, Part 1, 39-52 (with S.P. Ó Riordáin).
'Folk Tales from Co. Limerick', *Béaloideas*, vol. 17, 201-25.
'Béaloideas — Céad Pictiúirí', *Catalogue of Oireachtas Exhibition in TCD*.

1951

'Irish Folk Narrative on Sound Records', *Laos*, vol. 1, 180-6.

1952

'A Sweathouse in Co. Tyrone', *Journal of the Royal Society of Antiquaries of Ireland*, vol. 82, Part 2, 179-80 (with A.T. Lucas).

1953

'Christmas', *Ireland of the Welcomes*, vol. 2, no. 4, November/December, 18-20.

'Across the Fjaell', *Mungret Annual*, 9-12.

Review of *The Thatched Houses of the Old Highlands* by Colin Sinclair (London, 1953), *Béaloideas*, vol. 22, 198-201.

Review of *Gaelic Folksongs from the Isle of Barra*, recorded by J.L. Campbell, edited and translated by J.L. Campbell, Annie Johnson and John MacLean, and published by the Linguaphone Institute for the Folklore Institute of Scotland, in *Béaloideas*, vol. 22, 201-2.

Review of *Singing Flails: A Study in Threshing-Floor Constructions, Flail-Threshing Traditions and the Magic Guarding of the House* by Albert Sandklef, FFC 136 (Helsinki, 1949) in *Béaloideas*, vol. 22, 202-3.

1954

'Saint Brigid's Crosses', *Ireland of the Welcomes*, vol. 2, no. 5, January/February 1954, 10-11.

1954-55

'Representations of Ploughs on Grave Slabs at Claregalway Priory', *Journal of the Galway Historical and Archaeological Society*, vol. 26, nos. 1-2, 14-18.

1955

'The Holy Wells of Co. Limerick', *Journal of the Royal Society of Antiquaries of Ireland*, vol. 85, Part 2, 193-217.

'The Flail and other Threshing Methods', *Journal of the Cork Historical and Archaeological Society*, vol. 60, no. 191, 6-14.

'A Pot under a Kitchen Floor', *Journal of the Cork Historical and Archaeological Society*, vol. 60, no. 192, 128.

'The Bodhrán, a percussion instrument', *Journal of the Cork Historical and Archaeological Society*, vol. 60, no. 192, 129-30.

'Stand und Aufgaben der Hausforschung in Irland', *Bericht uber die Arbeitstagung des Arbeitskreises für deutsche Hausforschung e.v. in Schleswig vom. 3 bis 6 August.* (Münster), 29-50.

1955-56

'Semi-Underground Habitations', *Journal of the Galway Archaeological and Historical Society*, vol. 26, nos. 2-3, 75-80.

'The Bed-Outshot in Ireland', *Folk-Liv*, vols. 19-20, 26-31.

1956

'Cócaireacht gan Cistin', *Galvia*, vol. 3, 16-18.

'Irish Farmyard Types', *Arctica, Essays presented to Åke Campbell*, (Uppsala), 6-15, (Studia Ethnographica Uppsaliensia, 11).

'Three House Types', *Ulster Folklife*, vol. 2, 22-26.

'The Irish Traditional House', *Papers of the International Congress of European and Western Ethnology, Stockholm 1951* (Stockholm), 95-100.

'Irish Yesterdays', *Cultural Relations Committee Exhibition Catalogue*.

'The Magic Islands', *Ireland of the Welcomes*, vol. 5, no. 1, May/June, 20-3.

'Whitewash and Thatch', *Ireland of the Welcomes*, vol. 5, no. 3, September/October, 26-9.

'Samhain', *Ireland of the Welcomes*, vol. 5, no. 4, November/December, 17-20.

'Holy Wells in Co. Limerick', *Our Catholic Life*, July, 11, 22, October, 26-7.

1957

'Holy Wells in Co. Limerick', *Our Catholic Life*, Easter, 3-4.

'Materials and Methods in Irish Traditional Building', *Journal of the Royal Society of Antiquaries of Ireland*, vol. 87, Part 1, 61-74.

'Some Distribution Patterns in Irish Folk Life', *Béaloideas*, vol. 25, 108-23.

'Hallowe'en', *The Kerryman*, 26 October.

'Lake Monsters', *Ireland of the Welcomes*, vol. 6, no. 4, November/December, 15-18.

1958

'That Yew Tree's Shade', *Ireland of the Welcomes*, vol. 6, no. 5, January/February, 25-8.

'Time and Calendar', *Biatas*, January, 493-6.

'Spanish Ships Wrecked off Sligo Coast', *Sligo Champion*, 15 February.

'February Festivals', *Biatas*, February, 565-8.

'The Month of March', *Biatas*, March, 625-8.

'Et Perrexit . . . Patricius', *Ireland of the Welcomes*, vol. 6, no. 6, March/April, 20-21 (also in *Éire Ireland*, no. 400, 17 March, 6-7).

'April', *Biatas*, April, 45-9.

'May Day', *Biatas*, May, 97-100.

'June', *Biatas*, June, 145-8.

'The Month of July', *Biatas*, July, 217-20.

'August', *Biatas*, August, 277-80.
'The Days of the Week', *Biatas*, September, 365-8.
'The Last Sheaf', *Biatas*, October, 402-5.
'November', *Biatas*, November, 462-4.
'Happy Christmas', *Biatas*, December, 556-8.
'The Holy Wells of North Co. Kerry', *Journal of the Royal Society of Antiquaries of Ireland*, vol. 88, part 2, 153-64.
'Bread', *Ulster Folklife*, Vol. 4, 29-32.

1958-59

'The Holy Wells of Co. Dublin', *Reportorium Novum*, vol. 2, no. 1, 68-87.
'Holy Wells of Co. Dublin, A Supplementary List', *Reportorium Novum*, vol. 2, no. 2, 233-5.

1959

'Thatch and Whitewash', *Biatas*, April, 25-8.
'Fires, Fireplaces and Cooking', *Biatas*, May, 125-9, 137.
'Our Daily Bread', *Biatas*, June, 204-8, 225.
'What did our Ancestors Eat?', *Biatas*, July, 269-72, 300.
'What did they Drink?', *Biatas*, August, 340-3.
'What our Ancestors Wore', *Biatas*, September, 434-40.
'Changing Times in Transport', *Biatas*, October, 498-504.
'Weighing and Measuring', *Biatas*, November, 577-81.
'Hunting the Wren', *Biatas*, December, 667-72.
'Holy Well Legends in Ireland', *Saga och Sed*, 35-43 (= *Folkloristica*, Festskrift till Dag Strömbäck, 15 August, 1960, 35-43).
'A Wayside Incident in Co. Limerick c. 1740', *The Irish Sword*, vol. 4, no. 14, 71.
'The Quarter Days in Irish Tradition', *Arv*, vol. 15, 47-55 (published 1960; also in *Estudios . . . Almeida* 1960, see infra).

1960

'The Quarter Days in Irish Tradition', *Estudios e Ensaios Folkloricos em Homenagen a Renato Almeida*, (Rio de Janeiro), 299-307.
'Toibreacha na Naomh', *Irisleabhar Mhuighe Nuadhat*, 21-6.
'The Holy Wells of Corkaguiney', *Journal of the Royal Society of Antiquaries of Ireland*, vol. 90, Part 1, 67-78.
'Holy Well Legends in Ireland', *Saga och Sed*, 35-43.
'Notes on Irish Dwellings of Traditional Type', *Royal Archaeological Institute of Great Britain and Ireland Programme of Summer Meeting 1960 at Dublin*, 8-10.
'Room to Rhyme', *Biatas*, January, 765-70.
'The Blessed Well', *Biatas*, February, 817-22 (republished in *Munster Express*,

Christmas Supplement, 9 December.)
'Our Names', *Biatas*, March, 921-6.
'Our Surnames', *Biatas*, April, 19-24, 43.
'The Gentle Places', *Biatas*, May, 139-44, 150.
'Treasures', *Ireland of the Welcomes*, vol. 9, no. 1, May/June, 19-22.
'The Summer Pastures', *Biatas*, June, 193-7.
'The Dairy in Days of Old', *Biatas,* July 276-80.
'Wandering People', *Biatas*, August, 351-6.
'Standing Stones', *Biatas*, September, 424-8.
'The Flail', *Biatas*, October, 500-4.
'The Light and Fire', *Biatas*, November, 588-92.
'And Ghost Stories', *Biatas*, December, 653-7.
Review of *Bagpipes* by Anthony Baines, (Oxford, 1960) in *Béaloideas*, vol. 28, 125-6.

1961

'The Penal Laws in Irish Folk Tradition', *Proceedings of the Catholic Historical Committee*, 10-16.
'The Irish Folklore Commission', *The Archivist*, vol. 4, no. 1, 1, 4.
'Spreading the News', *Biatas*, January, 732-6.
'The Wake', *Biatas*, February, 811-15.
'The Plough and Spade', *Biatas*, March, 875-9.
'Travel by Water', *Biatas*, April, 44-8.
'The Water Diviner', *Biatas*, May, 109-12.
'The Forge', *Biatas*, June, 208-12.
'Castles', *Biatas*, July, 258-61.
'The Hedge School', *Biatas*, August, 326-9.
'Inside an Old Irish Kitchen', *Biatas*, September, 394-7.
'Highwaymen — they robbed the rich .. !', *Biatas*, October, 484-7.
'In Memory of the Dead', *Biatas*, November, 534-7.
'There's a long story behind . . . That Christmas Cigar', *Biatas*, December, 606-9.

1962

'The Family in Irish Tradition', *Christus Rex*, vol. 15, no. 3, 185-96.
'History and Folk Tradition', *Irish Hibernia*, 41-5.
'Change in the Irish Landscape', *Ulster Folklife*, vol. 8, 65-71.
'Come all ye gallant Irishmen . . .', *Biatas*, January, 660-3.
'Choose your Weapons', *Biatas*, February, 798-802.
'Proverbs, Every Proverb is a Saying, But . . .', *Biatas*, March, 726-9.
'Haste to the Wedding', *Biatas*, April, 16-19.
'Faction Fights', *Biatas*, May, 92-5.
'Castles', *Ireland of the Welcomes,* vol. 11, no. 1, May/June, 12-15.
'The Funeral Years Ago', *Biatas*, June, 164-7.
'The Terror of the Whiteboys', *Biatas*, July, 224-7.

'One for Sorrow, Two for Joy', *Biatas*, August, 314-7.
'The Foot of the Rainbow', *Biatas*, September, 374-8.
'The Gabled House, A Basic Architecture', *Forgnán*, September/October, 17-21.
'Those Magic Islands and Sunken Cities', *Biatas*, November, 492-6.
'Stand and Deliver', *Ireland of the Welcomes*, vol. 11, no. 4, November/December, 12-15.
'The Last of the Woods', *Biatas*, December, 572-6.
In Ireland Long Ago (Cork), 189 pp. (The series of articles brought together in this book first appeared in *Biatas*, 1959-62).
Review of *Ulster Folklife*, vol. 8, 1962 in *Béaloideas*, vol. 30, 166-7.

1962-63

Review of *Tótamas in Éirinn* by Seán Mac Suibhne, (Baile Átha Cliath, 1961) in *Éigse*, vol. 10, Part 3, 254-5.

1963

'Grosbrittanien und Irland', *JRO Volkskunde* (München), 157-74.
'The Spade in Ireland', *Béaloideas*, vol. 31, 98-114.
'The Long Memories', in Gorman, Michael (ed.), *Ireland by the Irish* (London, 1963), 10-18.
'An Corcán Óir', *Our Games Annual*, 106-8.
'Mountain Dew', *Biatas*, January, 616-19.
'Water Monsters', *Biatas*, February, 684-8.
'Black Cat and Broomstick', *Biatas*, March, 752-5.
'Four Footed Neighbours', *Biatas*, April, 28-32.
'The Butter Stealers', *Biatas*, May, 96-100.
'The Hungry Grass', *Biatas*, June, 164-7.
'. . . Song of the Crickets', *Biatas*, July, 232-6.
'The Night of the Big Wind', *Biatas*, August, 310-15.
'The Ancient Healers', *Biatas*, September, 368-72.
'The Master', *Biatas*, October, 432-6.
'The Cooper', *Biatas*, November, 495-500.
'Currachs', *Biatas*, December, 560-4.

1964

Gentle Places and Simple Things (Cork), 125 pp. (The series of articles brought together in this book first appeared in *Biatas*, 1960-63).
'Chalk Sunday', *North Munster Antiquarian Journal*, vol. 9, no. 3, 123-6.
'The Combined Byre-and-Dwelling in Ireland', *Folk Life*, vol. 2, 58-75.
'Meitheal', *Meitheal*, June.
'Comhar', *Meitheal*, July.
'Our Landscape', *Biatas*, January, 622-6.

'Birds in Irish Tradition', *Ireland of the Welcomes*, vol. 12, no. 5, January/February, 9-12.
'Don't Cross your Bridges . . .', *Biatas*, February, 686-90, 695.
'A Rainbow in the Morning . . .', *Biatas*, March, 732-5.
'The Widow's Curse', *Biatas*, April, 28-32.
'The Tall Ships', *Biatas*, May, 96-100.
'A Short Guide to the Little People', *Ireland of the Welcomes*, vol. 13, no. 1, May/June, 21-5.
'The Thatcher', *Biatas*, June, 151-6.
'The Horseman's Word', *Biatas*, July, 196-200.
'The Tailor', *Biatas*, August, 258-63.
'Silk of the Kine', *Biatas*, September, 337-41.
'The Stone Mason', *Biatas*, October, 410-14.
'Man's Oldest Friend', *Biatas*, November, 478-82.
'The Plague', *Biatas*, December, 540-44.
'The Dog Fair of Newcastle West', *The Monthly Observer*, December.
Guide to Bunratty Folk Park (English and Irish versions).

1965

'Farm and Field Gates', *Ulster Folklife*, vol. 11, 76-9.
'Distribution Patterns in Irish Folk Tradition', *Béaloideas*, vol. 33, 97-113.
'Folk Tradition Questionnaires', *An Múinteoir Náisiúnta*, vol. 10, no. 6, 23-5.
'Company on the Road', *This is Ireland*, (Bord Fáilte), 32, 89, 93.
'The Word of Power', *Biatas*, January, 612-16.
'Traditions of Dublin City', *Ireland of the Welcomes*, vol. 13, no. 5, January/February, 11-14.
'The Byre', *Biatas*, February, 704-8.
'Jack is Alive!', *Biatas*, March, 756-60.
'Games at Wakes', *Biatas*, April, 22-6.
'Country Childhood', *Biatas*, May, 98-102.
'Bunratty Folk Park', *Ireland of the Welcomes*, vol. 14, no. 1, May/June, 27-30.
'The Feet Water', *Biatas*, June, 181-5.
'The Fair Day', *Biatas*, July, 260-4.
'Fences and Gates', *Biatas*, August, 346-50.
'The Labouring Man', *Biatas*, September, 392-6.
'The People of the Sea', *Biatas*, October, 487-91.
'Hunting for Husbands on Hallowe'en', *The Kerryman*, 30 October.
'The Blacksmith', *Biatas*, November, 542-6.
'The Light of Christmas', *Biatas*, December, 614-18.

1966

'Irish Country People' (Cork), 127 pp. (The series of articles brought together in this book first appeared in *Biatas*, 1963-65).
'Faction Fighting in Co. Limerick', *North Munster Antiquarian Journal*, vol. 10, no. 1, 47-55.

'The Irish People', *Éire-Ireland*, vol. 1, no. 4, 6-12.
'The Basket Maker', *Biatas*, January, 697-700.
'The Wee Blue flower', *Biatas*, February, 789-93.
'The Dancing Master', *Biatas*, March, 856-60.
'The Family', *Biatas*, April, 22-4.
'Draw Up a Chair', *Biatas*, May, 78-80.
'The Herb Doctors', *Biatas*, June, 120-22.
'An Corcán Ceolmhar', *Comhar*, Iúil, 22-3.
'The Soup Kitchens', *Biatas*, July, 168-70.
'Gold under the Furze', *Biatas*, August, 216-18.
'The Gamblers', *Biatas*, September, 264-7.
'The Healing Art', *Biatas*, October, 312-14.
'The Luck of the House', *Biatas*, November, 360-2.
'King of All Birds', *Ireland of the Welcomes*, vol. 15, no. 4, November/December, 27-30.
'The Storytellers', *Biatas*, December, 417-19.
Review of *Irish Art in the Early Christian Period to A.D. 800* by Françoise Henry (3rd edition, London, 1965) in *The Sunday Press*, 16 January.

1966-67

'Some Notes on Traditional House Types in County Kildare', *Journal of the Co. Kildare Archaeological Society*, vol. 14, no. 2, 234-46.

1967

'The Bothán Scóir' in Rynne, Etienne (ed.) *North Munster Studies,* Essays in Commemoration of Monsignor Michael Moloney (Limerick), 489-98.
'Irish Folk Custom', *Éire-Ireland*, vol. 2, no. 1, 7-15.
'The Dress of the Irish', *Éire-Ireland*, vol. 2, no. 3, 5-11.
'The Local Tradition', *Clonmel Nationalist* (Commemorative Number), 14 January.
'The Twelve Swans — a traditional Irish Folk Tale', *Biatas*, January, 456-7.
'The Tailor of Rathkeale — a traditional Irish Folk Tale', *Biatas*, February, 494-6.
'Carrol the Carman — an Irish Folk Tale recalled', *Biatas*, March, 547-9.
'The Servant Boy and Farmer — a folktale recalled', *Biatas*, April, 20-22.
'The World Under the Ground', *Biatas*, May, 76-9.
'The Singing Bird — a folktale from Co. Limerick', *Biatas*, June, 106-8.
'The Wise Men of Muing an Chait', *Biatas*, July, 176-7.
'Tuppence and Thruppence — a tale from the Rambling House', *Biatas*, August, 214-15.
'The Story of Máirín Rua', *Biatas*, September, 270-2.
Folktales of the Irish Countryside (Cork), 139 pp. (It includes folktales which appeared in *Biatas*, 1967-8).
Review of *Irish Folk Ways* by E. Estyn Evans (fourth impression, London, 1967), in *The Sunday Press*, 22 October.

1968

'A Timber-framed House from County Meath', *Ulster Folklife*, vol. 14, 24-7.
'Animal Droppings as Fuel', *Folk Life*, vol. 6, 117-20.
'The Poachers', *Biatas*, January, 452-5.
'All the Colours of the Rainbow', *Biatas*, February, 504-7.
'Eachtra Mheargánta — Aonach na Madraí', *Feasta*, Márta, 5-6.
'The Murrain', *Biatas*, April, 21-2.
'Gold under the Furze', *Biatas*, May, 76-9.
'The Griffin, A Folk Tale', *Biatas*, June, 124-7.
'King Whiskers — A Folk Tale', *Biatas*, July, 178-80.
'The Workhouse', *Biatas*, September, 274-6.

1969

'The Gaeltacht', in Ó Cuív, Brian (ed.) *A View of the Irish Language* (Dublin),
   112-21.
'Representations of Houses on some Irish Maps of c. 1600', in Jenkins, Geraint
   (ed.) *Studies in Folk Life*. Essays in honour of Iorwerth C. Peate, (London),
   91-103.
'Thomas Crofton Croker' — Introduction to *Researches in the South of Ireland*
   (Irish University Press facsimile reprint of first edition, London, 1824, Shan-
   non), V-VIII.
'The Dog Fair of Newcastle West', *Ireland of the Welcomes*, vol. 17, no. 5, January/
   February, 15-17.
'Christmas Rhymes', *Ireland of the Welcomes*, vol. 18, no. 4, November/December,
   22-6.
Review of *The Original Australians* by A.A. Abbie, (London 1969), in *The Irish
   Press*, 2 August.

1970

The Pleasant Land of Ireland (Cork), 88 pp. (The text of the Telefís Éireann
   Series 'The Hearth and Stool and All', January-February 1967).
Folktales of the Irish Countryside (illustrated), (New York), 103 pp.
'The Use of the Spade in Ireland' in Gailey, Alan and Fenton, Alexander (eds.)
   The Spade in Northern and Atlantic Europe (Belfast), 49-56.
'Irish Vernacular Architecture in Relation to the Irish Sea' in Moore, Donald
   (ed.) *The Irish Sea Province in Archaeology and History* (Cardiff), 98-107.
'The Flail in Ireland', *Ethnologia Europaea*, vol. 4, 41-55.
'The Irish Language in Co. Clare in the 19th Century', *North Munster Anti-
   quarian Journal*, vol. 13, 40-52.
'The Luck of the House', *Ulster Folklife*, vols. 15-16, 20-7 (*Studies in Folklife
   Presented to Emyr Estyn Evans*).
'Stories and Storytelling', *Automobile Association Handbook of Ireland*, 26-7.
'Pity the Poor Monster', *Ireland of the Welcomes*, vol. 19, no. 2, July/August,
   36-8.

1971-73

'Auxiliary Family Names', *Béaloideas*, vol. 39-41, 228-32.

1972

The Year in Ireland (Cork), 274 pp.

'Traditional Forms of the Dwelling House in Ireland', *Journal of the Royal Society of Antiquaries of Ireland*, vol. 102, Part 1, 77-96.

'Folk Tradition and Literature', *Journal of Irish Literature*, vol. 1, no. 2 (Newark, Del., U.S.A.), 63-76.

'The Death of a Tradition', *Topic*: 24, (Washington), 5-18 (reprinted in *Studies*, Autumn 1974, 219-29.

1973

'St. Brigid's Cross', *Ireland of the Welcomes*, vol. 2, no. 5, January/February, 15-18.

'The Nine Irons' in Escher, Walter, Gantner, Theo and Trümpy, Hans (eds.) *Festschrift für Robert Wildhaber* (Basel), 471-6.

'Dónaill Ó Conaill i mbéalaibh na ndaoine', *Studia Hibernica*, no. 14, 40-66.

Review of *Irish Popular Superstitions* by W.R. Wilde, (Irish University Press facsimile edition of the text of the first edition, Dublin 1853, Shannon, 1972), in *Hibernia*, 11 May.

Review of *West Irish Folk-Tales and Romances*, by William Larminie (Irish University Press facsimile edition of the text of the first edition, London 1893, Shannon, 1972), in *Hibernia*, 11 May.

1974

'The Village Pump', *Ireland of the Welcomes*, vol. 23, no. 1, January/February, 16-19.

Review of *Tyrone Folk Quest* by Michael J. Murphy, (Belfast, 1973) in *Education Times*, October.

1974-76

'Some Marriage Customs and their Regional Distribution', *Béaloideas*, vols. 42-44, 136-75.

1975

Ireland's Vernacular Architecture (Cork), 82 pp.

'Emigration from Co. Clare', *North Munster Antiquarian Journal*, vol. 17, 69-76 (*Féilsgríbhinn Éamoinn Mhic Giolla Iasachta*).

'Le Masque en Irlande', in Glotz, S. (ed.), *Le Masque Dans La Tradition Européene* (Binche), 193-7, 337-81.

1976

Editor, *Folk and Farm*, Essays in honour of A.T. Lucas, (Dublin), 277 pp.

'Ethnological Mapping in Ireland with a linguistic contribution by G.B. Adams', *Ethnologia Europaea*, vol. 9, 14-34 (with Alan Gailey).

Review of *Irish Settlements in Eastern Canada*, by John J. Mannion (Toronto, 1974), in *Journal of the Royal Society of Antiquaries of Ireland*, vol. 106, 135-6.

1977

'Calendar Customs and Festive Practice in Ireland', in Feder, A. and Schrank, B., *Literature and Folk Culture, Ireland and Newfoundland.* (Papers from the Ninth Annual Seminar of the Canadian Association for Irish Studies, at Memorial University of Newfoundland, February 11-15, 1976, St. John's), 110-28.

Review of *Classic Irish Houses of the Middle Size,* by Maurice Craig (London, 1976), in *Irish University Review,* vol. 7, no. 1, Spring, 122-3.

1977-79

'Irish Tower Houses and their Regional Distribution', *Béaloideas*, vols. 45-47, 158-63.

Review of *Life and Tradition in Rural Ireland* by Timothy P. O'Neill (London, 1977) in *Béaloideas*, vols. 45-47, 274-6.

Review of *Österreichischer Volkskundeatlas*, sechste Lieferung, erster Teil, (Vienna, 1978) in *Béaloideas*, vols. 45-47, 276-7.

1978

'Farmer and Labourer in pre-Famine County Limerick', *Limerick Association Handbook.*

'Stories and Storytelling in Ireland', in Norton, E.S. (ed.) *Folk Literature of the British Isles* (New Jersey and London), 107-14.

A Bibliography of Irish Ethnology and Folk Tradition (Dublin and Cork), 95 pp.

Review of *Castles of Ireland*, by Brian de Breffny (London, 1977), in *Irish University Review*, vol. 8, no. 2, Autumn, 261-2.

Review of *Castles and Fortifications of Britain and Ireland,* by J. Forde Johnston (London, 1977) in *Irish University Review,* vol. 8, no. 2, Autumn, 261-3.

Review of *To Shorten the Road* by George Gmelch and Ben Kroup, (Dublin, 1978) in *The Irish Independent*, 8 December.

1979

'Oral Tradition and the Printed Word', in Harmon, Maurice, (ed.) *Image and Illusion*. Festschrift for Roger Mac Hugh (Dublin), 31-41. (Also vol. 9, no. 1, Spring, of *Irish University Review*, 31-41).
'The 'Schools' Collection', *Ros*, Summer, 2-3.
'Green Corn', *Sinsear*, 1979, 82-4.
'At the Foot of the Rainbow', *Ireland of the Welcomes*, vol. 28, no. 6, November/December, 18-20.

1980

'Snaidhm na Péiste', *Sinsear*, 102-8.

1980-81

'Cottier and Landlord in Pre-Famine Ireland', *Béaloideas*, vols. 48-49, 154-65.
'Supplement to a Bibliography of Irish Ethnology and Folklore', *Béaloideas*, 48-49, 206-27 (with Patricia Lysaght).

1981

'Bread in Ireland', in Fenton, Alexander and Owen, Trefor M. (eds.), *Food in Perspective*, Proceedings of the Third International Conference on Ethnological Food Research, Cardiff, Wales, 1977, (Edinburgh), 57-67.
'Mass Rocks', *Sinsear,* vol. 3, 21-4.
'Sound Recording of Folk Narrative in Ireland in the Late Nineteen Forties', *Fabula*, 22. Band, Heft 3/4, 312-15.
'Foreword' in O'Dowd, Anne, *Meitheal A Study of Co-operative Labour in Rural Ireland* (Dublin), 13-14.
'Irish Folk Tradition and the Celtic Calendar', in O'Driscoll, Robert, (ed.) *The Celtic Consciousness* (Toronto and Dublin), 217-42.
Irish Stone Wall Calendar 1982, Introduction. (Belfast).
'Farmyard Forms and their Distribution in Ireland', *Ulster Folklife*, vol. 27, 63-75.
Review of *The Holy Wells of Ireland* by Patrick Logan, (London, 1980) in *The Irish Independent*, 25 April.
'An Rí (The King): An Example of Traditional Social Organisation', *Journal of the Royal Society of Antiquaries of Ireland*, vol. III, 1981, 14-28.

The Photographic Record — a Selection of Caoimhín Ó Danachair's Pictures

PLATE I. Making a seine boat, Dungegan, Co. Kerry. 1947

PLATE II. House, Teelin, County Donegal. 1946

PLATE III. Woman at hearth, Maam, County Galway. 1935

PLATE IV. Haymaking, Waterville district, County Kerry. 1946

PLATE V. Naomhóga, Dunquin, County Kerry. 1968

PLATE VI. Oat Stacks, Kilrealig, County Kerry. 1946

PLATE VII. Hay Stacks, Kilrealig, County Kerry, 1946

PLATE VIII. Oats growing in ridges, Glenmore, County Kerry. 1946

PLATE IX. Lobster pots, Annascaul, County Kerry. 1947

PLATE X. Seaweed rake, Feohanagh, County Kerry. 1947

PLATE XI. Turf-cutting *meitheal*, Ballyferriter, County Kerry. 1947

PLATE XII. 12th July celebrations, Rathfriland, County Down. 1947

PLATE XIII. Wren boys, Athea, County Limerick. 1947

PLATE XIV. Landscape, Teelin, County Donegal. 1946

PLATE XV. Sheep-gap in stone wall, The Burren, County Clare. 1946

PLATE XVI. House, Rathnew, County Wicklow. 1935

PLATE XVII. Houses, Curracloe, County Wexford. 1947

PLATE XIX. Dresser, Maam Cross, County Galway. 1935

PLATE XVIII. Children's clothes, Garumna, County Galway. 1935

PLATE XX. Family, Iveragh, County Kerry. 1946

PLATE XXI. Bread in pot oven, Dunquin, County Kerry. 1947

PLATE XXIII. Donkey with panniers, Glenmore, County Kerry. 1946

PLATE XXII. Pump, Kilsallaghan, County Dublin. 1962

PLATE XXIV. Cows drinking, Coumeenole, County Kerry. 1968

PLATE XXV. Goats with ladder, Lisduff, County Longford. 1946

PLATE XXVI. Preparation for recording, Cloonaghlin, County Kerry. 1947

PLATE XXVII. Collecting information, Bishop's Quarter, County Clare. 1946

Applied Folk-life Study - a Personal View

G.B. THOMPSON

Having been appointed in 1959 the first Director of the Ulster Folk Museum — a new institution established some months earlier by act of parliament — I was in the privileged position of being able from the outset to influence the development of policy. Such ideas on policy as I had at that time owed much to the inspiration and example of certain personalities responsible for my academic training, my entry into the museum profession, and the course it has since followed. One of these was my good friend Kevin Danaher.

We first met in 1951 at Liverpool Street station in London. We were en route to Stockholm to attend an international folk-life congress. It was my first trip abroad and the fact that I was making it at all was the result of a recommendation to my employers from Professor Séamus Delargy, Director of the Irish Folklore Commission, that I should accompany two members of the Commission's staff, Kevin Danaher and Seán O'Sullivan, to the congress and use the opportunity to see something of Scandinavian folk museums.

It was a fortuitous arrangement; I was a relative newcomer to folk-life study, blinkered by inexperience and inclined to see folk-life as an esoteric preserve in which specialists communicated with specialists — a mistaken notion which could well have become consolidated had I travelled alone to the congress and met only certain delegates. Happily, my arrival in Stockholm was prefaced by a journey lasting the best part of three days and two nights in the company of two companions already widely experienced, internationally known, and, in Kevin's case, compulsively communicative. In a conversation initiated at Liverpool Street, interrupted only by a few hours' sleep, and terminated by our dispersal in Stockholm to separate living quarters, I gained new insights into folk-life study which have been of lasting value to me ever since. In particular they directed me towards the belief — the belief strengthened by subsequent experience — that folk-life study is not, as some see it, solely a pure subject, but is also an applied subject. In stating this I do not deride those who engage only in research; their contribution is essential to the advance of knowledge, but unless it is to remain a self-indulgence among specialists, there must also be those who take it upon themselves to relay it to the layman. In other words, where folk-life study is concerned, the community at large should be both the basic supplier and the end consumer, and it is, I feel, the sharing of this belief that has contributed significantly to the bonds of friendship and professional relationship with Kevin Danaher that have endured to my enjoyment and advantage for more than thirty years.

Fig. 1   The Shannon farmhouse, as reconstructed at Bunratty Folk Park

In any assessment of Dr. Danaher's contribution to the general study of folk-life, and that of Ireland in particular, his interest and ability in popularising it (I use the term in its best and broadest sense) must rate highly. Unlike myself, whose eventual appointment as Ulster Folk Museum Director established that I was, and still am, professionally required to cater for the layman since the institution is by definition a public amenity, Kevin Danaher has popularised the subject by inclination rather than obligation; strictly speaking, his professional commitments have been concerned with collection and archive development, and more recently with university teaching. His achievements thereafter in presenting folk-life to the public at large as an author, lecturer, television personality, adviser and consultant, are the products of a personal conviction voluntarily and enthusiastically translated into practice. Appropriately one of the most impressive developments with which he has been associated as official adviser is located near Limerick, his native county. I refer to Bunratty Folk Park, an institution which for obvious professional reasons is of particular interest to me.

The folk museum and the folk park (they are not necessarily synonymous) are manifestations of applied folk-life. The father of the folk museum movement, the Swedish educationalist Artur Hazelius, saw them as a means of achieving self-knowledge and understanding by bringing people together in a setting illustrative of their own cultural tradition. As we know, it was the start of a movement that is now international in its spread. It is, however, symptomatic of the fact that in

Ireland applied folk-life study is still in its infancy that a folk institution for the layman has found a foothold only recently. In 1951, when Kevin Danaher and I first met, Ireland had no folk museum, though proposals that such an institution be established in Ulster were under consideration. Admittedly, too, in Dublin the Irish Folklore Commission in which Kevin Danaher was employed was already of international repute, but by no stretch of imagination could it be seen as an institution dedicated to popularising, and applying within the general community the information embodied in its considerable archives.

Thirty years ago, therefore, anyone in Ireland interested in translating folk-life study into a popular community movement was encouraged more by hope than prospect. Seen in this perspective the situation today is undoubtedly gratifying, and while Kevin Danaher and I cannot claim responsibility for it we can, at least, appreciate having an involvement in it which has enabled us to give practical expression to a mutual interest.

It often happens in Irish affairs that events are somewhat paradoxical. The development of such public folk institutions as exist at present is no exception; paradoxically it is in Northern Ireland that a state folk museum has emerged with full central government support, whereas in the Republic of Ireland developments to date are attributable to local rather than national initiative and of these the most significant so far is Bunratty Folk Park.

Fig. 2   Hill-farm from Coshkib, Glens of Antrim, with surrounding fields, as reconstructed at Ulster Folk and Transport Museum, compares with the Shannon farmhouse.

Fig. 3   Village street nearing completion, Bunratty Folk Park

The contrast between north and south goes further. The origins of the Ulster Folk Museum are traceable to an academic source and the pioneering work of Estyn Evans, first Professor of Geography at the Queen's University of Belfast. Thus established, the Ulster Folk Museum — now part of a composite folk and transport museum — has been developing, without prejudice to a basic academic research function, a general community role in which the recognition of commercial and promotional techniques and objectives are of late becoming increasingly important.

Bunratty Folk Park (the term 'museum' was deliberately avoided at the beginning) on the other hand originated as the by-product of commercial enterprise aimed at counteracting the threatened decline of Shannon airport. Plans for a runway extension necessitated removal of a farmhouse representative of local vernacular building. Instead of destroying the house, it occurred to developers, keen to add to the tourist attractions of the area, that if the farmhouse were to be moved and reconstructed adjacent to a restored Bunratty Castle, it would provide an interesting contrast — a conjunction of the extremes of local domestic life in the past. Thus the Shannon Farmhouse, as it is now known, came not only to be transplanted, restored and preserved under the specialist oversight of Kevin Danaher (Figs. 1 and 2), but came also to initiate the development of a small six-acre folk park in which a range of buildings illustrating the social history of the

Shannon areas of south Clare and north Limerick would eventually be featured.

By an interesting coincidence the Ulster Folk Museum and Bunratty Folk Park were each officially opened to the public in the summer of 1964, notwithstanding a very modest stage of development in each instance. It could be said, therefore, that two projects starting from different points of origin — one the statutory endorsement by government of an academic proposal, the other an element within an imaginative commercial undertaking — converged momentarily in terms of a simultaneous public launching and a forecast of future physical growth. These in time have led to a situation today where there is a convergence of objectives.

Today, Bunratty Folk Park is in course of becoming a twenty-acre establishment and is well on its way to featuring between twenty and thirty replica buildings. Already, buildings representative of dispersed rural settlement are complemented by an emergent village settlement (Figs 3 and 4). The furnishings and fittings displayed in context within traditional buildings are augmented by the Talbot Collection of agricultural machinery presently housed in the farm courtyard of Bunratty House, an early nineteenth-century dwelling which, itself, adds yet another period and another social stratum to the folk park.

Initially Bunratty Folk Park's role was promotional, reflecting its commercial origins and concern for the local tourist industry. Its objectives, therefore, though worthy were restricted; but more recently it has come to appreciate its educational potential as a resource of local social history, and its plans for the future extend beyond mere physical expansion towards the academic function which in most folk museums elsewhere, including the Ulster Folk Museum, was an original element. For some years past its curator, Chris Lynch, and his colleagues have been establishing working relationships with other museum professionals and the resultant exchange of ideas is increasingly evident in the policy which now directs the folk park's activities and its future objectives. Though still owned and administered by Shannon Free Airport Development Company Limited and still regional in its coverage, it can already claim a national significance. As a means of applying folk-life study to community life its influence and achievements extend well beyond the region it represents. It has, therefore, a capacity and an inducement to devise and accomplish programmes and exert influence undreamt of at the time of its opening. It remains to be seen how far, and in what respects, it succeeds in doing so, but of the several advantages it enjoys none is more valuable than the services of its official adviser, Kevin Danaher, whose own extensive knowledge is still at its disposal and who also provides a link with the resources and personnel of the Department of Folklore at University College, Dublin. It is to be hoped that this link having been established while Dr. Danaher was still in post, will survive his retirement from the Department's staff.

I have already suggested that in the past few years there has been a convergence of objectives between Bunratty Folk Park and the Ulster Folk Museum. There is still, however, a considerable contrast in scale and activity. While this is due partly to the former being a regional establishment and the latter a provincial institution, with a consequential difference in financial input, there are other factors to be taken into consideration. Notwithstanding the fact that during the Evans regime the Department of Geography at The Queen's University, Belfast, was in effect a training ground for professional ethnologists, there is yet no teaching department at tertiary level in Northern Ireland comparable to the Department of Folklore at

Fig. 4 Workers' terrace housing in the developing village area, Ulster Folk and Transport Museum, which will compare with the Bunratty exhibit village.

University College, Dublin. The Ulster Folk Museum, therefore, has sought partly to fill the void by placing initial importance on development of a research function and by adopting a comprehensive view of folk life as embracing both material and non-material aspects.

Nor must one ignore the pluralist nature of the Ulster community and the fact that for the latter half of its history the Ulster Folk Museum has been evolving in the midst of violent social upheaval. It seemed evident, therefore, that priority should be given to putting into practice as a matter of urgency a teaching role that responded to the demands of a disturbed and disrupted community. By force of circumstances the museum has made considerable strides in identifying and implementing educational programmes relating to the whole spectrum of education from primary and secondary schools, through tertiary colleges to the general field of adult education. Cultra Manor, the focal point of the estate in which the museum has been evolving since 1961, having recently been superseded as the museum's administrative centre, is now the home of the museum's Education Department. It is anticipated that in time it will be supplemented by a new accommodation block by which the museum's education centre will become residential. This will go a long way towards equipping the institution to fulfil a policy based on the belief that there is no activity, no profession, no field of endeavour concerned with the present and future well-being of the community that could not be practised more effectively with a fuller knowledge and understanding of its folk life. It is equally so that in a community where for so long a sense of cultural identity has been submerged beneath those of religious persuasion and political aspirations, a new and fuller awareness of a folk tradition that speaks more of unity than division would be both welcome and timely.

There is immense scope in Ireland, north and south, for the application of folk-life study to the social and cultural development of our respective communities. A start has now been made in converting theory into practice, and for those of us privileged to assist the transition it is, of course, gratifying. But it is still only a beginning and an imbalanced one at that. There is no cause for complacency for the signs within community life in general testify to a need for self knowledge and understanding greater now than at any time in the past. The achievements thus far of the folk institutions we now possess are still modest, but not so modest as to conceal the fact that there is a healthy public appetite for the information and services they are capable of providing and failure to respond fully to this demand would be an indictment of those with the power and ability to provide the means.

Contributions to the Study of the Irish House: Smokehole and Chimney

A.T. LUCAS

The siting of the hearth and the development of the chimney in the Irish traditional house have been exhaustively investigated by Ó Danachair.[1] His study was primarily devoted to the analysis and classification of these features in habitations of relatively recent times, but it included data about the location of the hearth in earlier centuries, chiefly drawn from sources of seventeenth-century date. In the absence of a chimney, smoke was normally vented from the house through a hole in the roof, and in the following notes an attempt has been made to explore the evidence for the existence of a smokehole in houses of the Early Christian period and to trace its survival down to modern times.

The literary evidence shows that in Early Christian and medieval times and in some districts down to the seventeenth century, the characteristic Irish house was a structure with walls made of posts and wattle coated with daub, or, perhaps lined with mats of straw or similar material to render them wind- and weather-proof. The roof was thatched with grass, rushes, reeds or straw. In plan, the house was either circular or rectangular but there is little doubt that the latter type was by far the commoner. It should be borne in mind, however, that remains of horizontal mills preserved in a significant number of waterlogged sites, which have been securely dated to the Early Christian period, demonstrate the practice of sophisticated carpentry techniques, and there is considerable literary and some pictorial evidence for the existence of timber-framed churches of rectangular plan with plank-built or boarded walls and shingled roofs. It is possible that some domestic buildings inhabited by persons of high social status were built in this fashion during the same period but the literary evidence for the preponderance of post-and-wattle dwellings is corroborated by the archaeological data from excavated habitation sites of contemporary date.

As the usual and, perhaps, the only type of fireplace in use was an open hearth bordered by a kerb of stones, an essential safety precaution was to locate it as far as possible from the inflammable walls of the building. If the house was round, the safest place for the fire was at the centre point of the floor; if the house was rectangular, the fire had to be somewhere along the middle line of the length, equidistant from the side walls, and if not in the centre, which was the ideal position, at least at a prudent distance from the nearer end wall. As the roof of a round house was highest in the centre and that of a rectangular one highest along the mid line of its length, the central location of the fireplace also minimized the danger of the roof catching fire from flying sparks or a surge of flame from the careless use of some highly combustible fuel. The effect of these constraints on the location of the hearth are illustrated by a plan of the Assembly Hall at Tara, copies of which are to be found in the Book of Leinster (twelfth century) and the Yellow Book of Lecan (fourteenth century).[2] It shows an approximately square building divided into five aisles, the outer two of which on either side are sub-divided into compartments for the seating of the various ranks and grades comprised in the assembly. The centre aisle, which is in line with the single doorway of the building, is occupied by a lamp, a candle, a vat and three hearths. These last are indicated by rectangles evenly spaced over the part of the aisle farthest from the doorway. They occupy about one-quarter of the length of the aisle but it is likely that the original intention was to spread them over half of it and that they have been crowded together by the necessity to leave space for the comparatively large figures of the lamp, candle and vat which are drawn in profile. How far the plan may truly reflect the social conventions governing precedence in seating and choice of food at any period in Irish history need not concern us here but it is most probable that such details of domestic arrangements, like the position of the hearths, which appear in it were those familiar to the person who first drew it, whether he lived in the twelfth century or earlier. Of the three hearths which were considered necessary, either to meet the cooking requirements of such a large company or to supplement the illumination from the lamp and candle in what may have been a windowless building, one lies close to the centre of the floor which was the location of the single hearth in the family house of the time.

If the position of the hearth was primarily dictated by considerations of safety, its central situation afforded additional domestic advantages: all parts of the house had equal benefit of the heat which it radiated and there was unhindered access to the fire from all sides for cooking and other purposes. Moreover, since people could seat themselves in a circle around it, the central hearth permitted a greater number of persons to enjoy uniform conditions of comfort and conversation when they gathered round it at night-time or during inclement weather than if it occupied any other position on the floor. This last amenity is alluded to in an account of the Barony of Forth, County Wexford, written about 1684, where the writer, describing the houses of the district, states that formerly they had spacious 'halls' (living rooms): 'in the Center of which were fire Hearthes (according to the ancient English mode) for the more commodious extension of heat to the whole family surrounding it . . .'[3] A very ancient and extremely widespread sleeping custom, an Irish instance of which was recorded in the early seventeenth century, was, very probably, also a common practice in central-hearth houses of earlier times. Moryson, describing the makeshift houses occupied by men herding and guarding cows on pastures distant from their permanent settlements, recounts: 'And in such places, they make a fier in the middest of the roome, and round about it they sleepe upon the ground, without straw or other thing under them, lying all in a circle about the fier, with their feete towards it.'[4]

The archaeological evidence which indicates that the Irish house of the Early Christian period had a central hearth is corroborated by such data as can be gleaned from the contemporary literature. There is, however, neither archaeological nor literary evidence for the existence of a chimney to collect the smoke rising from the fire and conduct it out through the roof. On the contrary, the literary evidence leads us to believe that it escaped through a smokehole, an opening at the apex of the roof, which was, presumably, situated directly above the hearth. In the saga, The Destruction of Da Derga's Hostel, which appears to have been compiled in the eleventh century from two versions which were probably committed to writing in the ninth, Cormac delivered his infant daughter to his thralls with instructions to kill her. Instead, they brought her to the calf-fold of the cowherds of Eterscel where she was fostered in a wickerwork house without any door, having 'only a window and a skylight (*acht seinister ⁊ forléas namá*).' Eventually, news of her existence leaked out and a man looked in through the skylight (*forléas*) and saw her in the house.[5] The tale Tochmarc Étaíne or the Wooing of Étaín, relates how Midir abducted Étaín away from Eochaidh in his house at Tara: 'He takes his weapons in his left hand, and the woman he took under his right arm, and bore her away through the skylight (*forlés*) of the house. The hosts rose up in shame around the king. They beheld two swans in flight round Tara.'[6] In the medieval story Buile Shuibhne, the demented Suibhne came to Loingseachan's mill where the old woman who tended it gave him small morsels to eat. Loingseachan learned of his visits and being anxious to speak with Suibhne, put on the old woman's clothes and remained in the mill after she had left. Suibhne arrived as usual at the mill but, recognising Loingseachan despite his disguise, sprang away from him at once 'through the skylight of the house (*dar forlés an tighe amach)*'.[7] An anecdote recounts how Cuchulainn ordered the shield-maker, Mac Endge, to make a shield for him surpassing all the shields of Ulster in decoration. When Mac Endge protests that he has exhausted all his art in making shields for the Ulstermen, Cuchulainn threatens him with death if he does not produce one for him. While he was in this state of perplexity, a strange man appeared to Mac Endge and told him to cover the floor of his workshop with ashes to the depth of a man's foot. Mac Endge does so and then sees the man entering the workshop through the *forlés* with a fork (compass) in his hand with which he draws a design for the shield in the ashes.[8] The life of St. Mochuda or Carthach, which dates to the twelfth century, relates that his community at Rahan included a monk named Constantine, who was a son of Fergus, king of Alba. He was a man of gigantic strength and enormous appetite. On one occasion he was digging a trench while the other monks were having their meal and he was forgotten. 'He was angry at this and sent a shovelful of earth through the roof-light (*forlés*) of the refectory, so that some of it fell into the trencher and cup of every monk indoors.'[9] The feasibility of casting an object into a house through the *forlés* also appears in the Togail Troi, an Irish version of the medieval story The Destruction of Troy, a copy of which is found in the Book of Leinster dating to the second half of the twelfth century. Discordia, incensed because she was not invited to the marriage feast of Peleus of Thrace along with the other goddesses, planned to set them squabbling among themselves during the festivities. Having obtained a golden apple from the garden of the Hesperides, she wrote on it the inscription: 'This gift is for the most beautiful of the goddesses.' Then going to the house where the feast was in progress she 'flung it over the sky-light in such wise that it lay on the house-floor before them all (*foceirdsi dar forlés in tige co m-búi for lár in tigi inafiadnaissi uili*).'[10] In the saga called Táin Bó Fraích, there is a flamboyant account of the royal house at Cruachan, County Roscommon, into which Froech and his followers were invited by Ailill and Medb. Among the descriptive particulars is: *cuing umai darsa forlés*.[11] This has been variously trans-lated as: 'A yoke of copper across the roof-light,'[12] 'A tie of brass across the roof-light'[13] and 'There was a lattice of copper across the skylight'.[14] Although *cuing* means a yoke, a literal rendering does not help to explain the nature of the object in question. A 'tie' is more in keeping with the coupling function of a yoke than a 'lattice' and whatever metaphorical justification there may be for the former ver-sion, there seems to be none of any kind for the latter. It has, with more prob-ability, been suggested that in this particular context *cuing* connotes 'a frame'.[15] The word may have had a specialised application in the technical vocabulary of metalworkers or carpenters which is now undiscoverable. Whatever the loss of information about some detail or accessory of the *forlés* occasioned by our ignor-ance of the precise meaning of *cuing* in this passage, the text does show that the *forlés* was accepted as being a conspicuous and essential feature of a house in-habited by persons of the highest social standing. Since the archetype of this saga dates to the eighth century and a recension of it occurs in the twelfth-century Book of Leinster, the chronological setting of this *forlés*, like that of the others already mentioned, lies in the Early Christian period.

It is hardly to be expected that information about the existence or location of the smokehole could ever be obtained by archaeological excavation but there appears to be one source of physical evidence for it. There are extant a number of small bronze house-shaped shrines which are generally dated to the eighth century. The general type of these objects may derive from late classical sarco-phagi but their decorative details are all Irish in character. They closely resemble

All the contexts cited above imply that there was only one *forlés* in each build-ing, while three of them imply that it was large enough not to make it seem grossly improbable to imagine a person passing through it. It is also evident that it was open to view from the floor of the house and that a person looking down through it had an unobstructed view of the interior. Midir and Suibhne who made exit through it and Mac Endge who entered through it are all magical personages which seems to imply that it was too high up in the roof to make such feats possible or probable for ordinary mortals. It is clear, therefore, that the *forlés* was not a chim-ney. The various translators of the texts quoted render *forlés* by 'skylight' while the Royal Irish Academy's *Contributions to a Dictionary of the Irish Language* defines it as 'a roof window, the circular opening in the roof of an early Irish dwelling', although none of the references cited in the *Contributions* provides any information about its shape. While it is, of course, true that any opening in the roof would admit a certain amount of daylight and, to that extent, might be justifiably termed a 'skylight', this rendering obscures the primary purpose of the opening which was not for the admission of light but for the emission of smoke from the fire. The well-established name 'smokehole' reflects, therefore, the true function of the opening more faithfully than 'skylight' and this is substantiated by the fact that, although the word *forlés* is extinct in modern Irish, it survives as the ordinary name for a smokehole in Scottish Gaelic. The older type of Hebridean house, like the early Irish house, had a central hearth: 'The fire was placed on a stone slab or group of flat stones (*cagailte*) set in the middle of the floor of the main apartment. An opening (*farleus*) was formed in the roof, a little to one side of the fire, through which the peat smoke, floating through the house, eventually found egress.'[16]

It is hardly to be expected that information about the existence or location of the smokehole could ever be obtained by archaeological excavation but there appears to be one source of physical evidence for it. There are extant a number of small bronze house-shaped shrines which are generally dated to the eighth century. The general type of these objects may derive from late classical sarco-phagi but their decorative details are all Irish in character. They closely resemble the Temple of Jerusalem as it appears in the illumination in the Book of Kells depicting the Temptation of Christ and they are paralleled by the house-shaped terminals which crown the shafts of a number of the high crosses of tenth-century date, e.g. the Cross of Muiredach and the West Cross at Monasterboice, County Louth; the cross at Durrow, County Offaly, and the Cross of the Scriptures at Clonmacnois. Both crosses and shrines seem to reproduce a type of framed wooden building, with gables in the case of the crosses and a hipped roof in the case of the shrines. All the better preserved of these shrines have a decorated ridge-pole in the centre of which is a rectangular panel in relief. On one in the National Museum of Ireland which was found in Lough Erne, this panel is surmounted by a low truncated triangle rising above the upper line of the ridge, the whole feature resembling a miniature version of the shrine itself. The Emly shrine, now in the Museum of Fine Arts, Boston, USA, the Moneymusk shrine in the National Museum of Antiquities of Scotland and a shrine in the National Museum of Denmark, Copenhagen, have closely similar features in the centres of their ridge-poles. There are two ridge-poles from such shrines in the National Museum of Ireland. On one, which comes from County Roscommon, the top of the central panel takes the form of two spiral-decorated bosses inclining towards each other; on the other, the find-place of which is unknown, the whole panel has been replaced by a human head in relief. For the craftsman designing and making one of these reliquaries the panel in relief in the centre of the ridge formed a focus of interest at the summit of the shrine midway between the converging lines of the roof, imparting a visual finality to the design, emphasised by the relief in which it was executed and by the projection of the top above the upper line of the ridge-pole. But the writer believes that neither this artistic imperative nor the variations of the feature found on the surviving shrines and shrine fragments preclude the view that it originated as a representation of a wooden flange surrounding the smokehole above the central hearth of a frame wooden building. The presence of such a flange would have done something to increase the updraught to clear the smoke from the interior of the house and, at the same time, minimise down-draughts created by strong winds. In recent centuries chimneyless houses were sometimes provided with a similar flange around the smokehole as was recorded about squatters' cabins at Geashill, County Offaly, in 1857: 'They lived in mud hovels, generally without windows; a hole at one end of the roof, out of which stuck a piece of wickerwork like a badly-made turf basket plastered with mud, formed the chimney.'[17] A similar observation was made in 1898 about one-room dwellings in Garumna and Lettermullen Islands, County Galway: 'A house of this sort may appear from the outside to have a chimney, but this is merely a structure built around the hole in the roof at the gable which serves the purpose of letting out the smoke; there is no flue inside and the hearth is merely a few stones against the end wall of the house.'[18] The owners of these dwellings must have believed that the erections around the smokeholes were in some way advantageous as it is incredible that persons living in such deprived circumstances would have put them up merely to create the impression that they had chimneys. All their neighbours would have known that they had not and even if a passing stranger were deceived by the pretence, no social prestige would accrue to the occupants as a result. If the shrine feature is, in fact, a reminiscence of a square boxlike structure symmetrically positioned around the smokehole at the apex of the roof, the ridge-pole must have run across the middle of the aperture. It could be argued that this would have curbed the fancy of storytellers inviting their listeners to believe that persons, even if they had supra-normal endowments, could leave or enter by the smokehole but this objection would not arise if the hole were on one side of the roof just below the ridge-pole, in which case a flange to raise the point of exit of the smoke above the level of the ridge would have been even more desirable than if the hole had been at the apex. It must be remembered, however, that the vast majority of domestic buildings were post-and-wattle structures in which the location of the smokehole may have provided a more credible setting for the exits and entrances of the *dramatis personae* of the stories quoted above.

The central hearth with its accompanying smokehole remained in use for long after the Early Christian period to which all the evidence previously cited relates. As factual descriptions of houses or other aspects of the social environment are of rare occurrence in Irish literature, virtually all the data on the subject come from the works of commentators writing in English, the majority of whom were non-Irish and addressing themselves to a non-Irish audience. The consequent critical and often contemptuous tone of their observations does not, however, invalidate the correctness of the facts which they recorded. None of the sources of information known to the writer predates the seventeenth century and most of them relate to the poorer strata of Irish society. Although poverty was, undoubtedly, partly responsible for the retention of the smokehole even after the central hearth had been abandoned, it was still the continuation of an ancient tradition and not a revival of it induced by poverty.

Moryson (1607-17) has already been cited for the existence of the central hearth in semi-permanent Irish houses but he also vouches for it and its accompanying smokehole in the houses of the upper classes as well: 'And in like sort the chiefe men in their houses make fiers in the middest of the roome, the smoke whereof goeth out at a hole in the top thereof.'[19] Boullaye le Gouz (1644) states that Irish cabins are without chimneys and they 'make the fire in the middle of the hut, which greatly incommodes those who are not fond of smoke.'[20] The anonymous author of a tour in Ireland in 1672-4, referring to the poorer houses, says that: 'the hearth is placed in the middle of the house.'[21] Farewell (1689) describes an Irish 'crate' or cabin as having a door on either side and no chimney and continues:

> Betwixt the door there was a spot
> I'th' middle, to hang o're the pot:
> And had an Engine in the nick,
> For pair of Tongues, a broken stick.[22]

When John Dunton visited O'Flaherty, 'the most considerable man' in Iar-Chonnacht, County Galway, in 1698, he found him living, not in 'the proper dwelling or mansion house' but in 'a booley or summer habitation', newly erected on the hill pastures. He was told that they commonly built such a house every year in some place or other and thatched it with rushes or coarse grass. The house was 'a long cabbin, the walls of hurdles plaister'd with cow dung and clay . . . The house was one entire long roome without any partition. In the middle of it was the fire place with a large wood fire . . . It had no chimney but a vent hole for the smoake at the ridge . . .'[23] Moffet (1728) describes the house of Gillo, the Irish 'hero' of his poem:

> And when occasion did require,
> In midst of house a mighty fire,
> Of black dry'd earth, and swinging blocks,
> Was made enough to roast an ox
> From whence arose such clouds of smoak,
> As either you or me would choak:
> But Gillo and his train inur'd
> To smoak, the same with ease endur'd;
> By sitting low on rushes spread,
> The smoak still hover'd over head;
> And did more good than real harm,
> Because it kept the long house warm,
> And never made their heads to ake;
> Therefore no chimney he would make.
> And thus for smoak altho' 'twas dear,
> He paid four shillings every Year.[24]

Finally, an account of the Rosses district, County Donegal, dating to 1753-54, states that the houses of the inhabitants were 'chiefly of one room with the fire in the middle of it.'[25]

The concluding lines of the extract from Moffet's burlesque just quoted refer to the Hearth Money Act, 1662, by which a sum of two shillings per year was levied in respect of every hearth, fireplace or stove in each house of an annual valuation in excess of eight shillings.[26] This was amended in 1665 by a further act which included the provision that a house not having a chimney was to be chargeable with two hearths.[27] Dineley, writing in 1681, attributes to this provision the beneficient intention of bringing the owners of such chimneyless houses 'to the decorum of the English', going on to say that 'some rather pay double, then [than] by having a chimney to loose the benefitt of so much good smoak, which they say nourisheth and keepeth warme their children, in which these thatcht hutts abound.'[28] This alleged Irish aversion to chimneys and this reason for it were to be repeated by a number of independent observers during the two succeeding centuries. Moffet's reference of 1728 to the value put upon the warmth of smoke has been quoted above while Young, 1776-79, having remarked on the absence of windows and chimneys in cabins, says: 'these two conveniences they hold so cheap, that I have seen them both stopped up in stone cottages, built by improving landlords; the smoak warms them, but certainly is as injurious to their eyes as it is to the complexions of the women, which in general in the cabbins of Ireland has a near resemblance to that of a smoaked ham.'[29] Dutton, 1808, writing of County Clare, is quite specific on the point: 'Formerly there was scarcely a cottage, that had a chimney, and, where the landlord has built them, he has frequently found a flag or sod on top of the chimney to keep in the smoke, which, they say, keeps them warm; this I have frequently seen myself, and, as the lower part of the cottage has for three or four feet from the ground but little smoke, they seem not to feel it when they sit down.'[30] In a footnote he adds that 'the same custom prevails near Castlecomer and in other parts of the county of Kilkenny, where they burn nothing but that abominable, sulky-looking, suffocating Kilkenny coal.' Fitzgibbon, 1868, relates that Lord Lorton constructed fireplaces with chimneys in a number of cottages on his estate at Rockingham, County Roscommon: 'Some time after this improvement, the tenants sent a deputation to his lordship, complaining of the cold, and stating that all the heat of the fire escaped by the chimney, along with the smoke; adding an earnest prayer, that they might be allowed to place a flag on top of the chimney, and thereby confine both the smoke and the warmth.'[31]

For whatever reason, many of the poorer kind of houses continued to be unprovided with chimneys down to the end of the nineteenth century and in occasional cases till much later still. Madden, 1738, referring to the wattle houses of 'our cotters', states: 'Numbers of them have no Chimney, either for want of Wood, or skill to build one'[32] while Young's evidence just quoted shows a similar state of affairs towards the end of the same century. More localized information from the nineteenth century reveals that a significant proportion of the 'cabins' and 'cottages' occupied by labourers and other persons near the bottom of the contemporary social scale lacked chimneys. The existence of smokeholes in such houses is occasionally mentioned but as their presence was difficult to detect from the outside, a lack of reference to them need not necessarily imply their absence. Indeed, it may safely be assumed that the majority of chimneyless houses were equipped with smokeholes. The following data on the topographical distribution of such houses have been assembled cursorily and are neither exhaustive nor susceptible of statistical evaluation, but they do serve to indicate the late and widespread survival of the smokehole. As the longevity of that survival was, to a large extent, fostered by conditions of extreme poverty, the data are, naturally, more abundant and more persistent to a later date in districts of poor or marginal fertility. This accounts for the large number of instances from Connacht but the rapid increase in population in the first half of the nineteenth century leading to the colonisation of bog and wasteland tended to perpetuate the existence of the smokehole in certain areas of the other provinces during the period. It should also be remembered that the preponderance of data from the counties of the western seaboard arises, in some degree, from the fact that many of the instances are taken from the works of travellers and tourists who were more disposed to record their impressions of the mass poverty to be found there than of social conditions in the less deprived districts through which they passed en route.

LEINSTER

County Meath
County in general, 1802. Referring to the better-off labouring cottagers: 'Few of them have chimneys.'[33]
Between Trim and Navan, 1814: 'mud cottages without chimnies'.[34]

County Westmeath
County in general, 1812. Referring to cabins: 'A hole in the roof gives vent to the smoke.'[35]

County Kildare
Monasterevan district, 1813: a cabin 'with no other outlet for the smoke than the door, and a hole made in the roof of the hut above the fire by a stick having been bored through the thatch.'[36]

County Offaly
Geashill, 1857. Describes mud hovels of squatters in Digby estate as having: 'a hole at one end of the roof' for the exit of the smoke.[37]

MUNSTER

County Tipperary
County in general, 1775. Referring to cabins: 'Sometimes they have a hole in the roof to let out the smoke, and sometimes none.'[38]

County Clare
County in general, 1808: 'Formerly there was scarcely a cottage that had a chimney.'[39]

County Waterford
Lismore district, 1824: 'From these hovels the smoke of the turf fire has seldom the option of escape by a chimney.'[40]

County Limerick
Adare district, 1846. Squatters' cabins: 'There may be a hundred souls inhabiting some thirty mud cabins, all without windows or chimneys.'[41]

ULSTER

County Derry
County in general, 1802. Vaughan Sampson states that very many of the houses on the Derry side of the Bann lacked chimneys.[42]

County Donegal
Culdaff parish, 1816: 'The cottages . . . seldom have a chimney.'[43]
Glenveagh: 'the narrow aperture that served almost as much for a chimney as an entrance'.[44]
Gweedore district, 1845. Describes houses as having 'no chimney'.[45]
Brockagh district, 1892. Poorest houses have: 'Hearth at one end; hole in roof for chimney'.[46]

County Monaghan
Trough barony, 1822: 'Chimneys . . . are very little used.'[47]

County Armagh
Slieve Guillion district, 1835: 'The cabin had neither window nor chimney; a small hole served the purpose of the latter.'[48]

CONNACHT

County Mayo

Westport district, 1835. Referring to cabins: 'the only place for the light to come in at, and the smoke to go out, is through a small hole in the miserably thatched and sometimes sodded roof.'[49]

Achill Island, 1843: 'In the village of Dooagha, consisting of almost forty cabins, there is not a single chimney.'[50]

Castlebar-Westport road, 1852. Referring to cabin: 'There was no chimney but the door, . . .'[51]

Achill Island, 1856. Villages were clusters of cabins with: 'holes for chimneys'.[52]

Achill Island, Keel neighbourhood, 1891: 'very many houses have neither window nor chimney.'[53]

Mullet and Portacloy districts, 1894. Old turf cabins sometimes have no chimney, only hole in roof. In Fallmore: 'few of the dwellings have windows and few or none chimneys.'[54]

County Galway

Headford district, 1817. Formerly the cabins had 'no gables, or chimnies'.[55]

Omey Island, 1845. Village of stone houses: 'some with holes for the smoke to ascend, and some with no way for its escape but through the door'.[56]

County in general, 1859. 'The miserable huts of the peasantry, seen by the feeble light which comes through the doorway and smoke-hole'.[57]

Letterfrack district, 1892. Houses of stone without mortar: 'In many of the houses there are no chimneys, the smoke being conveyed through a hole in the roof.'[58]

Joyce Country, 1892. 'In some houses there are no chimneys, the only exit for the smoke being the doorway, or a small hole made in the roof directly over the fireplace.'[59]

Clifden district, 1892. 'They have no chimney, the fire being laid on the hearth, and a hole made in the roof to allow the smoke to escape.'[60]

Garumna and Lettermullen, 1898. Better houses contain kitchen and one or two rooms: 'This type of house, if two roomed, may or may not have a chimney.'[61]

County Roscommon

Lanesborough, 1832. Contains '67 cabins, thatched, 11 cabins without chimneys'.[62]

Ballyleague, 1832. Contains '47 cabins, thatched, 5 cabins without chimneys'.[63]

Boyle, 1832. 'About thirty of these cabins within the town of Boyle, might be classed as destitute of chimneys, that is, of chimneys appearing above the thatch of the roof; but it was not easy to distinguish between those which had a hole cut in the thatch for the escape of the smoke, and those which had no passage for it but the house door or window.'[64]

Roscommon town, 1832. Cabins on outskirts with 'no chimneys, no windows'.[65]

If, as the absence of references to it seems to imply, the chimney was unknown in Ireland during the Early Christian period, the earliest significant introduction of it must have taken place with the buildings erected by incoming monastic orders like the Augustinians and the Cistercians in the twelfth century. In a lay context the earliest examples must have appeared in the castles built by the Anglo-Normans following their invasion of the country in the same century. The potential influence of such examples was minimal since only a minute fraction of the population would have been aware of them and, in any event, a chimney incorporated in the wall of a stone building did not lend itself to easy adaptation for use in a wattle-walled house with a central hearth. It is, of course, virtually certain that the first steps towards the adoption of the chimney as a standard feature of domestic architecture took place in the towns and it is in these we find the first recorded instances of a type of chimney which was common in rural houses in many parts of the country in the last century.

The first mention of it which the writer has met dates from the end of the sixteenth century. In the towns of the time, when many of the buildings were framed wooden structures, some of them with thatched roofs and when fire-fighting equipment was at best elementary, the risk of serious conflagrations was a continuous preoccupation of the urban authorities. One of the matters which engaged their attention was the hazard attendant on what were called 'forest chimneys'. The Dublin Assembly Roll of 1599 records a lease for sixty-one years to Robert Ball of a piece of wall adjoining his ground in Burnell's lane 'whereupon he may byld a forest chymney', for which he was to pay two shillings a year.[66] An entry of 1612 in the same roll affords more information about the nature of this kind of chimney. Petition was made to the Assembly for some course of action to be taken 'for preventing the immynent danger that may happen by the nombers of noysome and dangerose forrest chymnies' within the city and suburbs. The Assembly ordered a survey to be made to discover what forest chimneys were ruinous or insufficiently repaired and further directed that no fire be made in any chimney which was found to be defective until it was rebuilt with brick or stone and that 'noe forrest chymny shalbe hensforth builded within the cittie or suburbes.'[67] It is evident from this ordinance that forest chimneys were not of brick or stone construction and that the fire hazard they constituted was great enough to warrant a total prohibition on their future erection. The inference is that they were made of inflammable materials and from the fact that they were regarded as being particularly dangerous when in disrepair it might be further inferred that they were funnels of lath- or wattlework coated with daub, the loss of which from an area of the inner surface of the chimney would leave the woodwork exposed to the risk of catching fire.

This is confirmed by the civic records of Youghal where, following a fire in 1616, the Corporation ordered that: 'any persons as have a forrest chimney built with timber or wattles within the walls of the Town and suburbs thereof, shall, between this and Lammas day next, pull it down and build another with stone; and no person to make any fire in any house but in chimneys made of stone, in default to be fined 5 li.'[68] In the previous year a bill dealing with forest chimneys and thatched houses was debated in the Irish House of Commons. Since thatched houses were also regarded as a serious fire risk, the bill presumably, sought to control or prohibit the erection of them or of forest chimneys in towns and cities but, as the Commons could not agree on procedure in regard to it, the proposal was dropped.[69]

A byelaw 'for dwelling houses in Birr without chimneys', promulgated in 1627 by Sir Laurence Parsons, refers to fire damage in towns and villages caused, especially, by fires without chimneys and ordered that no tenant or undertenant in the town should keep a fire within a dwelling house or smith's forge 'without having a stone chimney (if they bee tyed thereto by the tenor of theire leases) or els a forrest chimney wherein to make theire fires'. Defaulters were to be banished from the town.[70]

A 'forest' chimney, in the form of a four-sided funnel supported by two parallel cross-beams, could have been erected over a central hearth and Ó Danachair records the tradition of a chimney of this kind from Tuosist, County Kerry.[71] However, the Dublin ordinance of 1612 decreeing that damaged forest chimneys were to be rebuilt in brick or stone indicates that these were three-sided flues set against a wall as it is extremely unlikely that free-standing funnels would have been replaced in either of these materials. These references to forest chimneys indicate that the commonest type of the traditional Irish smokehood, made of clay-plastered wattles, laths or strawrope was of frequent occurrence in town dwellings at least as early as the end of the sixteenth century but the Birr byelaw of 1627 reveals that by no means all town houses were provided with chimneys of any kind.

There are no sources known to the writer which would provide information to make it possible to trace the adoption of the chimney in the country as a whole or to assess the proportion of houses furnished with it at any one point in time. Towards achieving the latter objective, the Civil Survey of 1654-1656 supplies the widest territorial coverage but, unfortunately, only a portion of it survives. It exists in full for seven counties (Meath, Tipperary, Limerick, Waterford, Donegal, Derry and Tyrone); nearly in full for three (Dublin, Kildare, Wexford) and for small areas of four others (Kerry, Cork, Kilkenny and Louth). Its value for our purpose is further reduced by the fact that data about houses are systematically recorded in respect of one county only (Tipperary) and appear only sporadically elsewhere throughout the survey. In the survey of Tipperary the specification of the lands held by individual proprietors usually includes a statement recording the number of 'houses' and 'cabins' on them. In the vast majority of cases there is only one 'house' and virtually all of these are said to be thatched. The number of 'cabins' on a parcel of land varies from three to twelve but, more usually, it is merely said that there are 'some.' In the terminology used in the Tipperary survey there is a clear distinction between a 'house' and a 'cabin'. The difference in status between them emerges in entries relating to two properties, the owner of which was Piers Butler, who is described as a gentleman and an Irish papist. One was in Ballynoran townland, Kilmurry parish, and upon it stood 'a thatcht house being the said Piers Butlers mansion house'.[72] The other was in Minorstown townland, Kilsheelan parish, and contained 'a house covered with thatch being the said Piers Butlers Mansion House'.[73] It is reasonable to conclude that all the other 'houses' mentioned in the Survey, almost always one to each holding, were buildings of the same status: the dwellings of the well-to-do proprietors of substantial estates.

The survey of Tipperary contains approximately sixty-eight references to 'houses' of this kind,[74] thirty of which are stated to have chimneys.[75] One house had 'two or three chimnies',[76] two had 'a double chemny'[77] and two had an unspecified number of 'chemineys'[78] but all the others appear to have had a single chimney each. There is one instance of a shingled ('singled') house with a chimney.[79] Remarkably, houses with chimneys are recorded only from the eastern and southern baronies of the county (Ikerrin, Ely, Eliogarty, Slieveardagh, Middlethird and Iffa and Offa) but whether this means that there were none in the rest of the county or whether it is the accidental result of some variation in the collection or presentation of the data, the writer is unable to say. Unfortunately, the diligence in recording 'houses' sited on holdings of land which characterises the survey of Tipperary is exceptional, the instances noted in the districts covered by the other surviving portions of the survey being much fewer. Houses with chimneys are mentioned in three localities in County Limerick;[80] four in County Kerry;[81] two in County Waterford;[82] three in County Cork, including 32 in the town of Macroom;[83] and four in County Dublin.[84] The description of the Barony of Rathcline, County Longford, states that it is 'inhabited with English in many parts thereof' and that in Ballymahon there are 'some chimney houses and Irish creats' and that there are also 'some chimney houses with Irish creats disposed in several places'.[85] The only information given about the nature of the chimneys in these houses is in the case of four dwellings in County Dublin, all thatched, one of which had two stone chimneys,[86] two a stone chimney each[87] and one a brick chimney[88] and in the case of two houses in the parish of Knocklong, County Limerick, with stone chimneys, apparently one each.[89] It looks as if these few stone chimneys were accorded special notice because they were different from the other chimneys recorded in the survey. If this was so, the normal type of chimney, to which these latter belonged, was, presumably, the wattlework or 'forest' kind discussed above.

Although the 'cabins' recorded in the survey far outnumber the 'houses', in no single instance is there mention of a cabin with a chimney. This might warrant the assumption that cabins did not have chimneys, an assumption which is strengthened by the numerous cases in which 'cabins' are juxtaposed with 'chimney houses' where chimneys in cabins might have been expected to attract notice if they existed. The fact that twenty 'small cabins' in the possession of 'divers poor persons' in Macroom town, County Cork, are stated to be 'without chimney'[90] may or may not lend further strength to the assumption, as the reference to the lack of chimneys in these cabins might imply either that this was the norm or that some cabins, perhaps less poverty-stricken ones, had them. In situations like this, where the evidence is so imprecise and slender, the danger of overinterpretation must be avoided but, taking the survey data in conjunction with those on the lack of chimneys from eighteenth- and nineteenth-century sources already cited, the writer takes the view that at the time of the survey in the middle of the seventeenth century the vast majority of 'cabins' were chimneyless. It is to be regretted that there is no means of knowing what the term 'cabin' imported in the vocabulary of the time or in the vocabulary of any individual writer. It was, obviously, applied to dwellings of the poorest kind but, since all the commentators who employed it inhabited houses greatly more commodious than cabins and radically different from them in plan and structure, they may have used it as a generic name for all dwellings of native type, whether large or small, whether lived in by the very poor or the reasonably well-to-do.

The information about the incidence of chimneys supplied by the Civil Survey is disappointingly slight and the conclusions which can be drawn from it must be correspondingly insecure. If the data it provides about the frequency of chimneys in the eastern half of County Tipperary in the middle of the seventeenth century are representative of the country as a whole — a matter which must remain in doubt — it would seem as if about half of the houses of the more prosperous inhabitants had chimneys while the cabins occupied by labourers, tradesmen and small holders had none. Petty, writing about Ireland in 1672, states that there were 160,000 families with 'no fixed hearths', 24,000 which had 'but one chimney' and 16,000 with more than one chimney.[91] The reference to 'fixed hearths' indicates that he must have based his estimate on the Hearth Money returns since, as previously mentioned, the act of 1665, which amended the act of 1662 that imposed the tax, added a provision that 'houses having no fixed hearth with chimneys' were to be charged for two hearths. Apparently, a hearth was not regarded as fixed unless it was accompanied by a chimney. That 'family' and 'house' were interchangeable units in Petty's calculations is evident from the fact that, in a succeeding set of figures on the valuation of houses, he classifies the 160,000 above as 'cabins without chimneys'.[92] The vast proportion of these must have been in rural areas where, as we have seen from the Civil Survey of Tipperary, they greatly outnumbered the houses with chimneys. Petty also found that of the 16,000 houses with more than one chimney, 9,400, or considerably more than half, were situated in Dublin and the other cities and towns.[93] Although he does not offer any estimate of the number of houses with one chimney in the cities and towns, it can be safely assumed that a significant fraction of the countrywide total of 24,000 such houses was also located in them, since social pressures and civic regulations must have accelerated the adoption of chimneys in town dwellings from late medieval times onwards. This concentration of houses with chimneys in urban areas would have increased the disproportion between them and chimneyless habitations in the rural areas. If, as appears to be the case, Petty arrived at his figures via the Hearth Money returns, his estimate is reliable only to the extent that the returns were trustworthy but, in any event, it was grounded on statistics infinitely more comprehensive than any now available for the period as only fragmentary portions of the Hearth Money returns are extant. The general impression left by his calculations is that chimneys had not yet been adopted in the great majority of rural dwellings in the closing decades of the seventeenth century. A comment by Stevens, writing in the Carrigogunnel district, County Limerick, in 1690, may record a change in that area at least: 'They say that it is of late years that chimneys are used, yet the house is never free from smoke.'[94] The instances of chimneyless houses cited above indicate that two centuries later the change had not been completed at certain social levels in some parts of the country while in May 1955 the writer visited a clean comfortable thatched house in a little settlement in bogland in the townland of Srahataggle, south of Portacloy, County Mayo, which had an open hearth at the foot of the kitchen gable wall with a smokehole in the roof-ridge above it.

These notes are offered as a tribute to Dr. Kevin Danaher in admiration of his numerous wide-ranging contributions to the study of the life of the Irish countryside — its dwellings, work, customs, pastimes and beliefs — and in happy recollection of our joint fieldwork of journeys through all the provinces of that countryside over many years.

REFERENCES

1. *Béaloideas*, 16 (1946), 91-104.
2. Reproduced in Macalister, R.A.S., *Tara: A Pagan Sanctuary of Ancient Ireland* (London, 1931), 65.
3. *Journal of the Royal Society of Antiquaries of Ireland*, 7 (1862-63), 72.
4. Moryson, Fynes, *An Itinerary*, IV (Glasgow, 1908) 202.
5. *Revue Celtique*, 22 (1901), 19; Knott, Eleanor (ed.), *Togail Bruidne Da Derga* (Dublin, 1963), 3.
6. *Ériu*, 12 (1938), 185.
7. O'Keeffe, J.G. (ed.), *Buile Suibhne* (London, 1913), 43.
8. *Ériu*, 5 (1911), 72.
9. Plummer, Charles (ed.), *Bethada Naem n-Érenn: Lives of Irish Saints*, I (Oxford, 1922), 301; II, 292.
10. Stokes, Whitley (ed.), *Togail Troi: The Destruction of Troy* (Calcutta, 1881), 84, 22.
11. Meid, Wolfgang (ed.), *Táin Bó Fraích* (Dublin, 1967), 3.
12. *Revue Celtique*, 24 (1903), 130.
13. *Proceedings of the Royal Irish Academy, Irish MSS. Series*, 1, 141.
14. *Études Celtiques*, 2 (1937), 3.
15. Royal Irish Academy, *Contributions to a Dictionary of the Irish Language*, s.v. cuing.
16. Sinclair, Colin, *The Thatched Houses of the Old Highlands* (Edinburgh and London, 1953), 20.
17. Trench, W. Steuart, *Realities of Irish Life*, new edn. London (n.d., Preface dated 1868), 326.
18. *Proceedings of the Royal Irish Academy*, 21 (1898-1900), 256.
19. Moryson, Fynes, *op. cit.*, 202.
20. Croker, T. Crofton (ed.), *The Tour of M. de la Boullaye le Gouz in Ireland, A.D. 1644* (London, 1837), 40.
21. *Journal of the Cork Historical and Archaeological Society*, 10 (1904), 93.
22. Farewell, James, *The Irish Hudibras, or Fingallian Prince* (London, 1689), 33.
23. Mac Lysaght, Edward, *Irish Life in the Seventeenth Century*, 2nd edn. (Cork and Oxford, 1950), Appendix B, 334, 335, 337.
24. Moffet, William, *Hesperi-Neso-Graphia, or the Western Isle Described* (Dublin, 1791), 7-8.
25. Walker, Joseph Cooper, *A Historical Essay on the Dress of the Ancient and Modern Irish* (Dublin, 1818), Appendix 1, 199.
26. *Analecta Hibernica*, No. 24 (1967), 5.
27. *ibid.*, 14.
28. Dineley, Thomas, *Observations in a Voyage through the Kingdom of Ireland* (Dublin, 1870), 18.
29. Young, Arthur, *A Tour in Ireland, 1776-1779*, ed. Arthur Wollaston Hutton, II (London, 1892), 47-8.
30. Dutton, Hely, *Statistical Survey of the County of Clare* (Dublin, 1808), 143.
31. Fitzgibbon, Gerald, *Ireland in 1868* (London and Dublin, 1868), 127.
32. Madden, Samuel, *Reflections and Resolutions Proper for the Gentlemen of Ireland* (Dublin, 1738), 34-35.
33. Thompson, Robert, *Statistical Survey of the County of Meath* (Dublin, 1802), 73.
34. Trotter, John Bernard, *Walks through Ireland, in the Years 1812, 1814 and 1817* (London, 1819), 228.
35. Wakefield, Edward, *An Account of Ireland Statistical and Political*, II, 781-2.
36. Hall, Rev. James, *A Tour through Ireland*, I (London, 1813), 57.
37. Trench, W. Steuart, *op. cit.*, 326.
38. Campbell, Thomas, *A Philosophical Survey of the South of Ireland in a Series of Letters to John Watkinson, M.D.* (Dublin, 1778), 146.
39. Dutton, Hely, *op. cit.*, 142.
40. Croker, T. Crofton, *Researches in the South of Ireland* (London, 1824), 128.
41. Manners, Lord John, *Notes of an Irish Tour in 1846*, new edn. (Edinburgh and London, 1881), 20.

42. Vaughan Sampson, Rev. J., *Statistical Survey of the County of Londonderry* (Dublin, 1802), 299.

43. Shaw Mason, William, *A Statistical Account or Parish Survey of Ireland*, II (Dublin, 1816), 156.

44. Otway, Rev. Caesar, *The Donegal Highlands*, 2nd edn. (Dublin, 1895), 162.

45. Hill, Lord George, *Facts from Gweedore* (Dublin, 1845), 15.

46. *Congested Districts Board for Ireland. Confidential Reports* (Dublin, 1892), 87.

47. Reid, Thomas, *Sketches of Ireland* (London, 1827), 162.

48. Binns, Jonathan, *The Miseries and Beauties of Ireland*, I (London, 1837), 206.

49. Barrow, John, *A Tour Round Ireland in The Autumn of 1835* (London, 1836), 179-80.

50. Hall, Mr. & Mrs. S.C., *Ireland: Its Scenery, Character, etc.*, III (London, 1843), 403.

51. Head, Sir Francis B., *A Fortnight in Ireland* (London, 1852), 145.

52. Special Correspondent of *The Times. Letters from Ireland, 1886* (London, 1887), 112.

53. Grant, Sir Arthur, *Eight Hundred Miles on an Outside Irish Car* (Aberdeen, 1891), 61-2.

54. *Proceedings of the Royal Irish Academy*, 19 C (1893-96), 627.

55. Trotter, John Bernard, *op. cit.*, 419-20.

56. Nicholson, Asenath, *Ireland's Welcome to the Stranger; or Excursions through Ireland in 1844 & 1845* (London, 1847), 395.

57. An Oxonian (Canon Hale), *A Little Tour in Ireland* (London, 1859), 57.

58. *Congested Districts Board for Ireland. Confidential Reports*, 449-50.

59. *ibid.*, 443.

60. *ibid.*, 459.

61. *Proceedings of the Royal Irish Academy*, 21 C (1898-1900), 258.

62. Weld, Isaac, *Statistical Survey of the County of Roscommon* (Dublin, 1832), 143.

63. *ibid.*, 143.

64. *ibid.*, 189, footnote.

65. *ibid.*, 397.

66. Gilbert, John T. (ed.), *Calendar of Ancient Records of Dublin*, II (Dublin, 1891), 332.

67. Gilbert, John T., *op. cit.*, III, 23-24.

68. Caulfield, Richard (ed.), *The Council Book of the Corporation of Youghal* (Guildford, 1878), 45.

69. *The Journals of the House of Commons of the Kingdom of Ireland*, I (1613-1661), (Dublin, 1753), 64.

70. Cooke, Thomas Lalor, *The Early History of the Town of Birr, or Parsonstown* (Dublin, 1875), Appendix 7, 387.

71. *Béaloideas*, 16 (1946), 97.

72. Simington, R.C. (ed.), *The Civil Survey A.D. 1654-1656. County of Tipperary*, I (Dublin, 1931), 113.

73. *ibid.*, 278.

74. Simington, R.C. (ed.), *op. cit.* I, 113, 125, 270, 278, 318, 326(2), 328, 336, 340, 342(2), 343, 352, 354, 364(2), 366, 367, 368, 369(2), 375(2), 387, 389; vol. 2, 217, 238, 246, 251, 253, 260, 261, 262, 263, 287, 288, 299, 300, 301, 302, 304(12), 305, 325, 336(2), 341, 342, 361(3), 363(2 or 3), 367(2), 384, 411.

75. *ibid.*, I, 113, 125, 317, 318, 326(3), 328, 336, 340, 342(5), 343(2), 352, 354, 364(3), 366, 367, 368(2), 369(2), 375(2).

76. *ibid.*, 113.

77. *ibid.*, 326.

78. *ibid.*, 369, 375.

79. *ibid.*, 375.

80. Simington, R.C. *op. cit.*, IV, 234, 387, 389.

81. *ibid.*, 496, 497, 508.

82. Simington, R.C. *op. cit.*, VI, 92, 114.

83. *ibid.*, 293, 305, 361, 362.

84. Simington, R.C. *op. cit.*, VII, 204, 233, 234, 240.

85. Simington, R.C. *op. cit.*, X, 48.

86. Simington, R.C. *op. cit.*, VII, 233.

87. *ibid.*, 204, 240.

88. *ibid.*, 234.
89. Simington, R.C. *op. cit.*, IV, 234.
90. Simington, R.C. *op. cit.*, VI, 362.
91. Petty, William, *The Political Anatomy of Ireland* (London, 1691). Reprinted in *A Collection of Tracts and Treatises illustrative of Ireland* (Dublin, 1861), 19.
92. *ibid.*, 20.
93. *ibid.*, 19.
94. Murray, R. (ed.), *The Journal of John Stevens* (Oxford, 1912), 139-40.

Welsh Cottages – the Literary Evidence

TREFOR M. OWEN

One must perforce use 'cottage' tongue-in-cheek in a *festschrift* for Caoimhín Ó Danachair, bearing in mind his clear dislike of the word because of its irrelevance to the Irish historical tradition. Its use is studiously avoided in his volume on *Ireland's Vernacular Architecture* in favour of alternative descriptions such as 'smaller house' or 'cabin', in spite of the fact that the book abounds in illustrations of what a Welshman would unhesitatingly identify as cottages! Nevertheless the point is taken that the word is too diffuse in meaning and extraneous in origin to be of any real value in a serious discussion of Irish vernacular architecture.

In the Welsh context, however, both 'cottage' and its modern Welsh counterpart 'bwthyn' are sufficiently specific (and recognized) to be used to refer to a small house without land, (other than possibly a small garden), standing on its own. Regional forms such as 'tŷ moel' (lit. 'bare house') in Caernarfonshire, and 'tai bach' (little houses) in Cardiganshire also occur, but the prevalent word is 'bwthyn'. Surprisingly, the first recorded use of this word, according to the University of Wales Dictionary, was as late as 1728, but the English word 'booth' from which it probably derived, occurs in the Welsh form 'bwth' as early as the fourteenth century and is translated in William Salesbury's Dictionary of 1547 as 'cottage'. In English dialect usage, however, 'booth' may refer to a cowhouse or dairy (west Yorkshire) or to a herdsman's hut (Lancashire); and in Scotland the cognate form 'bothy' signifies 'a hut or shed where agricultural labourers and hinds are lodged.'[1] The Welsh counterpart to 'bothy' in this sense, however, was not 'bwthyn' but 'llofft stabal' (stable loft) which fulfilled a similar purpose or, in an eighteenth century account 'the hinds' or ploughservants' room'.[2]

Literary references to cottages in Wales begin with descriptions of early tourists which were often scurrilous in nature and far from objective. Carefully used, however, these accounts, which were written by people belonging to a different social class and based on fleeting glimpses of the conditions to which they allude, provide valuable first-hand evidence, particularly during the period 1750-1850.[3] A parallel source of information is to be found in the works of the agricultural writers notably Walter Davies whose *General View of the Agriculture and Domestic Economy of North Wales* (1810) and the corresponding volumes on South Wales (1815) are written from a more objective standpoint. Official government publications such as the *Report on Education in Wales* (1847) and the monumental *Minutes of Evidence of the Royal Commission on Land in Wales* (1894-96) are often wider in scope than their official terms of reference. These are supplemented by later accounts in Welsh describing conditions which had disappeared with the rebuilding on agricultural estates in the middle of the nineteenth century or the subsequent depopulation of the countryside. In each case it is the detached position of the observer in time or place which leads to the social record. What was described was often too commonplace to be deemed worthy of notice by the inhabitants themselves.[4]

According to an account of Anglesey written in the middle of the seventeenth century the houses of the Penmynydd district of the island were 'but cotes, not fitt for a civil man to rest himself in for an hour or two, much less to lodge in'.[5] Almost a century later the traveller Torbuck commented in derogatory terms on the primitive nature of Welsh housing usually comprising 'but one Room, but that plentifully stocked with Inhabitants, for besides the Proprietor, their Children and Servants you shall have two or three swine and Black Cattle (white they are never without) under the same Roof . . . These houses have Holes dug in their sides that serve them for a double Purpose, both to let in light and to let out smoak; they represent both Windows and Chimnies. For should a Man have a Chimney perching on the Top of his Thatch'd Mansion there, he would stand in great Danger of being prick'd down for a High Sheriff.'[6] Torbuck noted the use of 'dirt' which was 'kneaded into Houses' which were 'low in stature so that a Man may ride upon the Ridge and yet have his legs hang in the Dirt'.[7] In another allusion to the practice of accommodating domestic animals in the dwelling house Torbuck describes a cottage in Dinas Mawddwy, Merioneth, as having 'the uppermost Room of the House (that had nothwithstanding a Clay Floor) which was hung with as noble and elegant Tapestry as ever Spider's Loom produced . . . It had two Beds at the Upper-end, a Goat and two Pigs at the Lower end, and a Fireplace in the Middle.'[8] Such an internal division is reminiscent of the dwelling-and-byre arrangement of the long-house of the period.[9] As late as the 1850s scores of houses in Dinas Mawddwy were said to have lattice windows usually of very small dimensions, and the practice was attributed to the high price of glass until 1851.[10] A traveller writing about the same district in 1775, however, comments more favourably on the houses he saw: 'The Cottages in general unpaved and un-glazed, but built of stone, or well-timbered and plaistered and covered often with Slate, and superior to the miserable Mud Hovels of Pembrokeshire and Carmarthen-shire, which are, I believe, the worst mansions of Human Beings on this side of the Tweed.'[11] Another contemporary description (written in 1796) makes use of the comparision with Scottish conditions. As one travels northwards from Cardigan town 'the Cottages have been dwindling away, almost to a Scotch hut but they are made something higher wider and lighter and more square than the High-landers.'[12] Housing conditions clearly varied from district to district, the pre-valent building material being that most readily to hand. The use of mud for walling is documented as early as the fourteenth century in Pembrokeshire and is doubtless of even greater antiquity,[13] and comparisons with English conditions are usually to the detriment of Wales.

> The Mud Houses in these Parts (i.e. Carmarthenshire) are of most wretched Construction. The Walls do not consist of Lath and Plaister, as in Suffolk, etc., but are entirely of Earth, and that not of Straw wrought up with it, but with sometimes a Layer of Straw; and the Chimneys, scarcely rising above the Roofs, are of conical wickerwork barely plaistered over. The Walls are often seen in the state of Vegetation; the Roofs universally

thatched, whereas in North Wales the Cottages are of stone covered with Slate, but they want those pretty little Gardens which the poorest Hovel here always has . . . Most of the Cottages are destitute of Glass Windows, instead of which neat Lattice-work.[14] (Figs. 1 and 2).

Travelling across central Wales from west to east in 1802 Walter Davies notes a comparable improvement in the quality of building, especially that of chimneys, after he has passed through Llangurig to the upper Severn Valley. 'The cottages are somewhat similar; the chimneys made up of hay-ropes. As soon as we draw nearer Llanidloes the face of the Country enlivens, the cottages have framed wooden chimnies, more common to Montgomeryshire than any other I know. An instance of once most plentiful building material of the Country, the greater number of the houses in the town of Llanidloes are cased with boards.'[15] Housing practices did not necessarily improve the farther east one travelled but reflected both social conditions and the available building materials. The Llanidloes area, however, had its 'clod hall' although by 1876 when its existence was recorded its original clods or sods had been replaced with more substantial material.[16] Even Shropshire was not without its 'clod houses', 'rude habitations constructed in the most primitive fashion of "clods" of turf, and though they generally consisted of but one apartment were sometimes inhabited by a numerous family, with the addition of a pig or two, a donkey and some poultry'. Two examples

Fig. 1   Interior of cottage, c. 1836, Dolgellau, Merioneth, by Edward Pryce Owen, 1788-1863

Fig. 2   Thatched cottage, 1931, near Pumpsaint, Carmarthenshire, showing two types of chimney

(since disappeared) were cited in 1876 at places within half a dozen miles of Shrewsbury.[17]

Further light is thrown on the building methods in north Wales by a description relating to Maentwrog, Merioneth, written in 1796:

> The materials and Manner of building in this Country is very singular, the Materials are a Mixture of large round Cobles, usually used whole, but sometimes split with Gunpowder and the spaces filled up, and whole Courses laid alternately of long Ragg Stones, all this for Cottages or farmhouses laid dry, and sometimes afterwards stuffed with Moss, and the better ones painted with lime Mortar, and then sand or rather the chippings of the rag stone thrown hard against the face of the mortar. The Rag Stones are got here of a great length, for on the Copeing of the bridge over the Dryryd (sc. Dwyryd) is one 15f 2in. long 1 and revet from 9 to 12 feet and then can be got of a great width and thickness, very excellent blue Slate is got near here.[18]

Some fifteen miles to the south, at Dolgellau, the masonry used in house construction attracted the attention of the writer Richard Fenton at the beginning of the nineteenth century.

> From time immemorial they have built with very large stones, even to the top, lifting the stones to the work from towards the middle course with an immense machine which takes above a day to erect, and worked by two men, every stone being of such a weight as to require a Lever of that vast power. *Quere* if this is not a dear sort of masonry. The Lintels of Doors and Windows are generally of immense Stones of a middling size are worked in regular courses and stones nearly of a size, they look well, as at Nanney, in the new house.[19]

Yet another variation in the building of walls was recorded in 1816 by Edward Pugh in the same county at Llanegryn, 'a mean and miserable village' near the coast. 'The houses are of a singular construction; the ends facing the sea are built of stones, rudely placed upon each other, as better calculated to bear the stones from thence; the sides also are built of the same materials to the height of one yard above the ground; and the remainder, to the straw roof, is made of well-tempered mud, intermixed with rushes which bind and render it durable. These huts have an uncomfortable appearance but the poor who inhabit them find them proof against the most rigid winter's cold.'[20] Elsewhere in the county of Merioneth, as in the Migneint moorland district bordering on Denbighshire, the cottages might be 'formed of stones and green turf'.[21]

The practice of whitewashing the walls of cottages was a feature noted in many areas but nowhere more frequently than in Glamorgan where it was described by Walter Davies as an 'universal custom'. Byng, writing in 1787 ascribes the practice, which he observed in one Cardiff district — where even the roofs of houses and churches were whitewashed — to the quantity of lime produced in the county.[22] Further west in the vicinity of Margam and Neath in the same county he comments on the same custom: 'Such is the whitewashing of this country, which gives a pleasant look (though they are dirty beasts) that they not only whiten their houses, but the pales, and any great stone that is at hand: the graves, from the whiten'd stones around their tops of little flowers, look like children's gardens.'[23] Despite the 'outside show of neatness by the white-washing of their houses', Glamorgan folk neglected the interior of their homes and 'it were well they should apply a tub of water for the cleanliness of the inside of their houses, which like their persons are ever in filth and nastiness.'[24] The prevalence and frequency of whitewashing was remarked upon by another traveller who visited Glamorgan in 1781 noting that 'there is scarcely a cottage to be seen which is not regularly brushed over every month.'[25]

Cottage interiors were far less accessible to travellers and were often viewed as we have seen in Torbuck's references, with a patronizing disdain. Some writers were obviously shocked by what they saw. Edward Pugh in a work published in 1816 describes a house which he visited between Llyn Du Bach and Ffestiniog in Merioneth: 'Rather lower down I entered a shed on the edge of the road, the most miserable dwelling the mind can conceive: something in the shape of beds occupied the ends of the room; in the centre, about two yards square was a fire of turf on the ground, and three little naked children running about.'[26] At Rhyd-y-fen in the same district the English writer described a similar scene in rather uninspired doggerel:

Arriving I crept through a hole in the door
Some stones were laid down and some not on the floor,
The whole was one dark room with three windows so small,
That the light down the chimney quite outstript them all.
But this great relief came to soften their cares
Neither sober nor drunk could they tumble downstairs;
Two beds graced the mansion, which made it appear
That cleanliness, prudence and order reigned there.
The tables and cupboards which opened to view
Shewed the hand of industry had polished them true.
The shelves and their crockery, both china and delph,

Were clean and were orderly ranged on the shelf;
Dad, Mam and nine children which fortune bestowed,
In harmony lived in this darksome abode;
Nor can we consent to call these people poor,
Where prudence steps in and bars want from the door.[27]

Hutton's evidence despite its rather mocking expression is nonetheless valuable. His account of the preparation for a wedding feast in Cwm-y-glo, near Llanberis, Caernarvonshire indicates how the hearth could accommodate a large number of cooking vessels, if required:

A fire of square peat and sufficiently dried,
Was spread on the hearth, and at least four feet wide;
Over which took their stations six kettles or more,
Which promised a feast, when they opened their store;
And round this flat furnace, to keep them quite hot,
Were plac'd twelve more vessels, which held — God knows what,
Four cooks in short bed-gowns, attend by desire,
Like the witches in Macbeth, to stir up the fire.[28]

In the same district of Cwm-y-glo, W. Bingley was taken by his friend the local clergyman and antiquary Peter Williams to inspect a typical cottage occupied by a smallholder. As in other quarrying areas slate slabs were used extensively in building construction; 'a large slate placed on one side, with its edge on the ground' formed a hay rick. In Llainfadyn cottage, built in 1762 and removed to the Welsh Folk Museum, a similar slate is used for the 'palis' or partition near the door protecting the small living room and hearth from draughts. The interior of the cottage described by Bingley was so dark he could hardly distinguish anything in the hut except the gleam of light that came down the chimney. After a while he could discern the 'frame of the roof . . . formed by branches of trees fixed to large timbers by straw or hay-bands. This frame was covered with sods, and the whole with slates, which in the mountains are obtained in great plenty.'[29]

This particular cottage was occupied by an old man living alone and was quite different in atmosphere from the spirited scene described by Pratt in a hut near the sea at Barmouth, Merioneth, occupied by a family of fourteen. The sides of the hovel were so thick with ivy as to conceal the presence of the one-roomed building. Its mud walls had never been whitewashed and more light came from gaps in the thatched roof than from the window. Most of the occupants were engaged in some useful activity or other: the father was making nets, the mother shaving one of the local innkeepers, the eldest son weaving ribbons, the eldest daughter weaving cloth, the second son mending a petticoat, the second daughter repairing breeches, the third daughter combing the hair of the fourth who was knitting stockings; the sixth girl was baking bread; the seventh making broth; the eighth was rocking the cradle of the youngest child with her foot and dangling another in her arms while the fifth daughter was making first experiments at the spinning wheel. The whole household slept in three miserable beds, only one of which had curtains, and in a bed of dirty-looking straw with a covering of old sacks. These were the only furniture and yet the large family struck Pratt as a particularly happy one.[30] No doubt in a farming district (as opposed to a fishing village) the older children would have been in service on the larger farms housed in the stable lofts and maids' quarters.

Although the conditions described by Pratt are those of an indigent peasant, the homes of persons of higher status were hardly better. During a tour made in 1802 Walter Davies, himself a clergyman, described a curate's house in the parish of 'Llan-n.d-a' in Pembrokeshire in somewhat cryptic terms. It was a

> thatched house with white-washed front, none other of that description being in the village . . . On knocking, the curate's wife left the churn to come and open the Door . . . Bed in hall, another in Kitchen, and another in parlour . . . and in three words more the inventory of the whole furniture might be completed. One storey Had a view of the three aptments and whole roof at once because partitions scarcely higher than those of pews in church or folds in a sheep market. The roof over was the most curious part of the fabric. It was not made of stucko but of hay ropes curiously woven, and covered with the gum of culm soot. But curious as it was it did not hold water well.[31]

It is interesting to note that Walter Davies's own home, Y Wern, near Domen Castell, Llanfechain, Montgomeryshire, was hardly less lowly. 'It merely comprised a kitchen and two "chambers" or sleeping apartments. These rooms were called "chambers" as being on the ground floor, on the same level as the kitchen, and also to distinguish them from the *llofft* which would be an upstairs room. These humble dormitories – for they were only in this class of cottages – were mostly unpaved and unboarded, having the simple soil, or a layer of yellow clay, as a floor. Such was the Wern . . . with its straw roof and whitened walls.' The Davies family incidentally, consisted of nine persons, of whom two sons lodged out.[32]

The most reliable descriptions of the cottage interiors of the nineteenth century are to be found in the government reports, particularly the Education Report of 1847, which contain numerous objective accounts of domestic conditions by clergymen, doctors, landowners and persons of similar status. Emphasis was placed on the absence of sanitation and on overcrowding. For example, a cottage in St. Clears, Carmarthenshire, which was only about eight feet square was said to be occupied by a mother and four – previously five – children. The single room was divided by a partition of wattle. The chimney descended from the roof 'like a bonnet or umbrella' and was made of plastered wattle but the orifice of the chimney was so large that a heavy shower would have put the fire out. The 'ceiling' consisted of poles resting in the wallplates, strewn with brushwood. One of the girls slept in a box with the lid off; the rest of the family shared the one bed.[33] Regional differences are occasionally stressed: the pigsties of Monmouthshire were said by one witness (a mason) to be better than the turf cottages of the Builth district of Brecknock, particularly those built on the commons.[34] According to the vicar of Llandeilo the cupboard beds found in the local cottages were shut up as soon as the occupants quit them and never opened again until night. The use of linen by day or night was 'until lately' almost unknown but was coming into fashion among the young people.[35]

The primitive conditions which they encountered and, fortunately for the ethnologist, described, were universally deplored by the respectable witnesses whose testimony is preserved in these official publications. Their prevalence was ascribed to persistent poverty and ignorance, and any indications of improvement were warmly acclaimed. During the second half of the nineteenth century many of the cottages of the kinds recorded for us by both travellers and government witnesses disappeared as the population moved into the developing industrial areas. Estate-built cottages with considerably better accommodation housed a declining agricultural labour force. Even those cottages which survived were transformed inside by the proliferation of Victorian bric-a-brac, and extended or raised in height as living standards improved, eventually ending their days as holiday cottages or week-end homes in tourist districts.

NOTES AND REFERENCES

1. Wright, J., *English Dialect Dictionary* (1898).
2. Jones, F., *Transactions of the Anglesey Antiquarian Society*, (1940).
3. Books by tourists visiting Wales are reported and discussed by Hughes, W.J., *Wales and the Welsh in English Literature* (1924).
4. Serious discussion of cottages in Wales began with publication of Hughes, H. Harold and North, H.L., *Old Cottages of Snowdonia* (1908). Notable contributions were made by Sir Cyril Fox in 'Peasant Crafts in North Pembrokeshire', *Antiquity*, 11 (1937), 427-440, and in Peate, I.C., *The Welsh House* (1940).
5. *Transactions of the Anglesey Antiquarian Society*, (1952), 1.
6. Torbuck, J., *A Collection of Welsh Travels and Memoirs of Wales* (1738), 6.
7. *ibid.*, 6.
8. *ibid.*, 17.
9. Peate, I.C., *op.cit.*
10. *Cymru*, 57 (1919), 9.123.
11. Vaughan, H.M., 'A Synopsis of Two Tours made in Wales in 1775 and in 1811', *Y Cymmrodor*, 38 (1927), 67.
12. National Library of Wales, MS 2258, 45.
13. *National Library of Wales Journal*, 4 (1945-6), 168. A nineteenth-century account describes the mud and thatch cabins near Aberporth, Cardiganshire in the following terms. 'These clod-made dwellings are quite out of date now, and the process of building is well-nigh forgotten. We learn that the red earth of which they were formed was mixed with water and made into a paste by treading it in the fashion in which culm is yet made, and then the paste was mixed with straw. Stones were sometimes used here and there in the walls but usually the mud was used from foundation to roof. The walls are, of course, very thick, and are rounded at the corners of the buildings. They are covered with thatch, bound — except in superior thatching — with visible straw ropes running across the roof, and the chimneys are mere round orifices with a neat straw-rope margin around them . . . These cottages may be seen in every stage of preservation or decay; the mud walls crumble into curious forms, and are gradually destroyed by the farmers, who find the substance of the walls the richest of manures.' Horsfall-Turner, E.R., *Walks and Wanderings in County Cardigan* (n.d.), 140-41.
14. Vaughan, H.M., *op. cit.*, 49.
15. National Library of Wales, MS 1730, 152-53.
16. *Bye-gones*, 15 Nov. 1876, 150.
17. *ibid.*, 25 Oct. 1876, 136.
18. National Library of Wales, MS 2258, 54-55.
19. Fenton, Richard, *Tours in Wales (1804-13)* (1917), 94.
20. Pugh, E., *Cambria Depicta: A Tour through Wales* (1816), 94.
21. Byng, John, *The Torrington Diaries*, III (1935, 1936), 262.
22. *ibid.*, VI, 280.
23. *ibid.*, I, 295.
24. *ibid.*, I, 302.
25. Wyndham, H.P., *A Tour through Monmouthshire and Wales made in . . . 1774 and . . . 1777* (1781), 151.
26. Pugh, E., *op. cit.*, 404.
27. Hutton, W., quoted in *Bye-gones*, 12 July 1882, 96.

28. *ibid.*
29. Bingley, W.R., *North Wales: its scenery, antiquities, customs etc.*, I (1804), 219-20.
30. Pratt, S.J., *Gleanings from Wales, Holland and Westphalia* (1797), 44-49.
31. National Library of Wales, MS 1730, 122-23.
32. *Byegones*, 26 Mar. 1876, 87.
33. *Report of the Commissioners of Inquiry into the State of Education in Wales* (1847), I, 244.
34. *ibid.*, 73.
35. *ibid.*, 229.

A Dumfriesshire Drystone Dyker

ANNE-BERIT Ø BORCHGREVINK

Oh, gie me the bield o' a dry-stane dyke,
when the win' blaws cauld and snell.
Oh, gie me the shade o' a dry-stane dyke
when the sun's as hot as hell!
Oh gie me the strength o' a dry-stane dyke,
sae rugged, sae stie, an' sae true.
Oh gie me a frien' like the dry-stane dyke
that I've been describen tae you.

This poem, written by Charles Scott Jardine (b. 1909) was first read to me by himself one fine May evening in 1979, when I was visiting his home at Auldgirth, Dumfries. Charlie, one of the 'grand old men' of drystone-dyking in Scotland, was then retired, but still in full activity as a dyking instructor at Agricultural Training Board courses all over Scotland. It was in this capacity that the writer first happened to meet him. As part of her researches in Scotland in 1979 on the traditional use of dykes and hedges as fences and boundaries, she found herself on a cold, windy morning in March among a handful of lads on a field in Dumfriesshire, trying their hands at drystone-dyking under Charlie Jardine's skilful guidance. Charlie, the first of many drystone-dykers encountered in Scotland, taught her the basics of dyking as well as giving her a share in generations' knowledge about a craft and a way of living.

The following pages give, in his own words, some of the information which he has given in two long, taped interviews. The account is an edited version of parts of the literal transcription leaving out the interviewer's questions, but otherwise sticking as closely as possible to the way in which Charlie was putting it. Whenever necessary for understanding, a word or two is put in between brackets by the writer. For any inconsistencies in the orthographic transcription, the writer is to blame.

Not all the topics touched on during the interviews are rendered here, only main parts of the story. However, it is believed that Charlie's account is a true and important description of a craft, its skills and the society it belongs to.

* * *

Fig. 1   Roadside dyke (double dyke) built by Charles Scott Jardine's grandfather, 120-130 years ago. Moniaive area, Dumfriesshire

Fig. 2   Charles Scott Jardine (left) setting the lines on the frame for rebuilding part of a dyke which has been stripped down. Note the plumb line on the frame. (Dyking course, Kirkland Farm, Courrins/Parkgate, Dumfries, March 1979)

Well, my name's Charles Scott Jardine. I live in Dumfriesshire and I've lived in Dumfriesshire all my days. I started to dyke when I left the school at fourteen year old.

I started dyking in 1923. I started when I was fourteen year old, and I worked for fifty-three years before I retired.

I served my time with my father. He was the third generation and I'm the fourth generation of stone-dykers in the Jardine family.

They were all stone-dykers, and they've been for centuries, four generations. In the district where I belong there was three villages, and there was about four or five families o' dykers in each village; about four and five men working in one family. And they worked in the districts that they belonged, and that's how your . . . got all the stones used up in these districts. It was ploughed up the fields. Quite a lot o' places they were quarried in quarries, and that gave a lot o' employment to other fellas that weren't dykers.

The village that I belonged to was Dunscore. There was one seven miles away — Moniaive. There's another one, five miles to the east — Penpont. And there was about four or five families of dykers in each village.

There was three villages, and there was thirty-two dykers in the three villages. It was one o' the main jobs. That was in Moniaive, Dunsker and Penpont. That was before the last world war. After the war was past, the biggest lot o' them never came back, and that's what did away wi' a lot o' the good dykers.

Well, in my father's time there could be more, there could be more dykers — in my father's time.

They'd all plenty o' work. Anyone able to dyke'll never run out o' a job.

I've worked at stone-dyking all my life, and mostly in the Dumfries area. Up to Lanarkshire border and down near Gretna. That's runs in about thirty miles either way. I worked in the Moniaive area for the first three years, I think, I served my time. We cycled every morning and back at night. It was seven miles to Moniaive. The first job we cycled to was five miles above Moniaive. So that was twelve, and we left home about half-past seven in the morning and it was about nine o'clock when we got to the job. Back at night, aye. Stopped at half-past four, and it took me an hour and a half to cycle home.

I worked with my father, oh, until I got married. I worked with my father for about fifteen years. And after that I started out on m'own. I'd another three brothers that was dykers. They worked with my father, and when I started off on my own I took another man on and we worked together.

I never worked with my grandfather. He was retired before I started. Much of the jobs on — he did quite a lot o' work on Maxton Braes that's on the Moniaive area. He built all the roadside dykes up through there and all the field dykes on Maxwellton Estate. And these are dykes today which will be 120, 130 year old. They're standing as straight as the day they was put up.

He worked in the same area. I don't know anything about his work, but every different family had a different style from another. You could go to a dyke and you could know who built that dyke, owing to the style it was. Some families used the hammer far more than another family and they broke up their stones and had far more small chips in it. Other families had the knack of putting the stones together without breaking them, and they didn't use the hammer so much.

It was just called the Jardine dyke. People know today, coming round, looking

Fig. 3   Charles Scott Jardine laying the foundation for rebuilding the dyke, March 1979

at the dykes, certain people — 'That dyke was built by the Jardines.' A family o' Blacks ... There was such a difference between the Blacks and the Jardines — and they all belonged to the same district — and you could tell, looking at the dyke whether it was built with Jardines or Blacks.

The Blacks used the hammers too much. The farmers used to crib at them for breaking up the stones so much to put them on. They didn't lift the big stones and put them on full size. They broke them up into small pieces.

You know their method and you know their work. Well, in every district there's different types o' stones. The method o' putting them together's always the same. Just the same, the method's just the same, and the style o' building is still the same. It's been all from one lot o' training. Well, the method o' putting the stones together and the way to handle stone, that's the art that's in the craft. That's one thing that's handed on. That's kept in the family.

The like o' the Blacks, the Jardines, and the Stewarts, Todds, all these dykers, — the father was the employer and it was the sons of the brothers, his brothers or his sons that worked with him. He did the paying and did the contracting for the work. All (were) employed by the head of the family.

It still keeps a family business. Dyking seems to run in the blood. They don't know how ... There was a saying long ago that to be a dyker you'd to be able to sleep with a dyker, which meant that you'd to be working with him for a long time before you could do the job.

There was two dykers mostly in each estate. But there was a lot o' the families, did contract work, and they went out in the morning and they worked long days. In my grandfather's time I've heard them saying they went away at six o'clock in the morning, and they weren't back until six o'clock at night. (With) a horse and a cart. My grandfather worked with a horse and a cart. He went away in the morning and (he'd) maybe travel maybe seven miles, and he'd come back at night.

Well, they were contractors. You heard of a job and you went out and saw the job and you put in an estimate for the job; and it was maybe three or four, maybe more estimates for the job, and it was the one that did the cheapest job that got the job. But they'd to be professional dykers in these days.

Mostly (they had to give) a written estimate. You'd all to have written estimates. When a job come up like that, some o' these big jobs, they'd put out a specification which the job had to be carried out to the specification. Certain things was to be done, and the work was to be well-done with a practical dyker. And to finish up with the job, it was examined by a man that knew about the dyke, and if it didn't pass he would turn it down, and you wouldnae get any pay. These old factors knew all about the job and how it should be done, and if it was done right.

The dykes was all measured up. They had a chain, and they measured it with the chain — twenty-two yards. That was a chain. That was the common way o' doing it. They measured drains and dykes with this chain. It was truer, truer for the man that was doing the job, working with a chain rather as a tape. A tape would shrink and it could stretch. But a chain, when you measured it with a chain along the ground, it fell into all the holes. You got the full measurement.

If you're with a good dyker it takes three years for tae learn the job and be able for to do as much as what'll make a day's work pay — so much a yard. You've got to be able to build so many yards, which makes your pay reasonable with other trades. Mostly dykers long ago, they all run in families and they follow it on from one to the other, and it seemed tae work in and they seemed to learn it far better. A fella who's start'n' off, whose father's been a dyker, he seems to pick up the job far quicker than if someone just taken a notion to the job, and coming and start'n' off.

In the time that I was a dyker, I was in business myself for about thirty years, and that time I'd twelve apprentices. 'Fore I finished off, two or three years before I finished off, I had seven and eight dykers working with me all the time. When there's two or three working together, you could always carry one or two apprentices.

Well, it was best working with a pair. To start off with, he got the job o' laying in the stones, how to lay them in and then the dykers would be building the sides, and the first job he got would be breaking stones and doing the packing. As he worked on he would get putting one or two stones in the side until he got into the way of it. Then he would get so much to do in front of the dykers so as the dyker could follow on behind him, and if the stones weren't right, they could take them off and put them right. If you take an apprentice on, you've got to keep him interested in the job all the time. If you leave him back and let him lag, he gets fed up and leaves the job. If you can keep him working in front o' you and keep him interested in what he's doing, and keep him right, you'll find that it keeps him on the job and it gives him a big interest in what he's doing. Once he's able to put on stones that he can stand back and have a look at and say, 'These are well-laid,' it gives him good encouragement for to go on and be able to learn the whole thing.

We were working in pairs, mostly. Oh, yes. Well, if possible, if you can get the mate, it's far easier working a' pair-working (than) as a single man, because wi' pair-working you stay on one side of the dyke, and you work on one side of the dyke. You've no jumping over the dyke from one side to the other. There's a man on either side, and if there's any big stones, you can get help to lift stones, wherefore you'd have be struggling yersel'. I've never, since I started, I've never been out of a job. There's always been plenty of stone dykes to build, and still the same today. Anyone that can build a dyke today — there ('s a) job for a lifetime . . . I've always had good health, and that's one of the main things.

The cold weather and bad weather never interfered with my work. We didna' work on wet days or anything like that. It'd come a wet day, we just stopped and wait until the rain went off and then start again. It didnae pay for tae get wet. The stones were difficult to handle. If you were working with big stones, when they got wet, they were like moss on them stones. The stones get slippery and you can't handle them the same, and you're apt to get your fingers hurt. If the stones arc big, they slip and you let them fall on your toes. And if you put coats on and work when it's raining, you sweat too much inside, inside the coats, and the next day you have a sore back.

Fig. 4 The double dyke has been built up to the level of the first lines (about nine inches) and Charlie is now. setting the lines at about twenty-one inches — the height of the first course. Note the tight packing (hearting) of the dyke

I worked all the year round. When you're contracting for work you get lots o' different jobs. Hill jobs you went to in the summer time, and worked in the summer time. But you'd always other jobs lying back which could be worked in the winter time — shelter jobs and dykes which was just struck down. The stones were fresh every morning when you took them down, and you could take them down as much as what you could build, and put them back up again. In the winter time never leave any stones lying on the ground, because if it'd come a hard frost at night ye couldn't lift them . . .

If there was young fellas starting off — maybe a boy or two boys starting, the young boys working along with them, they'd be taking the dyke down and stripping it out, and when they started to build it the boys did the heart'n' and packing. Dykers put on the outsides and got the boys behind them and worked side by side, and the boys did the packing until it come the day they had got knowledge for tae carry on and build the side. He started off a boy, that was one o' the first jobs he did — stripping the dyke down, and when the dyke was built he got peggin' it up and finishing it off and clearing up the stones.

You would all work together. In a morning you would strip the dyke down as much as you could put up in a day. If there was four or five working, you took, maybe, six yards per man down, and by night time you'd have that all built back in, and you'd have a good stretch o' dyke to show for every day.

Different parts o' the country you get different types o' stones. Some parts o' the country they're round; other parts they're quite flat, and other parts you get big stones, some parts you get small stones. It doesn't matter where you're working or what type of stone you work with, the method of puttin' a' together is just still the same.

Most of the farms all round here and all round Dumfriesshire, — most o' the stones have been ploughed out o' the ground and gathered off; and this was a way where a lot o' farms were to get rid o' the stones. They built boundary dykes and dykes round small parks rather as put the stones in a big heap and leave them in the centre of the field. It was a way o' get'n the stones out the way and they were useful once they were built into dykes. I started off with my father. First job we did, first job I did — were a march dyke over hill. We'd two mile to walk over the hill to this march dyke, which was 850 yards long. We walked over to that dyke for a whole summer, and there was only two days that summer we'd to come back home for rain. That was a good summer.

You don't need a lot o' tools for building a dyke: a pick and a hammer, and a spade, and a frame the shape o' the dyke. For a four-foot-six dyke, if it's double dyke, that's small stones built on either side, you need a frame of about three foot high. You dig out a foundation at the bottom, under the ground about maybe four to five inches. You lay in your foundation a' thirty inches wide. After you've your foundation laid in and hearted and packed up, you set your frame on, which is twenty-six inches wide at the bottom and this gives your dyke a good seat on your foundation, and won't slip off. If you don't make your foundation wider than what the dyke's gonna start off at, the stones are apt to slide out and fall off.

(You use) large stones (in the foundation). That's when you get rid of all the big stones to start with, big rough stones, and stones that you maybe wouldna' be able to lift higher up. You could put them in the bottom and get rid o' them

Fig. 5   The dyke being built up to the second line. Two pairs are working on this section, building against each other one on either side of the dyke. Note the slight batter in the face of the dyke and how the dyke is tied together by putting the stones across rather than along the dyke

that way. You're get'n a good foundation, and it gives you a good start to build the dyke. After your frame's set you start building off. If there's two o' ye's working, one on either side, you build in against each other and both sides o' your dyke are tied together. First course you build up to about twenty-one inches high from ground level and put your through-bands in. These are ties which go right through, and are set in at three-foot intervals. They should be out about two to three inches from the face of your wall, and if they're good flat stones it makes quite a good step for anyone want to climb the dyke. It gives you a good step over.

(The through-bands are at about) three-foot intervals along the dyke, along the side o' the dyke. If you've plenty of them, if you've plenty o' good flat stones, you could put in two rows. Quite a lot o' dykes have two rows of through-bands. One set may be fifteen inches from ground level, and the next one set about two foot three from ground level. That's like two rows of through-bands. If you have plenty of them. It makes your dyke far stronger.

One of the main things in laying the stone is when you lift the stone and have a look at it. Always find out the flattest bed in your stone. If you prepare your bed for your stones with packing the centre and levelling the side of the dyke, always lay your stone on the flattest bed, no matter what the top o' the stone's like. You can always get another stone to sit in the top o' it, once you have built it up again ready for the next stone going on.

We build stones together. You don't have joints running all the way up the wall. Make sure that one stone's laid on two, and two stones laid on one, and you'll always have a broken joint.

The small stones — you break them up and pack them in. You don't throw them in. And bring you heartin' — it can either be 'heartin'' or 'packin'', bring it up along wi' your sides. You've always got a bed for to lay your next stone on if you keep your 'heart' up, slightly up if anything, for to keep the stones to shed the water out. If it comes a wet time and the rain's hitt'n' the dyke, when the stones are laid right, it sheds the water out instead o' shedd'n' the water in. If the stone's right laid and right packed, once your dyke sets down, your stones will be all firm and tight in the outside joints and they'll be sitt'n' tight and firm in the centre. But if it's no a dyke that's been packed or hearted your stones fall down in the nose, in the centre of the dyke, and they're awful apt for slippin' out.

Once you have your double up to about three foot, if it's a four-and-a-half foot dyke, you put a row right along — what they call copestones. These stones go right across the top o' your double, protruding about two or three inches and they're all blocked tight together. Flat ones, always flat ones, or flat bottom anyway, so's it'll lie on the top o' the double. After these are on, that's it ready for to put your top on.

The top — that's where you select your stones for to put your top on. You select stones that'll be aboot the height and sit tight on an upright position. If you can build your top stones in, set them in and block the wall tight together and wedge them, they'll stay there for a long time, and you can key them up and wedge them up that they won't fall off. It holds all the rest of the stones together. Once the weight's on the top o' the smaller stones, it keeps the smaller stones all in position. It takes over a ton o' stones to the yard for a four-foot-six dyke, and that's quite a lot o' stones. A man dyking every day and building in six yards — if it's a rebuild dyke or even a new dyke — he's a lot o' handle in the stones. He handles aboot twelve ton o' stones a day. If it's a rebuild he turns six ton o' stones out if he's building six yards, and he builds them back in; therefore, he's handled twelve ton o' stones a day. If you reckon that out — five days a week for fifty-four years, you can find out how many stones he's handled in that time.

When I go to instruct at the colleges, some o' the lads often ask, 'How much dyke have you built in the time you've been at it?' Well, I've worked it out, and I mostly say, 'If you've worked say five days a week, takin' an average, — ye're a lot of days off — but if you work five days a week on an average for fifty-four years, and build six yards in a day, you'll find out that it runs aboot seventy-six miles.'

The farmers lifted the stones off the farms, which were mostly in heaps on the farm, and hauled them over to where the dyke was to be built and tipped them out. The dyker had to lay them out. It took a lot o' work laying the stones out on either side of where you were gonna build the dyke before ever you got to start on it.

Well, you lay stones down for the dyke. If you've a lot o' small stones, you lay the small stones nearer where you're gonna be building the side o' your dyke, and your bigger stones further out, so's that in rotation you build your double stones in to the height of three foot, then you put your covers on and your tops in. If you lay them out right, you can build the double stones in. You come to the next row of stones and they're all lyin' there, all in rotation, ready for putting on.

Sometimes you get dykes where there're just, maybe, twenty-one inches o' double on the bottom, with through-bands all laid firm and right together, and big single stones all set up on their edge and all blocked together. Quite a strong dyke, and there's quite a lot o' these dykes in Galloway, what they call the Galloway dyke — big, strong boulder dyke. A single dyke, in the top half, twenty-one inches in the double. Some places over the hills in Galloway it's big single stones all the way, right from the bottom.

That's one o' the main things you've got to learn — how to break a stone, how to look at the stone and find out how it's gonna break. Rather as (than) lay the stone down and hammer at it, and hammer at it all the time and it'll never break. You've got to be able to have an eye for . . . to look at the stone and know how it's gonna break, how the grain in the stone . . . there's a grain in every stone. Some stones are quite easy broken in the grain. Granite stone — you need quite a

Fig. 6 The through-bands are being put in, at about three-foot intervals along the dyke

heavy hammer, but you can break them still the same.

(You do) no more (splitting) than you can help, because if you get into the habit of cutting and breaking your stones up, it slows the job up quite a lot. You've got to get into the way of just lifting your stones and building them in. You've always got to break a certain amount for packing in the centre.

The quickest dyke to build's a single-stone dyke with, maybe, about two foot o' double in the bottom, double stones on either side, covers on the top o' the doubles, then single stones. A man working himself gets on faster with a job like this, as a double dyke all the way up. Once you get practised and able to do the job, you know right away whatever type o' dyke you're gonna build and how you're gonna build it.

If they're well put together they're just as strong — either the double or the single. I've built quite a lot o' granite stones, which is the Galloway-type o' stone. It's a big round boulder stone, and it's very sore on the hands to work with. But when it's right put together it'll stand there for long enough. Granite is very sore on the hands. You've got to work it very carefully. If one slips out of your hands it takes all the skin off your fingers.

Sandstone's nice'n' easy to work with, and it's no too bad on the fingers. If it's a wet time it can be bad, but if it's dry, if it's a dry time when you're building the dyke, the sandstone's quite easy on your hands. And your hands are always nice and smooth when you're finished off with the job.

Limestone's difficult to work with. It's a rugged face, and it's a stone that's very brittle. Throughout the years it breaks up and if you strip down a limestone dyke, there's a terrible lot lyin' on the ground when you're finished building it, because a terrible lot o' the stones just break up and they're no fit to be built back in. It needs quite a lot o' new stones put back in. You need a lot more stones to rebuild it back up to the same height.

Well, on dykes you'll find gates where they've got to have room for to have a tractor going through, and you've got to build up the end of the dyke in a way that it'll stand. There's different methods how to put the stones in across the end o' the dyke. If you start off with one long stone running right through the end of the dyke, you've got to have the next one running back from there back into the dyke. This retains the end o' your dyke and makes it solid and strong and it won't fall down. Just set one stone on top o' the other and dig a hole to put a post in for to carry the gate ear and the end o' your dyke'll just fall down; but if it's built the right way with stones running alternative across the face o' the dyke and back, maybe eighteen inches, two feet back into the existin' dyke, it'll hold the end o' the dyke up and it won't need the post to hold it — the end o' the dyke up.

Very often we put in the gates. You put in the gateposts and hung the gate before you built the ends o' your dykes, because if you built the ends o' your dykes first, and then started to dig holes, you'd come on a big piece o' stone which was maybe sticking in below the dyke. It loosened the whole foundation o' your dyke. So therefore, it was advisable for to dig your holes and set in your posts and hang your gate before you built the ends o' your dyke.

The farmer mostly supplied the gates. Maybe, other times you'd buy in gates, and maybe keep a stock o' gates with posts. If it was iron gates, you put in iron posts, and if it was wooden gates it was mostly wooden posts. The posts had to be about, for to carry the gate, they had to be at least three foot in the ground. The heels o' the posts, — there was no use putting the posts in and just flinging the soil in — you'd to put the posts in and you'd to heel them at the back so as the post wouldn't slip back into the soil when the weight o' the gate come on and pulled the top o' the post down. It had to be wedged in the heel on the back side, and when you come up near the top o' the hole it had to be wedged in the top, in the front side o' the gate so's it carried the gate without moving the post and letting the point o' the gate down. It was methods o' doing it.

Well, a 'lunky hole' is just a passage through the extent of the dyke with the top and the covers on the top making it a block for cattle, but sheep can get through. That's the Scottish name for the holes through the dyke, or a run hole. Lots o' them call them just running holes for stock. In the Dumfriesshire area they're always called the 'lunky hole'. This is a hole left in the dyke, mostly march dykes for stock that had strayed over the dyke. It was a way o' getting them back without taking them long distances round about it. The 'lunky hole' left in the dyke — this was an opening about two feet wide, with ends built up to about two foot six high and a big stone, cover stone, laid right across the top of it. This left an opening right through from one side to the other.

They'd just block up that hole, just roughly with stones, just maybe built a wee bit rougher, and leave a small hole in the top between the cover and what you've put in, so's it gives a guide for anyone looking along the dyke. A shepherd knows where they all are. Someone coming along and seeing this gap, if they just take a look, they'll see how this has been built up, ready for to strip out and put any stray stock through if it was required. It could be built in roughly again just to block up the hole.

They can do for . . . you can make them smaller which you can run drains through, or rabbits or hares or game run through from the woods into the fields. If you go into any estate and go round the woods where there's dykes, you'll find quite a lot o' small 'lunky holes'. This allows the game and rabbits to run through from the fields into the wood and back the other way.

Yes. If it's . . . one side of the dyke would be wet, maybe marshy ground and the other side dry, and they were wanting to run water from one side through, they dug a drain through the small 'lunky holes' down into the ground. This kept the water from running down the centre o' your dyke, and washing the foundation out o' your dyke. If you go on a hill dyke, very often where it's been built along a wet part, if the drains have got blocked up, you'll see where the water has run down and washed all the foundation out o' the dyke. The dyke'll be . . . it'll no be standing straight, it'll be tumbling one way and tumbling another way, because the sides o' your dyke have been washed out from the very bottom. If it's mossy ground they sink in quite a lot, but they can be built on any kinda ground. It doesnae matter whether it's mossy or rocky. You can build the dyke on anything. You can build the dyke on places where you couldnae put a post end to put a fence up. You can build the dyke along mossy ground and it'll stand there quite a long time if you don't break the top o' the soil. Through a moss — if you cut into the moss, it sinks far quicker, but if you build your dyke on the top o' the moss, which is very tough, your dyke will sit on the top o' that. It'll sink in throughout the years a wee bit, but it'll stand there for a long, long time. (It is important) not to break the surface, because if you go through a moss that's

Fig. 7 Charles Scott Jardine putting on the flat copestones. They are blocked tight together, covering the dyke and protruding two or three inches on either side

always about a foot, maybe a wee bit more o' strong, tough fibre and as long as you build your dyke on the top o' that fibre in that moss, your dyke'll stand, but whenever you cut that and go down into the black moss, your dyke just sits in. Go through some o' these mossy places, you'll get dykes sitting down about as far as fifteen and eighteen inches sunk into the moss. On the field, if you were building a new part o' a dyke, if you take the turf off the top and level it out to about four or five inches, it's quite ample for to carry the weight o' dyke, and it gives you a good grip in. If you build just on the top o' the turf, you're no able to make your dyke as solid as what you would be if you had cut a foundation and set it into the ground.

Well, if there've been dykes in the hills and you're rebuilding them, and you build them on the old foundation, if the old foundation's good, you'll build a far stronger dyke on the top o' the old foundation as (than) what it was the first time, because the foundation's set into the ground and it'll never move. Therefore, when you cut the foundation on some o' these hill dykes to take out the stones and build them back in, you very often find soft parts which would sink in again. If you can leave the foundation stone sitting, and rebuild the dyke on the top o' the stones that are lying there, it wouldna sink any more.

Well, you'll get these dykes running, a lot o' Scottish dykes running straight up are march dykes, running straight up the hill, and very steep ground. Well, when these dykes were built, people used to ask how they got the stones away up there to build these dykes. They never took the stones up. These stones were all dug up the hill and let down. If you go to one o' these dykes running up a steep face like that and look along the back o' the dyke, maybe about ten, twenty yards out from the dyke, you'll get a big hole every here and there where stones have been dug out, and they've been all brought down the hill and built into the dyke. They never were taken up. And the method was to start at the top of the hill and always build back, in against the hill, moving down and building back up the hill to meet the dyke that you'd built to start with.

If it was two o' yez working, you'd maybe take in ten yards at a time. That'd be quite ample for to work back up the hill. Ten yards, move your frame down ten yards every time if you're wanting to put on an area and build it back up. That's quite enough. When you build the ten yards up, and you've any stones left, it's easier shifting your foot-stones you've left down ten yards as what it would be moving them down twenty yards. These stones in these places, they were all mostly hand-barrowed in. Quite a lot o' work long ago for labour fellows working with dykers, digging stones and carrying stones to the dyke, two men with a hand-barrow. They could move quite a lot o' stones in a day.

I've built quite a lot o' 'stells'. That's out in the hills for shelter for sheep in stormy weather. That's what they call a stell. It can either by round or square or a dyke with four wings running in north, south, east and west. A cross dyke, it's like a cross on the hill. It doesnae matter which way the storm comes, the stock has always got shelter somewhere on one side. You'll get quite a lot o' stells built round, with a wing running out either way, and this gives them shelter the way the storm comes, and in the centre of the roundel you'll always, not so much now, but long ago, the shepherd mostly cut maybe two ton, or three ton o' hay and built it into a rickle in the centre o' the stell. This fed the sheep in the time o' stormy weather.

(They were) just about the ordinary height — four foot six, the most o' them, and no higher. A dyke four foot six, you can get a terrible lot o' shelter. On a stormy day if a dyke's four foot six high and you come out about two yards out from the dyke, you'll get more shelter two yards out from the dyke as what you'll get close to the back o' the dyke because the wind's always blowing through some gaps in the dyke. It's quite cold if you sit down at the back o' the dyke, but if you come out from the dyke a yard or two yards it's different altogether.

We used to build quite a lot o' sheepfolds. That's where they handled the sheep for the clippings and dippings and all these things. There was always built different sizes of pens for handling and clipping and one thing and another like that. And you could move the sheep from one pen, they were always built in a way that you could put the sheep, handle sheep in one pen, move them through into the other pens as they were required. These dykes were all built quite high, mostly five feet. That kept the sheep from climbing up them and jumping out. The pens were mostly square, but instead o' the corners being built square with stones making square corners they were all built roundel — round corners. This kept the sheep from crowding into the corner. If the corner was square a sheep could walk, just about walk up it if they were crowded in. But if the corners were built round they couldn't clamber over them.

Buildin' sheep boughts, you'd always build as many big stones into the face — as sheep would stand in it — as you could manage, because with the sheep rubbing right round about when they were standing packed in these pens, they could pull the stones out if they were too small. You'd to build a strong inside face with good flat stones. This kept the sheep from tearing the stones out when they were packed into these pens.

Well, clambering up, they (could) get their feet on them. If it's a sharp-edged stone, their wool catches and could turn the edge of a stone round. And once the stone was turned round, if it wasnae tight built-up — no time until they got their feet on it, it was no time to work. It was surprisin' how it worked out. When you built these pens like that, for handling sheep, you'd always to make sure that the inside o' your dyke was very firm and tight.

(The stells) never were too big. They were maybe about twenty yards across centre, diameter. That was quite ample, and maybe two wings running out. May- be, if a wing was running out east and west, that gave shelter from the north and the east. I've built quite a lot (of stells). Away out in the hills — quite a long ways to walk at times for to get out to these places.

Some of them are round, some of them are square, and there's maybe about a hundred to a hundred and fifty yards o' dyke in each one. Always built to the opposite way from the wind, where the wind blew. If the wind blew from the

Fig. 8   The topstones, sitting in an upright position on top of the copestones, are blocked tight together and wedged in, all built up to the line to give the dyke the contour. Note the little stones, 'pinnings' or 'peggings', put in to finish off the face of the dyke

west a lot, it was built from the south to the north. If the wind blew from the north, it was built from the south to the west. That was against the wind for shelter.

Well, when you're doing a circle ye don't work on a big length at a time, maybe about three yards. If you set your frame about three yards every time and work round, you will always put stones on for to keep your line to the right circle that you're gonna be working on. Start it off wi' putting pegs in the ground for to make your bend, and you follow it round with your foundation and you work it up that way, and put stones on to hold your line in position so's it keeps you your guide all the way round.

Always use a line. Well, it's mostly a cotton line. It's a soft type o' string, and you can put a stone in the top and it'll stand quite a lot o' pressure. If the string that you work with's too hard, if you touch it with another stone against a stone, it just breaks straight off. You've got to have a soft type o' string for to work with which will stand and you can use for quite a long time. Most o' them buy cotton builder's lines. For each line it's twenty-two feet long. Two pegs, two wooden pegs cut out, tapered with a sharp, well, not just a sharp point, but a flat point at one end, round at the top end, and about nine inches long, so as you can wind your line onto it and still have room left for to push the peg into the dyke. We call them 'pegs'. Two of them at one time — you've got to have one for either side.

You set them (the lines) on, if you work with a frame, with your frame marked to the levels that you set them on to work with. Once you can do the job, you put your line on to about twenty-one inches high on the frame, and you can build right along there, just by looking at it. If there's amateurs working, you've got to work with the line lower down to keep them a better guide, making sure that the lines are nice and firm and tight all the time. Never let them get slack, because if it's a windy day it blows them into a half-moon, and if you're building to your line your dyke'll be the shape o' a half-moon every now and again.

I would set it on for the foundation at about nine inches high to start with. I would move it from there to twenty-one inches high, that's the height o' the first course. After the through-bands were put across the first course, I would move it to the full height o' the double, which is three foot or four foot six level.

(You'd also) use it for the top. You'd line the top out, and if you were working on a length o' dyke, and if you can build up your double and put your covers on and leave it until you get that length ready for topping you can line it, that full length, to the same contour as the ground and the height you've got to build your dyke. And you'll have a far better and stronger top, and anyone looking along it'll see that it's just the same height all the way along and the same contour as the ground. The same height o' dyke follows the same contour on the ground. When I was in business and had six and seven men, we used to top about 150 to 200 yards at the time, and the dyke looked different altogether. You could sweeten it right through. Wherefore if you topped a small part, maybe it was running up or running down too much, but if you did a length you could make a far sweeter job on the top o' your length. What they call 'sweetenin' it out'.

There's a lot o' different names for the different ways o' putting in the stones and building the ends o' dykes and holes left in dykes, and all these different things. O, all different names for shoddy work and open work, all these kinds o' things; firm jobs, tight jobs; stones, how ye'll be able to put them together. If it's a stone that's put in the dyke with a round top, some people would say, 'Well, they'll never get a stone to stay on the top o' that.' Well, you can always get a stone to stay on the top o' any stone. A stone to stay on the top o' a stone with a round top, you've got to look for a stone with a basin-shaped bottom so as it sits over the top stone. It's surprising how many you can find if you go and look for something like that.

That's in the craft. A drystone dyke is a craft. A craftsman, it doesnae matter whether he's a gunmaker or what he is, whenever he touches the stone or the piece o' wood or the metal that he's going to be making something with, he knows what he's gonna do and he knows where it's gonna go. He'll learn that. That all comes in in the learning of the trade, or the art.

The Large Farm in Nineteenth Century Ireland

T. JONES HUGHES

The size of holdings or the scale of farming has long been recognized as an important criterion in the analysis and interpretation of spatial arrangements in rural areas. For Ireland the printed books of the Griffith Valuation of c. 1850 provide this information for every household together with data relating to land occupation and tenure. This daring exposure of an entire landholding system was published during a twilight phase when the country was emerging out of the throes of the Great Famine and entering upon a prolonged and difficult period which saw the dismemberment and demise of this system. The discussion that follows is mainly based on these data, particularly as they relate to the highest-ranking units of landholding, namely those whose land was valued at over £100. Such units formed a major component of Ireland's settlement fabric in the nineteenth century.

For the entire island a total of some 7,200 farm units of over £100 valuation was identified. Nearly half of these were located in the province of Leinster, more especially in Counties Dublin,[1] Meath, Louth, Kildare and Westmeath. Thirty per cent of the total were widely spread over Munster. The fifteen per cent in Connacht were mainly confined to the east of the province and the remaining ten per cent occurred in small clutches in Ulster. Four principal landholding elements were involved, namely the estate owner, the feeholder, the lessor or middleman and the tenant. The distribution of these large farm units is complex, and a wide range of factors must have gone into its making (Fig. 1). Our main purpose is to attempt to identify and interpret territorial preferences. For this purpose the compacting influence of insularity serves to emphasise the principal components of the pattern and helps us to place regional peculiarities in their more general setting. A basic dichotomy emerges. In the north and the west are areas of frugal subsistence farming which were protected from the planter[2] and his ways by their physical disabilities. Such areas were devoid of highly valued land units. In the market orientated economy of the south and east, on the other hand, the £100 holding was an outstanding feature in the nineteenth century. We shall review some of the leading characteristics of this farming group with reference to factors such as landholding structures, settlement frameworks, the quality of farmsteads and the ratio of planter to Gael among their occupiers. For this purpose it has been found useful to draw a distinction between a stock farming and tillage tradition in Munster and Leinster, on the one hand, and a pastoral tradition, involving sheep as well as cattle, in Connacht and Leinster on the other.

Fig. 1   Farms with land valued at over £100, c. 1850.

THE STOCK FARMING AND TILLAGE TRADITION

In the east and south of the island in the mid nineteenth century concentrations of £100 holdings were most frequently encountered in areas where cereal cultivation, including barley and wheat, was important. Such areas occurred intermittently in a belt from east County Cork through Waterford and Tipperary to Laois and Kilkenny. In County Wexford the large farms were widely diffused throughout the county but in Wicklow there were important concentrations in the coastal baronies of Rathdown, Newcastle and Arklow. By far the highest aggregates were recorded in north Leinster in Counties Kildare, Meath and Louth which shared in both the tillage and the pastoral traditions. In north Munster, in County Limerick and adjoining baronies in Cork and Tipperary, large units were associated with an emerging commercial dairying region which specialized in butter production.

On the great farms of the south and east tenants were always more numerous than feeholders and in Counties Wicklow, Meath and Kildare feeholders accounted for less than fifteen per cent of the occupiers. Locally the most influential element in the nineteenth-century landholding matrix was not the feeholder or even the landlord but the lessor or middleman. In Duleek parish in County Meath, for example, a total of twenty-six £100 farms were held from nineteen different lessors. Such complex leasing arrangements were the best indicators of the dishevelled and capricious state of tenurial patterns over widespread areas at the time. It meant that, with a handful of notable exceptions, the great estate was not the territorial integrating and stabilising force that we had anticipated. The chaotic leasehold system was particularly reflected in the way wealth and poverty were locally perpetuated alongside one another. In the baronies of Ardee in Louth and Balrothery in north County Dublin, for example, where tillage was immensely important, the large farm units were themselves entangled and buried among smaller landholding entities as well as the large number of landless families. The valuation books record the number of landless families that were linked to large farms. In Munster and Leinster the highest totals were in Counties Cork, Limerick and Louth where as many as a quarter of the £100 holdings had four or more landless families directly attached to them. In Counties Kilkenny and Laois, on the other hand, the ratio was reduced to about seven per cent. It is clear that there was no simple relationship between the intensity of tillage farming and the density of landless peoples.

In terms of their territorial preferences there were obvious correlations between the incidence of high farming and the physically superior regions as these found expression in high land values. Communities of large farmers were largely confined to regions where land values exceeded ten shillings an acre. They were particularly attracted to the widespread areas of rich calcareous loams such as are found in south County Tipperary. Concentrations of large farm units in the south were also found aligned along great valleys such as those of the rivers Blackwater, Suir and Barrow and the arterial routeways which followed them. Such alignments were a reflection of the tillage area's long-standing dependence on access to villages and towns and eventually to distant markets. In this way a more intimate relationship than elsewhere in the island had evolved locally between this class of farmer and the urban network which was itself largely a product of the landholding system. Mallow in County Cork may be an example of a town that derived much of its sustenance as a regional centre from three estate cores — Listowel, Egmont and Becher — each valued at over £10,000, that lay in its immediate vicinity.

The large-farm landscape of Munster and Leinster had acquired a glossy veneer with the building ferment of the later eighteenth century. Landowners and fee-holders endeavoured to express their superior status and tastes by erecting elegant country houses; such elegance and refinement had hitherto only rarely been found in conjunction with rural living. Country houses remain an outstanding feature of our settlement fabric but it is important not to overestimate their significance. If we assume that a farmstead incorporating a country house was valued at over £50 we find that they represented less than a tenth of the total number of £100 holdings. The typical large farmstead in Munster and Leinster was a much more rudimentary structure and in Counties Louth, Kildare, Wicklow and Offaly a third of the total were valued at less than £5, and in County Limerick two-thirds fell into this category. In nineteenth-century Ireland the quality of his dwelling house was no reliable guide to the relative standing of a farmer. This was especially true of families of Gaelic stock; invariably their farmsteads were of lower value than those of their planter neighbours.

The classification of human features is a difficult and dangerous task, especially if these features are drawn from the past. It is much easier to identify types of farms and farmsteads than their human content. Nevertheless in what was over-whelmingly a planter's world it seems desirable to establish some criteria that might serve to distinguish between families of planter and non-planter stock. Historians have continually reminded us that ethnic constraints were a key to the understanding of community relationships in colonial Ireland. In some respects the large farm units which we are discussing were the rural territorial lattices of this colonial world and their presence in such numbers helps us to understand how the style of landholding that accompanied them came to have such a grip upon a nation and a people. Outside Ulster it is fairly easy to distinguish between planter and Gael in terms of family names[3] as these are recorded for every house-hold in the valuation returns. This has not been attempted for Ulster because of the apparent difficulty of distinguishing between Gaels of Irish and Gaels of Scottish extraction. In the mixed farming regions the Gaelic element among the large-farm population was least numerous in those counties which had experienced systematic plantation during the modern period. Thus whilst in County Offaly they numbered less than a quarter of the total and less than one-seventh in County Wexford, in Counties Waterford, Tipperary, Kildare and Louth Gaelic families formed as many as a third of the occupiers of £100 farms. Such totals help us to place the impact of the planter population on rural Ireland in perspective. The planters formed only a tiny if influential minority in what remained essentially an Irish nation.

In Munster and Leinster stock rearing and tillage were conducted within well-worn territorial frameworks of fields, farms and townlands. It was in such areas that the large farm was the one unit of settlement that was most closely syn-chronized with the townland framework. Townland and farm were known by the same name. Occasionally in such areas this relationship between large farm and administrative entity was extended to include the historic parish and its settlement centre. Large farms located in parish centres could often trace their origins back to the medieval period, to the time when the parochial framework, as we know it, was initially laid out. Such farms were rarely occupied by families of Gaelic stock. In the Leinster counties of Kilkenny, Kildare and Louth, for example, we found that a tenth of the £100 holdings were, c. 1850, located in such historic centres. The location of such farms could therefore be regarded as part of the process of alienation of the parish network which, for the student of territorial relationships, had been one of the most far-reaching consequences of the sixteenth-century religious reformation. Farm, church, glebe house, grave-yard and school together came to symbolise the local presence of the planter in this most sacred of sites.

We know little of the structure of Irish society even in the nineteenth century. From the valuation returns it is however possible to identify the principal farm families by name. Thus in County Tipperary the Gaelic names that recurred most frequently among the occupiers of the £100 holdings were Meagher, Mulcahy, O'Donnell and Scully and in County Waterford they included Kearney, Phelan and Nowlan. Such families may well have been the upholders of traditional lifestyles. We find, for example, that in the baronies of Middlethird, Upper-third and Decies without Drum in County Waterford over half the occupiers of the most highly valued farms were of Gaelic stock. With this evidence in mind it is easier for us to understand why, in this county, and on the Curraghmore estate, and within a stone's throw of a large port city Irish was spoken by the majority of the population in 1851. Communities such as these may have re-tained a greater than usual degree of self-respect and self-confidence in the adverse conditions that prevailed in the Famine years and it was in such environments that the remodelled Catholic church made its greatest initial emotive impact, far away from its primatial city in Armagh. Munster however was a province of many contradictions in the nineteenth century. In the early modern Catholic tradition the parish had acquired greater significance as a community, secular as well as ecclesiastical, rather than as a precisely defined territorial entity. Yet counties such as Limerick had retained a strong parochial tradition on a territorial basis which was hinged on to an old and resilient village network. In a county where at least half of the strong farmers possessed Gaelic names there were already Catholic churches present in historic parish centres such as Knocklong, Bruree, Drumcollogher, Kilmeedy and Ardagh in mid century. In this county however commercial farming, including dairying, was operating against a back-cloth of poverty and the valuation books illustrate how large-farm units were themselves in great difficulties. Many had recently been vacated; others were in the hands of caretakers. Together with some other counties lying transitionally between east and west County Limerick was a restless area in the immediate post-Famine years.[4] In this kind of atmosphere it is important to recall that by the mid nineteenth century, even in the commercial farming regions, the Gael was hardly ever a landowner or a feeholder and his name appeared only infrequently among the lengthy lessor lists. In his own countryside the highest status that he could hope to attain at this time was that of a large tenant farmer.

The great farm regions of the nineteenth century, despite their substantial privileged planter population, need not have been, in origin at least, the by-products of ruthless modern colonial enterprises. In Ireland the study of town-land names may serve as a rudimentary guide to the former location of such strong farming areas. Such areas are believed to be found in association with a limited range of cultural name elements, elements which refer to items which are the products of human activity. In County Carlow, for instance, as many as two-thirds of the £100 holdings were found in townlands bearing one of the following name elements:- *baile, town, cill* and *ráth*. In County Down one-third of the total were located in *baile* townlands. On a larger scale there was an obvious correlation in Leinster between the large farm areas of *c.* 1850 and what has been referred to as the *town* zone and its *baile rim*[5] and in counties Louth, Kildare, Carlow, Wexford and Waterford over thirty per cent of the £100 holdings were found in *town/baile* townlands. In County Meath where half of the most highly valued farms fell into this category it was not difficult to identify families which could trace their descent to the occupants of medieval castles and tower houses on the same site.[6] Among the most famous of these were the Plunketts of Dunsany and the Parsons of Gormanston. In such circumstances it is important to stress that in the study of settlement structures there is always the possibility of a continuity of status as well of site. It therefore seems as if the territorial bases of the large farm regions in Leinster and Munster are remarkably old and stable.

THE PASTORAL TRADITION

In colonial Ireland political and strategic considerations had always favoured the pastoralist and areas of permanent pasture, involving sheep and cattle rearing and fattening, remained persistent in location and extent. Mid nineteenth-century census returns are inadequate for us to attempt to define precisely the territorial extent of this region where the typical occupant of a £100 holding was referred to as a grazier or a herd. The valuation books however list individual holdings which were in the charge of herds and we are therefore able to identify those regions where graziers were most numerous. If we exclude County Dublin some fifteen per cent of the total number of £100 farms in *c.* 1850 were grazier holdings and the great majority of these were found in a broad midland zone extending from north Leinster to east Connacht. In Ulster grazier farms numbered only seven per cent of the total and in Munster, if we exclude County Clare, only two per cent. In Connacht the principal grazier territory was easily recognised as consisting of those parts of Counties Roscommon, Galway, Mayo and Sligo where over forty per cent of the £100 holdings were in the hands of herds. In County Roscommon on its own the ratio was as high as seventy per cent whilst in the Munster county of Clare it was thirty-five per cent. Here therefore was the powerful western component of a pastoral heartland. Its corresponding area in the east Midlands was less easy to identify using this type of criterion but Counties Meath, Westmeath, Longford, Kildare as well as Carlow all had over fifteen per cent of their holdings in the hands of herds.

Within this spacious midland belt it was further possible to identify core areas of intensive dry-stock farming and such areas must have represented some of the most specialised farming regions in nineteenth-century Ireland. The first of these lay astride the Mayo, Galway and Roscommon borders and it embraced parts of the baronies of Carra and Kilmaine in Mayo, together with Ballymoe, Castlereagh, Roscommon and Athlone baronies in County Roscommon and Kilconnell, Longford and Clonmacnowen in east County Galway. The barony of Ballymoe in County Roscommon provided the stereotype where out of thirty-nine £100 holdings, twelve of which were over 300 acres each, thirty-three were grazier holdings. This gives an impression of the scale and intensity of this kind of activity in a core area in Connacht. Similarly specialised livestock regions had emerged in the baronies of Kells and Morgallion in the north and in Ratoath, Deece and Dunboyne in south County Meath. On the Lansdowne estate in the parishes of Ratoath and Dunboyne graziers occupied half of the largest holdings. In grazier country a sharp distinction had to be drawn between a landowner, fee-holder or preferred tenant in his country house on the one hand and the herd or shepherd in his cabin on the other. In east County Galway mansion and cabin were particularly persistent territorial companions. Together they represented the principal components of one of the most discordant of rural landscapes encountered in colonial Ireland.

Caledon, Abercorn, Castlestuart and Charlemont were names in County Tyrone which stood for estate cores that were among the most formidable features of the landholding structures of Ulster. Similar cores prevailed in the Connacht section of the grazier heartland. In east County Galway, for example, were based estates of over £10,000 valuation each, whose total valuation was £72,000. These include Clanricarde of Portumna and Clancarty and Pollok of Ballinasloe. In County Wexford, by comparison, the total valuation of £10,000 estates was less than £25,000. In Ulster large-farm structures and intact great estates did not necessarily go together. In east Connacht, on the other hand, we see how close was the territorial relationship between groups of great farms and estate cores. The high density grazier territory in north County Roscommon was sustained by the presence of no less than five estates cores whose valuation exceeded £10,000 each. These were the Dillon, De Freyne, King-Harman, Pakenham-Mahon and Sandford estates. Similarly on the borders of Counties Dublin, Meath and Kildare estate cores such as those of Leinster, Drogheda, Clonmel, Cloncurry and La Touche together furbished the magnificent park landscape of the lower Liffey basin. In both Ulster and Connacht the planter feeholder was a prominent element in areas where the great estates had remained intact. In Counties Tyrone and Cavan, for example, over half the occupiers of £100 holdings were feeholders. In Counties Galway, Sligo and Mayo they accounted for a third of the most valued holdings. Little is known about these planter graziers of Connacht but they appear to have been a disparate group, the flotsam and jetsam of colonial operations extending over several centuries. They were however an essential component of the estate matrix in its mature form.

The unbalanced social structure of the pastoral lowlands was echoed in the rudimentary nature of the settlement fabric. Contemporary observers continually drew attention in the nineteenth century to the contrasts in the quality of the farmsteads and enclosure networks in Ulster as compared with the adjoining counties in Leinster and Connacht. In a cross-section of Ulster from County Down through Armagh and Fermanagh to Tyrone as many as a quarter of the farmsteads on £100 holdings were valued at over £50 each. In grazier country, on the other hand, the typical unit of settlement was a herd's homestead devoid of both outbuildings and haggard and valued at ten shillings or less and thus ranking no higher than the dwelling house of a landless labourer. Parish networks too were coarse-grained and their settlement centres were ill-defined and difficult to identify. The average area of a parish in County Kildare, for example, was less than a quarter of one in County Roscommon. In Connacht modern landlord villages and towns, such as Newtownbellew and Laurencetown in east County Galway, often remained skeletal features that had little to offer the pastoral economy in which they were engulfed.

Within the pastoral heartland the ratio of planter to native among the £100 holdings varied greatly from place to place. In Counties Longford and Sligo three-quarters of the total may have been of planter stock and in this, as in many other ways, Sligo was the most alienated of the counties of the western seaboard. Elsewhere in Connacht herds rarely bore planter names and in Counties Galway and Roscommon, as well as in Clare, native names were as numerous as those of the planters and in County Roscommon those that recurred most frequently included O'Connor, McDermott, Flynn and Mahon. At a time when the anglicisation process was at its height in the Famine years the graziers of the midlands seemed to have been poor custodians of traditional values. By 1851 the westward retreat of spoken Irish was halted only where the grey limestone plains terminated against the boglands of Connacht. On the Roscommon, Galway and Mayo borders baronies where over eighty per cent spoke Irish were lying in juxtaposition with baronies where it was already a minority language. It was in such zones of cultural cleavage between east and west that the territorial anomalies that we associate with colonial Ireland were most evident. Both the Congested Districts Board and the Land Commission used these cleavage areas as initial bases in their ambitious attempts at transforming former grazier holdings to small family farms. Viewed from the air the stone walls that so decisively defined the rectilinear fields of the limestone lowlands seemed to have been superimposed on an older, less extravagant and more chaotic base. Yet in the nineteenth century the pastoral economy of the midlands was one of the most exclusive. Grazier and smallholder, for example, had little to say to one another. Territorially this exclusiveness found its finest expression crystallised in the administrative divide between the Leinster and Ulster provinces. Here a hardened contact zone had evolved along the southern edge of the drumlin belt where concentrations of large and highly valued holdings terminated abruptly against the hungry hills of Monaghan and Cavan.

The author is grateful to Dr. Kevin Whelan of Memorial University, St. John's, Newfoundland for his helpful comments on an earlier draft of this paper.

NOTES AND REFERENCES

1. Generally County Dublin is excluded from the discussion because of the exceptionally high land values that prevailed in the vicinity of the capital city.
2. The planters were British colonists and colonial Ireland refers to the country as it was settled and governed from Britain.
3. MacLysaght, Edward, *Irish families* (Dublin, 1972).
4. Clark, Samuel, *Social origins of the Irish Land War* (Princeton, 1979), chapt. 4.
5. Hughes, T. Jones, 'Town and baile in Irish place-names', in Stephens N., and Glasscock, R. E. (eds), *Irish geographical studies* (Belfast, 1970).
6. Bence-Jones, Mark, *Burke's guide to country houses, Ireland*, I (London, 1978).

Tools and Things: Machinery on Irish Farms 1700-1981

TIM O'NEILL

It is appropriate to write about Irish farm machinery[1] at this moment in time as Ireland is in the middle of a period of rapid change. Even to a casual observer the machinery used on Irish farms has changed completely since the end of the 1940s. In the 1940s most Irish farms relied upon the horse for ploughing, for transport and for a wide range of other uses. Then less than five per cent of farms had tractors but now, in most counties, the vast majority have made the transition. The rate of change was not uniform. By 1975 almost every farm over five acres in Wexford had a tractor while at the other end of the scale less than twenty-five per cent of farms in Mayo had made the transition.[2]

The change from horse to tractor had important consequences. No longer could machinery designed for use with horses be easily used and the purchase of a tractor involved the purchase of new ploughs, harrows, seed sowers and other machinery. The pattern of diffusion of tractors therefore is also a pattern of diffusion of a wide range of other implements which had to be purchased in turn. Fig. 1 illustrates the pattern of distribution for tractors[3] which hints at the diffusion of the innovation they represent and illustrates an aspect of Irish history which has been well demonstrated in Dr. K. Danaher's writing.[4] Studies of material culture in Ireland have shown that there is a cultural and economic division between east and west. The Irish language, older house types, gaelic pastimes and traditions and even agricultural practices such as the use of primitive corn-drying kilns survive longest in the western districts. The time-lag generally for Ireland for the introduction of tractors was twenty years after the rest of western Europe and this reflects the depressed state of agriculture in the 1930s and 1940s. Changes began in the late 1940s. Ireland received £47 million worth of Marshall Aid in the early 1950s. An Anglo-Irish Trade Agreement signed in 1948 benefitted Irish farmers and gross agricultural output began to increase steadily.[5]

Manufacturers realised very early on that Ireland was an expanding market. The Ferguson tractor, developed in Belfast by Harry Ferguson between 1917 and 1936, revolutionized tractor design worldwide. The hydraulic pump and three-point linkage system at the rear of the tractor allowed the operator to control an attached implement and drive at the same time. It became perhaps the most popular tractor in Ireland. Ferguson started a school in the Powerscourt estate to train both mechanics and farmers and provided the students with accommodation in the Summerhill Hotel in Enniskerry. A 'pay as you farm' plan was introduced by manufacturers in the 1950s and they published regularly the statistics of change.

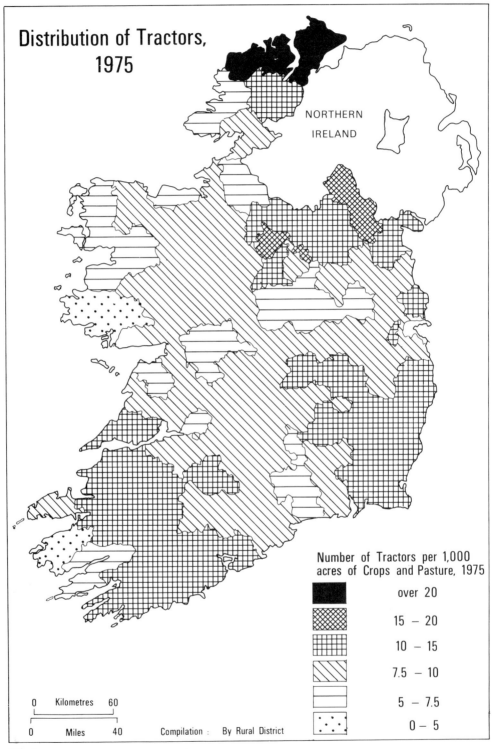

Distribution of Tractors, 1975

NORTHERN IRELAND

Number of Tractors per 1,000 acres of Crops and Pasture, 1975

over 20

15 — 20

10 — 15

7.5 — 10

5 — 7.5

0 — 5

0   Kilometres   60

0   Miles   40   Compilation :   By Rural District

Fig. 1

In a yearbook for 1954 Ferguson noted that there were 225 tractors on 15,695 holdings in County Clare and, with an eye to future sales, that there were 18,841 horses and ponies in the county.[6] Emphasis on sales by manufacturers, encouragement of agricultural advisors and increased prosperity all helped the transition from horse to tractor and the effect on machinery was dramatic.[7] Ireland's membership of the EEC and the financial benefits to agriculture accelerated the process[8] and by the end of the 1970s sales of tractors and machinery had grown into a £100-million industry though the dealers' association in 1979 complained that sales were down between ten and twenty per cent as a new economic phase for Irish agriculture began.[9]

The pattern of change in modern times is curiously similar to at least one aspect of change in the past when it is much more difficult to chart change. In the early nineteenth century improving landlords and agriculturalists believed that oxen were better draught animals than horses.[10] This view was no romantic return to the habits of an early age but was based on scientific experimentation. The statistical surveys of the period recorded how well people responded in the different counties and enable one example of innovation diffusion to be examined.

The revival of ox ploughing in the early nineteenth century was commonest in Leinster. In Kildare oxen were extensively used. Rawson reported, 'no man cultivates to any extent without oxen for the principal drudgery of ploughing.'[11] In other Leinster counties the surveys report oxen being used extensively on larger farms. In Munster oxen were less common. Bullocks and spayed heifers were widely used for ploughing in Waterford and Cork by the gentry while horses and mules were more common. In Kerry, Radcliff reported that most tillage was by spade and noted that some gentry worked bullocks though horses were more general.[12] Few oxen were used in Clare. There Dutton reported oxen 'are thought not to step quickly enough especially to meet the hurry of spring work'. In Connaught oxen were only used by a small number of experimenting landlords such as Lords Sligo or Lucan while in Ulster oxen ploughing also spread slowly. Even allowing for the different dates of these surveys the pattern of innovation followed the same general lines as the recent diffusion of tractors. The reasons for change are always complex depending on ability to purchase, influence of agricultural societies, example and an innovative mind and it is interesting to note that while ox ploughing disappeared generally in Ireland by 1900 it still continued into the twentieth century in parts of County Mayo.

Anyone interested in agricultural machinery in modern Ireland would obviously begin his search where the modern agricultural revolutions might be expected to have some effect. New approaches to agriculture developed in Holland and England in the seventeenth century. In England a conscious crusade to spread awareness of new farming methods was made from about 1730. Jethro Tull published his book on *Horse Hoeing Husbandry* (1733) to publicise his own methods and his invention of a seed drill replaced the old practice of scattering seed broadcast. Seed drills made the task of weeding the corn in neat symmetrical rows much easier with horse-drawn grubbers. The stories of Charles 'Turnip' Townshend, Robert Bakewell the sheep breeder and the Norfolk squire Coke of Holkham who raised his income from £2,000 to £20,000 were persuasive. Arthur Young described the improvers' methods from the 1760s to the 1790s and became the first secretary of a new English board of agriculture. Journals, shows and societies were all part of the new intellectual approach to agriculture. The Dublin Society, later the Royal Dublin Society, was part of this development. From Jethro Tull's seed drill and horse hoe of Queen Anne's reign the first significant advances in machinery were made. By the end of George III's reign ploughs, harrows, cultivators, rollers, seed drills and threshing machines had all been revolutionised.[13] Machinery was only one aspect of this revolution; experimentation in animal breeding, crop rotation, development of new crops, drainage and estate management also were carried on and were more significant.

In eighteenth-century Ireland these developments were widely known but not widely followed. There was little innovation and few new machines were either invented or imported. The availability of large numbers of manual labourers meant that labour-saving devices were not an economic priority. Where there is evidence of scientific farming it was usually concerned with drainage, reclamation, breeding, manures and improved crops.[14] There were exceptions and any paper on machinery in Ireland has to deal with rarities. John Wynn Baker working under the auspices of the Dublin Society built a factory in Celbridge, County Kildare. Yet the society was roundly condemned by Young who wrote that 'poor Wynn Baker, who settled in Ireland as the Dublin Society experimenter in agriculture — lived there for ten or twelve years in poverty and broke his heart because of the treatment he received.'[15] Baker's factory burned down in 1770 but his writings on scientific farming are among the few examples of an agricultural revolution in Ireland.[16] A constant complaint against the Dublin Society was that they offered the bulk of their prizes to manufacturers and too few to agriculture.[17] There were other eighteenth-century experimenters in machinery such as R.L. Edgeworth who invented a more efficient wheel,[18] amongst a wide range of other experiments.

Many factors should have encouraged improvements at the end of the eighteenth century: increased prices, more export opportunities and the availability of capital which was evident from the investment in canals, factories and grain mills. The greater availability of cheaper iron should also have affected agricultural implements. Cast iron was increasingly used in Ireland for domestic and industrial purposes but its use in agriculture spread slowly. Young commented upon the increasing use of iron in 1785 when 2,000 tons per year were imported from Russia to foundries in Enniscorthy, Mountrath, Dublin, Belfast and Newry.[19] Gradually change took place and the statistical surveys deliberately set out to record the use of new agricultural implements and machines.

The county statistical surveys show that seed sowers such as Cooke's Patent Drill Machine had been introduced.[20] Seed sown in drills did not become the norm and sowing seed broadcast either by hand or seed fiddle remained common until the 1920s. Much of what was recorded in the surveys was new and exceptional: improved harrows for corn and grass,[21] new designs for lime kilns and, most importantly, ploughs. Ploughs were extensively described and illustrated and improved British ploughs were the commonest implement introduced in the early nineteenth century.[22] Many ploughs in Ireland up to this time were heavy, ineffective and difficult to use. The older Irish ploughs required large teams of horses or oxen and usually required at least two people, one to lead the animals and a second to control the plough.[23] James Small of Berwickshire is credited with the main improvement in ploughs. His implements were basically a triangular frame formed by the stilts with a curved mould board which turned the sod efficiently.

Fig. 2   Tomb of Alexander Black (1826), Skreen, Co. Sligo

These were sometimes called a chain plough as Small fixed a chain to a hook on the underside of the beam to take up some of the strain during ploughing.[24] The chain eventually disappeared and this plough was known as the swing plough. Improved ploughs with wheels to control depth and width of furrow were introduced from England. They came into common use later than swing ploughs. In these ploughs, either made of iron or wood, careful alignment of beam, coulter and share with the land side of the plough reduced friction and this is basically the implement which was displaced by the tractor plough in recent years.[25] Scottish and improved English ploughs were gradually introduced during the nineteenth century and indeed the former came to symbolise quality in agricultural equipment.

The excess population hungry for work tied Ireland to spade tillage until well after the Great Famine. New ploughs were introduced however, as a grave stone in County Sligo shows (Fig. 2). These improved ploughs were copied by local blacksmiths and wooden copies were also made. Wooden examples were still made in County Galway in the 1950s (Fig. 3). The early nineteenth century was to witness many attempts at introducing new machinery. Scottish-style ploughs were given as prizes at ploughing matches.[26] The Royal Dublin Society organised many local agricultural societies and shows became common. In 1841 the Royal Agricultural Society was organised and gradually native manufacturers began to appear.[27] Their names can be seen in the catalogue of annual shows of the Royal Dublin

Fig. 3   Wooden/iron plough, Syllaun, Co. Galway, 1931

Society from 1834. In the early years Dublin manufacturers dominate: Courtney and Stephens of Blackhall Place, Keenans of Fishamble Street, Le Strange of North Street and the odd outsider like Chambers of Downpatrick. Pierce in Wexford, the best known Irish implement manufacturers, began operations in 1839[28] and their success was to induce other manufacturers to begin in Wexford also (Figs. 4 and 5). Star and Wexford Engineering were to follow. In the 1840s small foundries were established in many areas. Paul and Vincent and Henry Sheridan set up in Dublin.[29]

Fig. 4   Pierce wheel plough, Naul, Co. Dublin

Fig. 5   Pierce's foundry, Wexford, 1970

In the north large foundries, Gray's of Belfast and Kennedy's of Coleraine, were established in 1840 and 1842 respectively. By mid century the improved plough was well known, copies were being made and double mould boards were being added for opening drills.

In the same period as improved ploughs were being introduced, other implements were making headway. Threshing machines replaced flails in some areas.[30] Some of these were horse-powered while others were water-powered like one described from the Carrickfergus area.[31] Later native manufacturers were to make threshing machines suitable for one to four horses (Fig. 6). Until recently parts of these fixed in position could still be seen in many areas. Only rarely were they erected in outhouses in Ireland though such examples can be found. Allied with these early threshers were winnowing machines — called 'barn fans' in some northern counties. These machines sometimes made by local carpenters, replaced the older method of using a winnowing tray to separate the grain from the chaff. By mid century isolated examples of steam threshing were reported. Other innovations were also taking place. Scythes were probably first introduced into Ireland by the Normans. Before 1800 however these were mostly used for mowing hay. During the early nineteenth century reaping grain with scythes became more widespread. Sir Maurice Crosby of Ardfert, in Kerry is the first landowner reported as using corn stands which are still extensively used in County Galway. The

Fig. 6   Four-horse threshing machine, Co. Kerry

Fig. 7   Three horses pulling a reaper and sheaf binder, Ardmore, Co. Waterford

Scotch cart was also introduced with its spoked wheels rotating on the axle and its flat platform.[32] It replaced the traditional block-wheeled car in many areas.

As the nineteenth century progressed a second revolution in agricultural machinery took place in Britain. Year after year new inventions were patented and refinements were made to existing farm equipment. Experiments with reaping machines began as early as 1805 and credit for the first practical machine is given to Patrick Bell of Scotland and he was the first to incorporate the scissors principle in a larger machine in 1827.[33] In America Cyrus McCormick perfected his mowing machine by 1840. After 1850 new mowing machines were introduced and by the end of the century Irish manufacturers were competing with British and American manufacturers for the Irish market (Fig. 7).

A search of the Irish Patents Office failed to show Irish inventors active in this field. The occasional patent was taken out for an agricultural machine but many of these were impractical.[34] A notable exception was Mr. Hanson of Doagh in county Antrim who patented the first potato digger with spinning lifting forks in 1855. Most later potato diggers were developed from this design (Fig. 8).[43] There were other Irish inventors. It is claimed, not without dispute, that the inventor of the first power loom was Edmund Shanahan of Cork. In 1813 John Wately also of Cork invented a machine for grinding potatoes into flour for which he was awarded a gold medal by the Society of Arts in London.[35] When Irish manufacturers eventually patented their machines at the end of the nineteenth century their specifications usually concerned minor modifications to well-known machines.[36]

Farm machinery continued to improve in the period after the Great Famine. In the second half of the nineteenth century Irish farmers in general were better

Fig. 8   Potato digger, Nore valley, Co. Waterford

off and there was a gradual introduction of new machinery. Despite the decline in tillage, implements suitable for use on smaller holdings made rapid progress. Ploughs, improved carts, root cutters of various kinds, harrows and other inexpensive implements became popular. Sheridan of Dublin made a turnip slicer that cut the turnip by forcing it down through a box the base of which consisted of knives.[37] Such implements were an invention of the mid nineteenth century[38] and some survived in use till the 1960s (Fig. 9). After the famine shortage of labour in some areas, rising wages, and emigration made machinery necessary. There was some resentment against machines[39] but it would be easy to over-emphasise the rate of mechanisation. By 1891 many farmers in the Congested Districts of the west knew nothing of new farm machines and had never seen ploughs.[40] Improvers continued to advocate better implements. Instructors appointed by the Congested Districts Board sold potato sprayers at three-quarters of their cost price.[41] Spraying if not sprayers had a dramatic effect on yields.[42]

Some new inventions were very popular. An American horse-drawn hay rake known in Ireland as the 'tumbling Paddy' became popular in the late nineteenth century. Pierces made iron versions and country carpenters made wooden copies which may still be seen. On larger farms the most modern machinery was purchased. Horse-drawn manure spreaders or 'muck spreaders' were invented in Canada in 1878.[44] An early example survives near Newmarket-on-Fergus, County Clare but by 1912 there were a mere 1,800 in the country.[45] Of the larger more expensive horse-powered or donkey-powered machinery, threshers and churns were by far the most popular (Fig. 10).

Just as the statistical surveys give some idea of the state of agricultural machinery in the early nineteenth century a government report sums up the position in 1912. In that year there were 382,163 horses in use, almost a half million carts and a quarter million ploughs. There were over 300,000 harrows, 120,000 cultivators and grubbers, 115,000 land rollers, 62,000 potato sprayers, mainly of the knapsack variety and 62,000 seed-sowing machines, mainly the smaller barrow-like machines for turnips and mangels. For harvesting there were 97,000 mowers and reapers, 9,000 binders, 18,000 swathe turners, 65,000 horse rakes, 11,000 rick lifters and 9,000 potato diggers. There were 30,000 ordinary threshing machines, 2,000 combined threshers and finishers and 49,000 winnowers or barn fans. Machinery for preparing animal fodder was very popular. There were 104,000 root slicers and pulpers, 28,000 chaff cutters and 7,000 corn crushers. Six hundred and fifty seven water wheels and 116 windmills were still in use, 800 steam engines, 85 gas engines, 565 oil engines and 92 petrol engines were recorded. From these statistics a picture of Irish agriculture can be drawn. In 1912, 164,000 farms were less than fourteen acres in size and there were 406,000 holdings in the country. So almost every farm had a horse and a cart and most had a plough and harrow, and about one in three had a grubber and a root slicer or pulping machine. In relative terms this represented a very small amount of mechanisation and it is not surprising that one of the commentators in 1912 reported, 'I found a tremendous inefficiency on the part of farmers with regard to implements.'[46] It was not until the 1950s when tractors began to make progress that the next big period of change began.

In every community there are layers of agricultural implements stratified according to the status and economic strength of the owners. This paper has

Fig. 9   Turnip slicer, Co. Limerick

Fig. 10   M. Halpin's donkey-powered churn, Ardagh, Co. Longford, 1968

attempted to give an overall view of the innovators but the most important farm implements are always those in common use. Because of the slow rate of change in Ireland many older implements had a long period of supremacy in Ireland. It is only in recent years that many old implements have been abandoned (Fig. 11). Spades, already well recorded and described, were of great importance until the last quarter of the nineteenth century. Flails, straw-rope twisters, gorse lifters and choppers, thistle tongs and winnowing trays were the functional implements of the majority. Irish agricultural improvers rarely promoted improved machinery and the main emphasis was always on reform of tenancy arrangements, improvement of crops and animals and the organisation of co-operatives.[47] An older organisation of labour in communal work sessions has gradually given way before the advance of new machinery and new methods have destroyed the folk practices of older days. The last sheaf with its promise of renewal is summarily dismissed by the large combine-harvesters of the present day.[48] The difference between the farm implements of old and the new machinery is now reflected in the landscape. Modern large machinery operates standardized equipment made anywhere in the world and achieves its effect by power rather than by the acquired finesse of the older horse- or even hand-powered implements.

Fig. 11   Chaff cutter, Skibbereen, Co. Cork, 1979

NOTES AND REFERENCES

1. An earlier version of this paper was delivered as a lecture to the Merriman Summer School, Ballyvaughan, County Clare 1979.
2. Kennedy, R.E., *The Irish: Emigration, Marriage and Fertility* (California, 1973), 94-109.
3. Source: Agricultural statistics, Central Statistics Office. I wish to thank my Carysfort College colleague James Walsh who compiled this map. This distribution of tractors should be compared with that for 1970, *Atlas of Ireland* (Dublin, 1979), 59. At that time the east-west divide was even more dramatic. The number of tractors in Northern Ireland is much larger and the high distribution of tractors in border counties reflects this.
4. Ó Danachair, C., 'Distribution patterns in Irish folk tradition', *Béaloideas*, 33 (1965), 97-113; *Atlas of Ireland* (Dublin, 1979), 90-91.
5. Meenan, J. *The Irish economy since 1922* (Liverpool, 1970), 52-57, 88-130; Murphy, J.A., *Ireland in the twentieth century* (Dublin, 1975), 123.
6. Ferguson Ltd., *Dublin Year Book* (1954): National Library of Ireland, P. 2356.
7. Gailey, A., 'The disappearance of the horse from the Ulster farm', *Folk Life*, 4 (1966), 51-55.
8. Canning, J., 'Irish agriculture's gentle revolution', *Ireland of the Welcomes*, 28, No. 3 (1979), 8-12, and No. 4 (1979), 16-20.
9. *Irish Times*, August 23, 1979.
10. Lucas, A.T., 'Irish ploughing practices', *Tools and Tillage*, 2, No. 4 (1975), 204-7.
11. *ibid.*, 205.
12. *ibid.*, 206.
13. Fussell, G.E., *The farmer's tools: the history of British farm implements, tools and machinery before the tractor came* (London, 1952).
14. Young, A., *A tour in Ireland, 1776-1779*, 2 vols. (Dublin, 1780); Newenham, T., *A view of the natural, political and commercial circumstances of Ireland* (London, 1809), 309-19.
15. Young, A., *op. cit.*, II, 342-43; Baker, J.W., *To the Dublin Society: a remonstrance* (Dublin, 1770).
16. Baker, J.W., *Experiments in agriculture* (Dublin, 1769); *A short description and list of the instruments of husbandry made in the factory at Laughlinstown* (Dublin, 1769); *Practical agriculture, epitomised and adapted for the tenantry of Ireland* (Dublin, 1771); *Plan for instructing youths in the knowledge of husbandry* (Dublin, 1768); *Some hints on better improvement of husbandry* (Dublin, 1762); *Reclamation and cultivation of bog in county Kildare* (Dublin, 1773).
17. Newenham, T., *op. cit.*, 310.
18. Edgeworth, R.L., *An essay on the construction of roads and carriages* (London, 1813).
19. Young, A., *op. cit.*, II, 325-29.
20. Coote, Sir C., *Statistical survey of the King's County* (Dublin, 1801), 71.
21. Tighe, W., *Statistical observations relative to the county of Kilkenny made in the years 1800-1* (Dublin, 1802), 300-5.
22. Dutton, H., *Statistical survey of the county of Clare* (Dublin, 1808), 60-3; W. Tighe, *op. cit.*, 293-300.
23. Lucas, A.T., 'Irish ploughing practices', *Tools and Tillage*, 2, No. 2 (1973) and 2, No. 3 (1974).
24. Fenton, A., *Scottish country life* (Edinburgh, 1976), 38-45.
25. See collection of advertisement photographs from Philip Pierce and Co. Ltd. Wexford in Folklife Division, National Museum of Ireland.
26. Memorandum on Royal Dublin Society, August 3, 1855 (Larcom papers, MS. 7562 National Library of Ireland); *Munster Farmers' Journal*, 1812.
27. *Ireland: industrial and agricultural* (Dublin, 1902), 181.
28. James Pierce, a millwright of Kilmore, Wexford began to manufacture fire fans in 1830. These were very popular and by 1840 he had begun his agricultural machinery factory in Wexford town. One of the earliest machines manufactured there was a horse-powered threshing machine: *The Story of Pierce* (Dublin, n.d.), 1.
29. Kelly, M.J., 'Some old Dublin manufacturers of farm machinery' (typescript).
30. *Munster Farmers' Journal*, 1812.
31. Dubourdieu, J., *Statistical survey of county Antrim* (Dublin, 1812).

32. O'Neill, T.P., *Life and tradition in rural Ireland* (London, 1977), 68-82. Improved carts made little progress in the west: Dutton, H., *Statistical survey of the county of Galway* (Dublin, 1824), 92-93.

33. Fenton, A., *op. cit.*, 64-69.

34. See for example the following patents specifications: D.J. Murphy, Cork, Machine for cutting turning and pulverising ground (1852, no. 965); H. O'Connor, Limerick, Digging the soil by machinery with horse power (1853, no. 1426), and P. Kelly, Drogheda, Improved apparatus for cultivating, preparing and treating land and sowing seeds (1853, no. 2775). All of these were basically attempts to mechanise the principle of digging with a spade: Irish Patents Office, Merrion Square, Dublin.

35. *Cork Examiner*, September 22, 1934.

36. See Pierce and Co. Ltd., Wexford patents (Folklife Division, National Museum of Ireland).

37. *Catalogue of articles of manufacture* (Dublin, 1850).

38. Morton, J.C., *Cyclopaedia of Agriculture* (London, 1856).

39. Donnelly, J., *Land and People in Nineteenth Century Cork* (London, 1975), 235.

40. Hooker, E.R., *Readjustments of agricultural tenure in Ireland* (Carolina, 1938), 131.

41. *ibid.*, p. 133.

42. Lee, J., *The modernisation of Irish society* (Dublin, 1973), 101.

43. Fenton, A., *op. cit.*, 121; those who could not afford spinner-type diggers could use a plough with iron 'fingers' instead of a mould board to spread the potatoes.

44. Brown, T., 'The design and development of a farm implement', *Agricultural Engineering*, 16, No. 7 (1935), 261-67.

45. Implement statistics in *Department committee on food production in Ireland*, Parliamentary Papers, Session 11 November 1914-27 January 1916, V. 909. I wish to thank Dr. Cormac Ó Gráda U.C.D., for bringing this reference to my attention.

46. *ibid.*, 854-5 (T. Wibberley, I.O.A.S.).

47. *Report of the Recess committee* (Dublin, 1896), passim.

48. Gailey, A., 'The last sheaf in the north of Ireland', *Ulster Folklife*, 18 (1972), 1-33.

Traditional Dyestuffs in Ireland

BRÍD MAHON

Primitive man stained his skin and possibly his clothes by means of fruit juices, decoctions of flowers, roots and leaves, but the true art of dyeing began when man first learnt the use of a mordant to render the dye permanent. Alum is the most widely used mordant, but formerly crude native alum could be got from wood ash, human urine, sheep manure, oak galls, the sediment of certain pools containing alumina or iron and filtered smoke. In many parts of Ireland up to recent times chips of the oak or alder tree were used as a mordant called 'barking the yarn'.

Of all the traditional dyestuffs lichen was the oldest and remained the most popular. The knowledge of its use was never lost and continued down to our own times. Ordinary lichens require no mordant and yield a good permanent dye. The most common, often referred to as crottle, are *Parmelia saxatilis* and *Parmelia omphalodes*, much used by traditional weavers.

Natural dyestuffs were known in Ireland from prehistoric times. One of the earliest references to the craft of dyeing occurs in the Book of Leinster where King Tighernmas, the son of *Ollaig* is credited with first putting colour into cloth, namely brown, red and crimson with ornamental borders.[1] Whatever degree of credence may be given to this legend it is certain that in historic times colour played an important part in the social hierarchy, for the *Senchus Mór* lays down with some detail the colour to be worn by children in fosterage.

The first break in the long continuity of the craft came with the introduction of foreign dyewoods in the seventeenth and eighteenth centuries, and in many places the native plants were rapidly displaced. Their disuse was practically completed during the nineteenth century when chemical dyestuffs made their appearance. From that time onwards many of the old dyestuffs and the shades they represented were all but forgotten. Yet here and there a knowledge of some of the more common dyestuffs lingered on. A survey of the manuscript material in the Department of Irish Folklore, University College, Dublin, reveals that the dyestuffs either still in use or most commonly remembered include:

Bark and fruit of the elder tree, bark of the alder, oak bark, blackberries, bilberries, bulrushes, dogwood, dock, fuschia, foxglove, ferns, heather, lichens, laurel, meadowsweet, pennywort, shellfish, sloes, spurge, onion skins, wild madder, yellow weeds, residue of pools containing a deposit of permanganate of potash, hay water, soot, turf ash, as well as the non-native stuffs: indigo, madder, saffron, logwood and copperas for fixing dyestuffs.

A legend that throws light on an early taboo connected with the craft of dyeing has to do with St. Ciaran of Clonmacnoise who died AD 548. It is contained in the Book of Lismore, which was compiled from the lost Book of Monasterboice and other manuscripts in the second half of the fifteenth century.[2]

> On a certain day Ciaran's mother was preparing Glaissin. And when she had it ready to put the cloth into it, then his mother said to him. 'Go out, Ciaran,' said she, 'people do not deem it lucky to have men in the house with them when they are putting cloth down to be dyed.' The legend goes on to describe how Ciaran put a curse on the cloth so that there was no piece without a dark gray stripe, but later relented, blessed the *glaissin*, 'so that there was not made before it, a *glaissin* as good.'[3]

This legend is interesting not only because of the taboo, but because it describes how the cloth was dyed in one piece. It undoubtedly passed from oral tradition into the written word and then passed back again into folklore. A version from Bawnboy, County Cavan, in the manuscript archives of the Department of Irish Folklore says:

> Story of a boy who was a saint. His mother was dyeing clothes and told him to bring in some dyeing. The boy said he wouldn't. After a time he did but prayed it would come out an ugly colour and so it did. She then told him to go back and pray and it would come out a nice blue and so he did and it came out a nice colour. Then his mother found out he was a saint.[4]

O'Curry commenting on the taboo says,

> This superstition does not to my knowledge exist now, but there are certain days of the month and week upon which no housewife in Munster would put wool or cloth down to be dyed.[5]

A careful study of the manuscript material shows no evidence of the survival of either of these taboos into our own times.

One of the oldest and most expensive dyestuffs ever used was obtained from certain shellfish, principally of *Murex* and *Purpura lapillus* species. The Phoenicians who were skilled dyers were the legendary discoverers of this purple dye when a sheep dog belonging to the Phoenician God, Melkarth, known to the Romans as Hercules Tyrius decided to make a meal of shellfish. The animal's fangs were dyed a bright red and when Melkarth saw this he dyed a length of cloth with the shellfish which he presented to his mistress the nymph Tyros.[6] Like many myths the facts are changed to suit the story. It takes time and an application of heat, usually sun, to change the colourless liquid found in the shellfish, through varying shades to a purple that never fades. The Greeks knew of it. During the age of the Roman Empire it was known as the royal purple. Pliny the historian puts its discovery around 1400 BC.

By the Middle Ages the manufacture of this dyestuff was reputedly a lost art. In 1858 the French zoologist, Lacase Duthiers, sailing out of the port of Mahon on the Island of Minorca to study animal life in the Mediterranean 'was astonished to find the poor fisherfolk dyeing their linen with the juice of *Purpura lapillus*, the oldest and most costly of all the dyes'.[7] When knowledge of this dyestuff first came to Ireland we do not know, but archaeological evidence shows it was there in the seventh century. Dyehouses excavated by the Belfast archaeologist, F.J. Bigger in 1880[8] in Roundstone, Connemara, and by Dr. Françoise Henry in 1948 in Inishkea, north Mayo, revealed large mounds of the shellfish *Purpura lapillus* and

Murex sp. broken in such a way as to denote that they were used to extract the dye. Dr. Henry wrote,

> A cursory examination of some of the Donegal sand dunes has allowed me to find in a short time rubbish heaps of several other dyehouses.[9]

We have evidence of its existence a thousand years later. An Englishman, one William Cole who made a study of this dyestuff in the seventeenth century, said that he had heard of somebody living by the seaside in some port or creek in Ireland who dyed linen kerchiefs with some liquid taken out of a shellfish.[10] In 1800 Joseph C. Walker noted that the method of producing purple from a species of shellfish 'is still practised in the counties of Wicklow, Wexford and other counties on the eastern parts and also in Wales'.[11] Interestingly enough, knowledge of this dyestuff survived at least in folk memory down to our own times. In 1973, William McNeilis, fourth-generation weaver of Ardara, County Donegal, describing traditional dyestuffs, to the writer said:

> We used scrape crotal off the rocks and it would give us a black dye. There was a flower that grew in the corn and it was named Yellow Gabhar. We cut the flower and put it into the pot and it would give a yellow dye, and then we had what they call a heather dye, we used clip off the tops and put it into the pot along with the wool and that would give us a heather dye, and we had another called logwood and shoemaker that would give us a black dye. They used some class of shellfish that gave a red dye. It was a long time back and I don't know how they did it.[12]

Shellfish of *Purpura lapillus* are still to be found around the coast of Ireland, though *Murex* is not as plentiful as it was a century ago. A sepia dye could be obtained from the octopus squid, while sea slugs, two inches long were used to obtain purple dye. A somewhat similar colour to that obtained from shellfish could be obtained from certain lichens ground into a reddish violet paste, the colour being obtained by the action of ammonia of stale urine. This dyestuff appears to have been used in Ireland at a very early period. Walker describes it:

> These colours (crimson and purple) were obtained from a species of lichen growing on rocks and called by the Irish corcair, arcell and cudbear, in Erse, *corkir*. The crimson was obtained from the corcair of a finer kind resembling a thin white scurf which they scraped from the rocks, dried and then reduced to powder, then infused it in urine for three weeks or a month and so obtained a fine bright crimson dye. Considerable quantities are made up and frequently sold in the markets at Dingle.[13]

References to this dyestuff from the manuscript material include:

Beare, County Cork
Flannel for petticoats dyed a dark red. The dye was made from a sort of hard moss that grows on dry fences and in stony places and is called *Sraith na gCloch*. When boiled it makes a red dye.[14]

Delvin, County Westmeath
Cudbear, common lichen, which gives permanent purple with alum.[15]

Rosses, County Donegal
Carker scraped off the rocks made a very fine red.[16]

Crimson could also be obtained from various plants principally the bedstraws. Our Lady's Bedstraw (*Galium verum*), in Irish *rú Mhuire* or *baladh cnise*, gets its name from the folk belief that it was one of the herbs in Christ's manger at

Bethlehem. It is one of the few native plants to yield a red dye and is sometimes known as binnet or bindean, meaning rennet. The juice of the stem has the property of curdling milk and could be used for making cheese. *Galium verum* contains the same colouring matter as the Madder to which it is allied, both being of the family of the Rubiaceae. The flowers and stems are bright yellow.

Cultivated madder, *Rubia tinctorum*, was not a native plant, and it is possible that in many cases the wild madder, *Rubia peregrina* (common to the Burren) and field madder *Sherardia arvensis* were used. Madder dye is obtained from the roots of the plant which are peeled, reduced to powder for use and which give an attractive pink. Examples of the use of madder from the manuscript archives are:

> *Dunraney, County Cork*
> Alder, madder and logwood boiled together. The madder plant was obtained in bottoms and the strength of the dye was governed by the amount of different ingredients used.[17]

> *Kilnaughton, County Kerry*
> Roots of plants, maybe yellow roots, used to poison rivers, also used as a red dye. Very important for red things much in use.[18]

> *Killarney, County Kerry*
> Heather and madder used as dyestuffs.[19]

Roots of the common sorrel, *Rumex acetosa*, are frequently mentioned as red dyestuff.

Garments dyed yellow with saffron are constantly spoken of by writers as characteristically Irish. Saffron dye is got from the autumn crocus, *Crocus sativus*, but there is no evidence that it was known in early Ireland. According to tradition the first corms were smuggled into England by an artful pilgrim returning from a crusade; it is generally accepted that the plant was introduced into Britain sometime in the reign of Edward III (1312-77) and later introduced to Ireland. The early saffron was not the colour we recognise as saffron today, but a beautiful yellow obtained from the dried stigmas of the crocus. The yield was very small and though the plant must have been easy enough to grow it was very costly to use. It is improbable that saffron was much used on this account. An Englishman named Good, who taught for a while in Limerick in 1550 wrote:

> With the bough, bark and leaves of the poplar tree beaten together they (the Irish) dye their loose shirts of a saffron colour which are now much out of use, mixing the bark of the wild Arbut tree, salt and saffron. In dyeing their way is not to boil the thing but to let it soak for some days together in urine so that the colour may be deeper and more durable.[20]

Campion in his *History of Ireland* (1571) tells us that about this time saffron was beginning to fall into disuse.

No less than thirty-six different species of native plants as well as various lichens could produce shades ranging from bright yellow to a yellowy brown. Of the native plants the most widely used was the *buí mór* or weld (*Reseda luteola*). It was generally grown on waste land and poor pasture. Much grows wild but it was sometimes sown under barley and pulled out in the second year of growth. Weld needs mordanting and so treated yields a strong and lasting yellow. It was commonly called Dyer's Weed, Dyer's Rocket or Dyer's Greenweed, the latter because weld mixed with woad can produce green. Walker refers to it thus:

The truth is that the old English saffron does not mean crocus but any yellow colour, and generally distinguishes the weld, still retained in many parts of England and the very plant the Irish call *Buídhe Mór*, or Great Yellow. With this they dye their linen and fine woollen stuffs with different degrees of colour and fix the colour with urine. The yellow thus obtained is bright and lasting.[21]

References from the manuscript archives include:

Farney, County Monaghan
Buí Mór, a tall green plant, formerly used as saffron.[22]

Kilbeg, County Meath
Usual colour saffron, a dye made from *Buí Mór*, a herb or weed and the droppings of the sheep, the wool or garment dyed by this means. It was retainable and wouldn't lose colour by the sun or washing of the garment. It was the dye of the gallowglass uniform and was dark green in colour.[23]

(Note: Here the same effect as mixing woad and weld was achieved by mixing weld with sheeps' faeces).

Ardara, County Donegal
Flowers that grew in the corn named Yellow *Gabhar* or Yellow Weed. We cut the flowers and put it into a pot and it gave a yellow dye.[24]

Other yellow dyeplants mentioned include:

Carraroe, County Galway
Heather used to dye yellow. Also *Airgead Luachra* (Meadowsweet), which produced a pale yellow.[25]

Skibbereen, County Cork
Samhadh, sorrel gave yellow. Also gorse blossoms.[26]

Killarney, County Kerry
Onion skins and gorse blossoms gave gold. Also Mare's tail, called in Irish *Cáití Collagan.*[27]

Probably the nearest approximation to the colour we call saffron today was produced by a species of lichen. The Countess of Moira who appeared to be something of an eighteenth-century authority on dyestuffs wrote:

The saffron colour linen tunics in which Camden mentions Neil and his followers to have paid their visit to the (court) of Elizabeth of England, were not dyed saffron but a kind of lichen which grows on rocks and is prepared by the Irish as archil. I have seen this dye and it resembles in the mass the shade of yellow which borders on brown.[28]

In Carraroe they call this lichen *Féasóg Ghabhair*:

Féasóg Ghabhair, a lichen which grows on stones, light saffron. Also *Airgead Luachra* — Meadowsweet, gives pale yellow.[29]

The Neale, County Mayo
Lichen called *Dath na gCloch*. Used for dyeing woollen socks and ganseys. The result a yellowish brown.[30]

Lichen was usually gathered off the rocks in July and August, preferably after rainfall, dried in the sun and used to dye wool without any preparation. The boiling time might take anything up to four hours. For best results an iron dyepot was used.

Ardara, County Donegal
Well everybody had a huge big pot or maybe two of those pots for dyeing. They would

hold up till maybe twelve or fourteen pounds of wool. Well, first of all you put a layer of crotal down again till the pot. Now the fire you see was generally outside, for the pot was so big you needed a terrible big fire underneath it, like for to boil it, and after that it would be left for about an hour and a half and it would be taken off the fire, and the pot would be dumped outside. They'd be shaking the wool then to take the crotal out of it, the wool and after that the wool was washed.[31]

The craft of homespuns survived longest in places where lichens were plentiful; in Galway, Mayo, Donegal, in parts of Kerry. Some of the finest browns used in the dyeing of tweeds could be got from crotal. From the manuscript archives:

Gleann Cholmcille, Contae Dhún na nGall
Cuirtí dath ar an olainn, ar an tsnáith agus ar an éadach. Crotal — luibh a fhásas ar char-raigeacha agus ar chrainn. Dath donn a ghníthear as.[32]

Ardara, County Donegal
The dyes were got from herbs and a lichen called *crotal* that grew on the rocks. I never see it to this day and it's plentiful now that I don't think of those days that we spent scraping it into a bucket with a spoon and it dyed a very nice dark brown, a colour that was very popular with the London buyers of those days. All this was before the period of 1910.[33]

Carraroe, County Galway
Crotal gave light brown.[34]

Ibracken, County Clare
Lichen for home dyeing, dyed brown.[35]

Dualla, County Tipperary
Lichen a nutritious moss found in the bark of trees or stones near water was utilised for dyeing.[36]

Other brown dyestuffs in the manuscript material include:

Kilbeg, County Meath
People would dye at home, boiling the sloe bushes or dreenandun (i.e. *Draighneán Donn*) for a colour that was brown.[37]

Carraroe, County Galway
Briar roots and water lily gave light brown. *Veronica*, pale brown.[38]

Ibracken, County Clare
Bark of cherry gave brown.[39]

Roots of the bogbean or buckbean and the roots of the common bramble or black-berry were traditionally used as brown dyestuffs. Bramble roots are still occasion-ally used in the west of Ireland for dyeing stockings and other woollen fabrics. The non-native logwood also widely used gave various shades of brown. The colour for cloth or wool used for frieze was generally obtained from alder branches. In Dunraney, County Meath they gave this combination: 'To dye frieze use a liquid made from alder, *madar* and logwood boiled together.'[40]

Before the introduction of indigo, the oriental blue dye into Europe, the dye-plant woad was commonly used. It is referred to in Irish as *glaisín*, but it is possible that this was also a generic term for dyestuff. Woad was known in England as far back as pre-Roman times and while not indigenous to Ireland it was probably introduced here early on. However it is a deleterious crop greatly injurious to arable land and for that reason, no doubt, was never popular. While indigo largely re-placed woad from the seventeenth century onwards, O'Curry tells us that towards the end of the nineteenth century, a Mr. Francis O'Mahony of Limerick made a handsome fortune by cultivating woad.[41] Indigo was a popular dyestuff on the Aran Islands up to recent times and was also used for the dyeing of tweeds in cottage industries.

Gleann Cholmcille, Contae Dhún na nGall
Chuirtí ruamann fraoich nó ruamann de chineál ar bith de chúig chineál san éadach agus i ndiaidh sin chuirtí dath indigo air. Gheibhtí an indigo i nDoire.[42]

Carna, Contae na Gaillimhe
Bhíodh an t-éadach dathaithe le plúirín, dath breá gorm nach dtréigfeadh choíchin.[43]

Though *plúirín* is generally given as the Irish for indigo, it can also describe several wild plants. The Misses Galways of Rathronan, County Limerick who were skilled in dyestuffs in the early days of this century used what was probably wild pansy: 'The leaves and stem of the *goirmín* when fermented gave a blueish colour to the homespuns of the Misses Galloways [sic].'[44]

Various combinations of dyestuffs gave green: the yellow of weld mixed with the blue of indigo; by dyeing the cloth first with bedstraw or some other yellow dyestuff, and then passing it through a vat of woad. Yellow Flag, *seileastram* or *feileastram* gave green. Other green dyestuffs referred to in the manuscripts include:

Clonkeen, County Galway
People used dye wool by boiling heath and then boiling the woollen cloth in the water. This gave a dark green.[45]

Mohill, County Leitrim
Whin blossoms for lemon colour; nettles for dark green; dockens for light green.[46]

Drumshanbo, County Leitrim
Dye made from cuckoo saryl (sorrel) which gave a green colour.[47]

Of black dyestuff Walker had this to say:

The other colour (than yellow) in general used among the lower orders was black; their trouse and mantles were principally of this colour, also their caputia or cloaks. Cambrensis who remarked on this circumstance attributes it to the wool of the black sheep, but all of their sheep are not black and those clothes made of this black wool were generally dyed a deeper tint. The materials used for this colour were a kind of bog mire, consisting of decayed vegetables of an astringent nature and wet with urine. The colour produced was a perfect black which neither time nor weather would tarnish, but retained its original brilliancy as long as a piece of the cloth remained.[48]

This traditional method of dyeing black was still in use, or at least had survived strongly in folk memory up to the 1940s.

Murher, County Kerry
Used black sort of sediment found in grapes and used as a black dye. People who did not have it in their own place would go to where it was.[49]

Perhaps the best description of how this dye was used comes from the south-west.

Killorglin, County Kerry
They skimmed the iron mould from a stagnant pool and took the sediment from the bottom of the pool (a very dark substance) and brought it home in timber cans and put it into timber barrels to store it up. Then they got the bark of the alder and broke it up and boiled it in some of the iron mould in a pot for two hours or so. Then they put the articles to be dyed in a cool on the floor and poured the contents of the pot on the article and allowed it to rest for two hours or so to soak. Then they took it out and put it on the

fence for two or three hours. Then they washed it in the river and in the cold water and when they had it drained the article was jet black.[50]

Rathronan, County Limerick
Blue and black got by steeping linen or flannel in the *Poll an Bháite*, a spring in Keale, supposed to contain a deposit of permanganate of potash.[51]

Abbeyfeale, County Limerick
A permanent black dye obtained from the bogs.[52]

Islands, County Clare
A special sort of mud which was obtained in Balleen Lake, or in Inchbeg.[53]

Gleann Cholmcille, Contae Dhún na nGall
An poll dubh — poll mór sa talamh agus chuirtí an olann isteach ann trí lá agus trom os a chionn. Nuair a thigeadh sé amach as an pholl, bhíodh sé daite dubh nó níos cosúla le gormdhorcha.[54]

Cloghaneely, County Donegal
There is a well in Carraig an Fhia (Carrickanea, Falcarragh, P.O.) which dyes black. Garments are placed in it at sundown and were taken out at next sundown when they were found to be dyed a deep rich black.[55]

Ardara, County Donegal
The first black they got was called *Dubh an Phortaigh* or *Dubhach* got in the bottom of black bogs and that dyed a glossy black and later on they were able to buy copperas and shoemaker and logwood and they hadn't the trouble of taking soft mud from the bottom of the bog.[56]

It is not surprising that persons skilled in the use of dyestuffs very often had reputations as herbalists or folk doctors, and very many of the dyestuffs given were also used in folk medicine. *Crocus sativus* was a cure for measles. Sheeps' faeces, called in Irish *cróch na mbánta*, used to fix saffron dye was another cure for measles. In parts of Leinster the name *cróch na mbánta* is given to the crocus. The berries of the mountain ash were a remedy for rheumatism. *Veronica*, speedwell known in Irish as *Lus na Banaltra* as the name implies was a cure for sore breasts in nursing mothers. Wild pansy was not only a well known laxative, but once used as an ingredient in cancer cures. Foxglove, *Digitalis purpurea* was used in cures for certain swellings; digitalis used for cardiac diseases is well attested. Pennywort, *Umbilicus rupestris*, was a popular folk remedy for many ailments ranging from chilblains to consumption, while ivy was said to remove warts. Nettles were used in the treatment of rheumatism, sciatica and pleurisy, in addition to being a good spring tonic for the blood.

There was a strong link too between dyestuffs and the supernatural world. In Uibh Ráthach, Contae Chiarraí they never let children wear white underclothes lest they be swept away by the *púcaí* and as a safeguard they picked *sceochan na gcloch*, to dye the garment a yellowish brown.[57] It was believed that each time a supernatural being passed by, the foxglove, in Irish *méaracán na mban sí*, either waved fingers in greeting or bent a head in respect. The foxglove was said to resemble both fairy thimbles and fairy headwear. Roots of the yellow flag were associated with changelings. A changeling would turn into ferns or flaggers if immersed in a boggy pool. Such pools were said to have a forbidding effect on the fairies, possibly because of the residue of iron contained in them. (Iron was anathema to otherworld beings generally.)

Today it is true to say that the very names of many of the old traditional dyestuffs and the shades they once represented are all but forgotten. Perhaps the final word should be left to an informant in An Spidéal, Contae na Gaillimhe. When speaking of dyestuffs in 1940 he said:

Bhí na daoine in ann dathú a dhéanamh i gcónaí agus tá fós. Bhí an dath le fáil i luibheanna agus caonach mar atá an scraith chloch. Bhí daoine áithrid ann agus bhíodar an-mhaith ag meascadh dathanna. Bhí dathanna eile ag muintir an tsléibhe: rua-dhonn agus buídhearg, as fraoch áithrid a bhí siad le fáil. Bhíodh na daoine ag coimhlint le chéile faoi na dathanna céanna agus ní ligfidís a rún lena chéile — mar sin cailleadh eolas ar go leor de na luibheanna.[58]

The people were always able to dye and still are. The dye was to be got in plants and mosses, as on mossy stone. There were certain people who were very good at mixing dyestuffs. Mountainy people had other colours, reddish-brown and yellowish-red which could be got from certain kinds of heather. The people used compete with one another over the same colours and they would not divulge their secret to each other. Because of this, knowledge of many of the plants has been lost.

NATIVE IRISH DYESTUFFS

PURPLE

Common name	Botanical name	Irish name
Flora		
Dandelion (roots dye a magenta)	*Taraxcum officinale*	Caisearbhán
		Caol dearg
Danesweed:	*Sambucus ebulus*	Lus na nDanar
Dwarf elder		Péith bhog
Deadly nightshade	*Atropa belladonna*	Miotóg bhuí
		Lus mór coilleadh
Elder (berries with alum)	*Sambucus nigra*	Trom
Sundew	*Drosera rotundifolia*	Drúichtín móna
		Rós an tsolais
Bilberry or Whortleberry	*Vaccinium myrtillus*	Fraochán
Purple loosestrife	*Lythrum salicaria*	Eireaball caitín
		Créachtach

Lichens
Orcil and Cudbear (strictly speaking these are preparations of lichens, not the lichens themselves).

Shellfish
Principally *Purpura lapillus* and *Murex*. Also octopus, squid and certain sea slugs.

GREEN

Common name	Botanical name	Irish name
Flora		
Bracken (crumpled buds of the leaf fronds)	*Pteridium aquilinum*	Raithneach
Dock Sorrel	*Rumex acetosa*	Samhadh bó
Elder	*Sambucus nigra*	Trom

Flowering Rush	*Juncus* sp.	Luachair Bogbhuinne
Privet (berries and leaves with alum)	*Ligustrum vulgare*	Tor luathfás Primhéad
Foxglove	*Digitalis purpurea*	Méaracán na mban sí
Nettles	*Urtica dioica*	Neantóg
Horsetail	*Equisetum telmateia*	Eireaball capaill Feadóg

Lichens

BLUE

Common name	Botanical name	Irish name
Flora		
Devil's bit (leaves prepared like Woad)	*Succisa pratensis* (*Scabiosa succisa*)	Úrach bhallach Greim an diabhail
Elder (berries)	*Sambucus nigra*	Trom
Privet (berries with alum and salt)	*Ligustrum vulgare*	Primhéad
Red bearberry	*Arctostaphylos uva-ursi*	Lus na stalóg
Whortleberry or bilberry	*Vaccinium myrtillus*	Fraochán
Woad	*Isatis tinctoria*	Vód Glaisín
Yellow Iris (roots) Yellow Flag "	*Iris pseudacorus*	Seileastram Feileastram
Sloe Blackthorn	*Prunus spinosa*	Draighean
Mountain pansy	*Viola lutea*	Goirmín sléibhe

BLACK

Common name	Botanical name	Irish name
Flora		
Alder (bark with copperas)	*Alnus glutinosa*	Fearnóg
Blackberry (young shoots with salts of iron)	*Rubus fruticosus*	Sméara dubha Driseog
Dock (roots)	*Rumex obtusifolius*	Copóg
Elder (bark with copperas)	*Sambucus nigra*	Trom
Iris — Yellow Flag (roots)	*Iris pseudacorus*	Seileastram Feileastram
Meadowsweet (roots)	*Filipendula ulmaria*	Airgead luachra
Oak (bark and acorns)	*Quercus petraea* and *robur*	Dair

Sediments of marshy or boggy pools containing alumina and iron.

Lichens

BROWN

Common name	Botanical name	Irish name
Flora		
Alder	*Alnus glutinosa*	Fearnóg
Birch	*Betula pubescens*	Beith
Bogbean	*Menyanthes trifoliata*	Bearnán lachan Báchrán
Bilberry or Whortleberry	*Vaccinium myrtillus*	Fraochán
Onion (skins)	Some natural, some introduced.	
Hop	*Humulus lupulus*	Lus an leanna
Oak (bark)	*Quercus petraea* and *robur*	Dair
White waterlily (roots)	*Nymphaea alba*	Duilleog bháite
Veronica – Speedwell	*Veronica beccabunga*	Lus na banaltra Seamar chré
Larch (pine needles collected in autumn)		

Dulse – seaweed

Lichens

YELLOW

Common name	Botanical name	Irish name
Flora		
Agrimony	*Agrimonia eupatoria*	Airgeadán Méirín na máighe
Ash (fresh inner bark)	*Fraxinus excelsior*	Fuinseog
Birch (leaves)	*Betula pubescens*	Beith
Bog asphodel	*Narthecium ossifragum*	Bliocáin
Bog myrtle (or sweet gale)	*Myrica gale*	Raideóg Railleog
Bracken (roots, also young tops)	*Pteridium aquilinum*	Raithneach
Bramble	*Rubus fruticosus*	Driseog
Broom	*Cytisus scoparius*	Giolach
Buckthorn (berries and bark)	*Rhamnus catharticus*	Ramh Draighin Maide bréan
Common dock (roots)	*Rumex obtusifolius*	Copóg

Crab apple (fresh inner bark)	*Malus sylvestris*	Úll fiain
Autumn crocus	*Crocus sativus*	Cróch an fhómhair
Dyer's Weed	*Reseda luteola*	Ruachan buí Buí mór
Dogwood	*Cornus sanguinea*	Crann coirnéil Crann muchóra
Gorse (bark, flowers, young shoots) Furze, Whin	*Ulex europaeus*	Aiteann
Heath (with alum) Ling, Heather	*Erica tetralix*	Fraoch
Marsh — woundwort	*Stachys palustris*	Duilleog na saor
Kidney vetch	*Anthyllis vulneraria*	Meoir Mhuire Cosán uain
Marsh marigold	*Caltha palustris*	Lus buí Bealtaine
Meadow rue	*Thalictrum flavum*	Riascbhláth órdha
Marsh ragwort	*Senecio aquaticus*	Buachalán buí
Marestail	*Hippuris vulgaris*	Snáithe báite Cáiti collagan
Moss		
Nettle (with alum)	*Urtica dioica*	Neantóg
Pennywort	*Umbilicus rupestris*	Carnán caisil Lus na pingine
Privet (leaves)	*Ligustrum vulgare*	Tor luathfás
Red shank	*Polygonum persicaria*	Glúineach dhearg
Teasel	*Dipsacus fullonum*	Lus an fhúcadóra
St. John's Wort	*Hypericum* sp.	Luibh Eoin Bhaiste
Sundew	*Drosera rotundifolia*	Drúichtín móna
Tormentil (roots)	*Potentilla erecta*	Néalfartach Beinidín
Yellow Wort	*Blackstonia perfoliata*	Dréimire buí
Yellow Weed	*Reseda luteola*	Buí mór
Yellow fumitory	*Corydalis lutea*	Dearg thalún
Water pepper	*Polygonum hydropiper*	Glúineach

Lichens
These dyes give varying shades of yellow from buttercup through lemon and saffron to yellowy brown.

RED

Common name	Botanical name	Irish name
Flora		
Bedstraw (roots)	Galium sp.	
Common sorrel (roots)	Rumex acetosa	Samhadh bó
Lady's bedstraw (roots)	Galium verum	Rú Mhuire
		Baladh cnise
Wild madder (roots)	Rubia peregrina	Madar
Field madder (roots)	Sherardia arvensis	Baladh cnis Chon Chulainn
		Dearg faille
Tormentil (roots)	Potentilla erecta	Néalfartach
		Beinidín

Acknowledgement: I am much indebted to Dr. James White of the Department of Botany, and Dr. B. Healy of the Department of Zoology, University College, Dublin for their help in identifying native Irish flora and shellfish used as traditional dyestuffs.

REFERENCES

1. O'Curry, E., *Manners and Customs of the Ancient Irish*, III (Dublin, 1873), 88.
2. Stokes, W., *Lives of the Saints* (1890), 267.
3. O'Curry, E., *op. cit.*, 121.
4. Irish Folklore Collection, Department of Irish Folklore (hereafter IFC) MS, 749, 162.
5. O'Curry, E., *op. cit.*, 121.
6. Born, Wolfgang, *Purple in Classical Antiquity, Mediaeval Dyeing* (1880), 111.
7. Duthiers, Lacaze, 'Mémoire sur la pourpre', *Annales des Sciences naturelles, Zoologie*, 12 (1859), 5-84; see also Born, Wolfgang, *op. cit.*
8. Biggar, F.J., 'Investigations of the Prehistoric Settlements near Roundstone, Connemara', *Proceedings of the Royal Irish Academy*, 19 (1899), 727-30; 20 (1900), 433-437.
9. Henry, Françoise, 'A Wooden Hut on Inishkea, Co. Mayo', *Journal of the Royal Society of Antiquaries of Ireland*, 82 (1952), 163-77.
10. *Philosophical Transactions*, 1685, 1288: ref. in Henry, Françoise, *op. cit.*, ref. 9 above, 175.
11. Walker, J.C., 'Materials used by the Ancient Irish', in idem, *Memoirs of the Irish Bards* (Dublin, 1818), 161-66.
12. Collected Bríd Mahon (B.M.), Ardara, Co. Donegal, 1973.
13. Walker, J.C., *An Historical Essay on the Dress of the Ancient and Modern Irish* (Dublin, 1788), 145.
14. IFC MS, 751, 128.
15. IFC MS, 748, 233.
16. Walker, J.C., *op. cit.* (1788), 148.
17. IFC MS, 751, 128.
18. IFC MS, 753, 433.
19. Collected, B.M., Kerry, 1975.
20. McClintock, H.F., *Old Irish and Highland Dress and that of the Isle of Man* (Dundalk, 1950), 70.
21. Walker, J.C., *op. cit.* (1818).
22. *Irisleabhar na Gaedhilge (The Gaelic Journal)*, 12 (1902), 26.
23. IFC MS, 748, 65.
24. Collected, B.M., 1973.
25. IFC MS, 1833, 96.
26. IFC MS, 751, 469.
27. Collected BM, 1975.

28. Walker, J.C., *op. cit.* (1818), 161-66.
29. IFC MS, 1833, 96.
30. Reference from my colleague, Mr. L. Corduff.
31. Collected, B.M., 1975.
32. IFC MS, 751, 207.
33. Collected, B.M., 1975.
34. IFC MS, 1833, 96.
35. IFC MS, 752, 77.
36. IFC MS, 745, 463.
37. IFC MS, 748, 64.
38. IFC MS, 1833, 96.
39. IFC MS, 752, 77.
40. IFC MS, 748, 194.
41. O'Curry, E. *op. cit.*, 120.
42. IFC MS, 755, 196.
43. IFC MS, 160, 368.
44. IFC MS, 745, 262.
45. IFC MS, 746, 392.
46. IFC MS, 747, 521.
47. IFC MS, 747, 500.
48. Walker, J.C., *op. cit.*
49. IFC MS, 753, 359.
50. IFC MS, 753, 274.
51. IFC MS, 745, 201.
52. IFC MS, 745, 152.
53. IFC MS, 752, 238.
54. IFC MS, 755, 270.
55. IFC MS, 755, 412.
56. Recorded, B.M., 1975.
57. IFC MS, 34, 83.
58. IFC MS, 746, 309.

Waulking the Cloth

A. FENTON

When the goodwife took her wool to the weaver to have the pattern set, she took with her 'a cogful of meal, some butter, a kebbuck of cheese, a braxy ham,' or whatever was most plentiful at the time, so that he would work cheerfully and leave a blessing in the cloth.[1] When the web was woven, it was taken home, ready for waulking or fulling.

Waulking was a job for the women of a village or community. When the web came home, and the fulling-day was due, word was sent out and the waulking women, *na mnathan luaidh*, assembled at the house after breakfast, at the invitation of the owner of the web. A table was laid ready with whisky, bread, butter, cheese, cold mutton and so on. Tea was often given at the beginning and again half-way through. Dumplings were always in great favour. Whilst the older women examined the web and discussed its colours, pattern and texture, the younger ones carried stoups of stale urine, called *maighstir* or *mac-a-mhaighstir*, from neighbouring houses. The web was tramped in a mixture of soap, urine and water in a tub, and waulking could then begin.[2]

This was done on a fulling frame, called *cleith, cleith-luaidh* or *cliath-luathaidh* in Gaelic. Since the first element is the name applied to a hurdle or wicker frame, it is possible that fulling frames were originally made of wicker. Wicker or basket-work fulling frames have been observed by several writers. J. Robertson saw a 'long piece of basket work of watling which is laid on the floor, upon which they place the Cloth,' in the Hebrides in 1768.[3] They were still in use there in 1793,[4] and survived in the parish of Kilmuir, Skye at least up to the mid nineteenth century.[5]

In eighteenth-century Argyll the wicker fulling frame was said to be the common property of the village.[6]

Equally if not more common by the later 1700s was a fulling board made of deal planks, cut with longitudinal ribs to provide the necessary abrasive surface, the work proceeding across the ribs. Such a board was in use at Talisker, Skye, in 1772,[7] and they were evidently not substitutes for but alternatives to the wicker fulling board.[8]

Possibly some boards were hollowed in the middle, like shallow baskets, for a visitor to South Uist in the early twentieth century noticed fulling boards at three places there, in the shape of 'shallow wooden troughs'.[9]

In later days when waulking was beginning to die out, less care was taken with the fulling frame and a strong door taken off its hinges could serve.[10] Around

1881 at Braes in Skye, when the last recorded waulking took place there, the web was stretched across the forms in the school and waulked on boards laid over them. Waulking had therefore to be done on Saturday when the school was free.[11]

The number of women in the waulking team was conditioned in part by the size of the fulling board. Sizes mentioned are 10 by 3 ft (Hebrides),[12] 2½ to 3 ft wide by 8 to 9 ft long (Argyll),[13] and up to as long as 24 ft.[14] Where team numbers only are given, a calculation based on an allowance of two feet per person gives an approximate indication of its length. The calculation applies to only half the team, however, since the women sat opposite each other in pairs. The earliest Hebridean record, of late seventeenth-century date, refers to a team of ten, arranged five on each side of the board which was, therefore, ten feet long.[15] Captain Burt saw a team of six or eight working in the open air, near a water course, in the 1720s,[16] in the 1770s Pennant saw twelve to fourteen in Skye, and in the 1840s the minister of Kilmuir in Skye referred to teams of nine, ten, or twelve.[17] Teams of sixteen or eighteen are referred to for the Argyll mainland in the eighteenth century.[18]

For the most part, teams consisted of even numbers of women, but occasionally there was an extra one. This was usually an aged or infirm woman, with long waulking experience, who would sit at the end of the board and lead the singing, though without taking an active part in the work. She was called the *bean dhuan*, 'song-woman'. Her function could also, of course, be undertaken by an active worker.

Another team-member was the *bean luathaidh*, the woman who led the actual waulking. A third participant, the *bean dhlighe*, the woman of ceremony, led the various ceremonial processes in their correct order.

This group gave the waulking operation a strong internal cohesion, and also allowed for the development of special skills within the group, for the best workers and the best singers were chosen to take part in the waulking. There was, for instance, the 'Clann Pheidirein', or Patersons, in Coll, women famous for generations for their skill in waulking and knowledge of the songs. Before the evictions they were present at every waulking in the island. 'These Mac-Pheidirein women had a wonderful fascination over the workers and the singers at the waulking.'[19]

In latter days these elements were not necessarily fully observed, and there was only one overall leader, the most experienced and careful woman, who was in-stalled as mistress of ceremonies at the head of the frame to deal out the web and keep a general eye on the working of it. Opposite her, at the foot, might be a woman whose job was to fold the cloth as it passed round the end of the frame, and keep it soaked with the fulling liquid.[20]

Waulking is not a single, simple process; nor has the method remained unchanged through the centuries. This is particularly evident in the decline in the use of the feet, which is related in turn to the position of the fulling frame, low on the ground, or raised on stands.

On the basis of eye-witness accounts, the following stages took place. About a yard of the web was first unrolled by the one at the head of the table, soaked with the fulling liquid, and then worked slantwise across the frame. The women work, therefore, not towards their immediately opposite partners, but towards those diagonally across from them. The cloth moves along the table clockwise in a series of zig-zags, in a four-time rhythm, from woman to woman:

> At *one* she receives the cloth from her neighbour on the right, leaning forward and throwing it down at arm's length; at *two* she draws herself upright and brings it down again immediately in front of her, twisting it as she does so; at *three* she passes it, again at arm's length, to her neighbour on the left; and at *four*, once more upright, she brings her hands again in front of her, still beating time, and is thus ready for *one, da capo*, for the rhythm is ceaseless.[21]

In the Argyll practice, the diagonally opposite women rubbed and pounded the cloth between them, drawing it backwards and forwards, before passing it on to their neighbours.[22]

The zig-zag movement, the scouring over the rough wicker or ridged wood, the moisture and ammonia, all were necessary to raise and thicken the cloth, so that it would eventually appear as an equally coherent mass, without streaks.

Every action was in time to singing, and to such an extent was singing part of the task, that the length of the job was measured not by time but by the song. If the cloth needed more working, 'the women never said, "It will take another half-hour, or hour's work," but "It will take another song," or "It will take so many more songs." '[23]

As waulking proceeded, the moisture and movement had the effect of narrowing and thickening the web, a process called *a' dol a stigh*. Another effect was to raise the pile on the cloth, this being known as *casadh, basadh* or *basradh*.[24] The pile or nap was called *lòineag* in Lewis.[25]

Waulking went on till the cloth had shrunk about two inches, i.e. half the length of the middle finger. The shrinkage averaged an inch in the foot, the measurement being made on the back of the hand.

At this point another stage, called *bochdadh* in South Uist, was started. The women would wrap the tweed length by length round their hands and thump it against the board, in order to remove twists and wrinkles and keep the width even.

In Eriskay, when the first fulling stage was finished, two of the women stood up and rolled the cloth from opposite ends till they met in the middle. Then, keeping in time, 'four of them fall upon the roll and proceed to pat it violently, straightening out the creases, and those unemployed strike up another song, this time of different metre.'[26]

Where the board was at floor or ground level, the feet could be used at this point in the waulking, and then, 'sitting upon the ground, and tucking their petticoats up to their knees, the cloth is forthwith put under a course of more vigorous friction than before.'[27] The song changed for this operation.

In some places, after the first stage of 'hand-waulking', *luadh-làmh*, the cloth might be rolled up in web form, and a substantial tea was taken, of oat-cakes, scones, butter, cheese, crowdie, cold beef, fresh eggs, etc.

> The married women were expected all to take a full glass of whisky, whilst the maidens merely put the glass to their lips. There were no men at the table, and the hostess either said grace herself, or asked some pious matron to do so, and then came the extraordinary coaxing of them all to eat, making pieces for them, loading their plates with whatever was best, and all politely saying they were not hungry; all in high spirits, with radiant faces, interchanging witty remarks, quoting proverbs, repeating snatches of songs to illustrate or give force to their remarks, and this closed the first part of the day's work.

The married women then went home, and the next stage, 'foot-waulking', *luadh-chas*, was left for the maidens.

> This is their best time. Shoes and stockings are stripped off, and with petticoats kilted to the knees, they sit on two rows of stools with the cloth on the floor between them, and there they kick it with heart and goodwill, singing merrily the while, and keeping time with their feet to the rhythm of the song. Soapy suds are kept on the cloth, and the web is continually turned round to let the waulking benefit each part alike. The maidens are in high glee, and the special choruses sung at this work are fitted for giving any amount of improvisation.[28]

In such foot-waulking, the web was rolled different ways three times, so that it would be equally treated all over. It was after this that it was beaten and patted with the open hands for some time, to smooth it.

> Then some old woman shook it out of the roll, and with a charm put all the witches from having any power over it, saying — 'Roinn a h-aon, roinn a dhà, roinn a trì, roinn a ceithir, roinn a coig, roinn a sia, roinn a seachd, chan aodach so a shagart no chléir', etc. 'The first part, the second part, the third part, the fourth part, the fifth part, the sixth part, the seventh part, this is not cloth for priest or clergy' etc.[29]

Next the tweed was loosely rolled up and beaten by the hands to free it from surplus water. This beating was called *bualadh*. In Argyll this loose rolling was done on a thin straight board, a process called 'winding the cloth into a candle'. The board was a little longer than the width of the cloth. Winding was a careful job, to avoid creases and unequal overlapping of any selvedges. 'In this winding the cloth, the women kept slapping every inch of each fold with all their might, with the open palms of their hands.' The song sung for this had a different measure. It was called 'Port-nam-bas, the palm-chant, or rather palming-chant', into which the gossip of the countryside about real or supposed sweethearts was inserted. The songs were, therefore, also called 'pairing songs'. The candle of the cloth was left lying till next day, when it was soused in water and left to dry.[30]

In South Uist, a special song was sung during the beating of the roll. This was *òran nan gillean*, 'the lads' song', and the girls present in the work team were each named in turn in the song after a young man's name had been given.[31]

Etymologically, the word 'waulking' is the same as the verb 'to walk', which points to the early use of the feet in the process. Latterly, however, the work was done more by the hands than by the feet, and the fulling frame was raised on trestles or on stands rather than lying at floor or ground level. Martin noted in 1695 that both hands and feet were used,[32] and in the 1720s Burt saw six or eight women sitting on the ground as they waulked, 'with the wet Cloth between them; their Coats are tuck'd up, and with their naked Feet they strike one against anothers, keeping exact Time . . .' The rhythm was maintained by singing, or by bagpipe music.[33]

Waulking by Hebridean women observed in 1768 appears to have involved the sequence of first hands and then feet. The wicker fulling frame lay on the floor, and two rows of women sitting opposite each other regularly pulled the cloth to and fro between them, rubbing it hard the while on the basketwork of the frame. When fulling was nearly finished, they leaned back and pushed it violently against each other. Singing went on during the whole operation.[34] Similarly at Talisker in Skye waulking was done first with the hands and then with the feet,[35] and in the 1790s the same thing was observed, in each case the fulling frame being at floor or ground level. Some straw might be placed beneath both the frame and the workers to keep them off the ground.[36]

When the fulling frame was placed low in this fashion, there was no great problem about using the feet as well as the hands. Hand waulking was probably done in a kneeling position[37] in order to get the weight of the body behind the thrust of the arms, and the women would sit upright for foot waulking.

In more recent times the fulling frame has been raised from floor or ground level, making it as a rule impossible to use the feet in the waulking process. Where foot-waulking — *luadhadh leis na casan, luadh-chas* or *luadh-coise* — was a firm tradition, ways could be found of overcoming the problem. One Lewis family that waulked cloth up till the time of the First World War used a board six feet square that went from the dresser to the partition, and the twelve women who did the waulking with their feet actually sat on the board itself.[38]

There is an impression from some of the accounts that foot and hand waulking were separate techniques with their own areas of distribution. In South Uist, for example, foot waulking was said to be unknown[39] and in 1930 it was noted that hand waulking had been the only method used in Skye for several generations,[40] though earlier accounts show that foot waulking was also known there. Foot waulking survived, on the other hand, in Islay, and in Lewis, until about the First World War, though hand waulking, *luadh làimhe*, was also done.

It is likely that the distinction between hand and foot waulking is more apparent than real. Full-scale waulking required both methods in sequence. Home fulling, however, not only declined as the textile industry made ready-made cloth and clothes more easily available, but also changed in character as, with new social standards, the fulling frame was raised from floor level to nearer tabletop height. In areas where the older traditions were firmer, foot waulking remained in longer use, as part of a pattern of survival rather than as a simple alternative to hand waulking.

When the various fulling stages had been completed, washing followed. The web was often carried to a convenient burn in a hand-barrow. There, it was tramped by the women in plain water till all the soapy suds and urine was washed out of it, as well as any of the dye that had been loosened in the course of fulling. The web then got a second washing with soap, and the cloth was wrung out as well as possible. As it was washed, the web was laid in overlapping folds, a process called *coinnleachadh* or *cur chlò air choinnlean*, 'putting the cloth on the stick', though it was only after the folding that the cloth was rolled on a flat or round stick, 'slowly and carefully, bit by bit, hard and firm as the strong arms of the woman can make it, in order that the tension may be evenly distributed'. The rolling process had various names: *còrnadh, còrnadh a' chlò* or — *an aodaich,* 'to roll the cloth', *cur a' chlò air chòrn,* 'to put the cloth on the fold', *còrnaich an clò,* 'to fold or roll the cloth.'

Sometimes two or three strong men came in at this stage to stretch and roll the web as tightly as possible on the board, whilst it was still damp. It was left like that for several days to become smooth and stiff, and 'when it came off the stick with a sound that seemed like a declaration of its strength, it was called *fìor-aodach.* It was then unrolled to be dried in the sun, before being rolled up again ready for the tailor who would come to the house to make the suits for young and old.'[41]

In some areas, after washing and rolling, the web was taken back to the waulk-ing frame and was turned slowly clockwise along it, a verse being spoken at each turn, in a consecration ceremony. The members of the household for whom the cloth was intended were mentioned by name in the verses. The web 'is then spat upon, and slowly reversed end by end in the name of Father and of Son and of Spirit till it stands again in the centre of the frame'.[42]

The waulking of cloth was much more than just a job to be done. It was 'an elaborate and beautiful operation',[43] an integral part of the social structure and domestic economy of Highland life, a regularly recurring nodal point that helped to give a community cohesion. It had not only a strong internal structure, but also an external social function.

Women like the Patersons and others who were in constant demand at waulking had a high social status.[44] For young women, it was regarded as a serious slight not to be invited to a waulking, for it was there that they had an opportunity to meet young men.[45]

Waulking was properly a female prerogative, though in its latter days men might be present and there is a record in Barra of men helping out by singing a song if the women grew tired.[46]

A man at Carbost in Skye helped on one occasion to finish cloth, but it came out far too thick. The comment was: 'It will be perfect for mending the seats of the boy's trousers.' Men might also help with the rolling of the web after washing.

In Inverness-shire, there was a custom for each of the girls present at the waulk-ing to cut a knotted end of thrums off the corners of the web, and place it above the door. The first to put it there would get a husband of the same name as the first male who entered, and so on in sequence. This gave rise to a good deal of fun and chaffing.

If a young man dropped into a house where waulking was going on,

> ... he generally got a rough handling. He was summarily taken hold of by them and muffled up in the web, and thoroughly soaked with the luke-warm soapy water with which the web had been kept wet all the time. He might, on effecting his release, attempt to get a kiss from a pair of rosy lips, as a solatium for his tussle, but all hands were laid upon him, and he could not get it, nor was he at all displeased at his rough treatment from the bevy among which his own sweetheart was the one who delighted most in his discomfiture.[47]

Normally, however, male participation followed the waulking. When the lads gathered a piper came, and some suitable place such as the kiln-barn was tidied up for dancing. This was called the *bàl-luaidh* in South Uist, and might last until 1 or 2 a.m.[48] In some areas, such as Lewis, there was no dance after the waulking, however.

In singing waulking songs, one woman took the lead with the verses, and all joined in the chorus. The sound of the song, the rhythmic movements, the pungent smell of hot urine, and the lantern light all combined to make a unique and memorable occasion.

The songs, the *òrain luaidh*, were of various subjects, of love and war, of hunting, of sowing. Pride was taken in skilful singing. The Rev. Robert MacGregor, minister of Kilmuir in Skye thought that 'it is rather surprising how nature inspires them with such skill in the modulation of their rustic strains, that their music often appears as if composed by connoisseurs in the science. They observe flats and sharps with much precision, and also not unfrequently change their tunes from major to minor keys, and vice versa.'[49] Indeed, it was considered that if a woman with a hard metallic voice sang out of tune and overwhelmed the rest of the team, the *loireag*, a kind of water-sprite thought to preside over the operations of warping, weaving and waulking, would be especially wrathful at her.[50]

The woman who struck up the air of the song was sometimes called the *aon-bhualach* or *aon-ghuthach*, 'one striker' or 'one-voiced', in South Uist. She was selected by the waulking women, who then looked to her for guidance in voicing the air of the song.[51]

A late eighteenth-century writer said that iorrams and luinneags were sung at waulking,[52] the former defined by Dwelly as 'boat-song, rowing song' or 'song sung during any kind of work, by way of lightening its burden', the latter as a 'song, ditty', 'chorus', 'burden of a song', 'Gaelic song or catch'.

As waulking and singing proceeded, the cloth was tested from time to time to see if it had shrunk enough and if the texture was right. The middle finger was used as a gauge to test the shrinkage, and if necessary another song would be sung, the cloth being kept moist the while. When the cloth was ready, it was rolled, and beaten or clapped, when the *òran basaidh* or *coileach* was sung in quick 2/4 time, to end the waulking. 'The company would shout "Give them the *coileach*!" for the words of these last songs are to a great extent extemporised and consist of witty and ribald remarks about the people present with references to their actual or possible love affairs.'[53]

One of the things that the leader of the singing had to look out for was that no song should be repeated. If this should happen, the *loireag*, the gremlin of the waulking, would come and make the cloth as thin and uncompacted as at the beginning, and all the work would be wasted. When Carmichael, at a waulking in Mingulay in 1866, asked a girl to sing a certain song over again, she and the other women were embarrassed, and 'the leader said that were they to sing the same song twice at the same waulking the cloth would become thin and streaky and white as "rùsg na caora", the sheep's fleece, and there was no knowing what mischief might not befall the wearer of the cloth or the singer of the song.'[54]

Equally, it was considered unlucky to have a songless web, *clò bodaich*, and the waulking of a piece of cloth had always to be finished at one sitting.[55]

Waulking songs were once sung throughout the Gaelic-speaking parts of Scotland. Now waulking has disappeared from the scene and the songs as functional parts of that scene are rarely to be heard. Large numbers, however, have been preserved in several notable collections such as those of Alexander Carmichael, Margaret Fay Shaw, John Lorne Campbell, etc., but there is always the problem in recording that without the waulking team, a lone singer seems incomplete. This appears clearly from the technique as described by Margaret Fay Shaw in South Uist in 1955. The women sat at the waulking board, they started to work the cloth, and a one, two, three, four rhythm slowly began to emerge.

A woman will chant —

Far ail ill lò, hò ro hù a

and the others will join in with:

Hao ri *ò* 's na *ho* hì *iù* a
Far ail ill *lò, hò* ro hù a

and the first woman sings along:

'S *trom* mo *cheum*, cha *n-eil* mi *sunn*dach

(heavy is my step, Í am not joyful).

The soloist continues to sing the lines which tell the tale, and (in the case of this and similar songs) the first line of the chorus, the other women singing the other two. The choruses of waulking songs are usually meaningless, consisting of syllables that carry the air; but they have a mnemonic significance, and must always be sung correctly. The chorus is called the *fonn* or 'ground' and is the means by which the songs are popularly identified, as different versions of the same waulking song may begin with different lines. In order to make the waulking songs last long enough to do the work, each verse or *ceamhramh* (usually only a half-line, single line, or couplet) is sung twice, sometimes with a different phrase of the chorus after it the second time. When the verse has two lines or two half-lines, sometimes the second line of one verse is repeated as the first line of the following verse, sometimes the whole two-line verse is itself repeated. To sing a complete waulking song alone without anyone to take up the chorus imposes a very considerable strain on any reciter.[56]

Such songs, preserved without the functions and connotations that gave them their full meaning, must of necessity become art forms somewhat divorced from their origins.

I am indebted to Chrissie MacLeod, Lewis, for help with the Gaelic terms.

REFERENCES

1. MacKellar, M., 'The Waulking Day', *Transactions of the Gaelic Society of Inverness*, 13 (1886-87), 201-17.
2. *ibid.*, 202.
3. Society of Antiquaries of Scotland (hereafter SAS), Robertson J., MS. Tour 1786, 42.
4. Buchanan, J.L., *Travels in the Western Hebrides* (London, 1793), 84.
5. *New Statistical Account* (hereafter *NSA*), XIV (Edinburgh, 1845), 286.
6. Grant, K.W., 'Peasant Life in Argyllshire in the End of the Eighteenth Century', *Scottish Historical Review*, 14 (1918-19), 148-49.
7. Pennant, T., *A Tour in Scotland MDCCLXIX* (London, 1776), 328.
8. Buchanan, J.L., *op. cit.*, 84; *NSA*, XIV, 286.
9. Beveridge, E., *North Uist, its Archaeology and Topography* (Edinburgh, 1911), 322.
10. MacKellar, M., *op. cit.*, 202.
11. Maclean, C.I., *The Highlands* (London, 1959), 11.
12. Buchanan, J.L., *op. cit.*, 84.
13. Grant, K.W., *op. cit.*, 148-49.
14. Carmichael, A., *Carmina Gadelica, Hymns and Incantations,* I (Edinburgh, 1928), 306.
15. Martin, M., *Description of the Western Isles of Scotland, c. 1695* (Glasgow, 1884), 57.
16. Burt, E., *Letters from a Gentleman in the North of Scotland to his Friend in London*, II (London), 1759), 143.
17. *NSA*, XIV, 286.
18. Grant, K.W., *op. cit.*, 148-49.
19. Carmichael, A., *op. cit.* IV (1941), 89.
20. Grant, K.W., *op. cit.*, 148-49.
21. Goodrich-Freer, A., *Outer Isles* (London, 1902), 256-57.
22. Grant, K.W., *op. cit.*, 148-49.
23. *ibid.*
24. Carmichael, A., *op. cit.* IV (1941), 89.
25. MacDonald, D., The Historical Geography of North Tolsta, typescript, 1946, 32.
26. Goodrich-Freer, A., *op. cit.* 261-62.

27. Dwelly, E., *The Illustrated Gaelic-English Dictionary* (Glasgow, 1941), s.v. *luadhadh*.
28. MacKellar, M., *op. cit.*, 210.
29. *ibid.*, 215.
30. Grant, K.W., *op. cit.*, 148-49.
31. School of Scottish Studies (hereafter SSS), MacDonald, D.J., MS. 53, 4961/2.
32. Martin, M., *op. cit.*, 57.
33. Burt, E., *op. cit.* II, 143.
34. SAS, Robertson, J., *op. cit.* II, f.42.
35. Pennant, T., *op. cit.*, 327-28.
36. Buchanan, J.L., *op. cit.*, 84.
37. *NSA*, XIV, 286.
38. SSS, tape-recording SA 1967/31/84.
39. SSS, MacDonald, D.J., MS. 2, 140.
40. Nicolson, A., *History of Skye: a record of the families, social conditions of the island* (Glasgow, 1930), 319.
41. MacKellar, M., *op. cit.*, 215.
42. Carmichael, A., *op. cit.* I (1928), 307; IV (1941), 88.
43. *ibid.* IV (1941), 89.
44. cf. Maclean, C.I., *op. cit.*, 75.
45. *ibid.*
46. SSS, tape-recording SA 1965/99/5.
47. MacKellar, M., *op. cit.*, 215.
48. SSS, MacDonald, D.J., MS. 53, 4990.
49. *NSA*, XIV, 286.
50. Carmichael, A., *op. cit.* II (1928), 320.
51. *ibid.* VI (1971), 9.
52. Buchanan, J.L., *op. cit.*, 84.
53. Shaw, M.F., *Folksongs and Folklore of South Uist* (London, 1955), 7.
54. Carmichael, A., *op. cit.* II (1928), 320; IV (1941), 89.
55. Goodrich-Freer, A., *op. cit.* 256-57.
56. Shaw, M.F., *op. cit.*, 72-73.

Scottish Methods of Preserving White Fish

BRUCE WALKER

Scotland is a country with a very long coastline in relation to its land mass. This coastline has many natural harbours serving coastal waters at one time teeming with fish. In such a country, one would expect a historical fishing industry with well-established fishing ports, curing premises and traditional markets, all well documented from the medieval period onwards. Instead we find an industry only established on a national basis in the eighteenth century[1] in parallel with the agrarian and industrial revolutions, and not reaching its full expectations till the late nineteenth century − the halcyon days of the herring industry − and already declining as governments extend their territorial waters, excluding British boats or restricting the fish caught by strict quota systems.

In the medieval period, the waters round Scotland were the fishing grounds of the Dutch even although the Scottish Crown did its best to break the Dutch hold on the industry.[2] Until the eighteenth century most attempts to set up a Scottish fishing industry were only partly successful, possibly due to the export restrictions imposed on the Scottish merchants and partly due to poor legislation.[3] All of these early attempts were modelled on the Dutch method of fishing[4] and all the sophisticated methods of fish preservation used in Scotland originate from Dutch recipes.[5]

The only exception was the salmon-fishing industry which operated successfully in Scotland during the medieval period, supplying pickled salmon to markets in various parts of Europe through the Atlantic, Baltic, Mediterranean and North Sea ports.[6] The union with England brought about a change in this pattern of trading, the Scots merchants supplying Billingsgate Market, London with 'kitted'[7] salmon, only sending the surplus as pickled salmon to the traditional European markets.[8] Salmon were also 'kippered' or 'smoked' for more immediate home consumption.[9]

The white fish industry appears to have been at the poor end of the export market although fish such as saith, mackerel, and sprats were ignored as possible export material. The preservation methods used for white fish were much cruder and less costly than those applied to salmon and herring. These cures are directly linked to the traditional methods of fish preservation used by communities depending on fish as a major part of their diet.

The processes traditionally used can be classified under six main headings: drying, salting, smoking, exclusion of air, application of vinegar or other acid, and the application of ice or cold.[10] Not all of these methods were commonly applied to white fish and some of the preservation techniques used involved the combination of two or more of the basic processes.

DRYING

The simplest method of drying fish was simply to cut it open and hang it up in the air. One of the earliest references to fish dried in this way appears in a description of Orkney in 1573.[11] Fish dried in this way were still being offered for sale in the major Scottish cities in the nineteenth century[12] and can still be found in some parts of Scotland.[13] Fish 'haiks' can still be seen attached to the walls of many coastal cottages, the haik being a frame with protruding nails onto which the fish were fastened.[14]

Fish dried without salt were known as 'blawen fish',[15] 'gozened fish',[16] 'reis-geadh'[17] or in Fife as 'Crail-capon'.[18]

Air drying was particularly popular for curing dog-fish which are so full of oil as to be easily dried even in the moist climate of the Hebrides.[19] The flesh of the dog-fish is somewhat strong-tasting and was largely used by the lower classes, being exported and sold without its skin as 'darwen salmon'[20] or 'rock-salmon'.[21]

Skate was also dried in this manner as the skin of the skate continues to exude mucus for some days after death and will not take salt. Skate dried in this way were well known as 'sour skate' and were very popular in the Highlands and Islands where its pungent taste and strong smell of ammonia made it a favourite food amongst a people with an otherwise monotonous diet.[22]

In the Northern Isles special stone-built huts called 'skeos'[23] were built to dry meat and fish:

> A skeo is a small square house formed of stones without any mortar, with holes through which the air may have free passage; for which purpose the building was erected on a small eminence, being at the same time protected from the rain by a roof. It was not long since it was customary before using beef or mutton, not to salt it, but to hang it up in one of these places, until the wind, by which it was penetrated, should, at the necessary degree of temperature, have so completely dried the meat as to preserve it from putrefaction... Fish was also hung up unsalted in a skeo, but in this case a slight degree of putrefaction was promoted . . . .[24]

> Cod and ling were then caught near the shore, and the best of them being intended for sale, under the name of 'Stock Fish', were hung up unsalted on poles within a drying house of this kind, that the wind, in issuing through its crevices, might cure them; but as these fish could not always be preserved from putrefaction they were at first, perhaps from necessity, consumed by families, until a relish for tainted food would normally result from their constant introduction at meals. It is probably then from this cause, that though skeos are now in ruins, fish in a semi-putrescent state, named 'Sour Fish' or 'Souked Fish', are at the present day as agreeable to the Shetlanders as the tainted flavour of venison is to an English stomach . . . .[25]

Caves into which the tide flowed were also used to cure fish. These were known as 'helyer' or 'hiallar'.[26] This was not in the strictest sense a non-salt cure as the spray from the sea would salt the fish naturally during the drying process. In some cases this natural salting was assisted and on Island Roan

> The fish would be split and boned, then washed very clean, then it would be soaked in pickle for about two hours. Afterwards, it would be tied up in couples and carried to the fish cave on the north side of the island where it was hung up on sticks to be dried and cured.
> The cave had peculiar curing qualities, because of a current of sea air continually passing through the slit between the walls where the fish were hung up. Strangely enough, the

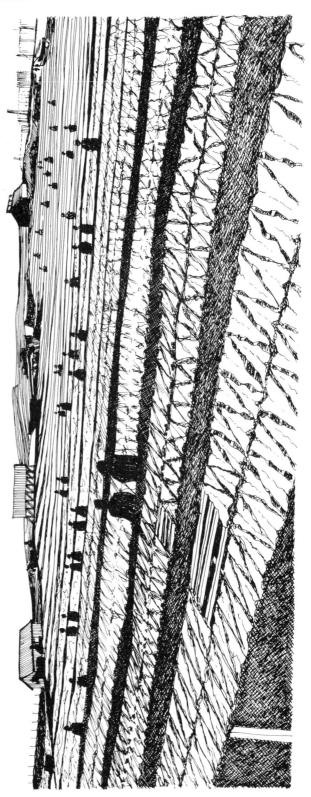

Fig. 1   Fish drying on trestles near Aberdeen (from a George Washington Wilson photograph)

fish, although perfectly cured in about a fortnights time would never get hard like ordinary salted fish when laid out to dry. It would remain soft and pliable after being removed from the cave and tasted like fresh fish with a lovely flavour which could not be obtained in any other way.

The general rule was, after curing, to take the fish home and pack it between layers of straw in boxes, ready for use at any time.[27]

Fish were also dried in the dwelling house by simply hanging them on a line above the hearth, or in later houses, over the fireplace.[28] This would result in a certain amount of smoking depending on the type of house and the type of fireplace.

SALTING

Salting was the most common method of preserving white fish and vast quantities were cured in this way.[28] A description of Sandness, Shetland, in 1774 gives a clear impression of the process at that date.

> Immediately as the boats came ashore, the fish are numbered, the splitters, washers and salters, set to work upon them: the first with a stroke or two of a large knife, cuts them open from the neck to the tail, pulls out half the bone, and throws the fish to the washer, who immediately washes them in the sea, and after they are drained, a pretty thick layer of salt is thrown in the bottom of a large chest (calked and pitched for the purpose), a layer of fish is laid in order so as to contain well, then a layer of salt, and so stratum super stratum till the chest is full. They commonly salt twice a week, Monday and Wednesday, but this depends much on the quantity got. They are all dried upon a beach; and where they have not this conveniency naturally, they force it by covering the green with stones. In clear weather, a little time drys fish, but gloomy, misty, or wet weather (and such is too common in Schetland) renders them brown and spoils them. A well cured fish is of a fine greenish colour, and when held between the eye and the light looks transparent.[29]

At Hamna Voe, Shetland

> The fish are split in a different manner here from the rest of Schetland, only the three upper joints of the back bone are cut out, being designed for the Irish market; whereas elsewhere they pull out one half.[30]

Care had to be taken when putting out the fish to dry and the weather conditions carefully monitored. If the fish were laid out on an already warm beach, the hot stones could blister the backs.[31] Too strong a sun after the fish were put out could have a similar effect[32] and any form of dampness, especially in the later stages of drying, could result in an attack of fish mites.[33] Because of this, some merchants refused to handle salt fish on a damp day, even under cover or indoors and storage rooms had to be dry and well ventilated.[34]

Gradually the drying facilities changed, especially those run on a large scale. Fish were dried on slatted trestles, provided with canvas covers which could be quickly pulled over the fish should the sun become too hot or there be any indication of rain or showers.[35] Misty weather and 'sea haar' still had to be avoided by experience.

The 'spelding cure' was practiced on the east coast of Aberdeenshire between Fraserburgh and Newburgh and in Orkney, Shetland and the Hebrides. The gutting and cleaning were carried out in the same way as other cures but the fish were not headed but split with the body of the fish. They were immersed an hour or more in strong brine then well washed in sea water and laid out to drip. After a day's good drying, they were gathered in small bings, and pressed down with weights for two days to ensure a good flat set then dried for another day. After the first week, the fish were allowed to remain in bing a few days at a time to sweat out the salt and make them a greenish-red colour.[36]

'Pickled' or 'wet cure' fish are prepared in the same way as dried fish. They are removed from the salt after forty-eight hours and the backs carefully scraped to remove the slime. The fish are well washed and repacked in tight pickle barrels with fresh salt. The fish are placed with the skin against the bottom of the barrel. The skin is normally placed downwards till the last fish which is reversed, with a full quota of salt between each layer. The barrels are allowed to stand overnight, then flagged, headed and laid on their sides to be filled with clean pickle through the pickle vent.[37]

Dried salted fish were known as 'salt fish'[38] or simply as 'salt cod', 'salt ling', etc. according to the kind of fish. Lightly salted sun dried haddocks were known as 'rizzers'.[39] Montrose salted fish were considered to be superior to those salted in other east coast burghs[40] and for those who wished to freshen the taste of salt fish, 'soaking in sour milk' was considered to be the quickest and best method.[41]

It was considered lucky to have fish in the house at Hogmanay[42] and salt fish served this purpose admirably. On Stroma, this was taken a stage further and salt fish and fried tatties were eaten for New Year's Day breakfast.[43]

Sugar could be used as a replacement for salt and 'sweet cured' fish were sold by some merchants.[44] Wet pickle, although popular in the salmon and herring trades does not appear to have been used to any extent for white fish.

SMOKING

The practice of smoking fish possibly began by simply hanging fish in the dwelling house to dry — and this in a house without chimneys would result in a smoky flavour. Chimneys were only introduced into most Scottish houses in the early eighteenth century[45] and therefore the practice had a long time to develop and the taste for smoked fish was still predominant when the Scottish fishing industry began to expand and develop beyond its traditional role.

Smoked fish can be broadly classified under two main headings — cold-smoked fish and hot-smoked fish.[46] Cold-smoked fish are by far the most common type. The main characteristic is that the fish are smoked in a cool smoke and remain raw. Hot-smoked fish are much less common and the fish are cooked during the smoking process.

Both classes of cure require fish in first-class condition. The best fish for smoking are those caught on sma' lines[47] and landed the same day as the act of disconnecting the hook tends to bleed the fish immediately and the class of boat using sma' lines tends always to land the same day. Merchants working with fish from larger boats perhaps staying out for several days or even weeks were prepared to pay more for fish killed and bled at the time of catching as the fish did not have 'black lugs'[48] and unsightly brown or black marks on the flesh where the flesh was in contact with congealed blood.[49]

In general smoked fish were referred to as 'reested'[50] and the framework of spars or ropes on which fish and meat were hung to smoke was known as a

Fig. 2   Finan kilns, in Mansefield Road, Aberdeen (from an old photograph)

'reest'.[51]

The best known of the cold-smoked fish are probably 'Finnan haddocks'.[52]

This special method of curing haddocks takes its name from the village of Findon, near Aberdeen. It was at first quite a home industry. Among the Kincardineshire villages the crews employed in the small line fishing usually divided each days catch of haddocks as soon as they landed. Each fisherman then took his own share home, where the fish were cured by the female members of the family, the smoking being done in the kitchen chimney or 'lum' which was especially adapted for the purpose.[53]

In the nineteenth century, the 'Finnan' or 'Aberdeen cure'[54] was only prepared on the small strip of coast between Stonehaven and Aberdeen and was traditionally smoked over fires made from 'soft grey peats'[55] but is now smoked over whitewood sawdust. The fish are gutted, headed and cleaned, carefully removing all the blood from the bone at the back of the 'sound'.

For Finnans, the fish are opened down the left side of the ventral fin . . . the ventral and anal fins are cut to the 'flag' side of the fish and the knife not passed out at the tail but stopped at the lower end of the anal fin. The splitter then half turns the fish round . . . and makes a long curved cut, down the bone next the dorsal fin. This has the double effect of allowing the salt to penetrate the fish better, and likewise, coupled with the short cut at the tail, has a tendency to broaden out the fish and give them a thick fishy look. . . . This cut along the bone is termed the 'gae feather'. The fish cut, they are hand-salted lightly and allowed to lie in salt overnight; then after being washed out of salt, they are, one by one laid out on frames or dykeheads to drouth previous to smoking. The drouthing dries up extra moisture and gives the fish what is termed a 'set' that is it fixes them in a broad open style which they would not have otherwise. After drouthing . . . they are spitted under the pectoral bone and fin, by one 'lug' only, and that on the 'flag' side, on wooden spits only, and taken to smoke.[56]

The fish on the wooden spits have to be moved several times during the smoking process to ensure that all are coloured correctly. The fish are removed when slightly lighter than the desired colour as the colouring process continues for a little time afterwards.

During the smoking . . . so constant has been the movement amongst the fire, keeping the peats from being covered amongst the ashes, and spreading the fire back and replenishing it . . . that a considerable amount of dust or 'coom' . . . settled on the fish rendering them rather unsightly. . . . A tub or trough of slightly warmed and salted water is set . . . fish washed singly, back and front, with a small rag. . . . They will keep sweet a good fourteen days in winter, and four in summer. . . .[57]

The making of Finnans was the most skilful and costly of all the cures practised in Scotland in the nineteenth century.[58]

A much cheaper cold-smoke cure was the 'Eyemouth' cure which cost less for the whole cure than the Finnan cost after smoking.[59] The Eyemouth cure was practised along the coasts of Berwick, the Lothians, Fife, part of Angus, part of Kincardine, Aberdeen, part of Banff, Moray and Inverness, and after the introduction of the railway, in Cromarty, Ross, Sutherland and Caithness. It was also used in the south-west in Argyll, Ayr, Wigton, Kircudbright and Dumfries. The fish are gutted, headed and cleaned.

In opening . . . care is taken to pass the knife down the right-hand side of the ventral fin. . . . In splitting, the fish is placed on its side, with the tail towards the operator, and the opened belly towards his right hand. Holding the fish firmly yet lightly by the upper lug the knife is passed down the upper side of the back-bone, close to the junction of the ribs with it, and severing the former at a rather obtuse angle till the extreme end of the abdomen is reached, when the angle at which the knife is held is changed to one more acute to the plane of the table. Continuing with one sweep till the tail is reached, the knife is passed right out thereat, leaving the ventral and anal fins all on the bone side of the fish when split. Then turning the fish partly round, with the tail towards the right, the splitter strikes off the small part of bone and fish, covering the clot of blood always found at the extreme end of the abdomen leaving it exposed ready for the next operation, which is termed 'seynding'.[60]

The clot of blood at the end of the abdomen is removed by scrubbing and the fish are immersed in a pickle tub. The pickle is made with clean cold water and sufficient salt to float a haddock. The fish are immersed for fifteen to thirty minutes and removed from the pickle by scoops and placed on drainers.[61]

> From the 'dreepers' the fish are lifted one by one, and being folded as it were backwards, are spitted upon either iron or wooden spits. . . . The spitting consists in passing the spit through both 'lugs' under the pectoral bone and fin sinews, and thereafter stretching the fish their full breadth on the spit . . . three to six fish according to size . . . conveyed to kiln. . . .[62]

The fires were made from 'cooperage chips' used to light 'billets of hardwood' then smothered with hardwood sawdust. The fish hang till the moisture ceases to drop from them which usually takes from half an hour to two hours. When taken down they have a 'scarcely perceptible tinge of colour and taste of smoke'.[63] They are packed in barrels for market and should keep four or five days in winter and two or three days in summer.

'Smoked speldings' are made from speldings cured in the usual way and are ready for smoking when about hand-clean. They are smoked in Eyemouth kilns, the speldings being laid three deep over iron spits to prevent them from curling. They are smoked to a light brown colour, then stored in a dry loft and covered from the air till marketed and keep for a long time.[64]

The 'Moray Firth' or 'Buckie cure' is made in all areas where merchants regularly make Eyemouths. The method is identical to the normal Eyemouth cure but the smoking continues for a full twelve hours and the fish come out well dried and a light golden-yellow colour not unlike Finnans and will keep from three weeks to a month in winter and a week in the summer.[65]

The modern 'Finnan' is often a version of the Eyemouth cure being soaked in brine rather than salting[66] and in some areas butter dye is added to the brine to give an even colour to the fish without the complex smoking arrangements of the traditional Finnan.[67] Butter dye is also used for boneless fillets known as 'block fillet' or 'golden cutlet' or for 'cod fillet'.[68]

A small variant of the Finnan is the 'Glasgow pale', a small haddock smoked to a pale straw colour with the backbone on the left side of the fish. These fish must be removed from the kiln just as they are beginning to develop colour,[69] as like the Finnan the colour continues to develop till the fish is cold.

The best known of the hot-smoked fish is the 'Arbroath smokie' originally known as the 'Auchmithie cure' or the 'lucken' or 'close fish cure'[70] in some areas. A small dried or smoked closed fish was also known as a 'pin-the-widdie'[71] or 'pinwiddie'[72] but this was not specifically applied to smokies. The fish are gutted, headed and cleaned in the same way as Finnans or Eyemouths but are not split.

On being scrubbed at the bone they are simply tied in pairs by the tails with stout twine, and either laid in dry salt or pickled for an hour. Then, if salted, they are washed out of it, or, if pickled, lifted out and strung across the spits (from twelve to twenty couple per spit) they are smoked on and set outside on frames to drouth . . . a good fire of small billets of hard wood, and that kind of peat known as 'stickly' peat is kindled on . . . the floor of the chamber in a pretty large heap. . . . This fire is allowed to burn pretty well down, partly to secure that half consumed fiery remainder of wood and peat fires known as 'iezle' and partly to heat up the chamber the better to cure the fish. The iezles are then spread through the chamber floor, and in this state give out a fair heat but little smoke. The fish are transferred from the drouthing frames to the chamber, fresh fuel, in the shape of cooperage chips, and billets, and peats, are added to the iezles, hardwood sawdust being thickly strewen over all . . . the light cloth is drawn over the top, and the whole left to smother in the closed in chamber for from forty to fifty minutes from the commence- ment according to the size and condition of the fish . . . the cloth is thrown off and the fish still on the spits are withdrawn from the chamber to the frames to cool. . . . The external colour is from a dingy brown to black, but the smoke flavour having to filter through the skin . . . leaves the flesh of a deliciously sweet taste, and quite white in colour. . . . The fish cured in this way are nearly all cured by the wives of the fishermen, and it is not usual for them to employ other than the primitive 'half-hogshead' as a 'smoke barrel' or kiln.[73]

Purpose-made timber smoke barrels were constructed in the early years of this century, these being gradually replaced by brick, particularly after the second world war.

In the same district identified with the Finnan Cure, there was formerly practiced, and very occasionally still is, a form of cure known as 'Bervies'.[74]

These fish were prepared in the same way as Finnans but were cured over a fire of stickly peat and yellow sods (recently formed peat) found overlying true peat. The yellow sods were added to the fire at the stage when Finnans would be con- sidered as overdone inducing a blaze thereby cooking the fish in the same way as smokies. They were then cooled and tied in threes by passing rushes through a hole especially made in the 'flag' side of the fish and tied round the bone. The fish are not washed but simply dusted. A Bervie will keep for a long time at any time of year.[75]

John Ross Jnr. gives some interesting descriptions of the types of kiln used for the above mentioned processes[76] and other less detailed but sometimes conflicting descriptions are also available.[77] These descriptions, combined with surveys of the surviving kilns are to be the subject of a separate study and could not be accommodated within the limitations imposed on this article. An old illustration of kilns is included, simply to indicate the richness of the subject. It should also be understood that many of the kilns were adapted or adaptable to different cures but always with limited success. Fish such as herring, mackerel, sprats, salmon and eels were also cured, sometimes using the same equipment as used for white fish and this again complicates the surveys of surviving kilns as these opera- tions were often on a very different scale and much more industrialised.

CONCLUSIONS

In the preservation of white fish we see a gradual change from the strong cures of the eighteenth and early nineteenth centuries, originally developed from necessity, to much lighter cures as transport became easier and the fish could be marketed more quickly. This is still happening and in almost every case the present-day version of the cure given in this paper is much lighter and more delicate to the palate.

The industry was originally a cottage one and although some of the larger fish suppliers have completely industrialised the various processes, a surprising number of small fish merchants remain, working in the traditional ways albeit with the help of the deep freeze and refrigerator.[78]

The white fish industry developed in parallel with the herring industry often sharing the same ports and fish-curing premises. This can create confusion when studying the surviving buildings and artifacts and a national survey is now required of surviving premises together with an archival survey for recipes and business accounts to reach a clearer understanding of the role of fish in the diet of the average Scot during the eighteenth and nineteenth centuries.

NOTES AND REFERENCES

1. Bremner, David, *The Industries of Scotland, their rise, progress and present condition* (1869, repub'd. 1969), 512-530; Dyson, John, *Business in Great Waters: The Story of British Fishermen* (1977), 33-88; Lythe, S.G.E. and Butt, J., *An Economic History of Scotland 1100-1939* (1975), 52-54.
2. Dyson, J., *op. cit.*, 49-54; Lythe, S.G.E. and Butt, J., *op. cit.*, 53.
3. Bremner, D., *op. cit.*, 513.
4. Dyson, J., *op. cit.*, 56.
5. Buchanan, Rev. John Lanne, *A General View of the Fishery of Great Britain drawn up for the consideration of the undertakers of the North British Fishing* (1794), 234-244; Smith, W. Anderson, 'Curing and Preserving Fish at home and abroad', in Herbert, David (ed.), *Fish and Fisheries . . . 1882* (1933), 97-98.
6. Bremner, D., *op. cit.*, 526-528; Douglas, Francis, *A General Description of the East Coast of Scotland from Edinburgh to Cullen* (1782), 147-148; Hoyes, John, 'Parish of Kinloss' (Morayshire), *Statistical Account of Scotland* (Commonly known as the Old Statistical Account, hereafter *OSA*), I (1791), 463; McCulloch, George, 'Parish of Loth' (Sutherland), *OSA*, VI (1793), 312; Peter, Alexander, 'Parish of Logie-Pert' (Angus), *OSA*, IX (1793), 36; Strang, John, *Glasgow and its Clubs* (1864), 30; Sutherland, William, 'Parish of Wick' (Caithness), *OSA*, X (1794), 4; Ure, David, 'Parish of Killearn' (Stirlingshire), *OSA*, XVI (1795), 122-124; Walker, William, 'Parish of St. Cyrus' (Kincardineshire), *OSA*, XI (1794), 93; Wilson, Mr., 'Parish of Gamrie' (Banffshire), *OSA*, I (1791), 472.
7. Douglas, F., *op. cit.*, 147-48.
8. National Library of Scotland, Acc. 5726: Richardson of Pitfour Papers. Surviving office books of the shipping and fish-curing enterprise of the Richardson family from 1763 to the second decade of the nineteenth century.
9. Robinson, James, *The Whole Art of Curing, Pickling and Smoking Meat and Fish* (1847), 61-64; Ross, John Jnr., 'Curing and Preserving Fish in Scotland and its Islands', in Herbert, David (ed.), *op. cit.*, 128-129; Smith, W.A., *op. cit.*, 101; Ure, D., *op. cit.*, 122-124; 'Viking' (Duthie, R.G.), *The Art of Fishcuring* (1911), 107-108.
10. Smith, W.A., op. cit., 94-95.
11. Settle, Dionyse, *A visit to Orkney in 1577. A true reporte of the laste voyage into the West and North-west retions . . . by Captaine Frobisher* (1577).
12. *Dundee Advertiser*, 27 June 1845.
13. *Scots Magazine*, new series, 112, no. 1 (1979), 92, illustration: 'Angus McAlister of Gigalum Cottages on the Isle of Gigha still hangs out fish to dry for the winter. He catches saithe locally and leaves them soaking in salt for a few days prior to drying. Before being eaten they are left in water overnight, then boiled and served with potatoes.'
14. Grant, William and Murison, David (eds.), *Scottish National Dictionary*, V (1960), 82:

heck, haik, hake: 'a triangular frame studded with spikes on which fish are dried'.

15. *ibid.*, II (1941), 162: blaw: to dry fish in the open air without salt.
16. *ibid.*, IV (1956), 255: gozen, gosen: to dry partially in the wind esp. of fish hung up to dry outside or in a specially constructed stone shed.
17. National Museum of Antiquities of Scotland (hereafter NMAS), Country Life Archive: Fish Drying: *reisgeadh*: the hanging of fish or flesh up to dry is from Norse *ruskeid*, split fish hung up to dry: N. Mackay, 1897, 95.
18. *ibid.*, Crail, Fife: dried haddock called Crail-capon: *Anster Fair*, canto, II, XX, 18.
19. Smith, W.A., *op. cit.*, 95.
20. *ibid.*
21. *Chambers Encyclopaedia*, XII, 462, s.v. 'shark': spotted or spiny dog fish . . . when beheaded and skinned sold as 'flake' or 'rock salmon'.
22. Smith, W.A., *op. cit.*, 95.
23. Low, George, *A Tour Through the Islands of Orkney and Schetland (1774)* (1978), 90; Monteith, R., *A description of the Isles of Orkney and Zetland . . . 1663* (1845), 46.
24. Hibbert, S., *A Description of the Shetland Isles . . .* (1822), 417, 563.
25. Brewster, David. *The Edinburgh Encyclopaedia*, XVIII (1830), 107.
26. *ibid.*
27. Mackay, John George, *The Story of Island Roan* (1962), 10.
28. Hall, James, *Travels in Scotland by an Unusual Route with a Trip to the Orkneys and Hebrides*, II (1807), 328, 339.
29. Low, G., *op. cit.*, 120-21.
30. *ibid.*, 137.
31. Ross, J. Jnr., *op. cit.*, 126-27; 'Viking', *op. cit.*, 73.
32. Ross, J. Jnr., *op. cit.*, 126-27; 'Viking', *op. cit.*, 73.
33. 'Viking', *op. cit.*, 85.
34. *ibid.*
35. Smith, W.A., *op. cit.*, 98.
36. Ross, J. Jnr., *op. cit.*, 119-120.
37. *ibid.*, 127-28; 'Viking', *op. cit.*, 59-67.
38. 'Viking', *op. cit.*, 77.
39. Grant, W. and Murison, D. (eds.), *op. cit.* VII (1968): 'risser': a lightly salted and half-dried haddock.
40. Douglas, Andrew, *A History of the Village of Ferryden* (1855), 47.
41. *The Fife Free Press*, 8 Jan. 1881, 5.
42. Personal recollections of the fishing community in Arbroath.
43. NMAS, Country Life Archive: information from Mrs. M. Simpson, Thurso (ex Stroma), Oct. 1969.
44. *Dundee Advertiser*, 3 Aug. 1855: 'Sweet Salted ling Fish on sale, of Summer catch and cure, at Peter Davidsons, No. 90 Seagate, Dundee. 1st August 1855.'
45. B.W., unpublished PhD research.
46. Burgess, G.H.O., Cutting, C.L. (in part), Lovern, J.A. and Waterman, J.J., *Fish Handling and Processing* (1965), 71.
47. Grant, W. and Murison, D. (eds.), *op. cit.* VIII (1971), 349-50: 'small lines' used to catch small fish such as haddock, whiting and flounders in distinction to the larger deep sea fish'. Sma' lines can have up to 1,400 hooks each spaced approximately a fathom apart.
48. 'Viking', *op. cit.*, 59.
49. *ibid.*, 59-60.
50. Grant, W. and Murison, D. (eds.), *op. cit.* VII (1968): 'reest, reist, riest, reast, rest, rist': 'To cure by drying or smoking': 'A framework of spars or ropes on which fish, meat, etc. are hung to dry in smoke above a fire, specifically in a smoking kiln or a farm cottage.'
51. *ibid.*
52. Burgess, G.H.O., Cutting, C.L., Lovern, J.A. and Waterman, J.J., *op. cit.*, 90-94; Ross, J. Jnr., *op. cit.*, 113-16; Smith, W.A., *op. cit.*, 99-100; 'Viking', *op. cit.*, 96-102.
53. 'Viking', *op. cit.*, 96.
54. Ross, J. Jnr., *op. cit.*, 113-14.
55. *ibid.*
56. *ibid.*, 113-15.

57. *ibid.*, 118-19.
58. *ibid.*
59. *ibid.*
60. *ibid.*, 109.
61. *ibid.*, 110.
62. *ibid.*
63. *ibid.*
64. *ibid.*, 120.
65. *ibid.*, 120-21.
66. Burgess, G.H.O., Cutting, C.L., Lovern, J.A. and Waterman, J.J., *op. cit.*, 94.
67. Common-place in Arbroath.
68. Burgess, G.H.O., Cutting, C.L., Lovern, J.A. and Waterman, J.J., *op. cit.*, 95.
69. *ibid.*, 94.
70. Ross, J. Jnr., *op. cit.*, 112.
71. Jamieson, John, *An Etymological Dictionary of the Scottish Language*, III (1880), 495.
72. Ross, J. Jnr., *op. cit.*, 112.
73. *ibid.*, 112-13.
74. *ibid.*, 119.
75. *ibid.*
76. *ibid.*, 106-29.
77. Smith, W.A., *op. cit.*, 93-105; 'Viking', *op. cit.*, 35-44, 77-82, 92-95, 99-102.
78. The smokie manufacturers in Arbroath still mainly work a form of cottage industry but recently combined to produce a leaflet giving the addresses of the various manufacturers.

Folk-life Study and the Ordnance Survey Memoirs

ALAN GAILEY

If the great Swedish ethnologist Åke Campbell through the inspiration of his visits to Ireland in the 1930s laid a corner-stone of the edifice of folk-cultural study in Ireland, then Caoimhín Ó Danachair constructed a major portion of the foundations. Over many years his writings have generated and maintained an appreciation of Ireland's folk culture amongst ordinary folk, and in more recent times he has been a source of inspiration for the first generation of students of the Department of Irish Folklore at University College, Dublin. His work, too, exemplifies the values of all of the sources of information used by the ethnologist; field data, archival resources and printed materials, the last especially from the nineteenth century. Hopefully, a contribution dealing with a major nineteenth-century documentary source relating to northern parts of Ireland, will serve as a fitting tribute to a colleague and friend whom I first encountered when, as an undergraduate, I visited the former Irish Folklore Commission a quarter of a century ago, seeking material on the Aran Islands in preparation for a geography degree dissertation. Then, as ever since, I met wide knowledge and an infectious, stimulating enthusiasm for folk-culture study. Also, I recognise the interest and concern Caoimhín Ó Danachair has shown for the successful development of my own institution which has become the acknowledged focus of folk-cultural research and exposition in the north of Ireland.

I

The latter half of the eighteenth century and first half of the nineteenth saw great interest in Britain and Ireland in the compilation of regional surveys of the details of physical and human environments. Amongst the best known examples are the county agricultural surveys of England and the great *Statistical Account* of Scotland, compiled on a parish basis under the supervision of Sir John Sinclair in the 1790s.[1] Indeed Scotland repeated the scheme in the early 1840s with the *New Statistical Account*, and since the 1950s has carried out the *Third Statistical Account* thereby pursuing the tradition down to our own time. In Ireland, the best known and most used contribution to this tradition is the series of county *Statistical Surveys*, carried out mainly in the first decade of the nineteenth century by the Royal Dublin Society, which regrettably was not completed for all the counties of the island.

When the large-scale topographic survey of Ireland commenced in the 1820s a plan developed to accompany the six-inch map sheets with a detailed physical, historical and human environmental survey, to be carried out on the basis of the civil parishes. It was intended that these surveys would be published. Data were collected both by the professional surveyors of the army ordnance service, and starting somewhat later, by a team of civilians including some well-known scholars of the day. This is not the place to detail the development and ultimate foundering of the scheme; the history of the project has been admirably recounted by J.H. Andrews.[2] Only one volume was published, for the parish of Templemore in north-west County Londonderry.[3] Its enormous bulk occasioned by the minute detail it contains, led to governmental worry as to the ultimate costs of continuing with publication of such memoirs, and the whole scheme was ended, though not before manuscript memoirs had been amassed for counties Londonderry and Antrim, for most of counties Down, Armagh, Fermanagh and Tyrone, for substantial parts of counties Donegal and Monaghan, and for a few parishes elsewhere, notably in County Cavan. Although by the time the scheme ended, topographic survey had extended farther south in Ireland, gathering of the historical and statistical material had lagged behind, thereby accounting for the dominantly northern provenance of the surviving Ordnance Survey Memoirs, most of the originals of which are in the library of the Royal Irish Academy, while a small quantity of the material is in the archives of the Ordnance Survey at the Phoenix Park headquarters in Dublin.[4]

By the early 1830s the military surveyors had been provided with an outline of the categories of information they were expected to gather systematically towards the memoirs. The first section dealt with physical definition of the parish area, including its name, a description of the locality and details of its topographic and other physical environmental features. The last section was to be a listing of its divisions, other than the administrative ones of townlands and larger units, and secondly a listing and description of the townlands included within the parish boundaries. Between these were two sections. One dealt with what was termed the 'artificial state' of the parish — divided into 'modern,' dealing with towns, buildings of all kinds and communications, 'ancient,' describing mainly what would now be termed ancient and historical monuments, and a description of general appearance and scenery. The other section dealt with the contemporary state of society and economy in the parish; under 'social economy' covering such topics as improvements and obstructions to them, the structure of local government, provision of what would now be termed social services, religion, 'habits of the people' which includes references to social custom and housing conditions, migration and 'remarkable events'; and under 'productive economy' dealing with industry, trades and crafts, commerce and exchange, and with agriculture and rural matters generally and coastal economy. Obviously for those interested in folk cultural studies, the potential for relevant material exists through much of these sections. However, the reality is conditioned by the thoroughness, interest and capacities of the individual surveyors involved. Partly in recognition of the limitations of some of the military surveyors in gathering data for the memoirs, the team of civilian memoir writers was set up. But because they came together on this work rather later, their memoirs cover a more restricted area than those of their military counterparts. Antrim and Londonderry were well covered by the civilian team, whereas almost the only memoirs in existence for Tyrone and Fermanagh are those compiled by the military surveyors. Here the problem of the different capacities of the individuals involved is most obvious. In some parishes in Fermanagh the memoir compilers obviously used their initiative and went beyond the bare structural bones given to them as a basis for enquiry. In others, the compilers slavishly followed what amounted to a rigid questionnaire, and in some cases they simply copied, word for word, large sections for adjacent parishes. Also, as mainly British surveyors working in Ireland, they had no background in Irish culture and could not therefore interpret the various guidelines given them. The case of the lighting of traditional bonfires is a good example of this. Bonfire lighting was obviously covered in the guidelines only in terms of 'Beal Tinne' or the 'lighting of the fires of Baal' and as a head of enquiry had obviously been conceived in terms of contemporary concepts of pre-Christian religion in Ireland. In spite of the fact that now one might expect such a denomination to refer to May bonfires, throughout the memoirs it refers to the midsummer (St. John's Eve) fires, and quite clearly no enquiries were made as to the lighting of bonfires on other annual occasions. All this said, however, the data collected in the memoirs on bonfires have proved sufficiently consistent for cartographic analysis, permitting their use as a datum for diachronic analysis of a wider body of material, including information recently collected by postal questionnaire in the north of Ireland.[5]

The quality and extent of individual parish memoirs varies considerably. Some have merited independent publication, and stand as major sources for local history study.[6] Others are so abbreviated as to be useful only for incidental references they may contain in a very few subject areas, and their significance rests in their place amongst the memoirs as a whole. Also, in an exhaustive study, whether carried out on a parish basis or on a thematic one, the memoirs must be taken in the context of their surrounding Ordnance Survey documentation, especially the name books and the letters, both of which contain valuable material. On the other hand, for at least a limited range of subjects, fairly consistent regional views may be constructed using the parish memoirs as a principal source. For example, extraction of data on the materials used in house building provides a picture broadly similar to that which has already been derived from a contemporary source, the Poor Inquiry of the mid 1830s.[7] The intent of this paper, then, is to examine a number of folk-life themes to discover how the memoir material surviving mainly from the 1830s may be regarded when taken as a whole, rather than on the level of the individual parish.[8]

II

The memoirs relate to all aspects of traditional life; material culture, domestic and community life, tradition, belief and language. For reasons already outlined, they are so variable in quality that no overall consistent view can be built up of most topics, and to attempt to deal with all of the available material would require a book, rather than the present article. Therefore, an indication of the nature of some material under four main subject areas is provided, and where on a theme of limited scope there may be regionally consistent material available, this will be indicated. To avoid burdening this article with large numbers of references, only the appropriate parish names will be used in the text; readers must, if they wish, refer back to the original documentation, using the parish name as a guide to discover the precise references themselves.

SOCIAL LIFE

In the section on 'Habits of the People' many sidelights on northern Irish life, especially rural life are provided. As might be expected, attitudes to strong drink, and to illicit distillation, provide support in western areas for the picture drawn by the late Professor Connell on this subject.[9] Poteen making is reported from the north Donegal parish of Mevagh, and in Templemore, north Derry, sale of illicit spirits is noted as being 'very extensive.' However, in some Fermanagh parishes (Tomregan, Magheraculomney, Kinawley, Galloon, Drumkeeran) poteen making is noted in the 1830s as having been either fairly recently discontinued, or much reduced in volume. This was especially true of the low-lying areas, but in parishes with mountainous districts like Cleenish, illicit distillation persisted in remote places, well away from the prying eyes of the Revenue police. From the Monea end of Devenish parish in Fermanagh comes the interesting detail that '. . . a great number of the inhabitants sell spirits without licences; this they make known to the neighbourhood by placing a jug or glass in the windows of the cabins.' By contrast there are almost no references to illicit distilling from east Ulster.

A different, and perhaps surprising attitude to drink emerges in some of the dominantly presbyterian parishes of south-east County Antrim. The stereotypical view of the presbyterian is coloured by the attitudes and experience of decades in the nineteenth century after the 1830s, and in particular after the 1859 Revival, when the temperance movement, which in reality often meant total abstinence, grew to importance. The memoirs, however, tell in Islandmagee parish that a '. . . remarkable trait among them, and one very unusual among Presbyterians, is their disregard for the admonitions of their minister, and the little respect which they pay either to his person, or to his counsels. They care not to be seen while intoxicated by him – and even on Sundays, they will, while in a state of inebrity, address him on the road.' Sunday drinking is reported for both Antrim parishes and from Kirkinriola to the north of Ballymena, and drinking 'between sermons', that is between morning and evening worship, from Islandmagee, Mallusk and Kilbride parishes. Towards an understanding of these practices, it is well to remember that gathering to religious services on Sundays provided one of the regular social meeting points in the pattern of rural life, and in a landscape organised without agricultural villages, with dispersal of farms throughout rural areas, it was perhaps inevitable that such gatherings would develop aspects other than the overtly religious pretext for their existence.

Such attitudes more probably illustrate differences in values and world view, to use an anthropological expression, and not necessarily disrespect for religion. In these same parts of County Antrim, there are references to the existence of singing schools where certainly the young folk (Mallusk) and perhaps others (Killead, Kilbride, Templecorran, Kilroot) were instructed in the singing of the psalms for use in church services, and they were prepared to pay for the privilege of being taught. Singing and music, however, were not restricted to the meeting house. In Glynn, 'they are fond of listening to music', and both here and in Carnmoney, close to Belfast, the violin is noted as the favourite instrument. Dancing to such music was a widespread recreation all over the areas covered by the memoirs; in Errigal Keerogue in Tyrone 'Their chief amusement appears to be playing musical instruments. In the evening, it is very common throughout the parish to hear some person playing the clarinet, flute, fife, etc. drum.'

The data on wakes perhaps catch the pattern of rural life as it was changing in the first half of the nineteenth century.[10] In dominantly Roman Catholic districts, like Upper Longfield in Tyrone, the older pattern obviously persisted, and elsewhere, like Duneane in Antrim, there are details of story telling, playing of games, smoking and drinking at wakes. In Kinawley in Fermanagh, keening survived amongst some families but the custom is 'nearly extinct', and a similar report comes from Culfeightrim in north Antrim. Also in north Antrim (Loughguile), the playing of wake games was reported as dying away, but in parishes farther south in Antrim such practices had clearly ceased. Wakes as events persisted, however, reading of the scriptures having replaced the more traditional activities in Carnmoney, and the singing of hymns rather than keening is commented on in Drummaul. However, whiskey drinking and the handing round of tobacco at wakes persisted in Islandmagee and also in Donegore, and in Kilbride in Antrim we learn that the wakes were 'conducted with much decorum'.

If wakes were in many places no longer being attended for amusement, both weddings, and perhaps more strangely, christenings, 'are generally conducted with becoming hospitality and hilarity' in the parish of Muff in Donegal. Weddings were, in fact quieter events than christenings in Donegore and Killead in county Antrim, and in the former parish those invited to participate in the latter were known as 'sitters'. 'Sitting up' is described in Islandmagee as a number of young men and women visiting the house in which an infant had arrived on the preceding day, and sitting up throughout the night, amusing themselves in a variety of ways; in Kilbride parish we are told that this was done 'without excess or intemperance'. Inevitably, in the same way that wakes provided opportunities elsewhere, such gatherings led to courtships and later marriages, as noted in Islandmagee.

Two county Antrim parishes – Carnmoney and Islandmagee – provide brief descriptions of another social event of the rural community, the 'quiltings', where young women gathered to help with the work of making quilted bedcovers, where young men gathered from about mid-day onwards, general conversation giving way to dancing as the evening wore on. Here is a good example of the problem posed by the Ordnance Survey memoirs, for museum collections of quilted bedcovers in Ulster clearly show that the activity of quilting, and almost certainly also the social event associated with it, were much more widespread in the first half of the nineteenth century than those two references would lead one to expect.

AMUSEMENTS

Social events like christenings, weddings and wakes concentrated on family occasions as settings for various recreations including dancing and singing. Communal occasions provided similar opportunities, and none more than the fairs which were an essential exchange point in rural economic life. References to people resorting to fairs for purposes of amusement are widespread. In Cavan in Drung parish 'a fair or market . . . will arrest industry in the most critical season.' Fairs and markets in Portadown and Lurgan attracted people from the nearby rural parishes of Drumcree, Loughgall, Seagoe and Shankill. Similarly there are references to resort to fairs for amusement in Fermanagh (Devenish and Inishmacsaint) and Tyrone (Kilskeery). County Antrim provides many similar instances. In Ballycastle (Ramoan parish) publicans set rooms apart on their premises specifically for dancing on fair days, while in Cushendall (Layde parish) the fairs ' . . . are resorted to as much for amusement as business, and until very lately each Public House regularly employed 2 fiddlers or pipers on Fair days, and two rooms in each of these houses were set apart for dancing.' However things were changing for the report sadly concludes, 'but dancing in this parish has been (by the Priests orders) discontinued.' Further south in east Antrim, in Islandmagee, a different reason was given for decline in attendance at fairs and indulgence in recreational activities like dancing. The early 1830s saw the rise of the flax spinning mills in the Belfast area and elsewhere leading to a sharp decline in the market for hand-spun yarn; consequently there was less money circulating in rural areas to be spent on recreation.

Evidence from Ballycarry village (Templecorran parish, County Antrim) shows that fairs could be less pleasant places than the references above suggest. A graphic account of faction fighting, its rise and decline over a period of about a generation in the late eighteenth and early nineteenth century could probably have been matched from many other places, for there is much evidence from all over Ireland for such disturbances.[11]

> The commencement of these faction fights was about 50 years ago in consequence of a dance which took place in Alexander Cinnamon's Public house in Ballycarry where a number of the Islandmagee females were invited but none of the males. This irritated the males so much, that 16 of them assembled armed with sticks and went to Bally-carry and set up an opposition dance in Billy Herdman's public house, and sent in to the other house to demand their females, when immediately the combat commenced, and the 16 from Islandmagee forming themselves into a circle fought manfully, and beat their opponents which were more numerous. So after the combat the Ballycarry men sought for revenge, and took the opportunity of beating them in every fair in Ballycarry — until about 16 years ago when the decisive battle took place — on Christmas day at Races in Islandmagee, where a number of the Ballycarry men came over, but the Island-magee men completely beat them from Jas. Wilson's public house, Gransha townland across the lake — the Ballycarry men returned with a reinforcement of both men and women — each of the men having a white handkerchief round his waist to distinguish themselves, it being by night at 11 o'clock which the Islandmagee men being apprized of this number hid, so the other returned victorious — Magistrates came to Ballycarry to administer justice but both parties made it up and are peaceable since.

In this connection, it is interesting that the memoir writer for Layde parish tells that a consequence of the priestly prohibition on dancing at fairs in Cushendall was an increase in 'drunken rioting'.

Dancing certainly seems to have been a favourite amusement everywhere, and as well as venues of the kind already mentioned, dances were held on the premises of the Doagh Book Club for its members,[12] and a dancing school is noted there and also farther east in Kilwaughter parish where it was attended mainly by girls. Another book club or library to have dances was one in Roughfort to the north of Belfast in Mallusk parish. There also, 'Among the better description of farmers, the assistance and services of a dancing master are indispensible, while among the lower class, a few steps accidentally picked up, are quite sufficient with their naturally good tastes and ears, to ensure their excelling in this lively accomplishment. Among the farmers quadrilles, country dances and reels, and with the lower classes the two latter figures are at present in vogue.'

Other popular recreational activities include a number involving animals in one way or another. Following hounds on foot is reported in Tartaraghan parish, county Armagh, and hunting is noted in Racavan, Magheragall and Glenwherry, all in Antrim. Horse racing is mentioned in Carrickfergus in the east and on Rosapenna sands in Mevagh (County Donegal) in the far west, while near Enniskillen in Fermanagh, Mill Lough near the town was surrounded by a racecourse which had been in use until the late 1820s. Near Derry city (Templemore parish) strand racing was occasionally interrupted by the tides. It had died away in the late eighteenth century, was revived, again suspended in 1834, and again revived the following year, these fluctuations seemingly due to opposition from clergy and the landed class.

Cockfighting was widespread, and comments from Tyrone parishes (Ballyclog, Ardstraw) and others in Fermanagh (Enniskillen, Devenish, Derryvullen and Cleenish) suggesting that it was on the decline underestimated its vitality as a traditional sport, for it survives surreptitiously at the present time. Another activity that would now be regarded as cruel was bull-baiting, reported from Carrickfergus. This seems to have been an urban activity, for the only other Ulster reference to it that I know is from Downpatrick in the late eighteenth or early nineteenth century,[13] and it seems likely that it died out in the middle of the nineteenth century.

Ball games were also popular, ranging from bullet throwing (i.e. road bowling) which is referred to in parishes in the Lagan valley (Magheramesk, Magheragall, Drumbeg, Derriaghy) and at Carrickfergus. Unfortunately, the poorer quality of the County Down and County Armagh memoirs probably accounts for the absence of references there, for it is likely that bullet throwing was more widespread than the memoirs suggest.[14] Hand ball is noted in Killyman parish, County Tyrone, but we are given no description of the game, and there was a circular bowling green, nearly an acre in area, on the demesne of Castle Dobbs in Kilroot parish in south-east Antrim established possibly in the early eighteenth century, but probably intended only for aristocratic use. 'A sort of hurling or "Cammon Playing" as it is called in the north is still kep up. . .' in Loughguile in north Antrim, 'chiefly among the Catholics', and is mentioned in the same area in Finvoy, and in Carrickfergus ('commons or shinny') and Magheragall in the south of the county.

A quite common Christmas activity was competing for a prize of fowl by shooting at a target, noted in Antrim in the east (e.g. Kilroot) and in Fermanagh (Tomregan) and Tyrone (Skirts of Urney and Ardstraw). A variation of this in Carrickfergus permitted shooting at the geese or turkeys themselves, for which 'each person pays a certain sum to the owners of the Fowl for a shot.' Other seasonal festivities cited include harvest homes or 'churns' in Islandmagee, eating of pancakes on Shrove Tuesday in Carrickfergus, parading by Ribbonmen in Loughguile on St. Patrick's Day, the Apprentice Boys' celebrations in Derry City in August and December, 12th July processions of Orangemen in Fermanagh (Enniskillen, Trory South) and the 'Sham Fight' at Scarva (Ballymore parish, County Armagh), the strewing of flowers about doorways on May Eve (Enniskillen) and the observance of St. John's Day, 14th June, by Freemasons (e.g. in Bally-rashane, counties Londonderry and Antrim), a secret society which at that time embraced people of all religions, to judge from the report from Enniskillen. As has already been noted, of course, there is widespread reporting of the lighting of St. John's Eve bonfires in the memoirs, with the principal exception of large parts of County Down from which the custom had disappeared by the 1830s.

Apart from midsummer bonfires, the memoirs provide more consistent data on Easter than on other seasonal occasions. A day or two days' holiday were usual, and amusements already noted, like cock-fighting, were common (e.g. Ballinderry, county Tyrone; Trory South, County Fermanagh). Easter fairs and other communal activities are reported in detail from parishes in south-east Antrim, others close to Antrim town, and from Toome Bridge in the west of the county,[15] and there are references to the rolling of dyed eggs on Easter Monday.[16]

HOUSING

A considerable body of material in the memoirs deals with housing, referring to farmhouses, the dwellings of labourers and cottiers, and urban houses. However, it consists of fairly generalised descriptions, and details of individual features are rare. A good illustration of the nature and potential of this material has already been published,[17] with reference to counties Fermanagh and Monaghan, and the value of data on building materials has been mentioned above. Indeed, building material information provides one of the definite instances where the memoir information is sufficiently consistent to be used throughout the total area to which the memoirs relate. Information on the use of slates, for example is excellent. It is obvious that the use of slates in towns was commoner than in the countryside, and that slates were more in use on farmhouses than on the poorer houses of labourers and cottiers. But this generalised picture must be qualified, for in an area like the Ards peninsula in east County Down, where a source of local slate had been exploited at least since the seventeenth century, the parish memoirs show the use of slate even on the single-storeyed houses in the towns and villages, a category of housing elsewhere usually thatched until much later in the nineteenth century.

There are many references in the memoirs to the types of timber used in building. Imported softwoods from north America and Baltic countries are noted in connection especially with urban building, and the use of bog timber was everywhere widespread.[18] In one instance, perhaps (Fig. 1), there is evidence pointing to innovation in the building of farmhouses. While information where it exists on windows in cottages exclusively refers to apparently fixed windows, sometimes commenting on the virtual absence of glazing, information on farmhouses falls in two categories, showing that fixed or lattice windows were common in most areas, except in a belt across south Antrim from Island-

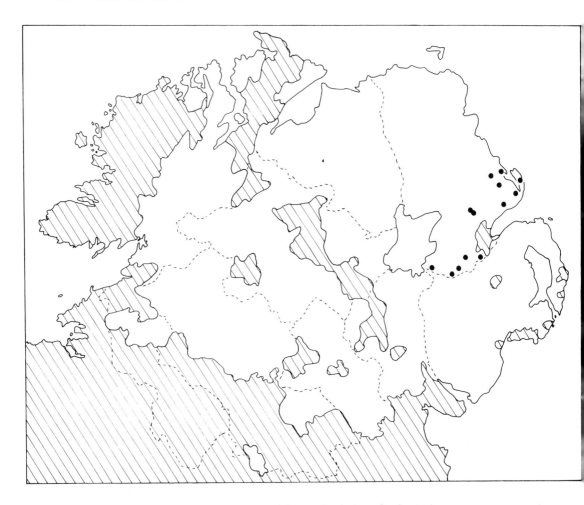

Fig. 1   Locations of parish references to sliding-sash windows in the Ordnance Survey Memoirs. The base map shows, unshaded, the parish areas for which memoirs exist

magee in the south-east to Aghalee in the south-west where the use of sliding sashes is noted. Almost certainly, however, a rather wider occurrence of this feature is missed, because of the poorer quality of the memoirs in Down and north Armagh. It looks as if the memoir information in this case is indicative, rather than truly definitive. The same situation may apply in the case of comments on two-storeyed farmhouses, which show a similar concentration across south Antrim, but the distribution is wider in this case, with outlying references from the Grange of Drumtullagh in north Antrim, in four parishes from Dunboe in the north to Lissan in the south but all in east County Londonderry, from Muckno in east Monaghan, Donacavey and Dromore in south Tyrone, and from parishes in east Donegal and east Down. Coming distributionally between these two cases, is the evidence for clocks as items of furniture in farmhouses, which again shows the concentration of evidence in south Antrim, but with extensions only into mid Antrim and east Londonderry. The problem of the unevenness of the quality of the memoirs is at play here for the conditions of south Antrim would certainly have been repeated at least in north Down; however, again, the evidence seems to point to innovation and change in the rural community at the time the memoirs were being set down.

By contrast, direct memoir evidence for features like the bed out-shot and the jamb wall, to the study of which Caoimhín Ó Danachair has contributed so much,[19] hardly exists. I have found no description of a jamb wall in any memoir, and only two of the outshot, of which that from Kilrea in County Londonderry must be regarded as suspect, for it refers to '. . . "outshots" or new bedrooms. . .' then being added to dwellings. The description from the area about Slieve Gallion in the east of the same county (parishes of Ballinascreen, Kilcronaghan and Desertmartin) is worth quoting in full. Referring to the houses of the 'lower and more numerous class of farmers', we learn that

> Their dwelling consists of two divisions, the kitchen with its *outshot*, a projection in the wall beside the fire, in which outshot the parents sleep, and an inner apartment seldom having a fire, though the floor is earthen.

Structural use of timber is noted too, in isolated cases. A clear description of crucks is provided for the village of Ballycarry in Templecorran parish, County Antrim,[20] and timber framing, deriving from English box-framing traditions imported into north-east Ireland in the Plantation of Ulster[21] are available from Carrickfergus, Antrim, and Coleraine, and perhaps also from the parishes of Derriaghy and Duneane in Antrim, and Ballyscullion and Lissan in Londonderry.

AGRICULTURE

The Ordnance Survey memoirs contain a great deal of information of crucial importance for the ethnologist, interested in the typology and the social context of agricultural technology, and for the agricultural and social historian. Understandably there is coverage of animals, crops and implements, of the presence or absence of enclosure, and of rotations and fertilisation of the land. More unexpected themes are dealt with too, like the practice of burning the land[22] and whether or not oxen were used by anyone for draught purposes. This last topic reflected what had been a matter of considerable interest during the late eighteenth century and into the first quarter of the nineteenth. Human aspects of agricultural life are mentioned too. There is much consideration of the conditions of farm labourers, and of the extent to which seasonal workers moved to Britain, mainly for harvesting. The activities of landlords in encouraging agricultural improvement are dealt with, sometimes at great length, and their role in the formation of farming societies is discussed. Perhaps most interesting of all is the fact that the memoirs preserve replies to a long questionnaire dealing with all aspects of agriculture which was distributed by the North-West of Ireland Farming Society to parish clergy in counties Donegal, Tyrone and Londonderry, but mainly the first two counties, between about 1815 and 1825. Taken together, these provide a remarkable record of the state of agriculture in the north-west at a crucial period, between the time early in the nineteenth century when much agricultural experimentation, which was costly, had been carried out by the landlord class, and the period of the famine when the entire rural scene was so fundamentally upset. These questionnaire returns would provide the basis for a fascinating monograph.

Indeed the memoirs more generally are important in this respect also, as is well illustrated in the case of threshing machines. The county *Statistical Surveys,* mostly of 1802 and 1812, referring to the northern counties show that the experimental stages of the adoption of threshing machines were then commencing. In the Down survey of 1802 we learn that a Mr. Christy was 'the first in this kingdom' to have one built on the basis of machines he saw in 1796 in Scotland, and by 1802 Mr. Ward at Bangor had one also.[23] The Cavan volume of the same year records one at Farnham.[24] Ten years later, seven landlords in County Antrim are noted as experimenting with the machines, some of them driven by water, and the comment is made that in that period the cost of a threshing machine had fallen from about the £100 which Mr. Christy had laid out on his, to less than £50 for which sum they could be had at that time in Scotland.[25] None of the other county surveys in the north at this time, for Tyrone, Londonderry, Donegal, Monaghan and Armagh, make any mention of this innovation. By the 1830s, however, the memoir evidence (Fig. 2) makes it clear that geographically the machines were now being installed more widely, for threshing machines are noted in the south Down parishes of Ardglass, Ballee and Kilmegan, in the west Armagh parishes of Tynan and Clonfeacle, and in at least the parish of Templemore in Derry, but also that tenant farmers as well as landowners were now installing them. In most cases the numbers involved were still small, although in Killead the comment is passed that they were 'becoming more general'. But the conclusive evidence that the next stage of the innovation acceptance had commenced is from the three east Antrim parishes of Kilwaughter which had three, one worked by water, Templecorran with seven, of which six were powered by horses, and Islandmagee, unlikely as it may seem, with no less than twenty of which only one was water powered. The significance here is that the more economical, smaller horse-driven machines, suited to the needs of the small Ulster farms, were now available, and it is interesting to see that the surge towards the widespread adoption of these one- to four-horse machines may have developed in south-east Antrim, in spite of the comment in the Templecorran memoir that the people there were not receptive to innovations. In fact, widespread acceptance of horse-powered threshing machines did not happen in Ulster until after 1850, and in the second half of the century foundries in Belfast, Larne, Ballymena, Coleraine, Newry, Omagh, Strabane and Derry city were all building and installing them in all districts. However, as in the case of evidence on other topics cited earlier, the memoir information on threshing machines seems to show that an area of rural innovativeness existed in east Ulster, certainly in south Antrim and, allowing for the problems posed by the variable nature of the memoirs themselves, probably in neighbouring parts of north Down at least.

A final theme, still within the subject matter of agriculture, illustrates clearly the relative value of the Ordnance Survey memoirs for folk-life study, and shows both that they must be considered alongside contemporary evidence of other kinds, but equally that they are ignored at peril of overlooking unique data. One of the earliest open-air exhibits at the Ulster Folk and Transport Museum

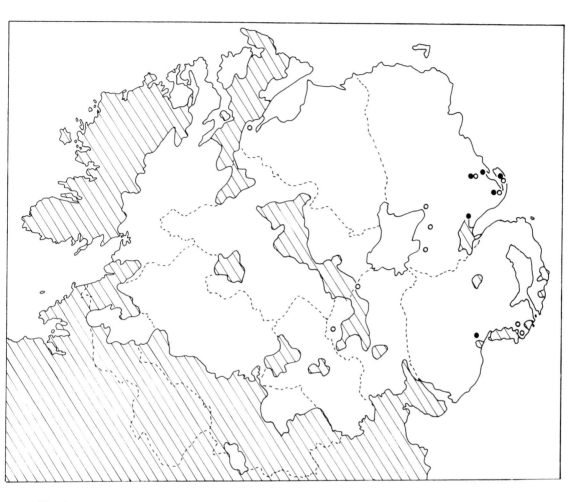

Fig. 2   Locations of parish references to mechanical threshers in the Ordnance Survey Memoirs.

was a water-powered spade mill, removed from Coalisland in County Tyrone. Associated research on the craft industry represented by this exhibit has revealed that at the time of compilation of the Ordnance Survey memoirs there were no less than thirty-eight of these mills working and three others already in ruins. Their significance for rural life in the 1830s is well documented by the memoirs themselves, for many comments, mainly but not exclusively for western parishes, make it clear that the spade was the common tillage tool for potatoes, and also for grain crops in Lower Longfield parish in Tyrone. Of course, as in Aghavea parish in Fermanagh social differences sometimes came into play, with spade tillage confined to the poorer farmers.[26]

The table below sets out the occurrence of references to these spade mills in the memoirs, on the contemporary Ordnance Survey six-inch maps, and in the first valuation of property in Ireland which was carried out in the 1830s but which was never published.[27] The data are tabulated by counties, the numbers in brackets being those mills noted as already in ruins in the Ordnance Survey sources, and these are additional to the working mills.

County	O.S. Memoirs	O.S. Maps	Valuation	Existing
ANTRIM	4	2	3	4
ARMAGH	3	6	7	7
DONEGAL	1	5	3	5
DOWN	0	0	0	1
FERMANAGH	1	1	0	1
LONDONDERRY	4 (2)	2 (1)	2	4 (2)
MONAGHAN	1	1	1	2
TYRONE	7	11 (1)	10	14 (1)
TOTAL	21 (2)	28 (2)	26	38 (3)

This table shows that no one of these sources provides exhaustive coverage of the spade mills; indeed taken together they fail to reveal the existence of one in Newry and another at Scarnageeragh (Emyvale) in Monaghan. However, the memoirs alone provide evidence for five mills: in Raloo parish (Antrim), Tamlaght Finlagan, Ballyscullion and Lissan parishes, the last of these being in ruins (all in County Londonderry), and in the town of Newtown Stewart (west Tyrone).

III

Information on social custom and material culture has been used in this article to attempt to illustrate the potential of the Ordnance Survey memoirs for folk-life study, and some of the problems inherent in using them. It would, however, be wrong to ignore the fact that many aspects of oral tradition are also dealt with, from widespread evidence for belief in fairy tradition, especially with reference to fairy thorn bushes, to a few instances of transcription of oral narrative, set down particularly in sections of the memoirs dealing either with historical tradition or with antiquities. The writer is conscious also that his present coverage of the memoirs is incomplete. Apart from abstracting data on housing throughout the memoirs, they have not been exhaustively scanned for other topics; in particular, the County Londonderry parishes remain to be indexed for all other topics. Also, a more searching coverage of the folk-life data contained in the memoirs for a single county has already been published, although without an attempt to address some of the problems inherent in the memoirs mentioned above. The sheer bulk of material in the Ordnance Survey memoirs is enormous. Some of the best parish memoirs have been published, as already noted, but the material as a whole would not warrant this exposure on account of its variable quality. A few other memoirs would justify separate publication where there is a major town, notably like Enniskillen. Eminently desirable, however, is the total abstraction of the memoirs and the subsequent subject indexing of the abstracts, to make this major research resource readily available for study, because the topographic arrangment upon which the memoirs are compiled militates against their ready use on a subject basis. This approach would be a major service, not only to folk-life study, but to many aspects of historical enquiry and to archaeology.

REFERENCES

1. Mitchison, Rosalind, *Agricultural Sir John* (London, 1962).
2. Andrews, J.H., *A Paper Landscape* (Oxford, 1975), chapter IV.
3. *Memoir of the City and North Western Liberties of Londonderry. Parish of Templemore* (Dublin, 1837).
4. Microfilm copies of the originals of the Ordnance Survey memoirs in the Library of the Royal Irish Academy may be consulted at the National Library of Ireland, Dublin; the Public Record Office for Northern Ireland; the Library, Queen's University, Belfast; and at the Ulster Folk and Transport Museum.
5. Gailey, Alan, 'The Bonfire in North Irish Tradition', *Folklore*, 88 (1977), 3-38, see especially map on 14.
6. *Ordnance Survey Memoir for the Parish of Antrim* (Belfast, Public Record Office for Northern Ireland, 1969); *Ordnance Survey Memoir for the Parish of Templecorran* (Belfast, Queen's University, 1972).
7. Gailey, Alan, 'The Housing of the Rural Poor in Nineteenth-Century Ulster', *Ulster Folklife*, 22 (1976), 34-58, see especially Fig. 12. Relevant descriptions of houses of the poor from the Ordnance Survey memoirs are printed on pages 53-55.
8. The only discussion hitherto published of the value of the Ordnance Survey memoirs for folk-life study will be found in Harris, Rosemary, 'The Ordnance Survey Memoirs', *Ulster Folklife*, 1 (1955), 43-52; her paper however deals only with County Antrim memoirs.
9. Connell, K.H., 'Illicit Distillation', in idem, *Irish Peasant Society* (Oxford, 1968), 1-50; see especially the map Fig. 2 which was based on an original prepared by Caoimhín Ó Danachair from data in the *Poor Inquiry (Ireland)*, Suppt., to Appendix E. An earlier version of this paper had been published in *Historical Studies III: Papers read before the Fourth Irish Conference of Historians*.
10. Ó Súilleabháin, Seán, *Irish Wake Amusements* (Cork, 1967).
11. O'Donnell, Patrick, *The Irish Faction Fighters* (Dublin, 1975); a fine fictional account of a faction fight is in Carleton, William, 'The Battle of the Factions', in his *Traits and Stories of the Irish Peasantry*, 4th edn. (London, 1836), 269-239.
12. Further information on the Doagh Book Club will be found in Adams, J.R.R., 'Reading Societies in Ulster', *Ulster Folklife*, 26 (1980), 56-64.
13. Pilson, Aynsworth, *Downpatrick Recorder*, 3 June, 1854.
14. Hicks, Dermot, *Road Bowls in Armagh* (Armagh, 1973); Murray, Raymond (ed.) *The Armagh Bullet Thrower* (Armagh, 1976).
15. A fuller discussion of these and other sources relating to Easter will be found in Gailey, Alan, 'Sources for the Historical Study of Easter as a Popular Holiday in Ulster', *Ulster Folklife*, 26 (1980), 68-74.
16. Another Easter custom associated with eggs, with a mainly northern provenance, has been discussed by Ó Danachair, Caoimhín, 'Distribution Patterns in Irish Folk Tradition,' *Béaloideas*, 33 (1965), 102-104; reference should also be made to his chapter on Easter in *The Year in Ireland* (Cork, 1972), 70-83.
17. Gailey, Alan, 'Vernacular Dwellings in Clogher Diocese', *Clogher Record*, 9 (1977), 187-231; see especially 212-20.
18. Lucas, A.T., 'Bog Wood. A Study in Rural Economy', *Béaloideas*, 23 (1054), 81-87.
19. Ó Danachair, Caoimhín, 'Some Distribution Patterns in Irish Folk Life', *Béaloideas*, 25 (1957), 109-111; idem, 'Traditional Forms of the Dwelling House in Ireland', *Journal of the Royal Society of Antiquaries in Ireland*, 102 (1972), 77-96.

20. For the wider vernacular architectural context of this reference see Gailey, Alan and McCourt, Desmond, 'A List of North Irish Crucks', *Vernacular Architecture*, 9 (1978), 3-9.
21. Robinson, Philip, 'Vernacular Housing in Ulster in the Seventeenth Century,' *Ulster Folklife*, 25 (1979), 1-28.
22. Lucas, A.T., 'Paring and Burning in Ireland', in Gailey, Alan and Fenton, Alexander (eds.), *The Spade in Northern and Atlantic Europe* (Belfast, 1970), 99-147, is an excellent example of how the Ordnance Survey material must be fitted into the context of data from all other available sources if it is to be properly understood.
23. Dubourdieu, Rev. John, *Statistical Survey of the County of Down* (Dublin, 1802), 52-53.
24. Coote, Sir Charles, *Statistical Survey of the County of Cavan* (Dublin, 1802), 63.
25. Dubourdieu, Rev. John, *Statistical Survey of the County of Antrim* (Dublin, 1812), 155.
26. Ó Danachair, Caoimhín, 'The Use of the Spade in Ireland', in Gailey, Alan and Fenton, Alexander (eds.), *op.cit.*, 49-56; idem, 'The Spade in Ireland', *Béaloideas*, 31 (1963), 98-114.
27. Data for the first valuation of property in Ireland in the 1830s may be consulted, for counties now in the Republic of Ireland, at the office of the Commissioner for Valuation, Dublin, and for counties now in Northern Ireland, at the Public Record Office for Northern Ireland, Belfast.

Rabbles and Runaways, Church Gates and Street Corners

TEMPORARY WORKERS AND HOW THEY FOUND WORK

ANNE O'DOWD

INTRODUCTION

In 1957 Kevin Danaher devised a questionnaire entitled 'Social Aspects of Work.'[1] Each of its eight questions was quite short yet the few hundred replies to it from all over the country yielded a wealth of information on co-operative work,[2] seasonal work and migratory labourers, women's work and farmers' relations with their workers. The questionnaire was circulated at a time when there were still many vivid and personal memories concerning the subjects queried, and the body of information received forms the basis for many individual studies of social organisation in rural Ireland. This paper utilises information from just one of these questions, that dealing with migratory labourers. The question as phrased on the questionnaire reads: 'Did migratory labourers go from your district to work elsewhere, or come to work in your district at spring work or harvest? What was the local name for such workers? From what place did they come, or to what place did they go?' As the replies show, this brief phrasing was sufficient to stir the correspondents' minds, in many cases, to write at length about the subject of seasonal and migratory labourers and hired workers, in general. Information was returned on areas worked in, wages received, conditions met with, the names the workers were called and of basic importance, how the temporary or seasonal work was found. The last of these is looked at in some detail in this paper and it is an indication of the tremendous work which Kevin Danaher has done over the years, that information received from just one question of one questionnaire of the many which he caused to be circulated, was the starting point for this study. The remaining information analysed is contained in the manuscripts in the Department of Irish Folklore[3] and two further questionnaires, one circulated by the Ulster Folk Museum in 1963[4] and the second by the Department of Irish Folklore in 1980.[5]

The temporary or seasonal workers were called many names and Fig. 1 shows the distribution of just some of these. Other names include 'thinners',[6] 'scoremen',[7] 'far downers',[8] 'connies',[9] 'bogeymen',[10] and 'puckadees',[11] The workers went to many places and the main movements within Ireland[12] were always from the poorer areas of the west to the richer farming areas in the east. In Donegal, for example, small holders in the Irish-speaking areas of the Rosses and Gweedore found work in the Laggan district of east Donegal; in Galway, men from Connemara travelled to Galway city and Athenry and were employed

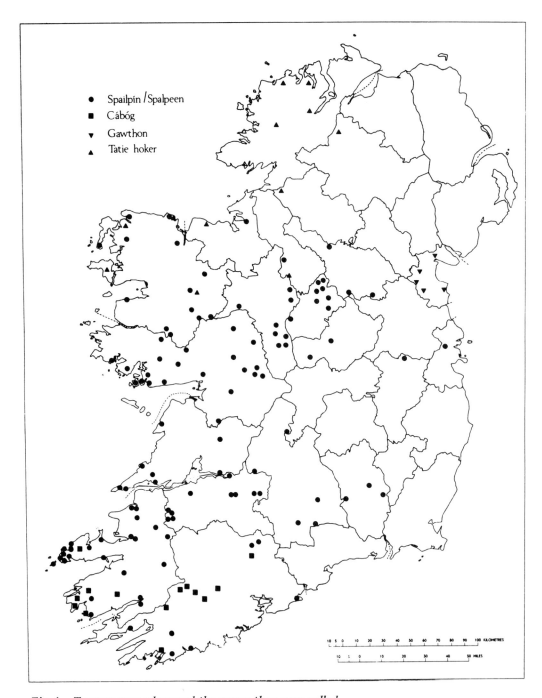

Fig. 1   Temporary workers and the names they were called

by farmers in east Galway; and in the south-west, potato diggers and other harvest workers found work in the farming districts of north Kerry, east Limerick and Tipperary. What follows is a discussion on how these people found work; the centres to which they travelled to be hired and the way in which the bargain was made with the farmer, their part-time employer. Although the purpose of all the hirings was to get casual employment at busy times of the year, the procedure and conditions varied.

1. THE HIRING FAIRS

> So come to the Dundalk hiring, be early and don't delay,
> And stand out for good wages like heroes bold and gay,
> Be staunch me lads and lassies when you go to town,
> And don't let the farmers your wages cut down.[13]

Hiring fairs were held in almost every market town in the province of Ulster. Some, however, were obviously more important than others and the significance of the hiring fair no doubt depended on the situation of the town and the size and viability of the farms around it. Fig. 2 shows the distribution of the larger hiring fairs. According to information received from the questionnaire and manuscript material, all of the hiring fairs in Ulster were held twice a year, once in May and again in November. The fair dates varied between towns but remained fairly constant for individual towns from one year to the next. In Ballycastle, County Antrim, the hiring fairs were on the last Tuesdays in May and in November;[14] in Antrim town[15] and in Ballyclare, County Antrim,[16] the hiring fair dates were May 12th and November 12th; in Letterkenny, County Donegal, hiring of workers took place on the fair day after the 12th of May and the 12th of November;[17] while in Newry, County Down, there were three hiring days on the first, second and third Thursdays of May and November.[18]

Although most of these fairs were called hiring fairs by those who replied to the questionnaires, it seems likely in all cases that the hiring of servants, both men and women, took place on the fair day of the month in question. Although the ordinary business of buying and selling livestock also went on, the main bargaining was with the workers. There is very little documentary evidence concerning hiring fairs in Ulster and pictorial representations and descriptions of the occasions — the bargaining, cajoling and trickstering — are few and far between. A mid nineteenth-century source does give us some idea of the purpose of the event even then and we see from it that hiring fairs were colourful as well as serious occasions.

> A curious custom is practised at the May and November fairs namely that of servants coming to them to be hired and both farmers and servants many of them residing 8 miles off, come (for) this express purpose. It matters not if the servant intends continuing with his former master, he comes to the fair, where his master re-engages him by giving him a shilling. The male servants who come to be hired carry a rod, the women have no sign of any kind. The numbers who attend the May and November fairs are very great, particularly in the former, and as they are chiefly for amusement, they present towards evening disgraceful scenes of drunkenness and brawling.[19]

It is not quite certain how common the idea of the hiring fair being a holiday was and it appears to have varied in different parts. In Ballymoney, County

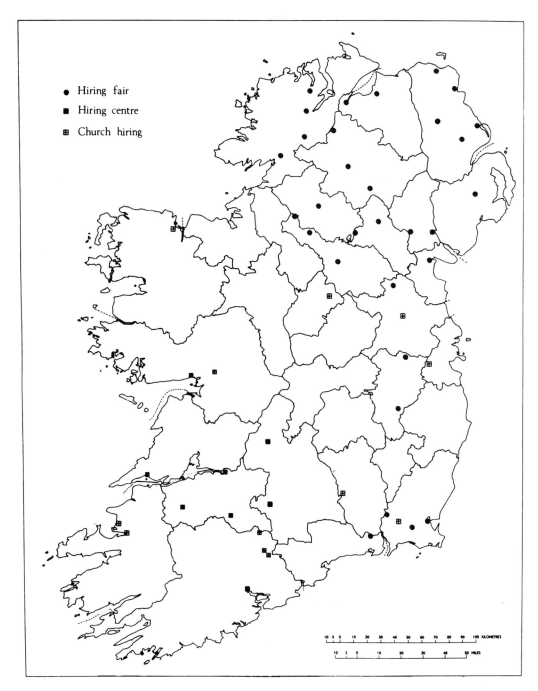

Fig. 2   Places where hirings took place

Antrim, most workers were actually engaged before the hiring day and the 11th and 12th of May and the 11th and 12th of November were holidays.[20] Of course, if the hired man was a good worker, the farmer would no doubt ask him to stay on before the hiring day.[21] A hint of enticement is seen in a report from County Monaghan in that the man who agreed to stay was given a week's holiday between terms.[22] There was probably a monetary reward in some places and good men would get extra hiring money to encourage them to stay on year after year.[23] Reports from some areas would indeed make one wonder why hiring fairs were held at all. One writer from Annahilt in County Down was hired with farmers from the age of sixteen years and he met and heard about many bad and good employers. In instances where the farmer was a reasonable man, the workers stayed on and there was no need for farmer or workers to go to the fair.[24]

As to the purpose of hiring fairs, however, it must be remembered that those attending often lived a good distance from the centre. In the case of the fair of Trillick, County Tyrone, people travelled to it from a twenty-mile radius at the beginning of the century. In the larger centres such as Derry, Strabane and Letterkenny, distances travelled were, no doubt, much greater. There were always new workers coming on to the market. There were also those who wanted a change and for these and others who might not have been known to the employers either personally or by reputation, the hiring fairs were a means by which they found work. When the farmer did attend the fair he, in many cases, only hired those men whom he knew by repute and the fair was the meeting place.[25]

> The merits of every farm boss for miles around the hiring village were known to everyone offering for hire. Of course, the farmers also knew, largely from gossip, the capabilities of every labourer: whether he was 'handy' with cattle, used with horses, a good spadesman, able to plough etc. etc. One or perhaps all of these features weighed with the farmer in making his contacts and these usually came about in this general fashion:
> A farmer strolling casually among the crowd would stop and ask someone he knew: 'Did you see Johnny so-and-so?' If that particular one had not seen Johnny the farmer would very soon, by dropping a query here and there, find someone who had seen him. 'He was standing outside so-and-so's shop as I came past a minute or two ago' or some remark of the kind would help to pin-point Johnny so that usually the farmer had little trouble in getting any contact or contacts he wished to make.[26]

Generally the workers simply stood about and it was obvious by demeanour and appearance that they were looking for work. Several reports indicate that an emblem was worn or carried as a sign that they were unemployed and Fig. 3 shows areas where this custom has been recorded.[27] The two main emblems were either a stick or a straw. The stick was sometimes described as a white rod, i.e. a peeled sally or willow rod,[28] though this was not always the case.[29] When a straw was the emblem, it was either sewn to some item of clothing,[30] or chewed in the mouth.[31]

The making of the bargain itself has been described by several writers in terms of the conversation which went on between the farmer and the prospective servant.[32] As with all bargain making this was a necessary part of the proceedings before a deal was made. Not so necessary, perhaps, was the physical abuse which some suffered and which caused one observer of the fair in Letterkenny to report that the farmer made the workers walk up and down 'just as they did with cattle'.[33] At the hiring fairs in Cushendall, Ballymena and Ballycastle, the farmers felt the

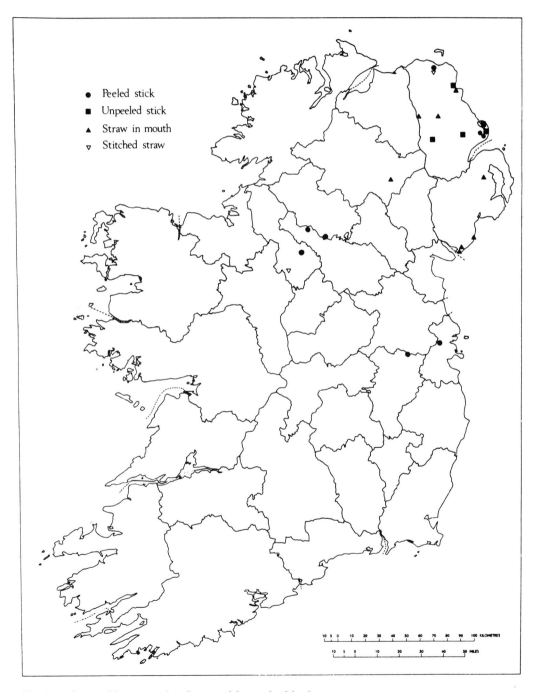

Fig. 3   Thus emblem worn by those waiting to be hired

boys' muscles[34] 'as when examining a horse in a fair and even made them some-times stride up and down.'[35]

If not hired at one particular fair one could continue to a hiring fair in another town at a later date. This happened particularly between the larger fairs or 'rabbles' such as Letterkenny, Derry, Strabane and Newry. Probably the most popular of all the 'rabbles' from the farmer's viewpoint was that in Derry as it was to here and to Strabane to a lesser extent, that the workers from west Donegal gathered and they always accepted lower wages than workers from elsewhere.[36]

Presumably one's chances of receiving a fair wage and a decent place diminished as one moved from fair to fair[37] and presumably also there was a greater chance of attracting an amount of ridicule if one was not hired at all. In County Louth this obviously happened on occasion which prompted one writer to say: 'If you stood in a hiring market and did not get an offer you must be a day ghost or a corner boy. The former meant a person who had TB or cancer and the latter a bad useless lout that even a workhouse would reject.'[38]

The possibility that one might not like one's employer was also catered for in the hiring fairs as special 'runaway' fairs were held in some places and those who had literally run away from their master got a second chance. In Newry, County Down, there were three days of hiring, all on Thursdays. The first was the 'releasing' or 'loosing'[39] day; the second was the main hiring day and the third was for runaways.[40]

Once the bargain was made, the usual procedure was to surrender one's bundle of clothes and arrange to meet the farmer later at a fixed spot. Generally the farmer and servant went home together from the fair although there are indica-tions that in the final years of the hiring fairs, those hired returned to their own homes for a week or so before commencing their new job.[41]

An important part of the concluding of the hiring agreement was the giving of a certain sum of money which was said to seal the bargain. In the quotation from the Ordnance Survey memoirs above we see that the farmer re-engaged the servant at the fair by giving him a shilling and thereby secured his services for the following six months and freed the servant from the temptation of accepting a higher offer from another farmer. A second reference to the Antrim hiring fair in 1838 refers to the shilling received as 'earnest'[42] and several more recent records of this word show it to have been closely associated with the binding of the hiring bargain (Fig. 4). In Antrim,[43] Armagh,[44] Cavan,[45] Derry,[46] Down,[47] Donegal,[48] Fermanagh,[49] Louth,[50] Monaghan[51] and Tyrone[52] the small money token was known as 'earnest' while the word 'earls'[53] or 'errols', also meaning the small payment at the hiring fair has been mainly recorded from county Antrim[54] but also from counties Derry,[55] Down,[56] and Tyrone.[57] The amount of this payment varied from one shilling to half a crown, to five shillings and even ten shillings, over the years.[58] It was 'money given as a token of good faith'[59] and although there were never written contracts at Irish hiring fairs,[60] both parties were expected to respect the verbal agreement.[61] Naturally, if a man, having accepted one offer, was approached with a better deal, he could return the money token and providing it was accepted, he was then freed from the bargain.[62] In other cases, once the 'earls' were accepted the bargain could not be broken.[63]

References to hiring fairs as described above, have not been recorded in any

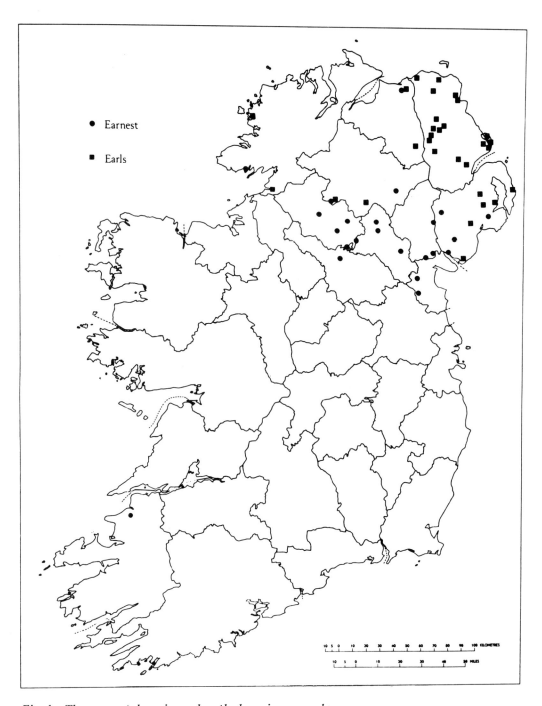

Fig. 4   The money token given when the bargain was made

significant numbers in the other three provinces and although those outside of Ulster are marked as hiring fairs on Fig. 1 as that is the name given to them by those writing about them, information in sufficient detail is lacking to allow any real comparison.[64] It seems that hirings were arranged at these fairs in May only[65] and unlike the hirings at the Ulster fairs, details of the duration of the term of employment, when given, state that the servant was under a twelve-month contract as compared to the usual six-month term in Ulster. When 'work-men' as distinct from servants were hired, their period of employment depended on the amount of work to be done and the generosity of the farmer. In 1956, a man from Kilcock, County Kildare, who was eighty-two years old when he gave his memories of the hiring fair there, said that some of the farmers kept some of the workmen even when the heavy work of harvesting was over. The men were engaged to dig drains and clean ditches etc. for the rest of the year.[66]

2. SERVANT BOYS AND GIRLS

> Now the winter is all over and the spring is coming on,
> When all the girls around must go and leave their mams,
> They are packing up their bundles with a fortnight or a week.
> Going to the market employment for to seek.[67]

Other than the hiring fairs discussed above, many of the hiring centres in Ireland were concentrated in the province of Munster. The more important of these included Newcastlewest and Kilmallock, County Limerick, Limerick City, Tralee, County Kerry, Mitchelstown, County Cork, Cork City and Kilrush, County Clare. Athenry, County Galway and Galway city were the important centres for Connacht and differences between the centres can be seen in terms of the kinds of workers who were employed. In Kilrush,[68] Kilmallock[69] and Newcastlewest,[70] the main hiring was that of servant boys and girls. In Newcastlewest, the main hiring day was on February 1, while elsewhere the servants, who were principally from Kerry, started arriving at the towns at the beginning of February and St. Patrick's day, March 17, was the day on which many bargains were made. The duration of employment was ten or eleven months and most returned to their homes before Christmas. Many returned to the same farmer year after year, some eventually settling in the places where they were hired out. In such cases it was very difficult for the men, in particular, to better themselves and few 'succeeded in raising [themselves] above the status of farm labourer'. The title 'servant boy' or 'servant girl' remained regardless of the worker's age.[71]

The work servant boys did depended on their age. Colm Danaher[72] explained the situation as he understood it for those hired from Newcastlewest by saying that 'the servant boys were of two kinds.'

> Firstly the one who could milk cows and go to the creamery and do light jobs. The second was the general worker who could plough and mow and face any kind of work whatsoever.[73]

Girls were usually employed for heavy domestic work and were paid less than their male counterparts. Often strong, well-built girls were hired in place of boys and the farmer by so doing could save himself a few pounds every year. Needless to remark, this was not too popular and the comment from one man, himself hired out to 'many a good house' from the hirings in Kilrush, County Clare, gives some idea of the reaction to such an occurrence.

> There used be servant girls at the hiring days too, and many a farmer would prefer to get a girl than a boy, and sure they used to have to do milking and everything too. Some of the lads that wouldn't be hired would say or shout at a farmer who was after hiring a girl 'I suppose you paid nine pounds for her, and you'll have a child with you for the Christmas.' They mean by this that the lady would fall by some fellow and have a child.[74]

3. CHURCH GATES AND STREET CORNERS.

> I made my way straight for Tipperary,
> Where I had been previously known,
> And I halted at 'meeting street corner'
> And put up my scythe to be shown.[75]

The remaining hiring places, including Cork City,[76] Mitchelstown, County Cork,[77] Galway City,[78] Nenagh, County Tipperary[79] and Tipperary town[80] and the places where hirings took place especially on Sundays and church holidays (Fig. 2) including Athenry, County Galway,[81] Killala, County Mayo,[82] Granard, County Longford,[83] Lucan, County Dublin,[84] Navan, County Meath,[85] Callan, County Kilkenny,[86] Newbawn, County Wexford,[87] Tralee[88] and Ardfert, County Kerry,[89] Kilworth,[90] and Kilmurry, County Cork[91] and also Limerick city,[92] were centres at which in general, more short-term hirings were arranged. The workers did not bind themselves by any contract to stay for a certain length of time. Rather they agreed to undertake a certain task of work and then leave to hire with another farmer. Most frequently in the accounts which are available, the work involved was potato digging and the 'spailpíns' and *cábógs*[93] thus employed did the work by 'task' or 'piece' work.[94] Workers were also employed on a short-term basis mowing and doing general harvest work.

Apart from Sundays in the spring and harvest seasons, the 15th August, which was a pattern day in the town of Athenry, was a popular day for 'spailpíns' to be hired. The majority of the workers who attended at the 'hiring market' in Athenry were from Connemara and they spent the months from about February to October working an average of two or three weeks with several farmers in east Galway. They set out from their own homes in Connemara in time to arrive in Athenry on a Sunday and stood around the market place there until hired. As soon as the work on one particular farm was finished, they returned to the market place again on a Sunday, looking for work. This was repeated several times throughout the months until October when the potato harvest was over and the farmers around Athenry had no further work to offer.[95]

In 1958, Colm Ó hUigín of Lettermore Island, County Galway spoke about his memories of these 'spailpíns' when he was growing up about the turn of the century. He remembered in particular that most of the workers brought their own loys with them as suitable working tools could not be found in Athenry.[96] As soon as the bargain was made with the farmer, the worker handed his new employer his loy as a sign that the bargain was agreed upon.

As Galway city[97] and Athenry were centres for men from Connemara, so Tralee, Limerick, Cork and Mitchelstown attracted workers from the poorer areas of Cork, Kerry and Clare. As was the case in Galway and Athenry, these people were true migratory labourers employed for short spells to dig potatoes and do other harvest work. In Cork[98] and Mitchelstown[99] the workers gathered at certain corners which were locally known as *crois na gcábóg* or the 'cábóg's' cross-roads and in Tipperary town those waiting to be hired stood at a point called 'Meeting Street Corner'.[100] Migratory workers from north Kerry especially stood at Ballsbridge in Limerick city[101] and during the days of the first world war, recruiting agents were to be found at the hiring stand 'and succeeded in inducing many prospective farm labourers to join the British Army'.[102] In Tralee a 'hiring market was held on the road-way outside the parish church [Catholic]. It started at 10.30 am and finished about two or three on each Sunday.'[103] And, in nearby Ardfert, workers gathered outside the church gates after first Mass on a Sunday.[104]

Although seasonal movements of temporary workers were more localised in Leinster than in the other three provinces, there are, nevertheless, a few records of centres in this province also at which short-term hirings were arranged and all of these were on Sunday (Fig. 2). In Callan, County Kilkenny, the workers assembled at the cross in the town and waited for the farmers to come in with their carts and select one or more of them to work for him.[105] From Newbawn in County Wexford in 1938 an eighty-seven-year-old informant remembered seeing workers from Kilkenny lining up outside the chapel door on a Sunday.[106] In Callan, Newbawn, Lucan[107] and Navan[108] the workers were all employed at harvest time, while in Granard, County Longford, potato diggers only gathered outside the Catholic church on Sundays after Mass.[109]

4. CONCLUSION

Of the kinds of hiring discussed, those arranged at the Ulster hiring fairs seem to have been the most organised and the most binding. The fact that special fairs were designated hiring fairs is evidence enough. However, other factors might also be taken into consideration. The distribution of records of workers carrying or wearing an emblem is plotted on Fig. 3 and shows that in nearly all cases this custom was associated with the hiring fair. The two references recorded from County Leitrim are to hiring fairs in Ulster.[110] From Swords, County Dublin, it is recorded that a sally stick, peeled in alternate rings, was carried as a sign that men were looking for work both at the hiring fairs and also at 'hiring corners in villages where farmers went if they needed extra men'.[111] A second record which shows that the custom of carrying or wearing emblems was not solely confined to the hiring fairs was recorded from Ballyhone, County Tipperary in 1938 and the informant, when talking about the hiring day in Kilmallock, said that each of the boys carried a straw in his hand waiting to be hired.[112] Elsewhere, unemployed workers were recognised by their bundle of clothes and in the case of potato diggers and mowers, by their spades and reaping hooks or scythes.[113] Reference has already been made to the workers from Lettermore Island in County Galway who brought their own loys with them to Athenry and how these were surrendered to the farmer as soon as the deal was made.[114] In Callan, County Kilkenny, until the turn of the century it was common to see the workers gathered with their reaping hooks on their shoulders and 'occasionally the farmer would take the hooks from the men in the town and bring them home with them. This was to ensure that the man whom he had hired would come to him.'[115] In Tralee, County Kerry, the farmer having spent an hour or two striking a bargain with the worker, 'always tried to get the man to come home with him because if he did not, he may be offered a shilling or so more by someone else in the meantime.'[116]

The money token known as 'earls' or 'earnest' in Ulster and which was given when the bargain was made, was not an important feature of hiring agreements elsewhere. 'Earlais'[117] and 'arles'[118] are recorded from Donegal in connection with advance payment to the girls and women who travelled in groups to fishing towns gutting herrings and two further answers to the 1980 questionnaire mention an unspecified sum of 'earlais' given to a newly hired *spailpín* from Connemara[119] and 'earnest and the price of a drink' given to workers at the market in Tralee.[120] In other cases 'earnest' referred to bargaining transactions in general.[121] In accounts where details concerning the sealing of the bargain at hiring centres are included, the farmer simply bought his man a drink.[122] No doubt there was a good deal of trickery and cleverness involved when bargaining. Colm Danaher recorded an amusing account of this in 1950.

> I heard a man saying that he was below in Newcastle one day hiring and there was a fellow from the town with him who had a stiff leg and two crutches. There did a farmer from the county Limerick come on to them. When the townie saw him coming on he put the crutches inside the wall and sat up on it. The farmer came on and stopped where the crowd were gathered together. 'Are any of you inclined to hire for the year, say.' The boys looked at him and *mo léir*[123] they didn't like his appearance at all. 'Oh!' says he, 'I have an easy place so anyone coming to me needn't be looking for high wages.' 'Twenty pounds 'til Christmas eve,' says one of the boys. 'Ochón,'[124] says the farmer, says he, 'half of it would be a lot.' They all saw immediately that he was a *buachaill*.[125] 'Wait a minute,' says the cripple. 'I'll go to you for ten pounds 'till the eighth of December.' The farmer was overjoyed and without much delay they struck a bargain. 'Come on now for a drink,' says the farmer and he delighted he met such a cheap boy. 'Oh toughen[126] a minute,' says the cripple sliding down off the wall, 'until I get my two assistants.' And, with that he pulled his crutches to him and began to hop after his man. The farmer looked back and nearly dropped when he saw the cripple and he as serious as could be hopping on after him. The crowd were in roars laughing at him so he only turned to make off from them. 'Where are you going,' says the cripple. 'What about the drink you promised me? Do you want to shame yourself?' The bystanders began to cheer at that and *faiteach*,[127] however miserable the farmer was the shame wouldn't permit him to go away and not stand the drink to the man after promising it to him. The people were charmed at the thought of the farmer getting a hand when he was so miserable.[128]

The money token given at the Ulster hiring fairs added a note of legality to the affair. Although there are reports of tricksters accepting the token from more than one farmer[129] it is doubtful that this was a frequent occurrence and some informants mention instances where the culprit was brought to court for such an offence.[130] No such cases have been recorded in the several hundred references to hirings in the rest of Ireland and all in all the implications are that they were much freer arrangements from both the farmers' and workers' points of view. In the few references to legal proceedings the actions arose as a result of bad conditions. All of these are related in anecdotal form and cannot, in all cases, be accepted as fact.[131]

There is no doubt that the true migratory worker, the potato digger, the mower and the *spailpín*-type worker were totally free of any restrictions. They 'took every day as it came',[132] 'they were hardy men and great workmen'[133] and had the freedom to choose to leave their employment if it displeased them in any way.[134] Several of them were renowned as workmen and many legends have survived recounting their skills against all comers.[135]

The hirings were accepted as means by which part-time work was found and those hired no doubt had a need for the money earned. Nevertheless, there are reports of mistreatment and the hiring fairs in particular, attracted much criticism. In Ardstraw, County Tyrone, a man who himself hired workers at the fairs acknowledged that while in some cases the girls hired 'were very well treated, fed and trained in many other cases they were treated like slaves.'[136] This attitude was echoed in connection with the hiring fair in Cavan town[137] while from Ardee in County Louth the hiring fair was likened to a 'slave market'. A proud boast was to be able to say that not one member of the family had been hired.[138] The strongest comment in this vein relating to hirings elsewhere comes from Corbally in County Clare where it was said that a servant going to work with a farmer for eleven months would be '1,000 times better off to take the shilling', i.e. to join the British Army.[139]

The hiring fairs were generally seen to be a training ground for youngsters, boys in particular, as many of them after a few years experience and with the knowledge thus gained, proceeded to work on a seasonal basis on farms in England and Scotland. That this choice was not available to those hired, especially at the hiring places in Munster, where there never was a strong tradition of seeking work outside Ireland, is perhaps one reason why criticism of the working conditions is not so strong. Alternatively, there are several instances of servant boys and girls settling in the areas to which they hired out in Munster[140] and this in itself is some proof that conditions were not so harsh.

The distribution of the larger hiring fairs in Ulster is seen on Fig. 2[141] and although hirings were arranged at fairs in many other towns[142] these latter were smaller and attracted mainly labourers from the local area. Some of the hiring centres outside of Ulster are also marked on Fig. 2. As with the hiring fairs there is no doubt that workers were employed at many other centres besides and both the questionnaire and manuscript material include lone references to places where men were hired for short periods. In County Cork these included Carrigtohill,[143] Charleville[144] and Rathcormack.[145] In Kerry in addition to Tralee, Listowel was mentioned by a questionnaire correspondent from that town who heard, but did not himself remember, that men were hired there on St. Patrick's day.[146] The village of Hospital in County Limerick was described as 'a convenient centre for [the 'spailpíns'] to come from Cork and Kerry.'[147] Apart from the hiring fair in Dundalk, County Louth, there were at least three additional places in that county where men were hired. Farmers from Grangegeeth and the Rathkenny-Slane area in County Meath went to Ardee and Drogheda in County Louth on February 1st and the workers they employed commenced their year's work on May 1.[148] What has been described as 'a hiring fair of sorts' was held in Knockbridge, County Louth where the 'gawthons' or local harvest workers (see Fig. 1) were employed.[149] Although the town of Cashel in County

Tipperary is mentioned by Eoghan Rua Ó Súilleabháin, one of Ireland's eighteenth-century poets, as a place where agricultural labourers were hired by farmers from the area,[150] no more recent references to this town as a hiring place have, as yet, come to light.

It seems certain that the Ulster hiring fairs had died out by 1945.[151] Michael J. Murphy reported that a hiring fair was still held in Ballycastle, County Antrim in 1956; however, it was a hiring fair in name only — the hiring of servants no longer taking place.[152] The hiring fairs in New Ross and Waterford seem to have finished sometime before the First World War.[153] In Taghmon, County Wexford up to the time of the First World War, the farmers still paid off their servants at the hiring fair on May 2. This, however, had changed by 1918 when servants began to receive a weekly wage.[154] In Kilrush, County Clare, the hiring of significant numbers of servants ended about 1910.[155] Newcastlewest, County Limerick survived as the major hiring place for the province of Munster up to 1945.[156] After this date the farmer called to the worker's house to inquire if he was available.

NOTES AND REFERENCES

1. The replies to this questionnaire are bound in volumes 1523, 1669, 1828 and 1829 of the manuscripts in the Department of Irish Folklore, University College, Dublin. Irish Folklore Collection manuscript references will hereafter be referred to as IFC MS.
2. See O'Dowd, Anne, *Meitheal, A Study of Co-operative Labour in Rural Ireland* (Dublin, 1981).
3. See Ref. 1.
4. Ulster Folk Museum questionnaire, *Hiring Fairs* (1963). Hereafter UFM/63/Q2a. For a discussion on hiring fairs in Ulster, see, Bell, Jonathan, 'Hiring Fairs in Ulster', *Ulster Folklife*, 25 (1979), 67-78. This present paper while concentrating mainly on the hiring procedure, develops certain points already mentioned by Bell.
5. Department of Irish Folklore questionnaire, 'Seasonal Workers' (1980). Hereafter IFC/Q80.
6. IFC MS 1829,54. Recorded from Graiguenamanagh, Co. Kilkenny in 1958. The workers who went to thin beet were mainly from Co. Mayo.
7. IFC MS 1523, 203. Recorded from Kilmacduane, Co. Clare in 1958. Some workers kept an account of the days worked on a piece of wood known as a tally — or a score-stick.
8. IFC MS 1753, 85. Recorded from Drumintee, Orior Upper, Co. Armagh in 1968. This was the name which Connacht and Munster men had for those from Northern Ireland.
9. IFC MS 1838, 58. Recorded from Garbally, Co. Galway in 1958. 'Cunnies' was also recorded from Caltragh, Co. Galway in 1980 (IFC/Q80). In both cases the name referred to workers from Connemara.
10. IFC MS 1458, 28. Recorded from Drumard, Co. Longford in 1956. These were the men who worked at the harvest in Co. Dublin.
11. IFC/Q80. Recorded from Ballyduff, Tralee, Co. Kerry. This name refers to one of the conditions which the servants wished to have in the bargain — to be free to attend Puck Fair in Killorglin, Co. Kerry.
12. The external movement of seasonal workers will not be discussed here. Generally, these workers found work by word of mouth, by receiving letters from farmers they worked with in previous years and occasionally by attending hiring fairs in the north of England in particular.
13. IFC/Q80. 'The Ballad of the Dundalk hiring': recorded from Ardee, Co. Louth; eight verses of the ballad were included in the questionnaire reply.
14. UFM/63/Q2a. Recorded from Monaclough, Armoy, Co. Antrim and Layde, Cushendall, Co. Antrim.

15. UFM/63/Q2a. Recorded from Glenavy, Co. Antrim and Donegore, Co. Antrim.
16. UFM/63/Q2a. Recorded from Whitehead, Co. Antrim; Ballymena, Co. Antrim and Ahoghill, Co. Antrim.
17. UFM/63/Q2a. Recorded from Letterkenny, Co. Donegal and Ballybofey, Co. Donegal.
18. UFM/63/Q2a. Recorded from Hilltown, Co. Down; Newry, Co. Down; Bessbrook, Co. Armagh. From Hillsborough in Co. Down it is recorded that there were hiring fairs in both Ballynahinch and Newry on the first and third Thursdays of May and November. Cf. Ref. 40 below.
19. Ordnance Survey Memoirs, Box 12, III, 2, 1838, 38-9. I am grateful to Alan Gailey for this reference and also 42 below.
20. UFM/63/Q2a. Recorded from Ballymoney, Co. Antrim. At the hiring fair in Comber, Co. Down most hiring had been arranged before the hiring day 'but by custom farm labourers were entitled to this day as a paid holiday': UFM/63/Q2a; recorded from Co. Down.
21. UFM/63/Q2a. Recorded from Moygashel, Dungannon, Co. Tyrone.
22. UFM/63/Q2a. Recorded from Castleblaney, Co. Monaghan.
23. UFM/63/Q2a. Recorded from Armoy, Co. Antrim.
24. UFM/63/Q2a. Recorded from Annahilt, Co. Down.
25. UFM/63/Q2a. Recorded from Kesh, Co. Fermanagh.
26. UFM/63/Q2a. Recorded from Greenisland, Co. Antrim.
27. The hiring of workers at centres other than the hiring fairs is discussed in the following sections.
28. IFC MS 1785,23. (Referring to hiring fair in Blacklion, Co. Cavan). Recorded from Carntullagh, Ballinagleragh, Co. Leitrim in 1970; IFC MS 1497, 43. Recorded from Kilcock, Co. Kildare in 1956; IFC MS 1442, 140. Recorded from Courtown, Kilcock, Co. Kildare in 1956; IFC/Q80. Recorded from Swanlinbar, Co. Cavan; UFM/63/Q2a. Recorded from Whitehead and Ballycastle, Co. Antrim and Teemore, Co. Fermanagh. In Ballycarry, Co. Antrim it is recorded that the men for hire carried an ash twig from which about three inches of the bark had been removed (UFM/63/Q2a). In Swords Co. Dublin a sally stick peeled in alternate rings was carried as a sign that the bearer was looking for work (IFC MS 1523, 261, 1958).
29. IFC MS 1361, 26. Recorded from Cushendall, Co. Antrim in 1952; IFC MS 1362, 234. Recorded from Cushendall, Co. Antrim in 1953. UFM/63/Q2a. Recorded from Mullagh-boy; Islandmagee; Ballyclare and Randalstown, Co. Antrim.
30. IFC/Q80 (Referring to Ulster hiring fairs). Recorded from Drumregan, Mohill, Co. Leitrim; UFM/63/Q2a. Recorded from Ballycastle, Co. Antrim.
31. UFM/63/Q2a. Recorded from Cushendall; Portglenone and Kirkinriola, Co. Antrim; Greencastle; Kilkeel; Saintfield and Mullartown, Co. Down; Kilskeery and Dungannon, Co. Tyrone.
32. See, for example, IFC/Q80 where James Rafferty from Ardee, Co. Louth gives a very detailed account of the conversation between farmer and workman at the hiring fair in Dundalk and IFC MS 1690, 195. Recorded from Drumintee, Orior Upper, Co. Armagh in 1964. See also Murphy, M.J., *At Slieve Gullion's Foot* (Dundalk, 1950), and MacGill, Patrick, *Children of the Dead End* (London, 1914).
33. IFC/Q80. Recorded from Tamney, Letterkenny, Co. Donegal.
34. IFC MS 1782, 149. Recorded from Forkill, Co. Armagh in 1970; IFC MS 1362, 234. Recorded from Cushendall, Co. Antrim in 1953. The practice was also seen at the hiring fair in Antrim town, UFM 63/Q2a. Recorded from Portglenone, Co. Antrim.
35. IFC/Q80. Recorded from Drumintee, Orior Upper, Co. Armagh; UFM/63/Q2a. Recorded from Creeslough, Letterkenny, Co. Donegal and Churchill, Letterkenny, Co. Donegal. There is a story told about a girl at the Newry hiring fair which sums up reaction to such behaviour. When asked to walk up and down she replies: 'I could trot a bit for you if it'd please you.' IFC MS 1690, 198. Recorded from Balnamadaa, Drumintee, Co. Armagh.
36. UFM/63/Q2a. Recorded from Priestland, Coleraine, Co. Antrim; north Antrim and north Derry and Aghadowey, Co. Derry.
37. An example of this was recorded in association with Rosslea hiring fair in Co. Fermanagh. 'Rosslea hiring fair was the very late one. The last Saturday in May and those who had missed the hiring or failed to turn up at other places were available there — usually at

very much reduced wages. To have been hired at Rosslea was a definite slur on both employer and employee.' (UFM/63/Q2a).

38. IFC/Q80. Recorded from Ardee, Co. Louth.

39. Hiring fairs in Clones, Co. Monaghan and Cootehill, Co. Cavan were called 'Loosing Fairs' (IFC/Q80), while in Castleblaney, Co. Monaghan the 'day when servants were free was known as loosing day and this was a week before hiring day for the new term.' (UFM/63/Q2a).

40. IFC/Q80. Drumintee, Orior Upper, Co. Armagh. This is corroborated by a questionnaire reply from Poyntzpass, Co. Armagh. However, in this report all the Thursdays in May and November were hiring days in Newry, the second hiring day being the most important (IFC/Q80). See also IFC MS 1744, 27. The hiring fair in Ballynahinch, Co. Down was known as the 'runaway' fair (UFM/63/Q2a and see also, Bell, J., *op. cit.*, 71). Cf. 18 above.

41. IFC MS 1697, 140-141. Recorded from Eshnanunmera, Co. Fermanagh in 1966, concerning the hiring fair in Fivemiletown; IFC/Q80. Recorded from Ardee, Co. Louth; UFM/63/Q2a. Recorded from Castleblaney, Co. Monaghan and UFM/63/2a. Recorded from south Donegal and south Fermanagh.

42. Ordnance Survey Memoirs, Box 12, III, 2, 1838, 54.

43. UFM/63/Q2a. Recorded from Greenisland, Co. Antrim.

44. IFC MSS 1690, 195; 1744, 27 and IFC/Q80. Recorded from Drumintee, Orior Upper, Co. Armagh in 1964, 1966 and 1980; IFC/Q80. Recorded from Poyntzpass, Co. Armagh; IFC MS 1782, 149. Recorded from Forkill, Co. Armagh in 1970. UFM/63/Q2a. Recorded from Kileavy Parish, Co. Armagh.

45. IFC MS 975, 102-3. Recorded from Urney, Co. Cavan in 1938.

46. UFM/Q63/2a. Recorded from Coleraine, Co. Derry.

47. UFM/Q63/2a. Recorded from Banbridge; Hilltown; Downpatrick and Warrenpoint, Co. Down.

48. IFC/Q80. Recorded from Killybegs, Co. Donegal.

49. IFC MS 1697, 140. Recorded from Eshnanumera, Co. Fermanagh in 1966; IFC MS 1711, 154. Recorded from Drummully, Co. Fermanagh; IFC/Q80. Recorded from Lisnaskea, Co. Fermanagh; UFM/63/Q2a. Recorded from Derrygore, Co. Fermanagh.

50. IFC/Q80. Recorded from Ardee, Co. Louth; IFC MS 1692, 64. Recorded from Louth, Co. Louth in 1965.

51. UFM/63/Q2a. Recorded from Monaghan town; Castleblaney; Clones, and Tedavnet, Co. Monaghan.

52. UFM/63/Q2a. Recorded from Kilskeery and Dungannon, Co. Tyrone.

53. Although the etymology of the word 'earnest' is obscure, it is believed to be possibly connected with 'arles', i.e. 'earnest, esp. in confirmation of a bargain, or an engagement of a servant — arle-penny, arles-penny.' Arles, from Middle English, erles and a dimunitive of Latin, arrha. see cf. *Chambers 20th Century Dictionary* (Edinburgh, 1981), 68 and 407.

54. IFC MS 1386, 141. Recorded from Glenariff, Co. Antrim in 1955; IFC MS 1362, 236. Recorded from Cushendall, Co. Antrim in 1953; UFM/63/Q2a. Recorded from Bushmills; Armoy, Cushendall; Toberagnee; Ballykeel; Whitehead; Ballycarry; Ballymoney; Ballymena; Glengormley; Ahoghill; Cullybrackey; Cloghfin; Drumminning; Ballylummin; Randalstown; Kirkinriola and Ballycastle, Co. Antrim.

55. UFM/63/Q2a. Recorded from Coleraine; Knockloughrim and Castledawson, Co. Derry.

56. UFM/63/Q2a. Recorded from Killyleagh; Saintfield; Drumaghlis, Kilkeel; Ballyhalbert and Ballylough, Co. Down.

57. UFM/63/Q2a. Recorded from Kilskeery and Augher, Co. Tyrone.

58. In the earlier years of the hiring fairs the amount must have been a lot less. A few lines of a song were recorded from Glenariff in Co. Antrim in 1955 purporting to refer to a time at least 80 years previously at which time the earls were three pennies (IFC MS 1386, 141).

59. IFC MS 1386, 141. Recorded from Glenariff, Co. Antrim in 1955.

60. Cf. Bell, J., *op. cit.*, 77, n. 18.

61. *ibid.*, 71. See also IFC MS 1695, 147. Recorded from Eshnanumera, Co. Fermanagh in 1966; IFC/Q80. Recorded from Drumintee, Orior Upper, Co. Armagh; UFM/63/Q2a. Recorded from Drumaghlis, Co. Down.

62. UFM/63/Q2a. Recorded from Drumaghlis, Co. Down; Castleblaney, Co. Monaghan; Cushendall, Co. Antrim. IFC MS 1697, 140. Recorded from Eshnanumera, Co. Fermanagh in 1966.

63. UFM/63/Q2a. Recorded from Kilkeel, Co. Down; Antrim and Knockloughrim, Co. Derry.

64. The hiring fair in Dundalk, Co. Louth is an exception here. Although it was similar to the hiring fairs in Ulster, it possibly was not as popular. Michael J. Murphy, a full-time collector with the Department of Irish Folklore, reported that few workers from south Armagh attended the hiring fair in Dundalk as 'the southern farmer was regarded as a more severe task master and not so attentive to the worker's food, bedding etc. (as) his northern (and usually Protestant) counterpart.' (IFC/Q80).

65. IFC MS 1497, 43. Recorded from Kilcock, Co. Kildare in 1956 and referring to the hiring fair in Kilmainhamwood, Co. Meath; IFC MS 1829, 23. Recorded from Kilcullen, Co. Kildare in 1958 and referring to the hiring fair in Calverstown; IFC MSS 1497, 43 and 1441, 429. Recorded from Kilcock and Ballycannon, Co. Kildare in 1956 and referring to the hiring fair in Kilcock; IFC MSS 220, 220; 406, 361 and 1399, 480. Recorded from Taghmon town, Clongeen and Ballinglee, Co. Wexford in 1936, 1937 and 1955 and referring to the hiring fare in Taghmon. IFC MSS 577, 297 and 631, 44. Recorded from Ballykelly and Ross, Co. Wexford in 1938 and 1939 and referring to the hiring fairs in New Ross and Waterford; IFC MS 220, 220. Recorded from Taghmon, Co. Wexford in 1936 and referring to the hiring fair in Wexford town.

66. IFC MS 1497, 45. Recorded from Kilcock, Co. Kildare in 1956.

67. IFC MS S 487, 465. Recorded from Carrickerry, Shanid, Co. Limerick in 1938.

68. IFC MS 1391, 190-193 and 241-2. Recorded from Kilrush, Co. Clare in 1955.

69. IFC MS 462, 382. Recorded from Ballyhone, Cappawhite, Co. Tipperary in 1938; IFC MS 610, 76. Recorded from Meenagishagh, Kilcummin, Co. Cork in 1939; IFC MS 1523, 59 and 429. Recorded from Granagh and Corduff, Co. Limerick in 1958; IFC/Q80. Recorded from Pallasgrean, Reaskmore, Co. Limerick.

70. IFC MS 1193, 424. Recorded from Athea, Co. Limerick in 1950; IFC MS 1523, 59. Recorded from Granagh, Co. Limerick in 1958; IFC/Q80. Recorded from Laharn, Tralee, Co. Kerry; IFC/Q80. Recorded from Newcastle, Co. Limerick.

71. IFC/Q80. Recorded from Pallasgrean, Co. Limerick.

72. Colm Danaher is Kevin Danaher's brother.

73. IFC MS 1193, 428-429. Recorded from Athea, Co. Limerick in 1950.

74. IFC MS 1391, 241-242. Recorded from Kilrush, Co. Clare in 1955.

75. IFC MS 1828, 26. Recorded from Reaskmore, Pallasgrean, Co. Limerick in 1958. Four additional verses of the song are included.

76. IFC MS 1523, 8 and 9. Recorded from Skibbereen, and Derrynaggart, Co. Cork in 1958.

77. IFC MS 107, 461. Recorded from Araglin, Co. Cork in 1935; IFC MS 128, 122-123. Recorded from Ballyard, Kilworth, Co. Cork in 1935; IFC MSS 516, 227-228 and 938, 56. Recorded from Ballyvourney, Co. Cork in 1938 and 1944.

78. IFC MS 1828, 51. Recorded from Killian, Co. Galway in 1958; IFC MS 1581, 292. Recorded from Ross, Co. Galway in 1961; IFC MS 1700, 179. Recorded from Spiddle, Co. Galway in 1965; IFC/Q80. Recorded from Carraroe, Co. Galway.

79. IFC MS 642, 292 and 303. Recorded from Carheen and Gortaveha, Feakle, Co. Clare in 1939; IFC/Q80. Recorded from Templederry, Co. Tipperary.

80. IFC MS 1828, 26. Recorded from Reaskmore, Pallasgrean, Co. Limerick in 1958; IFC/Q80. Recorded from Ballymacadam, Cahir, Co. Tipperary.

81. IFC MS 1546, 308. Recorded from Lettermore, Co. Galway in 1956 and 1958; IFC MS 1828, 51. Recorded from Killian, Co. Galway in 1958; IFC/Q80. Recorded from Carraroe; Caltra, Ballinasloe; and Aughrim, Ballinasloe, Co. Galway; IFC MS 1865, 551. Recorded from Rossaveel, Co. Galway in 1965.

82. IFC MS 1243, 455. Recorded from Rossport, Co. Mayo in 1943. (See also IFC MS 1245, 538).

83. IFC MS 1795, 94-95. Recorded from Dernaferst, Tullyhunco, Co. Cavan in 1956; IFC MS 1430, 41-42. Recorded from Smear, Granard, Co. Longford in 1956; IFC MS 1480, 70. Recorded from Ballinalty, Co. Longford in 1957; IFC MS 1480, 336. Recorded from

Derrycassen, Granard, Co. Longford in 1957.

84. IFC MS 1429, 157. Recorded from Clonelly, Dromard, Co. Longford in 1955.
85. IFC MS 580, 71. Recorded from Cannistown, Co. Meath in 1938.
86. IFC MS 1240, 85. Recorded from Callan, Co. Kilkenny in 1949.
87. IFC S MS 882, 542. Recorded from Newbawn, Co. Wexford in 1938.
88. IFC MSS 1718, 43; 910, 115. Recorded from Ballydavid, Co. Kerry in 1933/4 and 1943; IFC MSS 930, 298; 935, 311. Recorded from Murreagh, Co. Kerry in 1944; IFC MS 1167, 87. Recorded from Tullig, Trughanacmy, Co. Kerry in 1948; IFC MS 1167, 236. Recorded from Castlemaine, Trughanacmy, Co. Kerry in 1948; IFC MS 1530, 77. Recorded from Áith Caisil, Corkaguiney, Co. Kerry in 1958; IFC MS 1523, 42. Recorded from Ballyduff, Co. Kerry in 1958.
89. IFC/Q80. Recorded from Ballyduff, Tralee, Co. Kerry and Ardfert, Co. Kerry. (In both Tralee and Ardfert, servant boys and girls and short term workers were employed).
90. IFC MS 334, 233. Recorded from Crossterry, Bear, Co. Cork in 1937.
91. IFC/Q80. Recorded from Killinardrish, Carrigadrohid, Co. Cork.
92. IFC MS 118, 185. Recorded from Luogh, Co. Clare in 1935; IFC MS 642, 292. Recorded from Feakle, Co. Clare in 1939; IFC MS 1829, 27. Recorded from Reaskmore, Pallasgrean, Co. Limerick in 1958; IFC/Q80. Recorded from Reaskmore, Co. Limerick.
93. The distribution of the occurrence of these words is seen in Fig. 1. Both are Irish words; *spailpín*, migratory farm labourer; *cábóg;* migratory labourer (cf. Ó Dónaill, N., *Foclóir Gaeilge-Béarla* (Dublin, 1977), 1138 and 166).
94. Working by 'task' or 'piece' work was common practice amongst seasonal and part-time workers. The custom was explained clearly by one informant from Co. Longford referring to the migratory harvest workers from that county who went to work on the large farms in Dublin, Kildare and Meath up to the beginning of this century. 'They worked by task, i.e., they took a field of oats and made a bargain with the farmer to cut, bind and stook it for so much. They had no regular hours for work and often worked from daylight almost to dark.' (IFC MS 1480, 7. Recorded from Ballinulty, Columbkille, Co. Longford, in 1957).
95. IFC MS 1448, 226. Recorded from Lettermore Island, Co. Galway in 1956.
96. IFC MS 1546, 307-308. Recorded from Lettermore Island, Co. Galway in 1956. Mr Ó hUigín's explanation for this was that most men in Connemara were left-handed workers (see Gailey, Alan, 'The Typology of the Irish Spade' in Gailey, A. and Fenton, A. (eds.), *The Spade in Northern and Atlantic Europe* (Belfast, 1970), 35-44, for a discussion on the distribution of Irish spade types).
97. Temporary workers were employed at the weekly Saturday market in Galway city up to the 1950s.
98. Cf. 76.
99. Cf. 77, IFC MS 938, 60.
100. Cf. 80, IFC MS 1828, 26.
101. Cf. 92.
102. Cf. 92. IFC/Q80. Recorded from Reaskmore, Co. Limerick.
103. IFC MS 1523, 50. Recorded from Tralee, Co. Kerry in 1958.
104. IFC/Q80. Recorded from Ardfert, Co. Kerry.
105. Cf. 86.
106. Cf. 87.
107. Cf. 84.
108. Cf. 85.
109. Cf. 83.
110. Cf. 28 and 30.
111. Cf. 28.
112. IFC MS 462, 382. Recorded from Ballyhone, Co. Tipperary in 1938. The custom, however, no longer existed at the date of recording.
113. There are many examples of this in the traditional material. See, for example, IFC MS 463, 442. Recorded from Mitchelstown, Co. Cork in 1937; IFC MS 107, 461. Recorded from Kilworth, Co. Cork in 1935; IFC MS 1193, 420. Recorded from Athea, Co. Limerick in 1950; IFC/Q80. Recorded from Newcastlewest, Co. Limerick and Pallasgrean, Co. Limerick; IFC MS 1581, 290-291. Recorded from Ross, Co. Galway; IFC MS 334, 233

and 795. Recorded from Glengarriff, Co. Cork in 1937; IFC MS 217, 461. Recorded from the Beare Peninsula, Co. Cork in 1935; IFC MS 1116, 255. Recorded from Ballydavid, Co. Kerry in 1939; IFC MS 1225, 543. Recorded from Cahirciveen, Co. Kerry in 1952; IFC MS 1391, 241. Recorded from Kilrush, Co. Clare in 1955.

114. Cf. 96.

115. Cf. 86.

116. IFC MS 1523, 50. Recorded from Tralee, Co. Kerry in 1958.

117. IFC/Q80. Recorded from Meenmore, Co. Donegal.

118. IFC/Q80. Recorded from Ballyshannon, Co. Donegal.

119. IFC/Q80. Recorded from Connemara, Co. Galway.

120. IFC/Q80. Recorded from Ballyduff, Co. Kerry.

121. IFC/Q80. Recorded from Pallasgrean, Co. Limerick and Louisburgh, Co. Mayo; IFC MS 1573, 523. Recorded from Coolagarry, Cam, Co. Roscommon in 1960.

122. IFC MS 38, 33. Recorded from Luogh, Co. Clare in 1930; IFC MS 642, 292. Recorded from Carheen, Co. Clare in 1939; IFC MS 1828, 27-28. Recorded from Reaskmore, Co. Limerick in 1958; IFC/Q80. Recorded from Limerick city; IFC MS 1167, 87. Recorded from Tullig, Killorglin, Co. Kerry in 1948.

123. *mo léir* an expression translated by Ó Dónaill, N., *op. cit.*, 776, 'Alas! Woe is me!'.

124. *Ochón*, is an Irish expression similar to *mo léir, ibid.* (See Ó Dónaill, N., *op. cit.*, 919.)

125. *Buachaill*, the Irish word for a boy (see Ó Dónaill N., *op. cit.*, 150). In this context, it means a rogue.

126. 'Toughen', according to Colm Danaher, is a local west Limerick expression meaning 'wait a while'.

127. *faiteach*, fearful, apprehensive, timid, shy (see Ó Dónaill N., *op. cit.*, 511).

128. IFC MS 1193, 435-436. Recorded from Athea, Co. Limerick in 1950.

129. IFC MS 1744, 27-28, and IFC/Q80. Recorded from Drumintee, Orior Upper, Co. Armagh in 1966; IFC MS 1362, 236. Recorded from Cushendall, Co. Antrim in 1953. See also Bell, J., *op. cit.*, 71.

130. IFC MS 1697, 140. Recorded from Eshnanumera, Co. Fermanagh in 1966; UFM/63/ Q2a. Recorded from Drumaghlis, Co. Down.

131. See, for example, IFC MS 768, 132-133. Recorded from Co. Kerry in 1941; IFC MS 334, 797-8. Recorded from Inchataggart, Glengarriff, Co. Cork in 1937 and IFC MS 557, 574-6. Recorded from Ballyduff, Co. Meath in 1938.

132. IFC MS 436, 442. Recorded from Bawnanearla, Co. Cork in 1937.

133. IFC MS 1828, 25. Recorded from Reaskmore, Co. Limerick in 1958.

134. IFC MS 1193, 425. Recorded from Athea, Co. Limerick in 1950.

135. Several of these legends explain the worker's speed and dexterity by the fact that he had some power helping him, e.g. the devil in the form of a beetle in the handle of the implement being used. In others, a mower is reputed to mow an extraordinary amount in a day and unlikely looking workers are able to do more work than all the other workers in the field.

136. IFC MS 1321, 70. Recorded from Ardstraw, Co. Tyrone in 1951.

137. IFC S MS 975, 103. Recorded from Cavan town in 1938.

138. IFC/Q80. Recorded from Ardee, Co. Louth.

139. IFC MS 1436, 87. Recorded from Corbally, Co. Clare in 1955.

140. See, for example, IFC MS 1523, 52. Recorded from Ballybunion and Asdee, Co. Kerry in 1958; IFC MS 1741, 247. Recorded from Ballyneale, Carrick-on-Suir, Co. Tipperary in 1960; IFC MS 1391, 242. Recorded from Kilrush, Co. Clare in 1955; IFC MS 1436, 88. Recorded from Corbally, Co. Clare in 1955; IFC MS 1828, 34. Recorded from Pallasgrean, Co. Limerick in 1958; IFC MS 1193, 429 and 432. Recorded from Athea, Co. Limerick in 1950.

141. Those marked in Antrim are Ballymena; Larne; Ballyclare; Ballycastle and Cushendall. In Armagh: Newtonwhamilton and Newry. In Cavan: Swanlinbar; Blacklion and Cavan town. In Derry: Limavady and Derry city. In Donegal: Letterkenny; Milford; Ballybofey and Donegal town. In Down: Ballynahinch. In Fermanagh: Enniskillen. In Monaghan: Clones and Monaghan town and in Tyrone: Omagh; Strabane and Ballygawley.

142. The questionnaire material records that there were additional hiring fairs in the following centres: In Antrim: Ballymoney; Bushmills and Antrim town. In Armagh: Crossmaglen;

Hamiltonsbawn and Armagh town. In Cavan: Cootehill and Belturbet. In Derry: Kilrea; Coleraine; Magherafelt; Claudy and Dungiven. In Donegal: Carndonagh; Lifford; Castlederg; Raphoe and Falcarragh. In Down: Castlewellan; Comber; Ballywalter; Banbridge; Killyleagh; Newtownards; Kircubbin and Downpatrick. In Fermanagh: Irvinestown; Rosslea; Lisbellaw; Lisnaskea; Belcoo; Tempo and Derrygonnelly. In Monaghan: Ballybay; Scotstown; Carrickmacross and Castleblaney. In Tyrone: Trillick; Cookstown; Dungannon; Fivemiletown; Aughnacloy; Clogher; Fintona; Sixmilecross; Pomeroy; Carrickmore and Gortin.

143. IFC MS S 385, 282. Recorded from Carrigane, Co. Cork between 1934 and 1938.

144. IFC MS 1828, 13. Recorded from Banteer, Co. Cork in 1958.

145. IFC MS 1828, 7. Recorded from Roscarberry, Co. Cork in 1958.

146. IFC/Q80. Recorded from Listowel, Co. Kerry.

147. IFC MS 1828, 31. Recorded from Pallasgrean, Co. Limerick in 1958.

148. IFC MS 1535, 353 and 355. Recorded from Rathkenny-Slane and Grangegeeth, Co. Meath in 1959.

149. IFC MS 1693, 57. Recorded from Louth, Co. Louth in 1965.

150. Ó Duinnín, Pádraig, (ed.) *Amhráin Eoghain Ruaidh Uí Shúilleabháin* (Dublin, 1901), 54.

151. Cf. Bell, J., *op. cit.* 75-76.

152. IFC MS 1470, 179. Recorded from Ballycastle, Co. Antrim in 1956.

153. IFC MS 577, 297. Recorded from Ballykelly, Co. Wexford in 1938. The informant mentions that hiring fairs were held in the two places approximately 35 years before the date of recording.

154. Cf. 65. IFC MS 220, 220.

155. Cf. 68.

156. IFC/Q80. Recorded from Laharn, Tralee, Co. Kerry.

The Oldest on the Farm

ÅSA NYMAN

'Once upon a time there was a man travelling in an unfamiliar district. Night was coming and it was getting dark, so he set about looking for a night's lodging. But it was a very desolate area, the farms were far apart and he walked and walked without seeing a single human habitation. When he was on the point of giving up hope, he saw a light in the distance. He went in that direction and came in a while to a very large farm situated on a hill. It was completely lit up, light shining through all the windows and everything looked warm and inviting. Outside in the farmyard an old man stood chopping wood — he seemed to be chopping firewood for the night — and the man stepped forward to the old man and said:

"Listen, father of the family! I wonder if it is possible to get night-quarters here?"

"I can't reply to that," the old man said. "Ask my father, he is indoors!"

The man entered through the door and came into a large room, simply a large hall. Inside the door there was a big, open fireplace and there an old man was at work making a fire. He was very old, his hair and beard were white and he was squatting in front of the fireplace, blowing to set fire to birch-bark and split wood.

"Listen, father of the family!" the man said. "Is it possible to get a night's lodging here?"

"I am not the father of the family," the old man said, "and I can't promise you a night's lodging. You must ask my father. He is sitting at the table over there."

The man looked round and saw that there was a big table in the middle of the hall and that an old man was sitting at the table. He went up to him. He was a very old man. His face was wrinkled like a sack of birch-bark, his hair was as white as snow and so was his beard, which was so long that it was lying spread over the table. It looked as if he was freezing for he was trembling all over and his hands, leaning on the table, were shaking.

"Listen, father of the family!" the man said. "Will you kindly let me stay the night here?"

"I am not the father of the family," the old man answered, "and I can't promise anything, you must ask my father. He is sitting in the corner over there."

The man looked at a corner of the hall in the direction the old man pointed and saw that somebody was sitting there in a big armchair. It was a very old and decrepit man sitting in the armchair and he was so shrunken by age that there was room for another two such men in the chair and yet they would not have been sitting too close together.

"Listen, father of the family!" the man said to him. "I wonder will you give me permission to sleep here tonight?"

"I am not the father of the family," the old man answered with a very faint and pitiable voice — it was more like a rattle in his throat.

"I can't promise you a night's lodging, but you must ask my father. He is lying on the seat over there."

The man looked in the direction the man pointed with great difficulty, and saw an old dodderer lying on a bench below a window. He was so old that he looked just like a skeleton. He was quite bald and had a long white beard hanging down to the floor. It looked almost as if he was dead, his mouth was sunken and he was lying on his side with his eyes shut. The man went forward to him and then he saw that the old man was alive, for his lips were quivering at every breath.

"Listen, father of the family! Will you kindly let me sleep here tonight?" he said to the old dodderer.

It was some little time before he knew that the old man had heard what he had said — he lay for a long time unmoving. But at last he opened his eyes, looked at the man and said with a miserably weak and trembling voice:

"I am not the father of the family and I can't promise anybody a night's lodging. You had better ask my father. He is lying at the end of the bench here."

The man looked over the bench and saw that a cradle stood at the foot of it. He stepped up to the cradle. In the cradle something was lying that had the appearance of a human being. The being had the size of a child but after having found out more about it, he saw that it was an incredibly old man lying there. He was so old that he was quite shrunken and dried up. He had no hair and no beard, his face was wrinkled like that of a new-born baby and he was sucking a dummy teat.

"Listen, father of the family," the man said to him. "Will you let me, a poor traveller, have a roof over my head here tonight?"

The little old man in the cradle went on sucking his dummy teat and it looked as if he had not understood or heard what the man asked him. But in a little while he dropped the teat and moved his lips as if he was saying something. The man leaned over the cradle to listen to what he said and then he heard the old man answer his question with an extremely weak and quivering child-like voice.

"I am not the father of the family," the old man said. "You must ask my father, I am sure he will give you permission to stay the night here. He is sitting up on the wall."

The man looked up to the wall and saw that something was fastened high up there. It looked like a little basket or box of birch-bark. A little being moved in it and a tiny little face, shrunken as an old apple, looked over the edge and down at him.

"Listen, father of the family!" the man said to the strange being. "Will you kindly let me sleep here tonight? I have walked a very long way and I am too exhausted to go further."

The being moved and in a little while the man heard a voice from the basket — it was very, very weak, sounding like the croaking of a bat.

"You may do so by all means, my child!" that bat-like voice said. "Of course you may sleep here tonight, but first of all you must have food and drink after having been travelling such a long way. Nobody must sleep hungry in our home."

And when the voice had said this, food and drink without limit or moderation was put on a table, which was brought into the hall. And a wide and soft bed was made alongside one of the walls equipped with a fine mattress, cushions and excellent quilts.

And the man ate and drank until he was well satisfied and then he went to bed, content and happy to have met, at last, the father of the family and to have got his permission to eat and sleep in his house.'[1]

*   *   *

This story, recorded in the province of Värmland in western Sweden, is a folktale type known in oral tradition in many places in Europe as well as North America, but particularly in Scandinavian and North German tradition.[2] In a special form the tale is very common in Irish oral tradition.[3] Now and then it is mixed up with motifs or elements of other categories of oral tradition and so, depending on the elements emphasized, it can vary considerably. Sometimes it is told as an explanation − often with an educating or moralizing aim − of the advanced age of the old men, sometimes as a funny story about the old man weeping, because his even older grandfather had given him a good thrashing on account of something wrong he had done, sometimes telling us about the oldest one in the shape of a giant, who wants to try the traveller's strength. In Irish oral tradition the tale is told as a dream, in which the traveller visits Lochlann or Scandinavia, where inter alia he has to shake hands with a giant.

The Scandinavian form of the folktale has very few features of fairy tradition. In spite of the epic reiteration and the expressive description of the incredible age and appearance of the 'father of the family', the fundamental idea of the folktale − several generations living together under the leadership of the oldest master −- seems here, more clearly than in other redactions of the tale, to build upon the real circumstances that existed in older times of a patriarchal family system.

The extended family is a well-known ethnological phenomenon;[4] two or more related families live together in an economic union. This way of living probably once existed all over Europe, and even beyond. Its most consistent form existed among the Romans but also among the Teutons patriarchalism was known. Through the saga literature of Iceland we know that households with forty to fifty persons were common there during the saga period. The clans of the Scots until the eighteenth century were grouped in extended families and pretty much the same conditions obtained amongst the Irish.[5] In Europe the patriarchal family system still exists in a modernised form among the southern Slavs, called *zadruga,* but in most parts of Europe it ceased to exist during the first centuries of the Modern Age. Only in remote districts and among people where circumstances have favoured it, as among settlers, has the patriarchal system been extant until now in a more or less complete form, but more often as a transitional or temporary form. In Scandinavia the patriarchal family system has been maintained especially in the isolated Norwegian fiord valleys and in the ajacent districts of Sweden, above all in the province Jämtland.

In the last-mentioned province in the summer of 1945, I had the opportunity to meet some people who had grown up in families living according to the patriarchal system. They were all born in the parish of Borgvattnet in the eastern part of Jämtland but in different villages.[6] Two examples of this way of living are given here. The site plans (Figs. 1 and 2) are not based on measurements, since most of the buildings no longer existed at the time of investigation, but have been drawn according to the informants' descriptions. A special interest is given to the people's way of using the space of the farmstead.

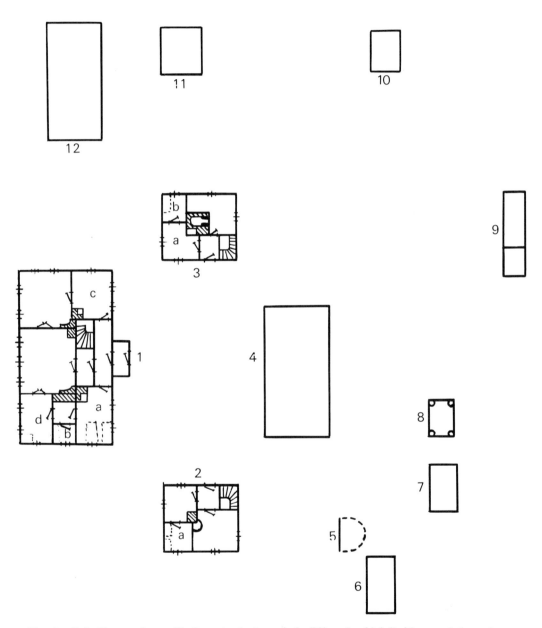

Fig. 1 Erik Magnus Bergvall's farmstead: 1, main building; 2, old folks' house; 3, brew house, also called summer house or baking house; 4, cow house; 5, cellar; 6, wood shed; 7, store house; 8, store house on posts; 9, summer cow house; 10, smithy; 11, cattle-food store; 12, cow house.

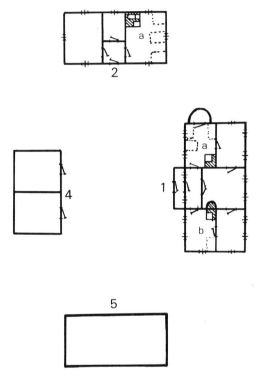

Fig. 2   Olov Henriksson's farmstead: 1, main building; 2, brew house; 3, servants' house; 4, store house; 5, cow house.

   In one of the farmsteads in the village of Boberg there lived at the beginning of this century no less than four generations as a working unit and the oldest of the men, Erik Magnus Bergvall, was the absolute master until his death in 1914 at the age of seventy-seven. The household consisted of:

1. Erik Magnus Bergvall (1837-1914)
    and his wife Brita Kristina (1844-1918)
2a Daughter Kristina (1862-1927)
    married to Erik Andersson (1851-1943)
2b Son Hakvin (1872-1920)
    married 1914 to Emelinda (1879-?)
3a Son of Kristina: Albert (1880-1937)
    married 1905 to Kristina (1883-?—

3b   Son of Kristina: Arvid (1890-?)
       married to a/Ragnhild (1892-1918)
                b/Gunhild (1901-?)
3c   Daughter of Hakvin: Frideborg (1915-?)
       married to Evert (1911-?)
4a   Son of Albert: Erling (1908-?)
4b   Daughter of Albert: Hedvig (1920-?)
4c-d Children of Arvid and Frideborg: all born later than 1923.
In the household several maids were also included, but no farm-hands since
there were enough men fit for work within the family.

As long as Erik Magnus was alive about fifteen people lived and worked together
as a unit. Every day they had their meals at the same table in the kitchen of the
main building (1a) during the winter, in the 'brewing house' (3a) during the summer — except the old housewife, who always ate sitting at the fireplace. At the
table everyone had his own definite place, the master at the end of the table below
the window. Nobody was allowed to take his place. The old housewife was responsible for the cow-house and her daughter, Kristina, for the cooking. Both of
them were helped by maids. The men worked in fields and woods according to
the master's instructions.
    The buildings of this farmstead were of the same type as those of farmsteads
for single families all over north Sweden. With the exception of the main building
there were another two dwelling-houses: a 'summer-house' also called 'brewing-
house' or 'baking-house' (3) and a house for the old folk (2). It was necessary to
use all the houses, including the summer-house, to have sleeping places for all.
Erik Magnus and his wife had their sleeping place in the old folks' house (2a),
Kristina and Erik in a small room behind the kitchen of the main building (1b),
Albert and Kristina in the summer-house (3b). As long as Arvid and Hakvin were
unmarried they slept in room 1d in the main building. Though Albert and his
wife had their sleeping place in the summer-house, the household, according to
the custom in North Sweden, had meals there during the summer months.
    The same year as Erik Magnus died, in 1914, Hakvin married. The old widow
then moved her sleeping-place to the second kitchen (1c) of the main building
and Hakvin and his wife took possession of the old folks' house (2). Arvid, when
married, occupied the upper floor of the summer-house. The maids had their
sleeping place in the common kitchen (1a) during the winter, and during the
summer in a little room in the upper floor of the summer-house. After the old
master's decease the younger generations managed the farm in co-operation but
acted as two households as to meals. In 1918 the farm was partitioned and in
1922 some of the houses were moved.
    In another village, Skyttmon, in the same parish, a farmer, Olov Henriksson,
governed his house and people until his death in 1901 at the age of ninety-two.
Not until then did his son Henrik, at that time fifty-seven years old, 'put his
feet under his own table'. Unfortunately he died in 1902, so he was master during only one year. After his death his two sons, Olov Peter (1876-1930) and
Nikolaus (1883-?), used the farm in co-operation to start with but very soon
they partitioned it and Olov Peter moved. Nikolaus became the owner of the old
farmstead. In 1902 he pulled down the 'brewing-house' and built a new one in

another locality. He also replaced the cow-house (Fig. 2).

The Henriksson family was never specially numerous. Olov Henriksson had only one son, who for his part had two sons. When the household was at its most numerous it consisted of seven members of the family plus three or four farm-hands and three maids. In the main building there was room enough for the family and the servants had a house of their own (3), where the farm-hands slept down-stairs and the maids on the first floor. The old master and his wife had their sleeping-place in one of the two kitchens of the main building (1a), Henrik and his wife in the other kitchen (1b). When the old master became a widower he changed his sleeping place with Henrik and his family. Nikolaus, who was un-married, slept by his father. The members of the family and the servants all had their meals in the kitchen of the main building during the winter and in the kitchen of the brewing house in the summer (2a).

Henrik's wife died in 1890 and the household was without a housewife until 1899, when Henrik's son Olov Peter married. His young wife — she was twenty-three years old — then became mistress of the household, responsible for both the cooking and the cow-house. Three years later, when the farm was partitioned, she moved with her family to her father's place as settler.

As already noted there were many people in this parish who had grown up in patriarchal families and it was generally known that the patriarchal system was common in all villages of the parish in older times. However, this way of living was not rooted in old tradition in this area but was rather the result of practical necessity. Colonization here is rather recent; the first settlement was probably in the middle of the eighteenth century and some were as late as the nineteenth century. The settlers were for a long time occupied with reclaiming land and so villages were not created through sub-division of holdings but by means of new settlements. The area was an isolated woodland. Until 1872 there were no real roads, only forest paths for pack-horses. At that time the woods became valuable and wood companies bought many of the farms.

Judging from the word for one of the buildings of the farmstead, the old folks' house (Swed. *undantagsstuga* or *födorådsstuga*), an alternative system to the patri-archal family was also known, and was prevalent in other parts of Sweden; when the master had grown old, his oldest son took charge of the farm on special terms, such as assured provision of house and other necessities for the old people. But the patriarchal system seems to have been so deeply rooted that the old master kept his position as leader of the farm, even if he had made such a contract with his son. It is notable that the families in question were not large and so there was no problem with succession.

One cannot leave out of account that stubborn retention of the farm leadership in recent times was due to individual conservative and dominating personalities. The description of the old master Olov Henriksson almost sounds like a tale, telling how every morning he went in person to the storehouse to share out the food for the day, anxious to prevent anybody else making decisions about management of the farm.

NOTES AND REFERENCES

1. Free translation of a manuscript in the Institute of Dialect and Folklore Research, Uppsala (ULMA 25125) recorded in the 1940s by R. Brobert from his mother, b. 1865.

2. Aarne, A. and Thompson, S., *The Types of the Folktale. A Classification and Bibliography* (F.F. Communications, Helsinki, No. 184, 1961), no. 726; Liungman, W., *Sveriges Samtliga Folksagor*, 3 vols. (Djursholm, 1950-52), 254: Lixfeld, H., 'Alten: Die drei Alten (AaTh 726)', in *Enzyklopädie des Märchens*, I (1977), 383.

3. Ó Súilleabháin, S. and Christiansen, R. Th., *The Types of the Irish Folktale* (F.F. Communications, Helsinki, No. 188), no. 726*.

4. Grosse, E., *Die Formen der Familie und die Formen der Wirtschaft* (1896), created the technical term *Grossfamilie* in his survey of the existence of the patriarchal family system. Mortensen, I., *Bondeskipnad i Norig i eldre tid* (1904), has elucidated the distribution of this system in Norway. In Sweden Erixon, S., *Gården och familjen. Bidrag till belysningen av storfamiljsystemets förekomst i Sverige* (Etnologiska studier tillägnade N.E. Hammarstedt, 1921); idem, *Bonden i högsäte* accepted the German term in Swedish translation, *storfamilj*. Gavazzi, M., prefers the term Mehrfamilie, 'Die Mehrfamilien der Europäischen Völker,' *Ethnologia Europaea*, 12 (1979-80), 158. Financial and historical research has also touched on the problem of the partriarchal family system.

5. Meitzen, A., *Siedelung und Agrarwesen der Westgermanen* (1895), 184; Arensberg, C.M. and Kimball, C.T., *Family and Community in Ireland* (Harvard, 1940); Leyton, E., *The One Blood* (St. John's 1975).

6. Some of the farmsteads in this parish were visited by S. Erixon before 1920.

Airgead Geal go Pras: Staidéar ar Rannscéal ó Chontae Luimnigh

DÁITHÍ Ó hÓGÁIN

Bhailigh Máiréad Bean Uí Dhanachair, máthair Chaoimhín, an scéilín seo a leanas i bparóiste Áth an tSléibhe, Contae Luimnigh, sa bhliain 1937:

Is minic do bhíodh Micheál Ó Longáin ar aonach le stoc a mháistir do dhíol, agus ba ghnáth leis bheith ag aonach Chroma gan teip gach Lúnasa. Duine des na baird dob ea Micheál, agus file maith, mar is eol do chách. Do bhíodh cruinniú na bhfilí gach uile bhliain ag aonach Chroma. Is mó cara a chasfaí ar Mhicheál na laetha san. Duine díobh san dob ea Liam Dall Ó hIfearnáin. Nuair a bhí Micheál i Luimneach lá ar obair an Ridire do bhuail sé le Liam sa tsráid, agus do bhí ana-sheanchas acu sa tigh tábhairne. Do bhí Liam ag maíomh ar a ghliocas — go dtéadh sé timpeall na Mumhan agus gan radharc na súl aige. Níor chreid Micheál ar fad an uile rud a dúirt sé, ach do chuir Liam geall leis go ndéanfadh sé amach puball Sheáin Uí Thuama ar aonach Chroma so chúchu gan aon treorú ó aoinne.

Abair ná raibh Micheál déanach an lá san, agus níorbh fhada go bhfaca sé féin agus na filí eile Liam Dall ag teacht. Ba ghnáthach le lucht díolta an óil agus lóin an t-am san a bpuball do thógaint i líne dhíreach i bpáirc an aonaigh — maide ina sheasamh ar aghaidh gach pubaill amach agus bratach ar an maide. Nuair a shrois Liam páirc an aonaigh bhí sé ag ciorcalú timpeall go dtí gur bhuail sé maide pubaill, agus dúirt sé os ard:
'Is bachallach glas an gas é seo os comhair do thí!'
Ní bhfuair sé aon fhreagra óna raibh istigh. Ar aghaidh leis gur tháinig sé ar mhaide eile, agus dúirt sé an leathrann céanna. Is é an freagra a fuair sé ná comhairle chun imeacht leis. Mar sin dó go dtí gur bhuail sé le maide Sheáin Uí Thuama, agus thug sé an leathrann:
'Is bachallach glas an gas é seo os comhair do thí!'
Agus fuair sé freagra ó Sheán féin:
'Ag mealladh na bhfear isteach im' phuball ólta dí!'
Ansan dúirt Liam: 'Dá mbeadh scilling im' ghlac is pras id' phuball d'ólfainn í!'
'Go maith is go ceart — tá an bhraich anso agus hóp gan díol!' arsa Seán á fhreagradh.
Thosnaigh Liam arís: 'Is minic sin mac dea-athar lá gan luach na dí!'
Agus do chríochnaigh Seán an leathrann mar seo: 'Is cuma — tá céad míle fáilte ag Seán Ó Tuama roimhe!'
Abair gur chuir na filí liú buaidh astu, agus do dhruideadar isteach agus do thosnaigh Comhdháil na mBard.[1]

Óna fear céile, Liam, a fuair Bean Uí Dhanachair an scéal sin. Chuir Liam Ó Danachair féin an scéal i gcló san iris *Béaloideas* i 1947.[2] Tá an rannaireacht focal ar fhocal mar an gcéanna ansiúd, ach amháin go bhfuil an tráchtaireacht i mBéarla. Ó dhuine darbh ainm Seán Ó Conchúir, ón gClais, Áth an tSléibhe, a chuala Liam an scéal thart faoin mbliain 1908. Rugadh an Conchúrach seo sa bhliain 1816, agus is óna sheanathair féin a fuair sé an chuid is mó de na scéalta a bhí aige. Ar an bhfeirm chéanna a raibh Seán féin ina chónaí uirthi a bhí a shean-athair ag cur faoi.³ Is léir as sin ar fad go bhfuil anseo againn fíorthraidisiún béaloidis a shíneann siar go dtí an 18ú Céad – sin, go dtí an tréimhse a raibh na carachtair féin atá i gceist sa scéal beo.

Ní miste cúpla focal a rá ar dtús faoi na carachtair úd. Ó Ghleann Chorbraí, in iarthar Chontae Luimnigh, ba ea Micheál Ó Longáin. Bhí cónaí air i mBaile Uí Dhonnchú, gar don Ghleann, agus bhí sé mar reachtaire ag Ridire an Ghleanna, Éamonn Mac Gearailt. Nuair a d'iompaigh an Ridire ina Phrotastúnach sa bhliain 1741, deirtear gur tharla titim amach idir é féin agus an file, rud a thug ar Mhicheál a aghaidh a thabhairt ar Chontae Chorcaí agus cur faoi ansiúd. Fuair sé bás tuairim na bliana 1770.⁴ Ó Shrónaill, i gCo. Thiobraid Árann, ba ea Liam Dall Ó hIfearnáin. Is cosúil gur thart faoi 1720 a rugadh é agus mhair sé go deireadh an chéid.⁵ I bparóiste Chill Bhríde, in oirthear Chontae Luimnigh, a rugadh Seán Ó Tuama sa bhliain 1709. Bhí tigh tábhairne aige i sráidbhaile Chroma ó thart faoi 1734 go 1739, agus ba mhinic an Chúirt Éigse á cruinniú sa tigh tábhairne úd. Níor éirigh go ró-mhaith lena ghnó i gCroma, agus b'éigean dó dul ag obair mar reachtaire go Baile Ó gCoinn, ar an taobh thuaidh de chathair Luimnigh. Níorbh fhada go raibh sé thar n-ais i gCroma, áfach – i mbun tábhairneoir-eachta arís – agus lean an Chúirt Éigse ar aghaidh tríd is tríd mar a bhí. Tuairim na bliana 1769 d'fhág sé Croma chun cur faoi ag Geata Mhungairid ar imeall chathair Luimnigh, agus d'éag sé ansiúd i 1775. Ba dhlúthchara leis an file eile, Aindrias Mac Craith (1709-93), ar a dtugtaí mar leasainm 'an Mangaire Súgach'. Bhí aithne ag an mbeirt acu ar a chéile as a n-óige, agus is dealraitheach gur in aonpharóiste a tógadh iad.⁶

Mar a tharlaíonn, tá leagan eile againn den scéal ó bhéaloideas Luimnigh. Bhailigh Tomás Ó Combá an méid seo a leanas ó Dhónall Ó Curtáin, ó Chnoc Uí Choileáin in iarthar Chontae Luimnigh i dtús an chéid seo:

> Tháinig file go dtí tigh tábhairne lá. Bhí a fhios aige gur le file eile an tigh tábhairne céanna, agus do theastaigh uaidh fear an tábhairne do thriail sa bhfilíocht. Chonaic sé sceach dheas ag fás ag ceann an tí, agus nuair a tháinig sé go dtí an doras do thosnaigh sé mar seo:
>> 'Is bachallach deas an sceach í seo aige tóin do thí!'
>> 'Tá, cheana, ag tarrac na bhfear isteach ag ól na dí!'
>> 'Tá scilling im' ghlaic agus ólfam í!'
>> 'Is maith an ceart, mar tá an tsraith agus an chóip le díol!'⁷

Tá roinnt difríochtaí suntasacha idir an leagan sin agus leagan an Chonchúraigh. Ar an gcéad dul síos, níl ainmneacha na bhfilí tugtha in aon chor i leagan an Churtánaigh. Chomh maith leis sin, ní mar a chéile an suíomh sa dá chás. Puball ar pháirc an aonaigh i gCroma atá i gceist sa chéad leagan, tigh tábhairne sa dara ceann. Agus tá difríochtaí áirithe idir na focail sa véarsaíocht. Chun go dtuigfí fás agus forbairt an scéil, ní fearr rud a dhéanfaimis ná díriú ar na trí bunghnéithe seo den insint agus féachaint conas a chuirtear i láthair iad sna leagan-acha éagsúla.

Tá flúirse leaganacha den rannscéal áirithe seo bailithe sa chéad seo, agus is i lámhscríbhinní Roinn Bhéaloideas Éireann atá a bhfurmhór le fáil. Baineann na leaganacha atá bailithe leis na contaetha seo a leanas: Luimneach, Ciarraí, Corcaigh, Port Láirge, an Clár, agus an Ghaillimh. Tá an dá leagan ó Chontae Luimnigh tugtha thuas againn. Bailíodh an scéal ó cheithre dhuine déag i gContae

Chiarraí, ó aon duine déag i gContae Chorcaí, ó bheirt i gContae Phort Láirge, ó chúigear i gContae an Chláir, agus ó thriúr i gContae na Gaillimhe. Níl amhras ná go raibh sé á insint ag i bhfad níos mó daoine ná sin, ach is leor an méid sin samplaí i gcomhair bunchomparáideachais agus tugann siad léargas dúinn ar scaipeadh geografúil an scéil.

Tosnaímis le leaganacha Chiarraí. Baineann seacht leagan acu le Corca Dhuibhne.[8] Ar pháirc ráis a thiteann an eachtra amach i gceann acu siúd, ar ráiseanna an Daingin i gceann eile, ar aonach Oileán Chiarraí i gceann eile, i dtigh ósta i gceann eile fós, i dtigh óil i dhá cheann, agus ní deirtear cén áit sa cheann deiridh. Níl ainmneacha na bhfilí tugtha ach i gcás amháin — Aogán Ó Rathaille agus Conchúr 'Cam' a thugtar orthu, ach tá dhá rannscéal eile ag teacht roimh an scéal sa chás sin, agus dá bharr seo ní féidir glacadh le hainmneacha na bhfilí faoi leith seo mar thraidisiún neamhspleách den scéal. Baineann dhá leagan le hoirdheisceart Chiarraí.[9] Aonach Chill Rois, sa cheantar sin, an láthair i gceann acu as Cill Choimín, agus pátrún i Sráid an Mhuilinn atá i gceist sa cheann eile — ó Ghleann Fleisce. Seán Ó Tuama an file a bhfuil an cábán dí aige sa dá chás, agus i leagan Ghleann Fleisce deirtear gur dall ba ea an file eile. Tá ceithre leagan den scéal againn ó iardheisceart Chiarraí.[10] Tigh tábhairne i sráidbhaile an láthair i dhá cheann acu siúd, tigh cónaithe i gceann eile, agus ráiseanna Chluain Meala i gceann eile. Níl aon ainmneacha tugtha ar na filí i gcás amháin, Eoghan Rua Ó Súilleabháin atá ag plé le file ná hainmnítear i gceann eile, Tomás Rua Ó Súilleabháin ag tabhairt cuairte ar 'Laoiseach' file síos amach atá i gceist i gcás eile, agus dall ar ráiseanna Chluain Meala is ea an cuairteoir sa chás deiridh acu. Tá leagan amháin eile againn a cuireadh i gcló san iris *Loch Léin* i 1904, agus is ríchosúil gur le Ciarraí a bhaineann sé.[11] Dá réir seo, bhí file darbh ainm Diarmaid Dall ag triall ar ráiseanna i gcathair Luimnigh, agus is amhlaidh a bhuail sé isteach i dtigh tábhairne a bhí ag Seán Clárach Mac Dónaill ar an tslí.

Tá dhá leagan bailithe ó iarthuaisceart Chorcaí.[12] Níl ach an véarsaíocht tugtha i gceann acu ón mBántír, ach i leagan ó Dhrom Tairbh deirtear go raibh Aogán Ó Rathaille i bpuball dí ag ól ar aonach Chnoc na Groí nuair a tháinig Eoghan Rua Ó Súilleabháin timpeall á rá go raibh scilling le caitheamh aige agus go raibh comhluadar óil uaidh. Ó Mhúscraí do cheithre leagan.[13] Cábán ar aonach nó ar chomhthionól atá i gceist i dhá cheann díobh, agus cábán ar na ráiseanna sa dá cheann eile. I dhá chás acu, is amhlaidh atá Eoghan Rua Ó Súilleabháin ag iarraidh teacht suas le mac tabhartha dá chuid, agus is é an mac sin fear an chábáin. Baineann eachtraí mar seo faoi Eoghan Rua agus a mhac le sraith eile rannscéalaíochta,[14] agus is léir go bhfuil siad ar iasacht sa rannscéal atá faoi chaibidil againn. I gcás eile, file Ciarraíoch agus file de mhuintir Chonchúir ó Bhaile Bhuirne atá i gceist, agus is léir gur forbairt dhéanach a leithéidí de charachtair a bheith páirteach sa scéal. An leagan ó Chill Mhichíl is spéisiúla, mar gur dealraitheach go bhfuil seancharachtar agus nua-charachtar araon le fáil ann. File áitiúil darbh ainm Seán Ó Fearghaile is ea an cuairteoir sa chás seo, ach is é fear an chábáin 'Seán Ó Luana an Rí' (< 'Seán Ó Tuama an Ghrinn'!). Tá dhá leagan bailithe ó dheisceart Chorcaí.[15] Baineann ceann acu le Cloich na Coillte, agus is é Seán Ó Tuama féin atá i gceist ansin — lena chábán dí ar aonach Thigh Molaige! De réir an leagain eile, ón áit chéanna, tigh tábhairne a bhí ag file i Ros Ó gCairbre, agus is é an cuairteoir an file áitiúil Séamas Ó Colmáin. Ní thugann an leagan a bailíodh i gCuan Dor[16] aon léargas breise — beirt fhile gan ainm ar aonach atá i gceist ansiúd – agus níl ach an véarsaíocht i gceist i leagan a bailíodh i mBéarra.[17] Baineann tábhacht faoi leith le leagan a bailíodh ar an taobh eile den chontae ar fad, áfach, i mBaile Mhistéala ar theorainn Chontae Luimnigh. Tá an dul céanna ar an insint anseo is atá ar na leaganacha Luimníocha:

> Bhí rásanna i gCaisleán Nua, i gContae Luimní, uair; agus mar ba ghnáth an uair sin bhí sraith de chábáin ann ina mbídís ag díol pórtair agus biotáille. Bhí cábán ag Seán Ó Tuama, an file, ann ina measc. Tháinig Liam Dall go dtí na rásanna, agus chuir fear éigin geall leis ná faigheadh sé cábán Sheáin Uí Thuama a dhéanamh amach. Chuaigh Liam Dall timpeall, agus thosnaigh sé mar seo ar aghaidh gach cábáin acu: 'Is bagarthach glas an beart os comhair do thí!'
>
> Bhíodh bata fada in airde os comhair an chábáin, agus ribíní glasa ina bharr, an uair sin.
>
> Fé dheireadh fuair sé mar fhreagra as ceann acu: 'Chun tarraingt na bhfear isteach ag ól na dí!'[18]

Bhí an rannscéal seo le fáil, chomh maith, i mbéaloideas na nDéise. I leagan ó Bhéal na Molt, Contae Phort Láirge, is amhlaidh a bhí cábán dí ag 'óstaer' file ar aonach an Chnoic Bhuí lá. Tháinig dall timpeall, agus chuir sé geall le fear a bhí ann go ndéanfadh sé amach cábán an fhile. Tríd an véarsaíocht a dhein sé amach é.[19] An chuma chéanna atá ar an leagan ó Bhaile Mhic Chairbre, ón gcontae céanna, ach amháin ná deirtear ann cá raibh an t-aonach ar siúl.[20]

Ó thuaidh linn anois go Contae an Chláir. I leagan ó Chill Bhaile Eoin, in iardheisceart an chontae sin, beirt fhile gan ainm atá i gceist agus cábán dí ag duine acu ar na ráiseanna.[21] Tá leagan i bhfad níos inspéise againn ón gCorrbhaile, sa cheantar céanna, áfach:—

> Bhí ráiseanna le bheith in áit éigin. D'fhiafraigh duine de Liam Dall Ó hIfearnáin an mbeadh sé ag dul go dtí na ráiseanna. 'Cad é an mhaitheas duit dul ann?' arsa an tarna fear. 'Cuirfidh mé galún puins ná bainfidh tú amach bothán Sheáin Uí Thuama!' Bhí bothán aige Seán i dteannta a lán daoine eile. Ba ghnáthach an t-am san sórt éigin rud glas a bheith in airde ar an gcábán á theaspáint don tslua. Do tháinig Liam, ach go háirithe, lá na ráiseanna. Do dhein sé fé dhéin an chéad chábáin. Seo mar a labhair sé: 'Is glas í seo, an chraobh ar thaobh do thí!'
>
> 'Is glas,' arsa fear an chábáin.
>
> Ní dúirt sé a thuilleadh. Bhí a fhios ag Liam nach bothán Sheáin é seo. Do dhein sé an rud céanna le gach ceann, go dtí gur tháinig sé go dtí an tarna ceann deireanach. Do thosnaigh sé arís: 'Is glas í an chraobh í seo ar thaobh do thí!'
>
> 'Is glas,' arsa an fear istigh, 'ag tarraingt na bhfear isteach ag ól na dí!'
>
> Labhair Liam arís: 'Tá scilling im' ghlaic, agus is pras a d'ólfainn í!'
>
> Labhair an fear istigh: 'Beidh fáilte ag Seán Ó Tuama roimpi!'
>
> Bhí a fhios ag Liam ansan gurbh é sin bothán Sheáin.[22]

An chuma chéanna – agus na carachtair chéanna ann – atá ar leagan eile ón gceantar sin, ach amháin an véarsaíocht a bheith mar a leanas: 'Is bachallach glas an gas é seo os comhair do thí'/'Ag mealladh na bhfear isteach ag ól na dí'/'Dá mbeadh scilling im' ghlaic is pras a d'ólfainn í'/'Maith an ceart, tá an bhraith is an hóp gan díol'/'Is minic mac dea-athar lá gan luach na dí'/'Tá céad fáilte ag Seán Ó Tuama roimhe.'[23] Níos faide ó thuaidh, tá an chuma chéanna arís ar leagan ón Leacht. Cábán Sheáin Uí Thuama ar aonach Bhaile Uí Chomhraí atá i gceist anseo, agus tugtar Dall Bán ó hIfearnáin ar an gcuairteoir.[24] Leis an dara leagan thuas a théann an véarsaíocht, cé gur truaillithe anseo í. Tá leagan eile fós bailithe ó Chontae an Chláir.[25] Ón Leamhach, Dúlainn, i bhfíorthuaisceart an chontae, don leagan seo. Óstóir agus cuairteoir ar an tigh ósta atá i gceist anseo, agus níl aon ainmneacha tugtha orthu ná aon chur síos pearsanta orthu.

Tá trí leagan bailithe ó Chontae na Gaillimhe,[26] agus tá gach ceann acu siúd ceangailte le rannscéal áirithe a bhí coitianta i gConnachta. Mar seo a bhíonn an chaint sa rannscéal Connachtach seo — File amháin: 'Seo ceist agam oraibh, a chomhluadair, agus feicimis fuasclaithe í — cé againn is deise, is gile, ná is áille gnaoi?' File eile: 'Tá fear againn dubh crosach, agus an fear eile mantach buí; agus níor mhaiseach an pobal a rachadh an cúpla thríd!'[27] Antoine Raifteirí agus Micheál Mac Suibhne is gnáthaí a bhíonn i gceist sa rannscéal seo. Is iad atá i dhá leagan den chumasc idir é agus an rannscéal atá faoi chaibidil san alt seo, chomh maith, agus is léir mar sin gur ó bhéaloideas an Chláir a thaisteal an rannscéal seo againne isteach go Co. na Gaillimhe. An Suibhneach agus file áitiúil ar a dtugtaí Conchúr Táilliúir atá sa leagan eile. Rud eile, níl ach an chéad dá líne den véarsaíocht i gceist sna leaganacha Gaillimheacha seo, viz. 'Is deas caol an chleaithín í sco ag doras do thí!'/'Is deas atá sí ag tarraingt amadáin isteach ag ól na dí!'

Is léir as na samplaí sin ó chontaetha éagsúla go bhfuil roinnt buntréithe ag baint leis an rannscéal seo. File amháin ag díol dí agus file eile ag tabhairt cuairte air an bunshuíomh, agus is gnáthaí gur cábán dí ar aonach nó ar ráiseanna a bhíonn i gceist. Is léir as comparáid a dhéanamh idir na leaganacha éagsúla gur le Seán Ó Tuama i gCo. Luimnigh a bhaineann an rannscéal go bunúsach. Is é sin a thugtar ar an tábhairneoir i leaganacha den scéal ó áiteanna i bhfad ó chéile i Luimneach, i gCiarraí, i gCorcaigh, agus sa Chlár. Ní miste anois iarracht a dhéanamh ar an scéal a rianadh siar tríd an 19ú Céad go dtí an 18ú Céad féin chomh maith agus is féidir leis na foinsí atá ar fáil.

Tosnaímis leis an scoláire Seán Ó Dálaigh, agus an insint a thug sé sin ar an scéal san eagrán dá mhórleabhar *Poets and Poetry of Munster* a d'fhoilsigh sé sa bhliain 1849.[28] Seán Ó Tuama agus Aindrias Mac Craith na carachtair atá i gceist san insint seo:

> One day, our friend, according to the custom of country publicans, had erected a tent on the race-course of Newcastle (or, as some assert, at the fair of Adare), which was surmounted by a green bough, as a distinctive mark of his occupation. . . He was eyed at some distance by Magrath who approached and accosted him, and the following short but pithy dialogue took place between the brother wits:
>> Magrath: 'Is bachallach glas an chleach so i dtóin do thí
>> Ag tarraing na bhfear isteach ag ól na dí!'
>> O'Tuomy: 'Airgead geal go pras a réidhfeadh slí,
>> Tá an charaid ag teacht, an bhraich is an hóp gan díol.'

Ní mar a cheile go díreach an leagan atá ag an Dálach i lámhscríbhinn dá chuid a scríobh sé thart faoi 1848. Tugann sé míniú ansiúd ar an gcúlra a deir sé a bhí laistiar den eachtra:

> When O'Toomy kept the public-house at Croom, one day that he was absent, Magrath — passing by with some friends — came in and treated them freely with drink. Not having a halfpenny to pay the reckoning which had already increased to a considerable amount, a stratagem occurred to him by which he was able to deceive his hostess (.i. bean chéile an Tuamaigh) and extricate himself from his present difficult position. He placed a sentinel at the door to give him notice when some loads of corn belonging to him would arrive — which were coming on after him on the way to the Limerick market. The boy, who kept watch for a long time — without seeing the corn, of course — made no announce-

ment. At which, Magrath was greatly enraged and rebuked him sharply for neglecting his duty and letting the cars pass by unnoticed. He told Mrs. O'Toomy that, however, it mattered little — as he would pay her immediately on his return. It is superfluous to add that this promise was never fulfilled, but so deep was the impression it made on the mind of the fair landlady that even the lasting friendship which it afterwards gave occasion to between O'Toomy and Magrath could never compel her to forget how grievously she had been imposed on.

But, in the following autumn, as Magrath and Wall (.i. Éamonn de Bhál) sauntered at ease through the racecourse of Newcastle — where O'Toomy had a tent — and eying him at some distance leaning leisurely on the pole to which the ropes were fastened and which was surrounded by a green branch, the distinctive mark of his position . . . they approached him. And the *Mangaire*'s address to him provoked the following interesting dialogue — the first introduction to that union which continued uninterrupted between them to the end of their lives:

> Magrath: 'Is bachallach glas an chleach so as taobh do thí
> Ag mealladh na bhfear isteach ag ól na dí!'
> Toomy: 'Airgead geal go pras a réidhfeadh slí —
> Tá an charaid ag teacht, an bhraich is an hóp gan díol!'[29]

Ní deir an Dálach cá bhfuair sé ceachtar den dá insint sin. Tá leagan níos faide de chuntas na bliana 1848 le fáil i lámhscríbhinn a scríobh Micheál Ó hAnracháin, ó Chill Rois, Contae an Chláir, sa bhliain 1856.[30] Díol suntais is ea go bhfuil an véarsaíocht ag an Anrachánach mar atá i gcuntas na bliana 1849, áfach. Is léir go raibh an tAnrachánach ag breacadh síos a chuntais sin agus *Poets and Poetry of Munster* os a chomhair amach aige, mar go bhfuil an prós beagnach focal ar fhocal aige mar atá sa leabhar sin. Níl an cúlra leis an eachtra tugtha ag an Dálach sa leabhar sin, áfach, rud a mhúsclaíonn fadhb láithreach. An amhlaidh ná raibh an tAnrachánach ach ag déanamh forbartha ar an gcúlra mar a thug an Dálach é in 1848? Nó arb é an tAnrachánach a thug an cuntas ar dtús don Dálach, agus an ag athscríobh as foinsí dá chuid féin maraon leis an *Poets and Poetry of Munster* a bhí sé sa bhliain 1856? Nó an raibh comhfhoinse ag an Anrachánach agus ag an Dálach? Is deacair na ceisteanna sin a fhreagairt. Tá gné shuntasach amháin den fhadhb ann, áfach. Tugann an Dálach le fios i gcuntas na bliana 1848 gur tríd an eachtra a chuir an Tuamach agus an Crathach aithne ar a chéile. Ach tá a fhios againn go raibh aithne ag an mbeirt fhile sin ar a chéile as a n-óige. Tá cuma níos iontaofa ar a ndeir an tAnrachánach. Tugann sé mar mhíniú ar an gcaint 'an bhraich is an hóp gan díol', 'the hops and malt are unpaid for still'; agus leanann air:

> This was to remind the *Mangaire* of his old scores, and how he had behaved to Mrs. O'Tuomy; which made him go forward and pay what he owed, and caused all parties to be well united. And no person enjoyed the joke better than Mrs. O'Tuomy, and especially as the *Mangaire* left her another guinea for his dealings with her before she left that place. And it is said that they were always good friends after that, and that she often spoke of the circumstance to the credit and honour of the *Mangaire*.

Míniú loighiciúil ar an eachtra a bheadh sa tuairisc sin, agus is trua ná fuil a fhios againn cá bhfuair an tAnrachánach é. Deir sé féin faoin lámhscríbhinn mhór a bhfuil an cuntas aige inti gur dhein sé an t-ábhar 'a thiomsú as mórán leabhar'.[31] Tá a fhios againn, ach go háirithe, go raibh leaganacha den rannscéal le fáil lasmuigh de Chontae Luimnigh féin go luath sa 19ú Céad ar a dhéanaí. Tá leagan againn a scríobh scoláire darbh ainm Éamonn Ó Sealbhaidh uair éigin nárbh fhada tar éis 1817. Is cosúil gurbh as comharsanacht Thulachair i gContae Chill

Chainnigh é seo, agus tá dlúthchosúlacht ag a leagan siúd le ceann de leaganacha Phort Láirge thuas, viz. 'Is cochallach glas an sceach seo i dtóin do thí' mar chéad líne. 'Mangaire le S. Ó Tuama' atá mar cheannteideal ag an Sealbhaíoch.[32] Tá leagan níos caighdeánaí de ag an ngrafnóir Cláiríneach Dónall Mac Consaidín i lámhscríbhinn dá chuid thart faoi 1840. Seo mar a deir sé:

> Andrew Magrath (*An Mangaire Súgach*), having been a long time in John O'Toomy's debt to the amount of a guinea, was walking along accompanied by Edmund Wall, at the racecourse of Newcastle – where O'Toomy had a tent, the sign of which was a green bough. Magrath approached and made the following remark: 'Is bachallach glas an chleach so os comhair do thí/Ag mealladh etc. etc.'[33]

Tá nóta inspéise ag an gConsaidíneach ag bun an téacs Gaeilge: 'Adeire drong le béalaithris gurb in aonach Chroma; agus d'fhág Tadhg Mac Cárthaigh, file den aimsir sin, scríofa i leabhar gurb in aonach Átha Dara do tharla an comhrá réamhráite.'[34] Bhí an tuairisc seo léite ag Seán Ó Dálaigh, mar go ndeir sé sin i bhfonóta lena leagan den rannscéal sa bhliain 1848: 'In an old Ms. written by a bard named Timothy McCarthy the fair of Adare is mentioned as the place where O'Toomy had the tent, when the dialogue occurred.'[35] Ach ní raibh mórán ar eolas ag an Dálach faoin ngrafnóir seo ('file fáidhiúil fíorfhoghlamtha ba ea an Tadhg Mac Cárthaigh so, agus do chónaigh i gCo. Thiobraid Árann nó Luimnigh, ach ní fios dom cá ham').[36] Mar a tharlaíonn, tá lámhscríbhinní againn ó pheann an Chárthaigh a bhaineann leis an tréimhse 1818-1827, agus bhí cónaí air i gCaiseal Mumhan.[37]

Tá foinsí níos luaithe ná sin féin ar fáil don rannscéal, áfach. Chuir an grafnóir Dónall Ó Briain an míniú seo a leanas leis an véarsaíocht i lámhscríbhinn dá chuid sa bhliain 1789: 'Magrath, John Toomy, and Edmond Wall, extempore at Adare fair.'[38] I bparóiste an Domhnaigh Mhóir, beagán mílte ar an taobh theas de chathair Luimnigh, a bhí cónaí ar an mBrianach seo,[39] agus is beag amhras ná gur traidisiún áitiúil Luimníoch a bheadh aige. Mar seo a thugann sé an véarsaíocht:

> '(Ls. doléite) glas an chleach so as taobh do thí
> (Ls. doléite) isteach ag ól na dí!'
> '(Ls. doléite) do réidhfeadh slí –
> (Ls. doléite) an bhraich is an hóp gan díol!'

Má ghlacaimid le substaint na seantuairiscí sin, dhealrófaí gurb iad an Tuamach, an Crathach, agus Éamonn de Bhál, na carachtair a bhí i gceist go bunúsach sa scéilín. Ach tá tuairisc againn atá níos sine ná aon cheann acu siúd – tagairt a chuirfeadh a mhalairt ar fad de chrot ar an bhfadhb dá nglacfaimis léi mar fhoinse iontaofa. Mar, de réir leagan den rannscéal a bhreac grafnóir darbh ainm Pádraig Ó Riada sa bhliain 1754, ba iad 'Seán Mac Dónaill' agus Seán Ó Tuama a bhí i gceist.[40] Seán Clárach Mac Dónaill (1691-1754), an file mór a bhí ina chónaí i Ráth Loirc, i dtuaisceart Chontae Chorcaí, an Dónallach úd, gan amhras.[41] Thug Seán Clárach cuairt ar Chúirt na hÉigse i gCroma tuairim na bliana 1735, agus cuireadh mórfháilte roimhe ann.[42] Bhí caradas agus comhfhreagras idir Seán Clárach agus an Tuamach, agus chum an Tuamach marbhna air nuair a d'éag sé ar an 7/1/1754.[43] Tharlódh gurb é sin ar fad ba chúis le Pádraig Ó Riada a bheith ag samhlú na beirte le chéile sa rannscéal agus é ag scríobh go gairid tar éis bhás Sheáin Chláraigh. Is cosúil gur Chláiríneach ba ea an Riadach,[44] agus tharlódh mar sin ná beadh eolas ró-chruinn aige ar fhilí Luimnigh. Is féidir easpa cruinnis mar seo a léamh as an leagan faoi leith den véarsaíocht a thugann sé dúinn:

> Seán Mac Dónaill: 'Is glas an chleach so amach as taobh do thí!'
>
> Seán Ó Tuama: 'Ag gairm na bhfear isteach ag ól na dí!'
>
> Seán Mac Dónaill arís: 'Tá airgead geal im' ghlaic, is dein (?) dom slí!'
>
> Seán Ó Tuama arís: 'Tá an costas ag teacht — an bhraich is an hóp gan díol!'

Ní thugann an Riadach aon eolas eile in éineacht leis an véarsaíocht seo, rud a fhágann gur cosúil gur ag plé atáimid le leagan béaloidis a chuala an Riadach féin. Agus leagan béaloidis atá comhaimseartha le Cúirt Éigse Chroma atá ann, leagan ná féadfadh bheith níos faide ón mbunús ná fiche bliain. Fiú má tá dearmad ar an ngrafnóir nuair a chuireann sé Seán Clárach in ionad an Chrathaigh, ní miste cuimhneamh go raibh an Tuamach agus an Crathach araon faoi bhun caoga bliain d'aois le linn don Riadach a bheith ag breacadh síos an leagain seo. Tugann leagan seo an Riadaigh léargas dúinn ar bhunghné amháin de chuid an scéilín — sin, gur scéal béaloidis a bhí ann ó thús. Ní gá ach féachaint ar an éagsúlacht atá idir na focail sa véarsaíocht féin sna leaganacha ón 18ú agus ón 19ú Céad chun sin a thuiscint. Fágann seo mar dhualgas orainn na snáthanna éagsúla i dtraidisiún an scéil a scaruint ó chéile.

Leanann ocht gcinn de cheathrúna eile ar an mbunvéarsaíocht i leaganacha an Bhrianaigh agus an Chonsaidínigh — ceithre cinn acu curtha i leith Aindriais Mhic Chraith agus dhá cheann an duine i leith Sheáin Uí Thuama agus Éamoinn de Bhál. Tá na hocht véarsaí seo — dar tús 'Nuair a théim go tigh an tábhairne níor chás liom fuireach oíche ann' — le fáil mar aon iarracht amháin ceapadóireachta i gcuid mhór lámhscríbhinní eile agus iad curtha i leith an Chrathaigh i gcónaí.[45] Is é is dóichí gur ceanglaíodh an dán eile seo leis an rannscéal de bharr an t-ól a bheith mar théama sa dá dhéantús agus de bharr an Crathach a bheith i gceist sa dá cheann chomh maith. Más ea, is léir go raibh an pátrún céanna á leanúint ag an mBrianach agus ag an gConsaidíneach. Is léir, leis, go raibh an pátrún céanna ó thaobh na gcarachtar á leanúint ag Seán Ó Dálaigh sa bhliain 1848. Fágann seo gur féidir féachaint ar na leaganacha seo mar aon snáth amháin traidisiúin. Ach, ós rud é nach mar a chéile téacs an rannscéil mar a thugann siad é, is léir gur ag tarraingt ar fhoinsí éagsúla a bhíodar i gcás na bhfocal. Dhealrófaí as seo arís go rabhadar neamhspleách ar a chéile chomh fada is a bhain leis an rannscéal agus go raibh an béaloideas seachas lámhscríbhinn mar fhoinse acu dó sin.

Ní miste cúpla focal a rá anseo faoi théacs na rannaireachta sa scéilín. Is féidir dhá bhundifear a aithint idir na léamha ar an gcéad líne: 1) 'Is glas . . . amach' v. 'Is bachallach glas'; agus 2) 'as taobh' v. 'os comhair' v. 'i dtóin'. Maidir leis na leaganacha béaloidis a bailíodh sa 20ú Céad — ag cur cúrsaí truaillithe san áireamh — tá samplaí againn ó chontaetha éagsúla de gach léamh acu siúd, agus roinnt eile curtha leo. Sa dara líne, baineann an bundifear le 'gairm' v. 'mealladh' v. 'tarraing' — tá 'tarraing' nó 'tarrac', 'mealladh', 'glaoch', agus 'bailiú' le fáil taobh le chéile ó áiteanna éagsúla sa 20ú Céad. Tá bundifear suntasach le fáil arís sa tríú líne. 'Airgead geal go pras a réidhfeadh slí' atá i ngach leagan sna seanlámhscríbhinní ach amháin i leagan an Riadaigh, mar a bhfuil 'tá airgead geal im' ghlac, is dein dom slí'. Is iad na leaganacha is coitianta sa 20ú Céad ná 'tá scilling gheal im' ghlac is ólfad í' agus 'tá scilling im' ghlac is is pras a ólfad í'. Chonaiceamar go raibh an focal 'costas' ag an Riadach sa cheathrú líne san áit a raibh 'caraid' sna seanleaganacha eile. Ach, in ionad 'tá an charaid ag teacht', is é is coitianta i leaganacha ó bhéaloideas an 20ú Céad ná 'is maith an ceart', a bhfuil samplaí againn de ó Luimneach, ón gClár, ó Chiarraí, ó Chorcaigh, agus ó Phort Láirge.

Fillimis arís ar na carachtair atá luaite sa scéal. Is léir as na seanlámhscríbhinní go raibh an eachtra suite i gContae Luimnigh. Tá an tuiscint chéanna le baint as na leaganacha a bailíodh ón mbéaloideas sa 20ú Céad. Filí na Máighe go díreach atá i gceist sa bhfurmhór de leaganacha an Chláir, mar a chonaiceamar, agus tá rian na bhfilí céanna siúd le brath go láidir ar thraidisiún Chiarraí, chomh maith. Léiríonn leaganacha Chorcaí go raibh seanchaithe an chontae sin den tuairim chéanna arís. Mar threise leis an gcruthú gurb iad filí na Máighe atá sa chúlra, tá na línte breise seo i gceist sa leagan a bhailigh Liam Ó Danachair in Áth an tSléibhe, Contae Luimnigh: 'Is minic sin mac dea-athar lá gan luach na dí!'/ 'Is cuma – tá céad míle fáilte ag Seán Ó Tuama roimhe.' Tá an dá líne chéanna sin bailithe, chomh maith, i gContae an Chláir, Contae Chiarraí, agus Contae Chorcaí. Is léir go bhfuil an chaint seo fásta as an rann atá curtha i leith Aindriais Mhic Chraith ag Micheál Ó hAnracháin ina lámhscríbhinn sin in 1856:

Más tú Seán is náir dhuit é mar shlí,
Is go bhfuil in airde ar chlár i mbuaic do thí
Dá mbeadh mac dea-athar lá gan luach na dí
Go mbeadh míle fáilte ag Seán Ó Tuama roimhe![46]

Freagra a bhí i rann seo an Chrathaigh ar an rann a bhí scríofa in airde ar chlár lasmuigh dá thigh tábhairne ag an Tuamach:

Níl fánach ná sáirfhear ar uaislibh Gaoidheal,
Bráthair den dáimh ghlic ná suaircfhear groí,
I gcás go mbeadh láithreach gan luach na dí
Ná go mbeadh fáilte ag Seán geal Ó Tuama roimhe![47]

Tugann seo i gceist beagán fianaise eile a shuíonn tigh tábhairne an Tuamaigh laistiar de na tuairiscí béaloidis. Bailíodh cuntas ón rí-sheanchaí Diarmaid Mac Coitir ó Bhaile Bhuirne, Contae Chorcaí, sa bhliain 1937, cuntas a chuireann síos ar an bhfile Eoghan Rua Ó Súilleabháin a bheith ag dul ag spealadóireacht 'ó Uíbh Ráthach síos go Luimnigh'. 'Ins an am so bhí file in áit éigin i gContae Luimnigh, agus fear tábhairne ab ea é', a deir an Coitireach. Chuir an tábhairneoir seo scríbhinn 'i Laidean' ar chlár os cionn a dhorais ag fáiltiú roimh Eoghan Rua. D'ordaigh Eoghan deochanna ó bhean an tábhairne agus fuair iad. Dhein sé iarracht ar imeacht ansin gan í a dhíol, agus ghlaoigh an bhean ar a fear céile – an file – chun é a bhac ó dhul amach. Labhair Eoghan Rua le file seo an tábhairne mar a leanas:

A fhile gan cháim is a sháirfhir shuairc an ghrinn
Des na folctha dob fhearr agus den dáil is uaisle a bhí,
Is é an friotal seo atá ar an gclár i mbuaic do thí
A thug mise ins an áit, cé táim gan luach na dí!

'Ó, míle fáilte romhat!' arsa fear an tábhairne, agus choimeád sé ar feadh seachtaine é 'ag seanchaíocht is ag comhrá is ag cumadh dánta.'[48] Is léir gurb iad Seán

Ó Tuama agus a bhean Muireann atá i gceist sa chuntas sin, agus go bhfuil Eoghan Rua Ó Súilleabháin curtha in ionad Aindriais Mhic Chraith. Tharlódh, ar ndóigh, go mbeadh an tuairisc seo ón gCoitireach bunaithe ar an insint a thug Pádraig Ó Duinnín ina leabhar *Filidhe na Máighe* sa bhliain 1906[49] — insint a bhí bunaithe ar lámhscríbhinn Mhichíl Uí Anracháin atá pléite againn thuas. Ach tá seans maith go bhfuil tuairisc an Choitirigh neamhspleách ar leabhar an Duinnínigh agus go bhfuil sí tarraingthe as gnáthchiste béaloidis a bhí coitianta faoi fhilí na Máighe. Ba é Seán Ó Tuama an lárcharachtar sa chiste béaloidis seo — ar an gcúis, gan amhras, go raibh a ainm is a shloinne luaite sna rainn ar a raibh an seanchas ag brath. Agus chinntigh éirim an tseanchais gur mar fhile a bhí ina thábhairneoir a chuimhneofaí ar Sheán, rud a chabhródh lena ainm a bhuanú mar charachtar sa rannscéal atá á phlé san alt seo.

Is léir as sin ar fad nach amháin gurb é Seán Ó Tuama an carachtar atá mar mhol ag roth na heachtraíochta seo agus é ag casadh trí lúb an bhéaloidis, ach gur bhain sé go dlúth agus go buan leis an scéilín luath agus déanach. Ach cad mar gheall ar na carachtair eile? Tá feicthe againn gur chuir Pádraig Ó Riada sa bhliain 1754 an file ó Ráth Loirc, Seán Clárach Mac Dónaill, isteach sa scéilín mar chéile comhraic ag an Tuamach; ach tá feicthe, leis, againn gur leagan diallach ón traidisiún é sin dá luaithe é. Ní miste a rá go bhfuil leagan diallach eile againn ó Chontae Thiobraid Árann. Mar seo don tuairisc atá i gceist, ó chomharsanacht dhúchais Liam Dhaill Uí Ifearnáin, agus dar dáta 1938: 'The meeting of Heffernan and Seán Clárach at the fair of Knockardon is very graphically described by an old man still living in the district. McDonnell had a tent, and in it the two right heartily enjoyed themselves.'[50] Bhí Seán Clárach triocha éigin bliain níos sine ná Liam Dall, ach mar sin féin bhíodar ceangailte le chéile i gcuid mhaith scéilíní béaloidis[51] agus b'fhéidir go raibh caidreamh acu lena chéile. Níl ach isteach is amach le fiche míle slí idir na háiteanna a raibh cónaí orthu, agus ní foláir nó bhí aithne nó clos trácht éigin acu ar a chéile, pé rud mar gheall ar iad a bheith ag bualadh le chéile ar an aonach le linn do Sheán Clárach puball (dí) a bheith ansiúd aige. Is suntasach an ní ná fuil Seán Clárach luaite mar charachtar sa scéilín ach anseo, sa tuairisc scaoilte (ó Chiarraí?) a cuireadh i gcló i *Loch Léin*, agus i lámhscríbhinn úd an Riadaigh ó 1754. Is féidir a rá go lom díreach ná fuil ceangal dá laghad idir an dá thuairisc dhéanacha seo agus an tseanlámhscríbhinn, áfach. Tá páirt Sheáin Chláraigh sa seanchas déanach le míniú tríd an mbaint a bhí aige sa bhéaloideas le Liam Dall agus ní ar aon tslí eile. Bhí an tIfearnánach luaite mar charachtar sa rannscéal go coitianta, mar atá feicthe againn. Is é éifeacht an scéil sna leaganacha a bhfuil sé i gceist iontu ná gur féidir leis an bhfile dall an file eile a aithint tríd an deacaint a chaitheann siad chun a chéile. Seo móitíf an aitheantais, agus breis béime curtha uirthi ag feiniméan na daille. Ach féach ná fuil aon mhóitíf den saghas sin curtha in iúl sa rannaireacht. Níl le tuiscint as caint na bhfilí lena chéile sa rannscéal go bhfuil an t-aitheantas mar mhóitíf i gceist in aon chor, gan trácht ar an daille. Ach bhí an mhóitíf úd an aitheantais dlúthcheangailte leis an íomhá a bhí ag Liam Dall sa seanchas de bharr é a bheith gan radharc na súl. Agus bhí Liam páirteach le filí na Máighe ina thuilleadh den seanchas,[52] rud a thabharfadh an chaoi do na seanchaithe mórfhuinneamh a chur sa rannscéal seo trí mhóitíf chomh húsáideach agus chomh hoiriúnach do shuíomh an scéil leis an aitheantas a thabhairt i gceist. Thug an mhóitíf seo breis brí — agus dá réir sin breis buanaíochta — don insint ar shruth fánach an bhéaloidis. Móitíf an-choitianta sa traidisiún Gaelach is ea filí a bheith ag aithint a chéile tríd an rannaireacht, móitíf a bhí i gceist i bhfad roimh an 18ú Céad — go deimhin, is í an lárphointe í i gceann de na rannscéalta is ársa atá againn sa Ghaeilge.[53] Leis an neart a bhí ag baint leis an móitíf seo sa traidisiún, mar sin, is furasta a thuiscint go sleamhnódh sí isteach gan mórán dua sa rannscéal atá faoi chaibidil againn anseo. Is rídhealraitheach gurb ar chomhchéim le Liam Dall a tháinig an ghné seo den insint i gceist.

Is féidir go raibh an tIfearnánach luaite mar charachtar sa scéal chomh luath leis an 18ú Céad féin — tá feicthe againn go raibh sé i gceist ann ag seanchaí a rugadh in iarthar Luimnigh sa bhliain 1816. Agus is léir as a ndeir Seán Ó Dálaigh in 1848 go raibh móitíf an aitheantais comhshamhlaithe leis an insint cheana faoin am a raibh sé sin ag scríobh. Tuairiscíonn sé, d'ainneoin go raibh sean-aithne ag an Tuamach agus ag an gCrathach ar a chéile de réir na staire: 'the following interesting dialogue — the first introduction to that union which continued uninterrupted between them to the end of their lives.' Thuig Micheál Ó hAnracháin an mhíloighic a bhain leis an móitíf i gcás na beirte sin. Tá an chuid sin de chuntas an Dálaigh fágtha ar lár aige ina lámhscríbhinn siúd, agus tá athrú suntasach eile aige a chealaíonn an mhóitíf. In ionad 'when O'Toomy kept the public-house at Croom, one day that he was absent, Magrath. . . came in' an Dálaigh, tá an méid seo a leanas ag an Anrachánach: 'Andrew McGrath happened to be going the way, and as Tuomy wished to avoid the reproach of his wife he hid himself in his room.' Tagann seo i gceart leis an gcomhthéacs mar a thuairiscíonn an tAnrachánach agus an Dálach araon .i. go raibh Bean Uí Thuama tar éis cosc a chur ar na filí sa tigh tábhairne de bharr an chailliúint airgid a ghaibh leo.[54] Is léir, mar sin féin, go bhfuil móitíf an aitheantais á cur i leataoibh d'aon ghnó ag an Anrachánach, mar go ndeir sé dá ainneoin féin nár aithin Bean Uí Thuama Aindrias. Ait go leor, níl an mhóitíf i gceist ag an Dálach i gcás na mná — is leor leis an t-iomrall aithne a chur i leith an Tuamaigh féin.[55]

Tá sampla suntasach eile againn de mhóitíf an aitheantais a bheith i gceist sa seanchas faoi fhilí na Máighe. Tá seo tugtha ag fear a raibh an-chur amach aige ar thraidisiún na bhfilí, an mórscoláire Eoghan Ó Comhraí. Ag scríobh thart faoi 1850, tugann sé cuntas ar conas a fuair an Crathach an leasainm 'an Mangaire Súgach.' Dá réir seo, bhí puball ag an Tuamach ag díol dí ar aonach Chroma. Thit cith trom báistí, agus tar éis an cheatha bhí Aindrias ag gabháil thar bráid nuair a chonaic sé an fear ag iarraidh an t-uisce a choimeád amach óna phuball le rámhainn. D'fhiafraigh an Crathach de cad a bhí ar siúl aige, agus dúirt sé sin gur ag déanamh cora a bhí sé. D'fhiafraigh sé ansin cen saghas éisc a raibh súil aige le breith orthu, agus d'fhreagair an fear eile gur bastúin a bhí uaidh. Níor fhan focal ag Aindrias, ach bhailigh leis agus ba bheag an mhoill air scata dá chairde a chnuasach. Thugadar aghaidh ansin ar an bpuball céanna chun achrann a tharraingt ann. Le linn dóibh bheith ag ól ann, tháinig an tábhairneoir isteach, agus d'fhiafraigh an Crathach de ar chuimhin leis bualadh leis cheana inniu agus freagra drochmhúinte a thabhairt ar cheist shibhialta. Ghlac an tábhairneoir go réidh é, agus chaith súil timpeall á rá gur éirigh go maith lena chuid iascaigh agus an méid bastún a bhí gafa aige tríd an bpuball a choimeád tirim! Bhain an comhluadar ar fad — agus Aindrias ina measc — ardthaithneamh as an bhfreagra seo, agus bhí mórscléip acu ag ól sa phuball sin go maidin. Chodail an Crathach an oíche sin i dtigh an tábhairneora, agus is nuair a dhúisigh sé ar maidin a fuair sé amach gurbh é Seán Ó Tuama féin an tábhairneoir a bhí aige. Agus is ar an ócáid sin a dhoirt an Tuamach crúiscín uisce beatha ar cheann Aindriais, ag baisteadh an leasainm 'an Mangaire Súgach' air![56] Is léir go bhfuil móitíf an aitheantais sleamhnaithe isteach san insint ansiúd arís; agus, ach an oiread le cuntais an Dálaigh agus an Anrachánaigh, níl aon ghá leis an móitíf do bhunchrot an scéil.

Tá Éamonn de Bhál le plé fós againn. Ó Dhún Guairne, in oirthear Chontae Chorcaí, ba ea an Bhálach (c1683-c1754).[57] Bhí dlúthcharadas idir é féin agus Seán Clárach Mac Dónaill,[58] agus tharlódh go mbeadh caidreamh aige leis an Tuamach chomh maith céanna. Tá dán fada againn de chuid Éamoinn, dán a chum sé mar mharbhna ar Ridire an Ghleanna, Seán Mac Gearailt, a d'éag i gCorcaigh ar an 10/8/1737.[59] Is léir as an déantús seo, maraon le caointe eile a chum filí nach é,[60] go raibh an Ridire céanna sin fial flaithiúil leis an aos dána. File ab ea é féin, agus deir an Bhálach ina mharbhna air go mba 'ghamhain cích deoil domhsa an fhlaith'. D'fhéadfaí a thuiscint as seo go raibh an Bhálach mar oide sa bhfilíocht ag an Ridire, agus tharlódh go maith gur chaith sé seal ar cuairt i dtigh an Ghearaltaigh uasail úd sa Ghleann, in iarthar Luimnigh. Is suntasach mar atá Micheál Ó Longáin mar an tríú carachtar sa leagan a bhailigh muintir Dhanachair in Áth an tSléibhe, sa chomharsanacht chéanna sin in iarthar an chontae. Bhí an Longánach mar reachtaire ag an Ridire a lean Seán Mac Gearailt sa teideal (a dheartháir, Éamonn).[61] Ós rud é ná fuil an Longánach luaite in aon leagan eile atá bailithe, tá an chosúlacht ar chúrsaí go bhfuil ionad duine eile glactha aige san insint. Ionad duine a raibh baint aige, chomh maith, le Ridire an Ghleanna? Is deacair a rá, ach is féidir a áiteamh go coinníollach gurb é an Bhálach atá laistiar den tagairt seo do Mhicheál Ó Longáin. Ní miste a rá, leis, go bhfuil deacrachtaí áirithe ag baint leis an Longánach mar reachtaire an Ridire agus Liam Dall Ó hIfearnáin a shuíomh le chéile sa scéal, mar atá déanta sa leagan seo. D'fhág Micheál Contae Luimnigh i dtrátha 1741, agus ní raibh Liam Dall ach bliain is fiche nó mar sin san am sin. Ba mhó fós an deacracht Liam Dall a shuíomh sa scéal in éineacht le hÉamonn de Bhál – b'óige fós Liam sa chás sin. Ach, mar a chonaiceamar, baineann Liam Dall mar charachtar leis an tsraith 'fhorbartha' den scéal nuair a bhí móitíf an aitheantais i gceist. Bhí 'an Dall Bán' mar leasainm ar Liam Dall,[62] agus thugtaí 'an Bhálach Bán' ar Éamonn de Bhál.[63] B'fhéidir gurb iad na leasainmneacha seo ba chúis le Liam Dall agus dá réir sin móitíf an aitheantais a theacht isteach sa scéal den chéad uair. Pé ar domhan de, is suntasach an ní go bhfuil file mar an Bhálach, a bhain le ceantar in oirdheisceart Chorcaí – os cionn leathchéad míle ó Chroma – i gceist sna luathinsintí. Níl de mhíniú follasach air seo ach gur bhain an Bhálach le bunús an scéil i ndáiríre.

Tá againn, mar sin, an Tuamach, an Crathach, agus an Bhálach mar charachtair sa bhunscéal. Ainm an Tuamaigh amháin a mhair go buan sa bhéaloideas. Thit an Bhálach ar lár as an insint de bharr é a bheith ina fhile stróinséartha i gcomhthéacs an tseanchais faoi fhilí na Máighe, agus is dealraitheach gur thit ainm an Chrathaigh ar lár de bharr mheath na Gaeilge i gCo. Luimnigh. Ní raibh a ainm siúd luaite sa véarsaíocht a bhain leis an seanchas faoi fhilí na Máighe mar a bhí ainm an Tuamaigh. Rud eile, bhain a íomhá siúd mar réice le saghas file atá coitianta sa bhéaloideas – baineann níos mó den indibhidiúlacht le file a bhí ina thábhairneoir. Is léir, áfach, go raibh cáil níos mó ar an gCrathach sa seanchas cúpla glún ó shoin.[64] Agus ní ceart a dhearmad gur mhair Aindrias chomh fada anall leis an mbliain 1793 .i. ceithre bliana tar éis do Dhónall Ó Briain ó Chontae Luimnigh a thuairisc a scríobh ag dearbhú gurb iad an Crathach agus an Bhálach an bheirt a bhuail leis an Tuamach san eachtra. Is féidir go leor den bhfianaise chomhthéacsúil a chur chun cinn maidir le páirt an Chrathaigh san eachtra. Tá an fonóta seo leis an scéal ag Seán Ó Dálaigh (1849): 'We should here observe that Magrath was somewhat deep in the books of O'Tuomy for certain old scores'. Mar atá feicthe againn, thug an Dálach (1848) agus an tAnrachánach míniú ar conas a tharla don scéal a bheith amhlaidh. Thuairiscigh Dónall Mac Consaidín go raibh giní sa scór i gcoinne an Chrathaigh le fada. Tagann seo go maith leis na tagairtí sna leaganacha éagsúla den tríú líne, mar a chonaiceamar.[65] Rud eile, lean Aindrias i bhfiacha leis an Tuamach de bharr luach na dí go ceann i bhfad. Tá seo soiléir as na dánta a chum an bheirt chun a chéile nuair a chuadar in aighneas le chéile i ndáiríre, agus sin go binbeach, thart faoi 1760.[66]

Filí na Máighe san 18ú Céad an bunús a bhí leis an rannscéal, mar sin, de réir mar atá dáileadh an scéil go geografúil, de réir stair na lámhscríbhinní, agus de réir na dtagairtí inmheánacha sa véarsaíocht féin. Ach an féidir go raibh an rannscéal le fáil coitianta sa bhéaloideas roimh ré fhilí na Máighe agus gur ceanglaíodh leo siúd é? Má bhí, níl pioc dá rian siúd le fáil ar na leaganacha atá againn. Rud eile, dá mba sheanrannscéal coitianta é tráth bheadh sé le fáil ar fuaid na hÉireann sa bhéaloideas — rud ná fuil is ar léir ná raibh. Arís, ní oireann na tagairtí sa véarsaíocht ná suíomh an scéil do thréimhse mórán níos sia siar ná ré na bhfilí atá i gceist againn. Ritheadh reacht sa bhliain 1683 mar a leanas: 'Sellers of ale or beer only. . . at fairs or during the fairs shall not be impeached for selling without licence. . . Every person licensed shall have a sign, stake or bush at his door, that travellers may know where they may receive entertainment for their reasonable money.'[67] Is ar éigean, mar sin, a d'fhéadfadh an rannscéal bheith ann in aon chor roimh 1683, gan trácht ar é a bheith inste faoi fhilí eile seachas filí na Máighe. Ach is í an argóint is fearr ar fad a d'fhéadfaí a chur ar son fhilí na Máighe mar bhunús leis an scéal ná na luathfhoinsí a bhí comhaimseartha leis na filí féin. Is suntasach an ní ná caitheann na foinsí sin amhras ar fhírinne an scéil ná ar na carachtair i gcoitinne a bhí páirteach ann. Níl de chnámh spairne sa ghnó, dar leo, ach cá háit go díreach ar thit an eachtra amach. Mar atá feicthe againn, tá trí láthair luaite leis an eachtra agus údarás áirithe ag gabháil leo — is iad sin Croma, an Caisleán Nua, agus Áth Dara. Aonach Chroma atá i gceist, agus tharlódh sin a bheith amhlaidh sa bhéaloideas de bharr an dáin mhóir a chum Seán Ó Tuama faoin aonach sin.[68] Is deacair a shamhlú go mbraithfeadh an Tuamach gá le puball chun bheith ag díol dí ansiúd, agus tigh tábhairne aige ar an mbaile céanna. Is deacair glacadh le ráiseanna an Chaisleáin Nua, ach an oiread, mar go mbeadh an Tuamach ag cleachtadh a ghnótha lena phuball dí sé mhíle déag ó bhaile sa chás sin. Aonach Áth Dara an láthair is oiriúnaí don eachtra, mar ná fuil an baile sin ach sé mhíle slí ó Chroma. Tá feicthe againn gurb é sin an láthair a thug an scoláire Luimníoch Dónall Ó Briain don eachtra agus é ag scríobh sa bhliain 1789. Más amhlaidh a bhí Éamonn de Bhál ar an bhfód agus é ar cuairt i dtigh Ridire an Ghleanna, dhealrófaí go mór gur roimh bhás an Ridire sin ar an 10/8/1737 a thit an eachtra amach. Timpeall ar an mbliain 1734 a chuaigh an Tuamach i mbun cheird na tábhairneoireachta, agus dá bhrí sin is é is dóichí gur am éigin sa tréimhse 1734-1737 ba cheart a chur síos don eachtra agus do phréamh bhunaidh an scéil. An 27ú Márta agus an 14ú Deireadh Fómhair na dátaí a bhí ag an dá mhór-aonach in Áth Dara san 18ú Céad.[69] Is léir, ach go háirithe, gur chuir filí na Máighe agus a gcairde spéis sa scéilín agus gur bhaineadar sult agus greann as. Ba mhar a chéile ag pobal na Mumhan é go ceann dhá chéad bliain ina dhiaidh.

SUMMARY

This article discusses one of the stave-anecdotes most popular with storytellers in Irish-speaking Munster. It concerns a conversation in verse between two poets, one of whom is selling liquor in a tent which he has erected at a fair. The anecdote has been collected in this century from the oral tradition of all six Munster counties, and in addition from County Galway. From both implicit and explicit references in these late versions, it is clear that the ancedote has to do with the Maigue circle of poets in eighteenth century County Limerick. The anecdote also occurs in traditional manuscripts of the eighteenth and nineteenth centuries, all of which have the Maigue poets as actors in the narrative. The earliest manuscript containing the anecdote dates from 1754, which is contemporaneous with the poets in question; but for various reasons, here discussed, this version must be regarded as partially inaccurate. The most important version from a historical viewpoint dates from County Limerick itself in 1789. It names the actors as Seán Ó Tuama (the Croom publican-poet who predominates in most versions), Aindrias Mac Craith (a celebrated rake and lifelong associate of Ó Tuama), and Éamonn de Bhál (a poet from County Cork). This is taken to be the basic form of the story. It is clear, however, that the story has always been an oral, rather than a literary one, and the syntax of the verse varies in an interesting manner from version to version. From early times, it tended to take on the traditional pattern of two poets recognising each other through their verse, and this process is discussed. In such secondary versions — which are widespread — the blind Tipperary poet Liam Dall Ó hIfearnáin takes the part of the visitor to the tent. Various evidence is adduced to suggest that Ó Tuama and Mac Craith were the participants in the original episode which gave rise to the story. The types of data used as evidence are chronological, geographical, contextual, and thematic. The article attempts to synchronise these multiple strands, and concludes that the anecdote is likely to have sprung from a real encounter between Ó Tuama and Mac Craith — the latter accompanied by de Bhál — at a fair in the village of Adare, County Limerick, sometime during the period 1734-37.

NÓTAÍ AGUS TAGAIRTÍ

1. Cnuasach Bhéaloideas Éireann (CBÉ) i Roinn Bhéaloideas Éireann S485, 326-8.
2. *Béaloideas*, 17, 63 (= CBE 93, 19, i lámhscríobh Chaoimhín).
3. *Béaloideas*, 17, 70.
4. Cf. Gaughan, J. Anthony, *The Knights of Glin* (Kingdom Books, 1978), 71; Ó Foghludha, Risteard, *Éigse na Máighe* (Baile Átha Cliath, 1952), 280.

5. Maidir leis, cf. Ó Foghludha, Risteard, *Ar Bruach na Coille Muaire* (Baile Átha Cliath, 1939), 13-35.

6. Cf. *Éigse na Máighe*, 35-66.

7. Lámhscríbhinn i seilbh Mhainchín Seoighe, Baile Thancaird, Cill Mocheallóg, Co. Luimnigh.

8. *Béaloideas 25* (1957), 75; CBÉ 218, 304 (an seanchaí céanna S423, 778-79); 256, 78-79; 387, 424-27; 702, 42; 772, 201-2; Téipeanna an Ollaimh Bo Almqvist, Roinn Bhéaloideas Éireann, 1970:3.

9. CBÉ S 460, 510; 862, 171-72.

10. CBÉ 126, 245; 964, 517-19; 995, 220-22; S466, 227.

11. *Loch Léin*, Eanair 1904, 96.

12. Lsí. Thorna, Coláiste Ollscoile Chorcaí 97, 123 (= CBÉ 845, 164); CBÉ 776, 536.

13. CBÉ 45, 323; 45, 355; 211, 108-9; 841, 246.

14. Cf. Ó hÓgáin, D., 'Friotal na hÉigse' (tráchtas Ph.D. d'Ollscoil Náisiúnta na hÉireann, 1978), 187-201. Tá gaol idir eachtraí mar seo agus Tíopa 873 in Aarne, Antti, Thompson, Stith, *The Types of the Folktale* (Helsinki, 1961). Cf., leis, Ó hÓgáin, D., 'Eoghan Rua, an File mar Laoch', *Feasta*, Feabhra 1980, 23, 25.

15. CBÉ 913, 20-1 (an seanchaí céanna S316, 125-26); S311, 202-3.

16. CBÉ S306, 88-89.

17. CBÉ 1283, 105.

18. CBÉ 54, 422.

19. CBÉ 84, 358.

20. CBÉ 85, 328.

21. CBÉ 861, 1046.

22. CBÉ 11, 52-53 (an seanchaí céanna 417, 98-9).

23. CBÉ 97, 148-50.

24. CBÉ S622, 70-71. Is cosúil go mba leasainm coitianta ar Liam Dall é 'Dall Bán'. Dhealrófaí gur saghas ailbínigh ba ea Liam — cf. CBÉ S580, 264, 271; agus *Ar Bruach na Coille Muaire*, 17-18, 34. Tagraíonn grafnóir ó Chill Síoláin, Co. Thiobraid Árann, sa bhliain 1827 (Lsí Choláiste Ollscoile na Gaillimhe 24:107-8) do 'Liam Bán Ó hIfearnáin Shrónaill' mar leanbh á luascadh chun codlata ag 'Liam Dall'. Ach ba ó Shrónaill Liam Dall, leis, agus is léir gur trí dhearmad nó de bharr grinn atá an dá phearsa déanta as ansiúd.

25. Ó Duilearga, S., Ó hÓgáin, D., *Leabhar Stiofáin Uí Ealaoire* (Baile Átha Cliath, 1981), 286-87.

26. *Irisleabhar na Gaedhilge*, 9 (1899), 334; CBÉ 182, 765-66; 811, 454-55.

27. I gcomhair thagairtí, cf. an Clár Cártaí i Roinn Bhéaloideas Éireann faoi 'Filí: Raifteirí' agus 'Filí: Mac Suibhne'.

28. Ar lgh. 10-11 den dara heagrán, a foilsíodh sa bhliain 1850.

29. RIA (.i. Lsí Gaelacha Acadamh Ríoga na hÉireann) 1386, 228i-228iii.

30. RIA 774, 316i-317ii.

31. Ar an leathanach teidil.

32. Lsí na níosánach, Sráid Líosan, Baile Átha Cliath, 1L 2, 212m. Is cósúil go bhfuil macalla ón rannscéal againn in amhrán ólacháin a bailíodh i gcomharsanacht Mhuileann na hUamhan, Co. Thiobraid Árann, sa bhliain 1863 (i gcló in Ó hÓgáin, D., *Duanaire Thiobraid Árann*, ((Baile Átha Cliath 1981), 41). 'A bhuachaill ó mo chroí, tá an bhraich agus *hop* go daor' atá i líne amháin de chuid an amhráin sin, agus tá aicill idir an 'go daor' ansin agus 'gan díol' i líne eile.

33. Lsí Choláiste Ollscoile Chorcaí 63, 776.

34. Lsí Choláiste Ollscoile Chorcaí 63, 777.

35. RIA 1386, 228ii.

36. RIA 28,1.

37. Cf. Catalóg an RIA.

38. Lsí Choláiste Phádraig, Má Nuad C62(g), 18i.

39. Cf. Ó Madagáin, Breandán, *An Ghaeilge i Luimneach* (Baile Átha Cliath, 1974), 28, 75-77.

40. RIA 722, 127i.

41. Maidir leis, cf. Ó Foghludha, Risteard, *Seán Clárach* (Baile Átha Cliath, 1933).

42. *Éigse na Máighe*, 78-79.

43. *Éigse na Máighe, passim* agus 136-8; *Seán Clárach, passim*.

44. Tá ainm Sheáin Uí Bhriain scríofa ar leathanach de chuid na lámhscríbhinne seo (RIA 722, 128). Tá ainm an scoláire chéanna breactha sa bhliain 1764 ar an lámhscríbhinn ó Cho. an Chláir Má Nuad MIII (lch 28).
45. Féach, mar shampla, na Catalóga do na Lsí Gaelacha san RIA agus i Musaem na Breataine. Tá téacs na véarsaí i gcló in *Éigse na Máighe*, 178-80.
46. RIA 774, 317i.
47. I gcló in Ua Duinnín, Pádraig, *Filidhe na Máighe* (Baile Átha Cliath, 1906), xxiv.
48. CBÉ S329, 134-37.
49. Lgh xxxii-xxxv.
50. CBÉ S580, 273.
51. Cf. RIA 907, 118; *An Claidheamh Soluis* 10/5/1903, 3; CBÉ 808, 3-4; S580, 262, 295. Ní miste a rá gur chaith Seán Clárach tamall ag cur faoi i gCo. Thiobraid Árann (*Seán Clárach*, 21, 61-62).
52. Cf. *Irisleabhar na Gaedhilge*, 17 (1907), 320; *The Irish Press* 19/8/1935, 4; CBÉ S580, 262.
53. Scéilín ón 9ú Céad mar gheall ar an bhfile cáiliúil Senchán Torpéist agus an bhanfhile Ingen Uí Dulsaine — i gcló in *Anecdota from Irish Manuscripts*, 4(1912), vii-xvii, 90-94.
54. RIA 774, 315-16i; RIA 1386, 227-28i.
55. De réir leagain den scéal seo a bailíodh ó bhéaloideas Luimnigh sa Chéad seo (CBÉ S498, 209-10), bhí an Tuamach as láthair nuair a bhuail an Crathach isteach ag lorg na dí le gliceas, rud a thugann tacaíocht do leagan an Dálaigh seachas leagan an Anracháanaigh. Is móide an tábhacht a chuirfear ina leith seo má chuimhnítear go raibh an insint in *Filidhe na Máighe* (a foilsíodh sa bhliain 1906) bunaithe ar leagan an Anracháanaigh. Is cosúil, mar sin, nach ar fhoinse chlóite atá an leagan Luimníoch seo — a bailíodh i mBrú Rí sa bhliain 1938 — bunaithe. Tá sé ráite sa leagan seo, leis, nár aithin Bean Uí Thuama an Crathach. Ní foláir nó bhí aithne mhaith aici ar Aindrias ag an am i ndáiríre, áfach, agus ní dócha dá bhrí sin gur leis an eachtra seo a bhain móitíf an aitheantais go bunúsach.
56. Catalóg 'H. and S.', le hEoghan Ó Comhraí san RIA, lch. 47.
57. Maidir leis, cf. Ó Foghludha, Risteard, *Cois Caoin-Reathaighe* (Baile Átha Cliath, 1946).
58. *Cois Caoin-Reathaighe*, 13, 61, 76-78; *Seán Clárach*, 18-19, 22-3; *Éigse na Máighe*, 60.
59. *Cois Caoin-Reathaighe*, 84-86.
60. Cf. *The Knights of Glin*, 69, 148-50.
61. *The Knights of Glin*, 69-71. Bhí dlúthchaidreamh idir an Longánach féin agus an Tuamach, ar ndóigh — cf. *Éigse na Máighe*, 227-30.
62. Cf. fonóta 24 thuas.
63. Cf. CBÉ 340, 327-9; 812, 418-20.
64. Bhailigh Seán Ó Cróinín leagan de iomarbhá eile i mBaile Bhuirne, Co. Chorcaí (CBÉ 573, 325). Níl aon ainmneacha tugtha ar na filí sa leagan úd, ach deir an Cróiníneach i bhfonóta gur airigh sé seanduine ag insint an scéil i bhfad roimhe sin agus gur 'Seán Ó Tuama an ghrinn agus an Mangaire Súgach (Aindrias Mac Craith)' a bhí i gceist ann. Baineann an leagan seo den scéal le file a d'aithin file eile a bhí ag díol dí ar na ráiseanna, agus is léir go bhfuil an suíomh seo ar iasacht ón rannscéal atá á phlé againn. Tá tagairtí eile béaloidis don 'Mhangaire Súgach' in CBÉ 1251, 130 (Co. Chiarraí), agus in CBÉ 1394, 249 (Co. Phort Láirge).
65. Ní miste a lua anseo, leis, go bhfuil an ceathrú líne i leagan amháin ó Phort Láirge (CBÉ 85, 328) an-oiriúnach don tuiscint seo, viz. 'Is maith an ceart, mar tá sí i bhfad sa chomhar gan díol!'
66. Cf. *Éigse na Máighe*, 60-65, 128-36, 157-60.
67. *Abridgement of All the Irish Statutes* (Dublin, 1736), 14.
68. *Éigse na Máighe*, 44, 77-78.
69. John Ferrar, *The History of Limerick* (Limerick, 1767), 463. Tá cúig dháta eile, maraon leis an dá cheann sin, tugtha in Lewis, Samuel, *A Topographical Dictionary of Ireland* (London, 1837).

Míthuigbheáil i Measc na nGael

SÉAMAS Ó CATHÁIN

Díol spéise iad cuid mhór de na scéalta atá cláraithe faoi Thíopa AT 1699 san *Types of the Irish Folktale*[1] ní hé amháin ó thaobh na scéalaíochta de ach ó thaobh na Gaeilge de chomh maith mar go mbaineann siad le ré na Gaeilge nuair ba láidre agus ba líofa ar na saolta deireanacha seo í i mbéal chainteoirí Gaeilge a bhí ar bheagán Béarla nó go mba daoine aonteangacha amach is amach iad.[2] I bhformhór mór na scéalta seo is idir cainteoirí Béarla agus cainteoirí Gaeilge a tharlaíonn na heachtraí ina mbíonn míthuigbheáil de chineál éigin i gceist, agus ní beag an léiriú a thugann an chaismirt seo ar mheon an phobail i leith theangacha na tíre seo gan trácht ar an léargas a thugann siad dúinn ar chuid de shainchomharthaí na gcanúintí Béarla agus Gaeilge ó cheann ceann na tíre.

Bhí sé d'ádh ar Chaoimhín Ó Danachair — agus is cinnte go ndéarfadh sé féin go raibh sé de phribhléid aige chomh maith — bualadh le mórán mór cainteoirí Gaeilge den tseort seo, daoine den chineál chéanna a mbíthí ag insean na scéalta seo orthu, le linn a chamchuairte ar Éirinn ar thóir an bhéaloidis, go speisialta ins na blianta a chaith sé ag triall ar ghleanntáin uaigneacha agus ar imeallacha iargúlta na tíre ag déanamh ceirníní do Choimisiún Béaloideasa Éireann.[3]

Cinnte cinnte casadh na cainteoirí Gaeilge agus na seanchaithe Gaelacha is fearr dá raibh in Éirinn san am sin air, agus maith mar a tharla, casadh leis chomh maith céanna ceann de na scéalta seo de chuid AT 1699 a bheas idir chamánaibh anseo — scéal nach bhfuil aon trácht ar bith ar Bhéarla ann ar chor ar bith, ach ina áit siúd scéal ina bhfuil cineálacha éagsúla Gaeilge ag dul chun spairne le chéile. Is foinse phléisiúrtha eolais iad na scéalta beaga seo ina bhfuil macallaí dubhacha mhórán cineálacha Gaeilge le haithneachtáil, agus is mór an trua nach bhfuil ach dornán beag uilig acu le fáil i measc ábhair uile AT 1699 in Éirinn.

I gcuideachta Thaidhg Uí Mhurchú, an bailitheoir iomráiteach béaloidis ó Uíbh Ráthach a bhí Caoimhín nuair a tharla an eachtra seo thíos:

We were in north County Clare — we were in Moloney's pub in Fanore, actually — and Tadhg Murphy said with regard to a storyteller who was there, he whispered to a man beside him and said:

'Cad é an t-aos atá aige?'
And the answer it was:
'Cad ab áil leis taos?'
Aos is masculine in South Munster, as you know. It is *aois* elsewhere.[4]

Níl a fhios agam ar tugadh míniú foirmeálta gramadúil ar dhá inscne an fhocail seo *aos* as a n-eascraíonn an mhíthuigbheáil seo ar an láthair inste an lá úd i gContae an Chláir. Ins an insint seo, glactar leis go bhfuil an t-eolas riachtanach sin ag an lucht éisteachta nó gur léir dófa fírinne an phointe gramadaí ar a bhfuil an scéal bunaithe, mar a thugann mana beag Chaoimhín 'as you know' le fios. Gan aon amhras, tá iarracht bheag den acadúlacht ag baint leis an scéilín seo agus, dá ndéarfainn é, le formhór na scéalta seo uilig; ach b'fhéidir gurb é sin is dual dófa — dreach bheag acadúil den chineál seo. B'fhéidir go ndéarfaí chomh maith gur ró-acadúil ar fad atá scéal mar seo chun go n-aireofaí ina scéal béaloidis ar chor ar bith é, agus gur sampla cumtha — scéilín uaigneach aonaránach — amháin é. Dálta chuid mhór scéalta arb é an breithiúnas céanna seo a tugadh orthu, ní hannamh go bhfaightear amach ina dhiaidh sin gur 'cumadh' faoi dhó nó faoi thrí iad sa chéad pharóiste nó sa chéad chontae eile. Bíodh is nach bhfuil aon tuairisc againn ar aon sampla eile den mhíthuigbheáil seo *aos/(t-)aos* — de thairbhe a laghad uaireanta a tugadh faoi deara ag macasamhail Uí Dhanachair agus Uí Mhurchú é seachas a laghad uaireanta a tharla a leithéid de chomhrá idir Cláiríneach agus Ciarraíoch — ní hionann sin agus a rá nach bhfuil fáil ar rudaí eile den chineál chéanna ón cheantar chéanna. Féach an scéilín seo thíos, mar shampla, a thóg an Br. M.S. Ó Flaithile síos i gContae an Chláir:

> Bhí file san áit seo fadó. D'airigh sé trácht ar mhuintir Chiarraí agus dúirt sé go raghadh sé chomh fada le Ciarraí go bhfeicfeadh sé cén sórt daoine a bhí ann. Bhailigh sé leis nó gur chuaigh sé isteach i bpáirt de Chiarraí. Tháinig an lá fliuch. Thóg sé lóistín i dtigh beag ar thaobh an bhóthair. Bhí ansin beirt ghearrbhodaigh agus pota beag prátaí beirithe acu. Chuireadar síos pota beag eile uibheacha. Bhí ansin an triúr ag ithe. Do bhain an file an barr den ubh agus nuair a bhí sé ite aige, do chaith sé an plaosc ar an urlár. Rángaigh don mhadra breith ar an bplaosc. D'uaidh sé é.
> 'Itheann do mhadra na huí (bheacha).'
> 'Itheann, agus itheann ina sheasamh,' a dúirt an gearrbhodach. . . .[5]

Ar an chomhfhuaim [nə hi:] atá an mhíthuigbheáil agus an greann ag brath sa scéal seo agus féach gur baineadh úsáid as féidearthacht eile de chuid na comhfhuaime céanna, mórán, mar seo thíos i mBaile Bhuirne:

> Bhí fear ó Bhaile Bhuirne ar aonach i Magh Chromtha uair. Bhí sé ina chodladh istigh i dtigh ar feadh na hoíche. Ar maidin níor éirigh sé in aon chor nuair a glaodh ar na daoine eile. Fé dheireadh, do tháinig fear go dtí an doras agus dúirt sé:
> 'An bhfuileann tú id' shuí fós?'
> Ach d'fhreagair an fear istigh agus dúirt sé: 'Dá mbeinnse im' thuí is fadó a bheinn ite ag na buaibh!'[6]

Ní cúrsaí canúintí, ach oiread, ach imeartas focal de chineál eile atá taobh thiar den ghreann agus den mhíthuigbheáil sa chéad scéal eile — sampla Corcaíoch eile ó Lámhscríbhinní na Scol:

> Lá amháin, bhuail buachaill beag óg isteach ag triall ar tháilliúir. Bhí culaith ghorm ar an mbuachaill. Dealraíonn sé ná raibh aon ró-fháilte ag an dtailliúir roimis. Seo mar a labhair an táilliúir leis:
> 'An tusa an buachaill beag gorm (beag orm)?'
> Thuig an garsún gur 'beag orm' a bhí ina chroí aige dó agus thug sé an chaint seo mar fhreagra air: 'Ní lú leat é ná é thú!'[7]

As Cuan Dor sa chontae chéanna don tríú scéilín seo ina bhfuil meascán eile

seachas meascán canúnach i gceist. Ó Sheán Ó hAodha a thóg Mícheál Ó Cuilea-
náin an scéal seo agus mar seo leanas a scríobh sé chuig an Seabhac faoin scéalaí:

> Fuaras an scéal agus na giotaí eile ó Sheán Ó hAodha ón gCreig láimh le Cuan Dor. Do
> saolaíodh agus do tógadh ar an mbaile sin é agus a athair roimis. Deir sé go bhfuil a mhuin-
> tir ann os cionn trí chéad bliain. Iascaire is ea é agus é dhá bhliain déag agus trí fichid
> d'aois. Bhí sé ina chaptaen báid tamall dá shaol agus níl aon chuid de chósta na hÉireann
> nach eolach dó. Do labhair sé Gaelainn le muintir Chonamara, le muintir Mhaigh Eo,
> muintir Thír Chonaill agus le muintir Ó Méith. Tá mórán focal Mainnise aige leis. Saor
> báid agus fear seolta a dhéanamh, leis, é. . . .[8]

Mar is léir, ba duine neamhchoiteanta an Seán Ó hAodha seo agus ní hionadh ar
bith go mba eisean a bhí ciontach leis an scéal seo a thugann Mícheál Ó Cuilea-
náin dúinn faoin teideal 'Crua-Ghaelainn'. Seo thíos anois é:

> Ní mar a chéile a labharthar an Ghaelainn in áiteannaibh eile. I gContae an Chláir agus i
> gConnachta 'fata' a deirtear in ionad 'práta'.
>   Bhí bád ag gabháil ó Thrá an Aonaigh go Port Láirge le hualach prátaí agus bhí bád
> ó Chontae an Chláir ag iascach taobh amuigh de Phointe an Ghealaí.
>   Cheap muintir Thrá an Aonaigh go mb'fhéidir go bhfaighidís beagán éisc uathu agus
> chuadar fé thómasc an bháid eile.
>   Tháinig duine des na Cláírínigh go taobh a bháid féin agus prátaí beirithe ar mhéis
> aige.
>   'Níos ás an fata,' a dúirt sé le duine den chriú eile.
>   'D'íosfainn go maith dá bhfaighinn é,' arsa an fear eile.
>   Chuir sé an cheist chéanna ar thriúr nó ceathrar acu agus fuair sé an freagra céanna.
>   'Níl caint úr ndúthaí féin agaibh,' a dúirt sé. 'Dúirt mé libh gur aníos a fhásann fata
> agus níor chreideabhair mé. Ar nóin, ní anuas a fhásfadh sé.'[9]

Is doiligh domh a chreidbheáil go n-inseofaí scéal mar seo taobh amuigh den
limistéar ina bhfuil an focal *fata* i réim — murab é leithéidí Sheáin Uí Aodha. Is
cinnte go bhfeilfeadh suíomh Connachtach i bhfad Éireann níos fearr dó ná
suíomh Corcaíoch agus seans gurab é aistriú an scéil ó dheas — más é sin anois an
rud a tharla — agus an t-athmhúnlú a rinne an scéalaí seo air chun lonnú logánta a
sholáthar dó is cúis leis an chiotrúntacht bheag a bhaineann leis mar scéal.[10]

Cleasaíocht focal eile — ach cleasaíocht nach bhfuil a oiread sin clisteachta ag
baint leis — seachas difríochtaí canúnacha atá sa chéad scéal eile. Ó Ultaibh a
thig sé seo agus ba é Énrí Ua Muirgheasa a chuir i gcló i *nGreann na Gaeilge* é sa
bhliain 1913. 'Fear Úr!' an teideal atá aige air agus seo thíos anois é:

> Fear a fuair bás uair amháin agus bhí a bhean ag greadadh agus ag caoineadh i dtigh na
> faire agus bhí a croí dá réabadh agus dá bhriseadh. Bhí sí ag greadadh is ag caoineadh:
>   'Faraor, faraor, a Mhichíl, go bhfuil tú i do luí ansin.' Bhuail bean glún ar mhnaoi eile.
>   'An gcuala tú sin?' a deir sí.
>   'Caidé sin?' arsa an bhean eile.
>   'An gcuala tú an rud atá an bhean adaí a rá i measc a cuid caointe — "fear úr, fear
> úr," agus gan Mícheál faoi fhód go sea aici.'[11]

Ós ag déileáil go príomhdha le hábhar ina bhfuil tús áite ag na difríochtaí
canúnacha seo atá muid, is mithid dúinn pilleadh ar an téad sin ar ais anois agus
ár n-aghaidh a thabhairt ar shampla maith den chineál cheart ó Chonnachtaibh.
Mar seo a thóg Tomás a Búrca (bailitheoir lánaimseartha) síos in Acaill é ó Mhícheál
Seoighe sa bhliain 1944:

Tá tamall ó shin, bhí fear as Co. Chiarraí nó mar sin as Co. Chorcaí – níl a fhios agam cé acu – ach bhí sé amuigh ar Oileán Acaill Beag. Bhíodh sé, leoga, ar na báid agus sílim gur ag míniú dófa leis na báid a oibriú a bhí sé. Nuair nach mbíodh siad ag iascaireacht, bhíodh sé ag fanacht i dteach ar an Oileán ar lóistín.

Bhí seanfhear sa teach agus gach uile oíche beo d'abraíodh sé an paidrín agus d'fhreagraíodh an mhuintir eile é. An oíche seo, ní raibh siad ag iascaireacht agus bhí an stráinséaraí istigh le haghaidh an phaidrín.

Bhí go maith. Chuaigh siad fríd an phaidrín agus nuair a bhí sé ráite acu, thoisigh an seanfhear ar Liodán na Maighdine Muire agus aniar ina dhiaidh d'abraíodh an stráinséaraí: 'Guí orainn, Guí orainn' – a d'abraíodh sé.

Bhí an seanfhear ag éisteacht leis agus níor mhoithigh sé a leithéid de chaint in am ar bith. Ar deireadh, chuaigh ar a fhoighid agus thiontaigh sé thart ar an stráinséaraí agus an-droch-chuma air:

'Ara, go mbascaí an diabhal thú,' ar seisean, 'nach bhfuil an tOileán ag fáil a sháith gaoithe gan tusa a bheith ag guibhe tuilleadh daoithi!'[12]

Ó Chorcaigh nó ó Chiarraí a tháinig an t-ainbhiosán stráinséartha seo, dar leis an Seoigheach úd, cé gur dóichí liomsa [gi:] Chúige Uladh ná [gi: g´] na Mumhan a bheith i mbéal an chuairteora mhí-ámharaigh seo ar an ócáid. Ní shin é is tábhachtaí le 'seanfhear' an scéil seo, ar ndóigh, ach go mba 'gaoth' (nó rud éigin cosúil léi) in áit 'guibhe' paidir an fhir eile.

Mar is léir, níl fairsinge mhór ar bith de na scéalta seo atá idir lámhaibh againn anseo le fáil in Éirinn agus ní miste cúis, nó cúiseanna, an tearcamais a lorg. An amhlaidh nach n-insítí go forleathan iad nó an amhlaidh nár bailíodh in am iad sular chlaochlaigh neart agus fairsinge na hithreach ina mbíodh siad ag fás? Nó an féidir i ndeireadh na dála nach eisceacht ar bith í an tír seo sa chomhthéacs seo mar go bhfuilthear ar an ghannchuid díofa seo, ní hé amháin in Éirinn, ach in áiteacha eile chomh maith – áiteacha ina mbeadh súil againn leo. San Fhionlainn, cuir i gcás, mar a bhfuil na cartlanna béaloidis ag cur thar maoil agus raidhse teangacha agus canúintí éagsúla in adharca a chéile le fada an lá?[13]

Má thógann muid an cheist dheiridh seo i dtús báire, is cosúil gur beag idir an Fhionlainn agus muid féin sa chás seo ins an mhéid is gur fairsinge go mór ábhar ilchineálach eile AT 1698 agus AT 1699 i dtraidisiún na Fionlainnise ná na scéalta áirithe sin atá idir lámhaibh againn anseo. Ina dhiaidh sin, is ceart a rá gur iomadúla go mór fada scéalta Fionlainnise de chineál na haiste seo ná an dornán beag samplaí Éireannacha díofa a léirítear anseo.[14]

Maidir le bailiú na scéalta seo in Éirinn, b'fhéidir gur leor a mheabhrú dúinn féin nárbh iad ba mhó go mbíthí ar a lorg agus gur minice i bhfad na bailitheoirí ar a ndícheall ag iarraidh scéalta fada Fiannaíochta sna ceantracha Gaeltachta ná sa tóir ar ghoblaigh bheaga mar iad seo dá bhlastacht iad. Thairis sin, is í páirt lucht inste na scéalta seo agus lucht a mbailithe araon is tábhachtaí liom ar fad. Iad sin is cúis leis an 'dreach bheag acadúil' ina ngléastar cuid mhór acu. Ba é an gníomhú catalaíoch seo ag Mícheál Seoighe[15] agus Seán Ó hAodha, ag Énrí Ua Muirgheasa agus ag an Bhráthair M. S. Ó Flaithile, ag Tomás a Búrca, ag Tadhg Ó Murchú agus, ar ndóigh, ag Caoimhín O Danachair a thug tromlach na scéalta seo chun tsolais ar an gcéad dul síos agus a sholáthraigh ag an am chéanna an cineál peirspictíochta a theastaíonn chun go bhfeicfí ina gceart ina dhiaidh sin iad.

SUMMARY

In Ireland, international tale types AT 1698 and AT 1699 encompass a wide range of material, including a number of stories based on comic misunderstandings which arise between speakers of different dialects of Irish. These anecdotes are the subject of this article. In Irish tradition, stories of such misunderstandings are rather rare, and are heavily outnumbered by stories of difficulties which arise between speakers of different languages – principally Irish and English. This situation of linguistic misunderstandings outnumbering dialectal ones is paralleled in Finland, where material of this kind has been more abundantly collected than in Ireland. The relative paucity of the Irish material may be due to its rather 'academic' quality – which would tend to make it less popular – and also to the fact that narratives of such brevity may not always have attracted the attention of collectors in Irish-speaking districts. The collectors were more accustomed to a diet of long hero-tales than to titbits such as these.

NÓTAÍ AGUS TAGAIRTÍ

1. Ó Súilleabháin, S., agus Christiansen, R.Th., *The Types of the Irish Folktale* (FF Communications 188, Helsinki 1963), 302-3.
2. Féach *Béaloideas*, 42-44 (1974-6), 120-35; agus 45-47 (1977-9), 84-117 áit a bhfuil cuntas ag údar an ailt seo ar mhórán scéalta eile de chuid AT 1698 agus 1699.
3. Tá cuntas suimiúil ar obair na mblianta sin le fáil in Ó Danachair, Caoimhín, 'Sound Recording of Folk Narrative in Ireland in the Late Nineteen Forties', *Fabula*, 22 (1981), 312-15.
4. Trascríobh ó thaifeadadh a rinne an t-údar ag Seimineár Iarchéime de chuid Roinn Bhéaloideas Éireann a tionóladh ar 25/2/1975. Scéalta AT 1699 an t-ábhar cainte a bhí ar siúl ann.
5. Cnuasach Bhéaloideas Éireann (CBÉ) i Roinn Bhéaloideas Éireann 103, 31. An Br. M.S. Ó Flaithile, Coláiste Chaoimhghin, Glas Naíon, Baile Átha Cliath a scríobh é seo sa bhliain 1936.

   Ach oiread leis na téacsanna eile anseo thíos, tá litriú agus poncaíocht an téacs seo athraithe agam lena gcur i gcosúlacht le Gaeilge na linne seo agus gach iarracht déanta agam ag an am chéanna gan aon ró-mháchail a dhéanamh ar na bunfhoirmeacha canúnacha.

   Cé nach gcuireann sé amach nó isteach ar bhunbhrí an scéil, is léir go bhfuil an chuid deiridh den insint seo in aimhréidh: is é an Ciarraíoch ar chóir dó "na huí" a rá agus ó cheart is é an Cláiríneach go bhfuil sé i ndán dó déanamh amach gur "ina shuí" a dúradh.
6. CBÉ S331, 343. Cáit Ní Shúilleabháin a thóg síos é seo ó Bhean Sheáin Uí Luasaigh (67), Carraig an Adhmaid, Baile Bhuirne, Co. Chorcaigh.

   Tá sé seo mórán ar aon dul le leagan eile den scéal a bailíodh ins an cheantar chéanna ó Phádraig Ó Coill (65), Na Millíní, Cúil Aodha, agus atá le fáil i CBÉ S330, 266.

   Is faoi 'Grinnscéalta' a cláraíodh an scéal seo (agus na scéalta eile ó Lámhscríbhinní na Scol a ndéantar tagairt dófa anseo) in Innéacs Chartlann Roinn Bhéaloideas Éireann agus ní faoi AT 1698 nó AT 1699 san *Types of the Irish Folktale*, op. cit.
7. CBÉ S314, 48. Humphrey O'Leary N.T. a thóg síos é seo ó Mrs. Crowley (80), Knocknagillagh, Bandon, Co. Cork.
8. Féach *Béaloideas*, 5(1935), 56.
9. Féach *Béaloideas*, 5(1935), 54.
10. Ní fheileann sé i gceart go n-abrann Cláiríneach 'fata' le Corcaíoch i gcomhthéacs an scéil seo agus é ag dréim go dtuigfear go réidh é. Tá brí an scéil ag brath ar éascaíocht tuigbheála agus ar an ábhar sin de d'fheilfeadh sé ní b'fhearr dá mba ag ceistiú na muintire seo aige féin a bhí an Cláiríneach seo in áit a bheith ag crá na gCorcaíoch a casadh air.

Faoi 'Cf. AT 1698' atá an scéal seo cláraithe ag Ó Súilleabháin, S., agus Christiansen, R.Th., op. cit., 301.

11. Féach Ua Muirgheasa, Énrí, *Greann na Gaeilge*, An Cúigeadh Cuid, An Dara Cló (Baile Átha Cliath 1913), 6.

Is ag brath ar an chosúlacht idir na fuaimeanna Ultacha [λː] agus [uː] atá greann doicheallach an scéil seo.

12. CBÉ 1012, 177-8. Tomás a Búrca a thóg síos é ó Mhícheál Seoighe (c. 55), H.A.O., Maigh Mhuilinn, Acaill, Co. Mhaigh Eo, 11/2/1944.

Déarfá go cinnte go mba macasamhail Sheáin Uí Aodha ó Chuan Dor 'Ciarraíoch' nó 'Corcaíoch' na heachtra seo — 'captaen báid', 'saor báid agus fear seolta a dhéanamh' a 'labhair. . . Gaelainn le muintir. . .Mhaigh Eo' agus gan 'aon chuid de chósta na hÉireann nach eolach dó' (feic lch 211). Níl ann ach caolseans gur Mac Uí Aodha a bhí ann, ar ndóigh. Níorbh nuaíocht ar bith iad stráinséirí den chineál seo aon am fud fad chósta na hÉireann agus ceird na hiascaireachta á teagasc acu faoi choimirce Bhord na gCeantar gCúng.

13. Tá flúirseacht scéalta bunaithe ar chúrsaí mhíthuigbheáil idir teangacha le fáil i gCartlann *Suomalaisen Kirjallisuuden Seura* (SKS). Lucht labhartha na Fionlainnise, na Rúisise nó na Sualainnise na dreamanna is coitianta a chastar ar a chéile ins na scéalta Fionlainneacha seo.

14. Tá na scórtha samplaí aonaránacha de scéalta den chineál seo le fáil ó mhórán gach uile chearn den Fhionlainn ach iad a bheith teoranta do cheantracha áirithe don chuid is mó. Ní hé amháin sin, ach is amhlaidh a bailíodh roinnt bheag de na scéalta seo chomh maith faoi dhó nó faoi thrí in áiteacha éagsúla thall is abhus tríd an Fhionlainn. Seo thíos leagan Gaeilge den scéal is flúirsí ar fad acu seo, scéal a bhfuil deich leagan de ar fáil i gCartlann SKS. *Sauna palaa* 'Tá an *sauna* trí thine' an teideal atá air agus míníonn sé an chaoi a ndeacha fear ó Oirthear na Fionlainne (Savo) a bhí ar cuairt in Iarthar na Fionlainne (Pohjanmaa) in abar i ngeall ar bhrí chanúnach an fhocail *palaa*.

Bhí fear ó Savo ar a bhealach isteach go dtí teach i Pohjanmaa nuair a chonaic sé go raibh an *sauna* i ndiaidh a ghabháil trí thine. 'Tá an *sauna* s' agaibhse trí thine,' (*sauna palaa*) a dúirt sé nuair a tháinig sé fhad leis an teach. 'Nach shin é go díreach mar is cóir dó a bheith!' a dúirt bean an tí. Nuair a thug muintir an tí an dóiteán faoi deara ar ball, seo mar a labhair siad: 'Go raibh tú ag an diabhal,' a dúirt siad, 'cad chuige gur dhúirt tú gur ina chaor (*palaa*) a bhí an *sauna* in áit a rá gur trí thine (*kyyttelee*) a bhí sé.'

15. Tá teipthe glan orm déanamh amach cad é an bhrí atá leis na litreacha 'H.A.O.' atá scríofa ag Tomás a Búrca i ndiaidh ainm an tSeoighigh seo (Féach Nóta 12 thuas). Is dóiche gurb é a bhí i gceist aige aitheantas a thabhairt do staidéas breise éigin a bhí ag siúl leis an tSeoigheach, agus ní bheadh a leithéid de chéim suas ag teacht salach ar íomhá chomónta lucht inste agus lucht bailithe na scéalta seo mar a léirítear san aiste seo é.

Baskets and their Uses in the Midlands

JAMES G. DELANEY

One of the most fascinating aspects of the fairy legend is the manner in which fantasy is woven into a tapestry of matter-of-fact and sometimes detailed everyday occurrences. Such a story is that from Donegal 'The Man Who Had No Story',[1] which tells of a professional basket-maker who found the rods for his baskets growing wild in his own district. Eventually, however, having exhausted this supply near home, he had to go farther afield to a deep and lonely glen, which because of its reputation of being haunted by the fairies, was shunned and avoided by all.

The description of the basket-maker in this story, the rest of which does not concern us here, struck the author as an exact portrayal of the basket-makers he has known in the midlands, and particularly in County Offaly. And to make the resemblance more striking, Bill Egan of Clonfanlough, of the latter county, who was himself a basket-maker, once showed me a place on the bank of the Shannon between Shannonbridge and Clonmacnoise, much like the lonely glen of the fairy legend above, where rods also were plentiful, but which was also shunned by men looking for rods, because they were 'in dread to go there'.

The author's interest in basket-making began in 1964 when he met Thomas Horan, then in his eighty-second year. Thomas lived in the townland of Ballyduff, in County Offaly, not far from the Westmeath border and only three miles from the Westmeath village of Ballinahown, where his parish church was situated. He told me that nearly every man in his young days could make his own baskets, of which there were various kinds, each for a different use, or as he put it, 'nearly every man could work rods'. He also told me that near every dwelling house, in addition to the usual kitchen garden, there was also a smaller garden, a special plot, set aside for the cultivation of osiers of different kinds, the golden osier and the green sally, or sallow, being the most common. This osier plot, or sally garden, was as well looked after as the kitchen garden, weeded regularly, and the rods pruned and kept in order with the greatest care. Even men who could not make their own baskets would still have their own osier plot, so that they could supply the material to the basket-maker when they needed his services.

Thomas Horan's father, a good basket-maker, was most assiduous in the care of his sally garden, and although he taught the craft to his son, he did not bequeath to him his own solicitude for the sally garden, which Thomas let fall into disuse. Times were changing and the 'skib' was going out of use. Certainly Thomas never made a 'skib', nor ever bothered to learn how, though he could, and frequently did make the heavier baskets so much used in his district, made from hazel rods, of which there was a plentiful supply to be had for the cutting. Thomas's son, Paddy, recently related that the little garden beyond the haggard, where the osiers were once grown, is still called 'the sally garden' though no osiers have grown there for many a long day.[2]

Only once, in Killeen townland, in the parish of Legan, County Longford, have I ever seen a sally garden, as described by Thomas Horan, though I have seen remnants of small ones in Carraroe, Connemara, County Galway. There are eight or nine stools of osiers in this garden, which is an extension of the kitchen garden, both being very carefully tended by their owners. Two kinds of osiers are grown, the green sally and the golden osier, but though they differ in colour and name, they both belong to the species known as *Salix viminalis*, or common osier, the variation in colour being due to hybridisation to which the latter is prone.[3] The rods are cut every year about November or December, made into neat bundles and placed against the wall of an outhouse, where they are left standing, exposed to the weather. In this way they mature slowly. Weak rods are not cut but left to grow for the second year, when they will be strong enough to use in the making of heavy baskets such as the 'cleeve', or back basket as it is sometimes called. In doing this the Kennys of Killeen were following the traditional custom handed on to them by their father.

Peter Byrne, of Treel townland, in the same parish of Legan, observed recently that it was essential to cut all the rods every year, except the weak ones, or 'they would grow into timber' and be useless for basket-making. He also said that sally gardens such as the Kenny's were not very common in the district in former times; that most men grew their osiers around the boundary fences of tillage fields, where they would be safe from marauding goats and donkeys, which were very common at the time.[4] There was one old basket-maker named Peter Clyne, in Byrne's district, who grew his supply of osiers in this way around the bounds of his one-acre labourer's plot evidently following the practice he was familiar with from his youth. He was nearing his ninetieth year when he died in 1979. However, in north County Longford 'most farmers had sally gardens, when I was young,' according to James Gilroy.[5]

Men like the Kenny brothers and Peter Clyne are exceptions, anachronistic if you like, and the growing of sallies for basket-making is a thing of the past, as are the traditional basket-makers who produced them. In the whole of the Irish midlands comprising an area within a fifty-mile radius of Athlone, the traditional centre of Ireland, it would be difficult to find more than two or three basket-makers like Thomas Horan, who learned the craft from his father, or Peter Clyne or Peter Byrne, who learned it from old basket-makers in their neighbourhood.

There were many types of baskets used in former times and even up to recently in north-west Offaly, where there were at least nine, each with its own particular name and function, associated with a custom and way of life that have disappeared forever, within the last forty or fifty years. The two baskets dealt with in this article survived into more recent times in isolated districts such as the north-west midlands and Connemara, County Galway, on the western sea coast 'beyond which no man dwells', as St. Patrick says in his *Confession*, where Gaelic is still the ordinary speech of the people. Though each of these baskets differed in the manner in which it was woven, and in shape, generally, yet they were often given the same name, 'skib', a word evidently cognate with the English 'skep', of which it is a Gaelic borrowing (Gaelic: *scib*), a sure sign of its antiquity and transmuted in the process and then retained in its Gaelic form, like many other words, in Hiberno-English. To avoid confusion here one type shall be named 'the cylindrical skib' and the other 'the boat skib'. The latter name is chosen because every one questioned about that kind of basket said 'it was like a boat.' However, in some districts, even in the midlands the word skib was unknown and the boat skib was known simply as a basket or sometimes potato basket because of the use to which it was put.

Sometimes before weaving the baskets, the rods were boiled and then peeled. The peelings came off in one piece, like taking off a stocking. That is how all the old men described it. An informant from County Roscommon who died about 1965 when in his nineties, observed how very strong ropes were made of these peelings, in the same way as making a thumbrope of straw or hay, and that they would last for years.

THE CYLINDRICAL SKIB

The cylindrical skib was a round flat-bottomed basket with a rim about three

Fig. 1   The cylindrical skib. The illustrations show a skib started with three rods at right angles to three, instead of twos as described in the text

inches deep so that in appearance it was very much like a sand riddle. It varied in diameter from about twenty inches to about twenty-four or thirty, and the weave for it began in the centre of the bottom around at least four rods, two of which were at right angles to the other two. They were kept firmly in place by making a slit along the middle of two rods and pushing the other two through at right angles approximately as far as their central points so that all four radians were of equal length (Fig. 1). The four rods were cut to the required length of the diameter of the bottom of the basket. The weave then began around the centre of the standards or radians, with a very light pliable rod (Fig. 2). According as the weave widened out stronger rods could be used. As the weave widened the radian rods were pulled wider apart, and other rods could be inserted if necessary to make more radians. When the bottom was finished two long rods were pushed in beside each radian (Fig. 3), one on each side, and these were taken at right angles to the bottom and tied together at the top of the basket (Fig. 4). The weave for the rim was begun through them to the required height of three inches or so. Then they were untied and woven through the rim to form what was called the 'binding'.

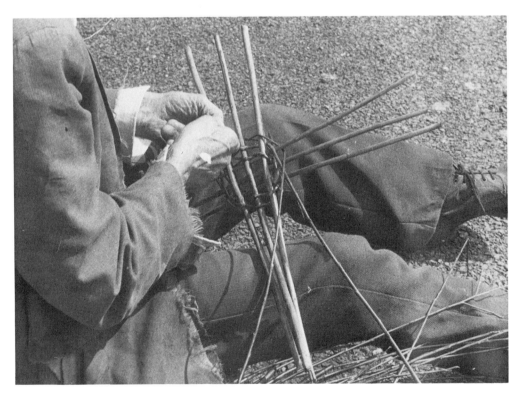

Fig. 2   The weave started

Fig. 3   Parallel rods being pushed in beside the radians

Fig. 4   The rods bent upwards to be tied at the top, prior to weaving the rim or 'binding'

THE BOAT SKIB

The word 'skib' was applied indifferently to the boat-shaped basket and to the cylindrical one in Roscommon and east Galway, while the word was not known at all in east Leitrim or north Longford, in both of which places the usual term was 'potato basket'. The make and weave of this latter basket were completely different from those of the basket already described. The basic requirements before starting the weave were a stout rim or 'hoop' as it was called, about an inch thick and long enough to be bent into a circular or oval-shaped hoop, the circle having a diameter about twenty-eight inches long; and five rods which served as standards or ribs. On this base the weave was made. The traditional hoop was what is known as a 'bucky brier', that is, a thick stem of the wild rose. In the course of time the bucky brier was no longer used, replaced by a strong hazel rod of the same thickness. Finally men began to dispense with the rod and used instead the rim of a bicycle wheel from which the spokes had been removed. However the description here is how it was made with the bucky brier, as that made by Peter Byrne of Treel, for the National Museum of Ireland on June 9, 1981.

Peter was asked to make the basket with the bucky brier hoop, as that was the oldest method known. He had great difficulty in finding a suitable one; such difficulty would explain why the briar went out of use. He found one at last though he was not too satisfied with it, but it was the best available. He left it for about a fortnight to allow it to season before he used it, and he had arranged with the author when to return, promising that he would not begin until he was present to see the entire work.

The bucky brier was seventy-two inches long and about an inch thick. This he bent into a circular hoop, overlapping three inches at each of the extremeties and tying them firmly together, having first pared them to form a lapped joint so that they fitted snugly into each other and made one continuous piece (Fig. 5). In former times this tying would be done with a strong wax-end, but Peter used a piece of binding twine from a used bale of hay. Next he took a strong rod about six inches longer than the diameter of the hoop and laid it across the hoop diametrically, so that there was an overlap of about three inches at each end. These overlaps he turned down over the rim of the hoop and looped then firmly around it, tying them with twine to keep them in place (Fig. 5). This was the main stretcher, as Peter called it. It was strong and not very pliable, so that, when fixed in place, it had only a slight curve. The curve on this rod obviously determines the depth the basket is to have. In the one under discussion the curve was slight, so that, when finished, it had the appearance of a shield or buckler of wickerwork, a shape that has given rise in some parts of Munster and in Wexford (which is Munster in its traditions and speech) to the Gaelic name, still retained in English speech, *sciath* or *sciathóg*.[6] (This word is unknown in the midlands.)

Having fixed the stretcher in place our basket-maker was ready to begin the weave. He took a rod and wound it around the hoop and around the stretcher, making two turns around the hoop for one around the stretcher. Another rod was woven around the hoop and stretcher at the other end in the same way, because in weaving this basket the weave is done alternately from each end and meets in the middle. When the weave was about two inches deep at each end he

Fig. 5   The boat skib. The rim or 'hoop' formed and the 'main stretcher' tied in place

took two more rods and pushed them into place in the weave at each end (Fig. 6). He then continued alternately to weave as before for three or more inches, when he inserted two more rods, one at each side of the stretcher. He wove through the five rods as before (Fig. 7) until both weaves met in the middle and the basket was finished (Fig. 8).

This then was the potato basket used in County Longford, up to about forty years ago, for straining the big pot of potatoes that were boiled every day for man and beast. The following description of how the basket was used is from James Gilroy, a native of the parish of St. Columbcille in north County Longford. He describes how the potatoes were boiled in a pot of four-stone capacity and when they were ready they were brought outside in the pot, with the basket, which

> was put on a flagstone by the drain leading from the kitchen door and the pot of potatoes was dumped on to the basket. The empty pot was taken inside and placed on the centre of the floor and the basket of potatoes placed on top of it, and the family sat around it on small stools. A plate with a large 'print'[7] of butter was put in the middle of the basket. Each person was given a porringer of buttermilk . . .
>
> When they were finished eating, any good potatoes were kept to make boxty and potato cake. The skins and the remaining potatoes were put back in the pot and pounded with meal for the hens.
>
> I was told that long ago people used to let the nails of their thumb grow long, and when they did not have knives they peeled the potatoes with the thumbnail. I know that they only took very little skin off, as they believed the best part of the potato was under the skin.[8]

Fig. 6   The weave proceeding, with the first pair of inner rods inserted

Fig. 7   The rods closest to the main stretcher in position

Fig. 8   The completed boat skib, held by the maker, Peter Byrne, of Treel, Co. Longford

This same basket, only more deeply curved was used also in Roscommon, where the cylindrical skib was also in common use. Here is a description of both skibs from County Roscommon from an old man, born about 1870, and who died about 1965. ('Teem' is from Gaelic *taomaim*, I strain off water, bale.)

> There were two kinds of skib, the boat skib and the clothes skib. The boat skib was shaped like a boat only roundier and was used for 'teeming' potatoes. The other skib was a big skib and the women used it for keeping clothes in, that they'd be after washing.[9]

The same informant gives a description of how this basket was used. The 'street' referred to is simply the portion of the yard outside the front of the house.

> When the potatoes were boiled, they used to bring the pot of potatoes out in the street, and they'd 'teem' the potatoes into the skib in the street. Then they'd bring the skib of potatoes and pot back into the kitchen, and put the pot in the middle of the floor, and the skib, full of potatoes on top of the pot. All the family would sit or kneel around the pot then. If they had a sup of milk they'd hould it under their oxters. Then they took the potatoes from the skib and peeled them with their fingers and ate them out of their hands.
>
> And that was how they ate the dinner. Very often they had nothing else to ate only the potatoes. I knew men eating potatoes three times a day. There were no knives or forks and the potatoes were peeled with the thumbnail.
>
> 'Dip one in the eye of the other' meant that one had nothing else to eat for any meal except potatoes.[10]

The Gaelic equivalent of this in Connemara was that one had *fataí agus scadán caoch* for dinner, that is potatoes and a blind herring, in other words nothing but potatoes. Another saying to which this condition gave rise was 'potatoes and dip'. The dip was whatever relish was to be had with the potatoes. In the lean years when every one had nothing but potatoes 'twenty-one times a week', as Patrick Kennedy puts it,[11] salt was the only dip available. Other substances were lard, bacon grease or salt herring, or in Connemara other salt fish such as eels or the local fish called *ballach* in Gaelic, or 'rock fish' in English, a species known as wrasse.[12]

Many stories in oral tradition have arisen from conditions prevailing at some particular time, and although they are very often apocryphal, the conditions which gave rise to them were all too true and known to all. It was this fact that gave them their peculiar piquancy and attraction. Such is the one which is known as 'potatoes and point'. The story is that one family had a small piece of bacon hanging up over the fireplace, more for show than anything else, as they could not bring themselves to eat it. And when they were eating their dinner of potatoes, they pointed the potatoes at the bacon, and that was the only relish they had.

Even in the 1890s in Thomas Horan's district, meat must have been a luxury for dinner, especially for the children. He used to take delight in telling how the young lads, his contemporaries, in the neighbouring townland of Bloomhill used to taunt him and his companions from Ballyduff with a derogatory chant, about the poor fare they had for dinner. Ballyduff at that time was given its original Gaelic pronunciation, the nearest English spelling to the probable dialectal form would be Balya Duh. So they sang out:

> Balya Duh, suh! suh!
> Colcannon and no dip![13]

They could not afford even butter for dip.

Although meat may have been scarce for youngsters in the closing decade of the last century, the diet was becoming a little more varied and oaten meal and oaten bread were plentiful to vary the monotony of the potato diet. But when meal grew scarce coming up to the beginning of harvest-time people had to rely on the potato again, especially the youngsters. Thomas Horan observed on one occasion: 'Many a time I ate my breakfast out of a skib before going to school.' That would be in the first years of the 1890s.

It is evidence of how quickly a custom dies out that men in the same district as Thomas Horan, and only about ten years his junior, never saw the skib being used to strain potatoes, nor saw children eating their dinner from it. One man who is about seventy-five years old told me that he used to see the skib used to strain potatoes at a thrashing, where there would be up to twenty men having dinner together in relays. The potatoes were strained through the skib and then the skib of potatoes was put on the table.[14]

Where the custom of sitting around the potato basket lingered on, as in north and south Longford, meat and vegetables were now part of the dinner. An informant in the parish of Drumard in north Longford, speaking of his youth in the second decade of this century, says that only a big farmer, and there were few in his area, could afford to kill his own pig, but the ordinary people bought cheap Russian bacon. Fried in slices on the pan, with whatever vegetables were in season, this was put on a plate or dish of some kind and placed on top of the basket of potatoes and all the children sat around on stools. The man of the house and his wife took their dinner at the table.[15]

Peter Byrne, mentioned above, related[16] that both the cylindrical skib and the boat skib, the latter known both as skib and a potato basket, were used in his district for straining and retaining the potatoes, but the latter was preferred for this purpose, as the potatoes spread out more evenly on it, did not break and dried more quickly. He never saw the potato basket in general use. But in his young days about fifty years ago in the months of September and October, the oats not yet being ready, and no oatmeal available for supper (it would never occur to them to buy meal) people used to boil a big pot of potatoes for supper, where there would be nine or ten children in a house. (Big families were usual in those days.) The potatoes when boiled were strained through the potato basket as already described and placed on the pot and all the children sat around on stools. A pan of fried bacon was placed on top of the potatoes. This cheap bacon imported from America, was very popular at that time. The children had a knife and fork each and a plate. Peter Byrne said he often saw this in houses to which he used 'to ramble' (visit socially) in his young days fifty years ago. So times had changed from the days of the salt 'dip'.

In Carraroe, a Gaelic-speaking district on the coast of Connemara, the custom of using the potato basket (Gaelic: *ciseog*) was observed up to about thirty-five years ago, an old man aged seventy-five related recently. All the family knelt around the basket which was placed on a wooden tub into which the water had strained. If there was salt fish for dinner, such as salted eels or 'rock fish' (*ballach*) the fish was boiled with the potatoes, and then placed on a plate on top of them. Each took a potato from the basket, peeled it with the fingers and dipped it into the fish before eating it. He also told about the *scadán caoch*, or blind herring which has already been mentioned above.[17] The custom died out during the infant years of the elder members of his family, so that now none of them remembers ever eating dinner from the *ciseog*. The *ciseog* is what has been termed the cylindrical skib and is the only form known in this district.

Patrick Kennedy (1801-73) wrote several books describing the customs and traditions of the district around Castleboro, in his native County Wexford. He gives details of the straining of the supper potatoes through a basket into a tub, on the top of which the basket of potatoes was left for a short time to allow them to dry out: then they were 'spilled out' upon a table on which a cloth had first been laid.[18]

In one particular story[19] he tells, incidentally, of 'a poor woman that was straining her supper in a skeeogue outside her cabin door'. In a note to the story he explains how 'the skeeogue or flattish wicker basket, having received the potatoes and boiling water, lets the liquid off to the pool at the bottom of the yard.' He also explains that the word 'skeeogue' is derived from Gaelic *sciath* (a shield) which he spells 'skiagh'. Throughout his books, particularly the biographical parts, he gives the reader to understand that the usual diet of the people, and of himself and his school fellows included, was the potato and nothing else, and this in a county that was better off, comparatively speaking than most. Even the parish priest's usual supper was the same as the poor neighbours' who came to him to be fed, and the only thing distinguishing his supper from those around about him was 'a print' of butter as relish. Sometimes Father James 'enjoyed the luxury of hot cake and tea'.[20] Kennedy never mentions sitting around the potato basket or eating from it. So the custom had either died out, or it was never known in Wexford.

Mrs. S.C. Hall, (1800-81) who was reared in Bannow on the south coast of County Wexford in the early years of the nineteenth century and a contemporary of Kennedy, says in one of her books that the food of the people was improving in quality. Then she refers 'in a great deal' to her 'recollections', obviously meaning, the recollections of her early childhood in Bannow, to describe the food of the people as she remembered it. She describes 'the lower class of Irish as existing, almost universally on the potato'.

> We have known many families who very rarely tasted flesh or fish, and whose only luxury was 'a grain of salt' with their daily meals; we do not speak of families in poverty, but of those who laboured hard and continually, the produce of whose labour barely sufficed to preserve them from utter want. Generally, however, they contrived to have a salt herring with their dinners; this was placed in a bowl or dish, water was poured on it, and the potato dipped into it obtained a relish.

Some few lines farther on she describes the straining of the potatoes:

> in the basket . . . from which they are thrown on the table seldom without a cloth, and around it the family sit on stools and bosses (the boss is a low seat made of straw); the usual drink is buttermilk, when it can be had.[21]

Alongside the above description is a picture of the pot in which the potatoes were boiled and the basket in which they were strained beside it full of potatoes. The basket is cylindrical as I have described above. So both types of skib, cylindrical and boat skib were known in County Wexford, in the very early years of the nineteenth century, the latter in Kennedy's district and the former in Mrs. Hall's. Neither uses the word 'skib', Kennedy using the Munster Gaelic *sciathóg* and Mrs. Hall the English 'basket'.

Under whatever name, these baskets were associated with the staple food, the potato, from that very early time, and probably for long before. According to most scholars the potato became the staple food as far back as the beginning of the eighteenth century.[22] As times improved around the end of the last century and the beginning of the present one these baskets began to go out of use. Although used in isolated districts, and even there only occasionally as described by Peter Byrne above, up to almost the middle of this century, finally the custom of using them to strain potatoes died out altogether. One old man in the Slieve Bloom district of south Offaly never heard of the custom in his youth and had only heard one person using the word skib, an old man who used to visit the house when he was a child and say to him and his brother that they were too lazy to bring in a skib of turf for the fire. He had not heard the word used since that time over seventy years ago, until I brought it back to his memory. Very few men are now found who can make either of the skibs described above; only three or four in widely scattered counties are known to the author.

That the word skib was at one time very much a part of everyday speech, in County Roscommon especially, and its shape associated in their minds with the boat, the following story illustrates.

> A young man from the parish of Athleague, on route to America in a sailing ship, was blown back home again to the Port of Cork, by a westerly gale when about three-quarters

way across. All the passengers were sent home, while the ship went into dry-dock to be repaired, and they were to be notified when the ship was again ready for sea. At last word came for the young man to rejoin the ship. When the father read out the letter to his son, the latter refused to go, saying he would never put his foot on the deck of a ship again as long as he lived, after the awful experience he had had. The father replied; 'Well, if you have to go in a skib, you'll go!'[23]

NOTES AND REFERENCES

1. I am indebted to Professor Bo Almqvist for giving me a copy of this story.
2. Personal communication from Patrick Horan, March 11, 1981.
3. Letter from Mr. Donal Synnott, National Botanic Gardens, Glasnevin, Dublin, to whom I submitted specimens of sallow from Cos. Offaly and Longford: October 3, 1972.
4. Personal communication from Peter Byrne, January 27, 1982.
5. Letter from James Gilroy, Carrick-on-Shannon, Co. Leitrim: March 31, 1982.
6. I am indebted to Dr. Kevin Danaher, in whose honour this essay has been written, for the data about Munster usage in naming the boat skib. See his interesting article on the basket-maker in *Irish Country People* (Cork 1966.)
7. 'Print' is the usual word for a large portion of butter. Patrick Kennedy also uses it in a passage quoted later in this article.
8. Ref. 5 above.
9. Irish Folklore Collections in Department of Irish Folklore (hereafter IFC), MS. 1507, 451-2.
10. IFC MS, 1506, 118.
11. Kennedy, Patrick, *Banks of the Boro* (Dublin, 1867), 113.
12. Peadar Sheáin Ó Dónaill, An Caorán Beag, An Cheathrú Rua, Co. na Gaillimhe, who told me this on Easter Day 1982.
13. IFC MS, 1708: 395.
14. Personal communication from Kieran Darcy, Clonascra, Co. Offaly, April 5, 1982.
15. Larry Mulligan, Enaghan, Co. Longford, IFC tape-recording of December 3, 1970.
16. Peter Byrne, January 27, 1982.
17. Ref. 12 above.
18. Kennedy, Patrick, *op. cit.*, 191-92; idem, *Evenings in the Duffrey* (Dublin, 1875), 65-66.
19. idem, *Legendary Fictions of the Irish Celts* (London, 1891), 132.
20. idem, *op.cit.* (1867), 192.
21. Hall, Mr. and Mrs. S.C., *Ireland: Its Scenery, Character, &c.*, I (London, n.d., but c. 1847), 83.
22. MacLysaght, Edward, *Irish Life in the Seventeenth Century* (Cork, 1956), 256.
23. The story is from memory. It was told to the author by an old man named Michael Healy from the parish of Athleague, Co. Roscommon, in 1960. IFC MS, 1574, 36.

Finally, after this article was completed, I was reminded that the boat-shaped skib, and the cylindrical skib or a variant of it, were used by egg merchants for putting country eggs into a crate, for export. Women in north Longford kept a special one for collecting eggs, and it was called a 'flake'. The same happened also in the County Leitrim parish of Carrigallen.

The Double-edged Sickle

ETIENNE RYNNE

Archaeology and folk-life studies are kindred subjects, the latter being in many ways an extension of the former into contemporary or near contemporary times. Evidence from folk-life studies can usefully widen the archaeologist's experience so that he is no longer limited to interpreting his material by normal archaeological methods alone. Such evidence is not necessarily used by the archaeologist to provide an immediate answer so much as to present a wide range of possibilities. It is just such evidence that is used to suggest an acceptable answer to the archaeological problem discussed in this paper, an attempt which it is hoped will give pleasure to Dr. Caoimhín Ó Danachair, an able practitioner in the field of folk-life studies, in whose honour it is humbly offered.

Bronze Age sickles/reaping hooks[1] from Britain and Ireland are of more than one variety. Although Fox has classified them,[2] and although they can be grouped broadly under socketed (laterally or vertically[3]) and non-socketed headings, there is another criterion which has not been used, a feature which may well be functionally diagnostic, namely whether their blades are single- or double-edged. Generally speaking, the socketed varieties have double-edged blades and the non-socketed ones single-edged blades, but this is not wholly the case, though almost so. The peculiarity of the double-edged blades of many Late Bronze Age sickles has usually been mentioned by writers dealing with the artifact type, but no one has yet endeavoured to explain the function of the sharp outer convex edge. Fox suggested that the vertically socketed variety derived from the socketed knife,[4] something which would explain the double-edged blade but not its function.

Fox doubted that Bronze Age sickles were primarily for reaping corn, suggesting that they were for more general use such as in thatching, and perhaps even for ceremonial use, quoting the late first-century BC Pliny reference to the druids cutting the sacred mistletoe with a golden sickle.[5] Dr. Sian E. Rees, the most recent commentator, goes so far as to state that 'There can be little doubt . . . that the bronze sickle was not the main tool used for reaping in the Bronze Age . . . It is more likely that composite flint sickles were used as normal reaping tools throughout this period . . . .'[6] She later developed this with the following statement, albeit concerning iron sickles:

> Certainly, the range of work that would be required of curved iron [cutting] tools on an early farm site is prodigious, — the gathering of roofing and flooring and other building materials, and materials for basket-working are examples of non-agricultural functions

[which] as well as the more specifically agricultural functions of weed clearance and fodder gathering all provide alternative possible functions for tools which we might glibly assume were evidence for arable agriculture.[7]

This statement, however, does not answer the question of the sharp outer convex cutting-edge of insular Bronze Age sickles. Indeed, her considered opinion is that 'Whether or not the [sharp] outer edge had any function is difficult to say.'[8] Although she offered no suggestions herself as to its possible function(s), her statement above does provide some leads as to where an answer may be sought.

Some years ago, when watching a German-made film of Alan Berg's opera *Wozzeck*,[9] a story based in the Leipzig district in 1821, the writer was suddenly startled by a scene (Act I, Scene 2) showing Wozzeck and his friend Andres 'cutting sticks' in a misty countryside with clumps of sally bushes all around. They were, however, not so much cutting sticks as cleaning already-cut bundles of sallies. Gripping the bundles under one arm, they were pulling and pushing handled implements, apparently double-edged slightly curved blades set laterally to the handles, up and down along the bundles in order to smoothen the rods by removing small branches and incipient buds (Fig. 1). Immediately the insular Late Bronze Age double-edged sickles sprang to mind, and I felt that at long last a possible answer to the question of their sharp outer edge may have been unconsciously demonstrated in that scene.

Fig. 1   Cleaning/stripping sallies with a double-edged sickle

Unfortunately, recent efforts to discover exactly what the two men were doing and exactly what the tool-type used was like, have so far failed to produce results, but irrespective of that the possibility that the Late Bronze Age double-edged sickles may have been used for cleaning or stripping down sally rods for basketry or wicker-work had suggested itself. It is clear that the sharp convex outer edge of such sickles could not have been used to reap corn and that, indeed, it must have been used with a pushing motion, something only possible against reasonably stiff material — such as osier or sally rods. The double-edged implements would be used with a pull-and-push motion, thus doubling the speed and efficiency of doing the job — the inner concave cutting-edge could, of course, be also used for reaping corn during the short harvest period, but for the rest of the year its purpose would be to function in conjunction with the outer convex cutting-edge to strip sally rods. In this regard, it must be remembered that Late Bronze Age pottery vessels are extremely rare in these islands. While wooden and leather vessels must have been used instead, there can be no doubt that baskets must have played a very important role as containers at the time. It is therefore not surprising to find that there may have been a specialised tool-type associated with the work.

The blades of some of the double-edged sickles are relatively straight (Fig. 2A), whilst those of others can be of very curved shape (Fig. 2B). The reason for this differentiation is not clear, but it is always possible (a) that the two types were not exactly contemporary, (b) that they may have been used with different stages in the growth of the sallies (*e.g.* whether the buds were incipient or well developed), or (c) that only the straighter ones were used for cutting and cleaning sallies, the more curved variety for something else altogether.

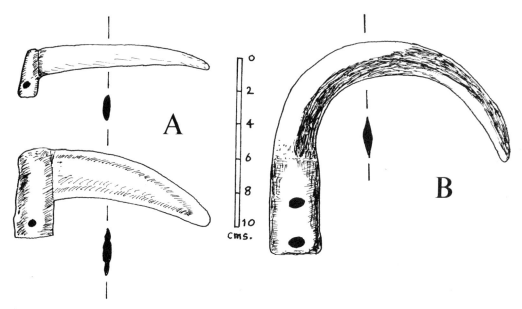

Fig. 2   Double-edged Late Bronze Age sickles: A — two varieties of the laterally-socketed type, with straight blade; B — vertically-socketed type, with curved blade

While the above-mooted suggestion may not be the correct answer to the problem of the double-edged sickle, it is offered in the belief that it provides a possible solution, one which might, at least, encourage re-thinking on the proper function of the tool-type.

NOTES AND REFERENCES

1. Strictly speaking, the term 'sickle' should only be applied to the balanced variety of short-handled cutting tool, the non-balanced or angular ones being more properly 'reaping-hooks'. The term 'sickle' has, however, become the standard one applied to all such prehistoric implements and so will be used throughout this article, especially as both types are involved in the thesis being discussed — see ref. 3 below.
2. Fox, C., 'The Socketed Bronze Sickles of Britain', *Proceedings of the Prehistoric Society*, 5 (1939), 222-248; idem, 'The Non-Socketed Bronze Sickles of Britain', *Archaeologia Cambrensis*, 96 (1941), 136-162.
3. The former (Fox's Group I) would be of reaping-hook type, the latter (Fox's Group II) more closely approaching the true sickle.
4. Fox, C., op. cit. (1939), 237, fig. 10.
5. ibid., 241-242.
6. Rees, Sian E., 'Agricultural Implements in Prehistoric and Roman Britain', *British Archaeological Reports*, British Series, 69 (1979), 448.
7. ibid., 450.
8. ibid., 449.
9. Adapted for television by Joachim Hess, with the Hamburg State Opera and the Philharmonic State Orchestra, Hamburg; the outdoor scenes were filmed 'on location'.

Gingerbread Hearts:
Symbols of Affection, Popularity and Honour

EDITH HÖRANDNER

Kevin Danaher is, on his own admission, very fond of Austria. Being familiar with the German language and the customs and way of life of much of Middle Europe, he must surely have come across the heart-shaped gingerbreads sold at local fairs which are often presented by a lover to his sweetheart, or brought home to those who could not attend as a token of remembrance. Generally, heart-shaped gingerbreads are also among presents to persons celebrating a jubilee, signalling the anniversary as well as being a symbol of affection; in connection with a group of performers (folk singers, or actors in folk plays, for example) these hearts stand for popularity with the common folk and the admiration of their followers.

The heart-shaped gingerbread can also be presented the other way round. For example, when the curator of the world-famous collection of engravings, the Albertina in Vienna, celebrated his sixtieth birthday, his guests were invited to his country house in Styria. Their celebrated host gave to each a gingerbread heart which had the name of his house written on it. Why are heart-shaped gingerbreads used in these contexts and how old is the practice?

The heart is commonly considered the centre of life and love, and therefore it is a basic motif of religious and profane iconography. The gingerbreads were produced from carved wooden moulds in which heart allegories and symbolism are found in abundance from the Baroque period onwards. They remained an integral part of the mould iconography, and later heart-shaped gingerbreads were achieved by other techniques.

The symbolism and allegories of the heart found on gingerbread moulds are applied in two ways. On the one hand the heart is part of a wider picture context, on the other hand the heart-shaped outline is in itself meaningful, enriched by additional motifs (often among them another heart) and scenes. Among the latter are floral ornaments, especially the 'tree of life', pomegranates and other symbols of life and fertility or, in Christian interpretation, of life everlasting.

The heart as part of a wider context usually refers to the love between two people. In a heart-shaped, round or rectangular frame there is often a scene which could well be entitled 'changing of hearts', a male and a female each holding a heart in their hands being about to exchange them. Very often these hearts show the flames of love, an iconographic conception dating from the beginning of the seventeenth century. Since the second half of that century (and the beginning of Baroque art) the 'heart in flames' (Fig. 1) has become the popular symbol of love of man, and also love of God. In the latter sense we find it as an attribute of saints

Fig. 1   The 'heart in flames' riding to the beloved person, spurred on by love and anxiety (the whip). This typical Baroque heart allegory was still familiar in the 18th and early 19th centuries. Detail from a mould in the Württenbergisches Landesmuseum, Stuttgart

on paintings and statues. The most famous 'saint with a heart' is St Augustine who is renowned for his 'language of the heart' (*Inquietum est cor nostrum usque ad requiescat in te, Domine!*).

Love is always considered to be 'hot' and 'burning', qualities which are adequately visualised by flames. There is, however, another heart symbol of love that was formerly also the attribute of saints, as of St Augustine again. It is also well-known from profane contexts. This is the heart pierced by arrows. The idea goes back to ancient times when the gods were thought of as sending good and bad things — love as well as plague — to man by means of arrows. These ideas were transposed into Christian ideology (cf. again St Augustine: *Sagittaversas tu [Domine] cor nostrum charitate tua et gestabamus verba tua transfixa visceribus*). The God of the Christians could also send epidemics and plague by means of arrows, as the well-known figure of St Sebastian shows.

The symbolic and allegorical language of the past was a rich and widely understood idiom. Some of it is still understandable without much trouble: thus the 'burning heart' riding on a horse and being spurred by love and anxiety (hence the whip) (Fig. 1), or the heart ripped apart (the saw!) by jealousy and anguish. Though the meaning of many allegories is evident, some need deciphering today when symbolic and allegorical language has been reduced to its rudiments. As far as heart symbols are concerned, we find mainly three: the heart itself, the heart with flames, and the heart hit and pierced by Amor's darts. Since the eighteenth and especially since the beginning of the nineteenth century and its products of memorial art and tokens of love and friendship, Amor was played down and the ancient god of love appears as a small and chubby putto.

The heart as a symbol of love was an appropriate present for engagements and at weddings. Besides gingerbreads in the shape of hearts and with appropriate signs and scenes on them we also know of heart-shaped white bread and of cakes baked in pottery or iron baking moulds in the form of hearts. Among the symbolism of the moulded 'engagement hearts' as they were formerly called, there were the two kinds of the 'hearts in love' already mentioned, the 'changing of hearts' between man and woman, the 'barred heart' (one closed with a big lock, a symbol of permanence alluding to the finality of marriage) and the 'handshake' (*dextrarum iunctio*). Marriage was considered to be a legal act and contracts were made by shaking hands. 'Handshake' used to be a synonym for both 'marriage' and 'engagement', since formerly the two ceremonies were identical (cf. the Scottish 'handfasting' regarded as a legal form of marriage).

Amongst the manifold variations of typical love symbolism only two more general principles need be pointed out. On the one hand, the heart held by a man and a woman (bridegroom and bride) signalling their union in love can be replaced by a lock or even by a babe-in-arms (the fruit of love), and on the other hand, instead of human beings, a pair of doves can have the heart between them. The pair of doves has been a symbol of lifelong affection and faithfulness since ancient times.

Equivalent to the love of man resulting in marriage is the love of God and the making of eternal vows. Accordingly, 'hearts of vows' were presented to nuns on the occasion of their spiritual marriage (Fig. 2). Of course these heart-shaped gingerbreads had religious symbolism on them, like the so-called 'monogram of Christ', IHS, the initials originally standing for the Greek *Iesous Christos Soter*, being 'translated' into German epithets with the same initials (*Iesus Heiland Seligmacher*).

Other religious symbols on these special hearts are the crown of thorns (often wound around a heart as symbol of the love of God for man), the nails of the cross (often three nails rising from a heart, the motif having some association with the tree of life in the form of a three-fold flower or branch, often coming from a heart instead of the typical vessel with two handles), and fruits that can be regarded as symbols of Christ or Christian virtues.

The heart as a symbol of the spiritual love of God became very popular during the Counter-Reformation when it was presented as gingerbread or shaped bread to nuns on their 'wedding day' as already mentioned. As an attribute and symbol of the mystical engagement with Christ the heart (with cross) is also found associated with female saints such as St Catherine of Siena (1347-80) and is referred to in legends; the motif of 'changing hearts' with Christ was reported of Catherine of Siena and also of St Luitgard of Tongern (1182-1246).

An outline of the heart can also be used to frame a scene on a mould and so on the gingerbread. In this strongly formal way the gingerbread heart can incorporate any motif at all, for example religious themes like the birth of Christ (Fig. 3), or scenes of the Easter liturgy (passion, resurrection) and profane themes such as the double eagle, coats-of-arms, the tree of life (Fig. 4), and many others. The motif was carved and the respective gingerbreads bought and presented on suitable occasions (Christmas, Easter, official banquets, when offering congratulations and good wishes at anniversaries or festivals).

Brief reference may be made to the fact that the gingerbreads were sometimes coloured and even gilded. This additional decoration heightened the glamour of the gift, and at the same time served to make coats-of-arms fully understandable and enhanced the overall symbolic effect. These colourful pictures and gilded

Fig. 2   'Heart of vows' presented to nuns on the day of their 'engagement' to, or 'wedding'
with Christ, their spiritual bridegroom. Mould in the Steirisches Volkskundemuseum, Graz

Fig. 3   Heart-shaped gingerbread mould showing the birth of Christ. Typical scene with infant Jesus in the crib, Mary (larger due to importance), Joseph and a shepherd, ox and donkey, the telling comet and the angel above the scene. Detail from a mould in the Heimat-museum, Feuchtwagen

Fig. 4   Heart-shaped gingerbread mould with stylised 'tree of life' and the typical pair of birds. The bird is a symbol of the soul, and a pair of birds live – as legends and myths tell – always near the tree of life, picking its fruits and drinking from the spring at its roots, thus obtaining eternal life. The motif could be universally used as a wish for fertility (engagement, wedding) or general well-being (generally or, with special relations, at New Year, on birthdays, etc.) It was also used with regard to spiritual occasions like baptism. Gingerbread mould in the Museum Calw

reliefs were used as wall decorations (like paintings) and they were put into glass-fronted cupboards as show pieces, but they could also be eaten. Colours applied were not always those suited to foods, which led to prohibitions the frequent repetition of which shows that they do not seem to have been effective.

For the festive official occasions of the noble and rich, marzipan was used instead of gingerbread and was moulded and gilded or coloured in the same way.

Gilding made the product shine resembling a metallic work of art, but it was also considered an appropriate means of presenting a saint in a becoming way. Saints are among the more frequent motifs cut into moulds since they were in continuous demand; gingerbreads showing the patron saint were presented by parents and godparents to children and vice versa. As in all other cases, these gingerbreads were bought at the small shops the bakers of gingerbread ran, which could be found even in small towns and villages, or at the various fairs they attended where they put up a stall.

The merely moulded and baked gingerbread showing the brown relief had a sober and even disillusioning effect by comparison with the coloured and gilded one, a contrast which led to coinage of the phrase 'to take the gilt off the gingerbread' which is still heard (or at least understood) today.

Towards the end of the eighteenth century moulds were carved which had space left for adding a name (in sugar decoration or by sticking on a slip of paper with the name written upon it) (Fig. 5). Gingerbread hearts presented at a wedding banquet very often carried the names of bride and bridegroom. In the early decades of the nineteenth century a period called 'Biedermeier' in Middle Europe, and especially in the realm of the Austro-Hungarian monarchy, people used to copy out or compose appropriate poems, small verses, 'home-made' lyric poetry, dedications and congratulations, and so on, in fine embellished handwriting on slips of paper and stick them on to gingerbreads, and also to other minor art forms then in vogue. All were presented and received as tokens of friendship, love and remembrance among all ages.

The first half of the nineteenth century saw widespread decline in the art of carving gingerbread moulds, but other forms of gingerbreads arose and they should be appreciated in their own right. As far as the heart-shaped mould is concerned, the space for icing and applied decoration became bigger and bigger, the carved motif of the mould being reduced to a garland following the outline (Fig. 6). Finally, merely the shape of the heart, at most accentuated for example by indentation, was used to mould the dough. Understandably this primitive mode of shaping demanded too much work when cut into wood, considering that an identical result could be obtained much more easily by using a metal cutter. These cutters were made much more quickly than the moulds and their production also demanded much less skill.

Since development of these late forms, wooden moulds have rarely been used in shaping gingerbreads, until they started to become collectors' items and were again employed to produce moulded reliefs in wax or other materials for decoration and often to be coloured or at least covered with some kind of patina.

Gradually the variety of motifs was reduced. However, around the time of the First World War the stock of cutters and printed motifs was still considerable, comprising hearts, riders, infants-in-arms, ladies and gentlemen, soldiers, watches, etc. Religious motifs were rare but not entirely unknown; for example it was

Fig. 5   Heart-shaped carved gingerbread mould, the circle being assigned for entering a name or wish, dedication or rhyme in sugar-icing or on a slip of paper on the moulded dough after baking. Excellent and rare example of the change from the carved mould (where even the words were carved and so unalterable, to be used only on identical occasions) and the later form where the heart was simply cut out of the dough and the words and decorations were put onto the baked gingerbread heart using a spout with white or coloured sugar ice. Wooden gingerbread mould, private collection

Fig. 6. Heart-shaped and garland-framed gingerbread mould, carved in wood, the empty area within the shape assigned for entering names, mottoes or verses. The carving is very much reduced, the form being very near the merely heart-shaped outline achieved by using a stencil and knife or a cookie-pattern. Carved wooden mould, collection of the German Bread Museum, Ulm

customary to present gingerbreads with a confirmation scene to a boy or girl being confirmed. These printed motifs came in big sheets, the single motif being repeated a few dozen times, each connected with the others by small 'bridges' of paper. When required the motif was cut off and stuck to the gingerbread by means of sticky sugar-ice.

New motifs were developed. Engelbert Humperdinck's opera *Hänsel und Gretel* generated a particular line of 'gingerbread renaissance'. The gingerbread house (*Knusperhäuschen*) of the witch became famous and was copied by housewives and even more by gingerbread bakers and confectioners, often presented as the masterpiece at the end of their apprenticeship. This holds true today. Hänsel and Gretel and the witch became popular motifs for gingerbread pictures, and at the same time were also 'painted' on gingerbread 'plates' with sugar-ice in white and various colours. Painting on gingerbreads was very much in demand in the 'twenties and 'thirties of this century, and reached its peak in the so-called 'artists' gingerbreads' of Munich where the new trend had started. Manufacture of such edible paintings has not survived. Printed pictures also went out of fashion except for two motifs, St Nicholas and his companion, the 'devil'. Down to our own time, around December 6 (the feast of St Nicholas, the day when children are presented with gingerbreads, nuts, oranges and small presents) the windows of bakers' and confectioners' shops are filled with oblong gingerbreads showing the figure or at least the face of the saint, and the devil in colour prints. These figures or faces, and small rectangles with verses on them are the only printed motifs still in general use. Whereas the old sheets of motifs are much sought after by collectors, the modern nostalgic movement stimulated sheet-production of motifs once again; it is still too early to judge whether it will last.

Generally, three motifs outlived all others: the heart, the rider, and the infant-in-arms. They were already popular when the last of the carved moulds were still in use and became more and more dominant as the painted and later forms of gingerbreads gained favour. Finally, apart from the special gingerbreads for St Nicholas's day, only the heart form survived. Since the former usually takes the form of a rectangular gingerbread plate decorated by the figure of the saint, so far as special shape is concerned, the gingerbread heart is the only significantly surviving outline.

Brief reference may be made to the general tendency to revert to old folk-art symbols and signs and to revive them. This movement was very strong in the 'thirties and 'forties and led to developments in the field of symbolic gingerbreads. Stencils (usually of cardboard) were cut at home or in the bakery, according to the suggestions of followers of the applied folk-art movement, and then decorated in symbolic detail by sugar-painting or icing. Similar examples are still made or have survived within individual family traditions.

The heart-shaped gingerbread, however, did not need any support to survive. The outline today is usually mechanically produced, the decoration often standardised, but its social contexts are as varied as ever (Fig. 7). It is — as it used to be — an integral part of the various fairs (parish fairs, seasonal fairs such as at Christmas, etc.) and can be bought at the numerous stalls around places of pilgrimage to bring home as a token of the pilgrimage, often carrying the inscription 'Memory of [place-name]'. In the Upper Austrian town of Gmunden it is presented as a 'gift of friendship' to everyone including tourists. Here, the decorated ginger-

Fig. 7   Typical stall of sweets including decorated heart-shaped gingerbreads, at a fair, Maria Enzersdorf, 1981

bread heart is an integral part of a custom which dates back to former times when the 'Corpus Christi Brotherhood' — members of which were well-to-do citizens of the town — presented the poor of the town with gifts. This was called 'to present love', and so it is called today. The custom took place on the fourth Sunday in Lent (*Lätare*), a day important in similar contexts in other parts of Europe. In England it was 'Mothering Day', when children went to visit their parents. The old custom fused with the new 'Mother's Day' which is celebrated in England on *Lätare*, and not on the second Sunday in May as everywhere else. 'Presenting love' in the form of a gingerbread heart in the revived version in Gmunden dates from after World War II.

Gingerbread hearts are a symbol of popularity, of affection, and of bestowing honour. They are still presented between lovers, to a person celebrating a jubilee, to a prominent visitor and to an honoured guest. They are given as private or official gifts, handed out to persons touring in Austria, and even if they are not as elaborate in their pictorial details as the moulded ones, their symbolism and functions are still fully alive. This article symbolises such a heart, presented to Kevin Danaher for his seventieth birthday, to the prominent scholar, the amiable personality, the helpful friend and, not least, the lover of Austria.

Note: This article is based mainly on material gathered in connection with the author's book *Model* ('Moulds'), published by Callwey Verlag Munique, 1982. The book contains an extensive list of relevant source materials.

An Crios Bríde

SEÁN C. Ó SÚILLEABHÁIN

Nós a bhaineann le comóradh traidisiúnta Lá Fhéile Bríde in Éirinn is ea nós an Chrios Bríde. Tá nósanna eile, leis, ag baint leis an lá sin; agus chun léiriú a thabhairt ar an mbaint atá ag an gCrios Bríde leo tugtar i dtosach báire anseo coimriú de phríomhghnéithe an lae sa saol traidisiúnta.

Is é Lá Fhéile Bríde, 1ú Feabhra, an chéad cheann de cheithre mórfhéilte ráithe na bliana faoin tuaith in Éirinn. Is iad Bealtaine, Lúnasa agus Samhain na féilte eile. Tá nósanna agus piseoga faoi leith ag baint le gach féile díobh. Ba é *Imbolc* nó *Oimelc* an t-ainm Ceilteach págánach a bhí ar thosach an Earraigh. Cé go bhfuil go leor eolais ar fáil faoi na féilte ráithe eile sa ré phágánach níl mórán eolais againn faoi *Imbolc* nó *Oimelc*, ach de réir dealraimh bhí baint ag an bhféile le séasúr bhreith na n-uan agus le níochán nó ionú. Cé go n-úsáidtear ainmneacha págánacha na bhféilte ráithe eile fós, tá *Imbolc* nó *Oimelc* imithe i léig le fada an lá mar ainm ar thosach an Earraigh agus úsáidtear Lá Fhéile Bríde ina ionad. Sa seanchas tráchtar mar a leanas ar ráithí na bliana:

> Ráithe ó Lá Fhéile Bríde go Bealtaine,
> Ráithe ó Bhealtaine go Lúnasa,
> Ráithe ó Lúnasa go Samhain,
> Agus ráithe ó Shamhain go Lá Fhéile Bríde.

Is í Bríd, Muire na nGael, ban-ab agus bunaitheoir Chill Dara, an naomh a chomórtar ar an gcéad lá d'Fheabhra. Mhair sí sa dara leath den chúigiú haois agus sa chéad cheathrú den séú haois agus is í an duine is cáiliúla de scata naomh den ainm céanna. Is cosúil gur ghlac Naomh Bríd chuici féin tréithe a bhain le bandia phágánach darbh ainm Bríd. Déanann roinnt scríbhneoirí tagairt dó sin, mar shampla:

> . . . it is in the person of her Christian namesake St. Brighid that the pagan goddess survives best. For if the historical element in the legend of St. Brighid is slight, the mythological element is correspondingly extensive, and it is clear beyond question that the saint has usurped the role of the goddess and much of her mythological tradition. The saint's *Life* infers a close connection with livestock and the produce of the earth.[1]

Ag tagairt do thréithe págánacha a bhaineann le ceiliúradh Lá Fhéile Bríde deir údar eile:

> The main significance of the Feast of St. Brigid would seem to be that it was a christianisation of one of the focal points of the agricultural year in Ireland, the starting point of preparations for the spring sowing. Every manifestation of the cult of the saint (or of the

deity she replaced) is closely bound up in some way with food production. . .[2]

Mar a deirtear ansiúd agus de réir údar eile, ba é Lá Fhéile Bríde tosach an Earraigh sa saol traidisiúnta in Éirinn.[3] Bhí dóchas i gcónaí ag cách, go mór mór na feirmeoirí agus na hiascairí, go dtiocfadh feabhas mór ar an aimsir ón lá sin amach. Deirtear sa seanchas gur gheall Naomh Bríd: 'Gach re lá go maith ó mo lá-sa amach'. Bhíodh lá saoire acu in áiteanna ar Lá Fhéile Bríde, go mór mór sna ceantair ina raibh paróiste, teampall nó tobar beannaithe coisricthe di. Bhí cosc faoi leith in áiteanna éagsúla ar aon obair a bhain le casadh; mar shampla, ní raibh sníomh, treabhadh nó obair le trucail ceadaithe. Deirtear sa seanráiteas: 'Bíonn Lá 'le Bríde ina shaoire ar chastaíbh.'

Is iad na Croiseanna Bríde, an Bhrídeog, an Ribín nó Brat Bríde agus an Crios Bríde na príomhghnéithe de chomóradh traidisiúnta Lá Fhéile Bríde in Éirinn. I ndáiríre chleachtaítí na nósanna seo ar an oíche roimhré, is é sin le rá Oíche Fhéile Bríde, mar chuireadh na Ceiltigh an oíche roimh an lá. De ghnáth bhíodh na croiseanna á ndéanamh ar Oíche Fhéile Bríde agus gach bliain chrochtaí ceann úr ar an díon nó ar an mballa sna tithe cónaithe, agus i gceantair éagsúla sna cróite leis, ionas go mbeadh an líon tí, na hainmhithe agus an fheirm go léir faoi choimirce Bhríde i gcaitheamh na bliana a bhí le teacht. In áiteanna ba cleachtais a bhí scartha óna chéile iad nósanna na gcroiseanna, an bhrait agus na brídeoige, ach in áiteanna eile ní raibh an deighilt sin eatarthu, mar ba ranna éagsúla de chleachtas amháin iad déantús na gcroiseanna, nós an bhrait, agus macasamhail

Fig. 1. Crios Bríde, Cill Rónáin, Árainn, Co. na Gaillimhe. Is as féar atá an crios déanta agus tá crois amháin air déanta as adhmad le píosaí deasa éadaigh uirthi.

Bhríde a thabhairt isteach sa teach. Tá cuntas maith ar an ngné seo le fáil i dtuarascáil ó Thír Chonaill a cuireadh chuig an gCoimisiún Béaloideasa i 1942, mar fhreagra ar cheistiúchán faoi Lá Fhéile Bríde. De réir an chuntais sin chaithfeadh duine as gach teaghlach dul amach tráthnóna agus beart luachra a bhaint. Bhéarfaí an beart abhaile agus d'fhágfaí é amuigh ar chúl an tí. Chaithfeadh gach duine ball éigin dá chuid éadaigh a chur amach mar bhrat Bríde agus chuirfí iad go léir i gcliabh lasmuigh. Ina dhiaidh sin d'éireodh gach duine as an obair. Nífidís agus ghlanfaidís suas iad féin chomh maith is dá mbeidís ag dul ar an Aifreann, agus chuirfidís orthu cibé éadaí maithe a bheadh acu. Phiocfadh an t-aos óg na prátaí i gcomhair an bhrúitín. Nuair a bheadh an suipéar réidh rachadh duine éigin amach chun an luachair agus na héadaí a thabhairt isteach. Chuirfí an luachair sa chliabh leis na héadaí agus thiocfadh an té a bheadh lasmuigh go dtí an doras leo. Chnagfadh sé ar an doras agus déarfadh sé:

> Gabhaigí ar bhur nglúine,
> Agus fosclaígí bhur súile,
> Agus ligí isteach Bríd!

Bhéarfadh an mhuintir istigh "'Sé beatha" mar fhreagra. Déarfadh an té amuigh an t-impí céanna dhá uair eile agus déarfadh an mhuintir istigh "'Sé beatha' an dara huair agus "'Sé beatha, 'sé beatha, 'sé beatha na mná uaisle' an tríú huair. D'éireodh fear an tí ansin agus d'oslcódh sé an doras agus ligfeadh sé isteach an té a bheadh amuigh leis an gcliabh. Bhainfí an luachair amach agus d'fhágfaí í ina luí i lár an urláir. Bhéarfadh gach duine leis a bhall éadaigh féin ansin agus bheadh dóchas acu go sábháilfeadh an brat Bríde iad ar gach caill agus gach urchóid ar feadh na bliana. Nuair a bheadh an brúitín réidh le n-ithe d'fhágfaí an pota ina shuí i lár an urláir agus shuífeadh an teaghlach uile thart air. Choisricfeadh fear an tí an bia agus déarfadh sé an t-altú bia. Tar éis an tsuipéir thosóidís ar na croiseanna a dhéanamh.[4]

Is léir ón tuarascáil sin go raibh an-tábhacht ag baint leis an bhféile. D'ullmhaítí suipéar faoi leith Oíche Fhéile Bríde. Roimh an mbéile chuirtí fáilte roimh Bhríd agus thugtaí macasamhail di, punann tuí nó luachra, isteach sa teach. In áiteanna dheintí crois i gcomhair gach seomra sa teach cónaithe agus i gcomhair gach cró leis, ach in áiteanna eile ní dheintí ach crois amháin, an ceann don teach cónaithe, nó dhá cheann, is é sin ceann don teach cónaithe agus ceann do chró na mbó. De ghnáth ghreamaítí na croiseanna leis na frathacha nó leis an scraith faoi dhíon an tí. Cé gur tógadh anuas an tseanchrois gach bliain in áiteanna, ba ghnáthaí na seanchroiseanna a fhágáil ann agus an ceann úr a chrochadh suas in aice leo. Dá bharr sin is iomaí teach a bhféadfaí a aois a áireamh ó líon na groiseanna a bhí sáite sa díon. In áiteanna eile ba ghnáth le lánúin nuaphósta sraith nua a thosú, agus i gcásanna mar sin d'fhéadfaí a áireamh ó na croiseanna cén fad a bhí lánúin ina gcónaí i dteach áirithe. Bhí dóchas ag na daoine go gcoimeádfadh an Chrois Bhríde an líon tí agus an fheirm slán ar feadh na bliana. Is mór an éagsúlacht atá ag baint le dearadh na gcroiseanna ó áit go chéile, le modh a ndéanta agus leis an mbunábhar atá iontu.[5]

Is é atá i gceist i nós na brídeoige ná dream daoine, ar a dtugtar *brídeoga* mar ainm, ag dul ó theach go teach ar Oíche Fhéile Bríde le macasamhail de Bhríd á hiompar acu agus bronntanas éigin á fháil acu i ngach teach. De réir na dtuairiscí is seanda is iad na páistí, go mór mór na cailíní, ba mhó a chleacht nós na brídeoige.[6] Cibé pástí nó daoine fásta, ba ghnách don dream a bheith i mbréagriocht don ócáid. Chaithidís éadaí ildathacha agus aghaidheanna fidil nó hataí tuí ag clúdach na haghaidhe. In áiteanna, chun cur leis an mbréagriocht, bheadh éadaí ban á gcaitheamh ag na fir agus éadaí fear ag na mná. Déanann roinnt de na tuairiscí tagairt d'éadaí déanta de thuí ar fad. An bhrídeog a thugtar ar an mhacasamhail Bhríde a bhíodh á hiompar ag na brídeoga. Chuirtí fíorchaoin fáilte rompu sna tithe agus measadh gur ceart bronntanas éigin a thabhairt dóibh. Fiú amháin mura mbeadh aon ní eile ag bean an tí le tabhairt dóibh chuirfeadh sí biorán sa bhrídeog. Deir an chuid is mó de na tuairiscí is seanda gur uibheacha nó prátaí nó bia de shórt éigin ba mhó a thugtaí do na brídeoga, agus chun deireadh a chur leis an oíche bheadh cóisir acu i dteach éigin leis an mbia seo. De réir tuairiscí eile roinntí idir baill na buíne an t-airgead a bheadh bailithe nó faighte de thoradh an bia a dhíol. Deir a lán de na tuairiscí a bhaineann leis an nós mar a chleacht daoine fásta é gur ghnáthach an t-airgead a úsáid chun rince agus cóisir feadh na hoíche — ar a dtugtaí *biddy-ball* — a bheith acu tamall ina dhiaidh sin i dteach éigin.

Ba ghnáthach in áiteanna ar Oíche Fhéile Bríde ribín nó giota éadaigh nó ball éadaigh a chur in áit éigin taobh amuigh den teach. I gceantair áirithe d'fhágtaí amuigh ar feadh na hoíche ar fad é. Bhí an nós seo forleathan ar fud na tíre. Chreidtí gur tháinig Bríd ar an ribín nó ar an éadach nuair a bhí sí ag taisteal mórthimpeall na tíre an oíche sin agus gur choisric sí é. Nuair a thógtaí isteach é chuirtí i dtaisce go cúramach é in áit shábháilte agus d'úsáidtí mar ba ghá i rith na bliana é mar bhíodh dóchas mór ag na daoine go raibh leigheas ar thinneas agus cosaint ar chontúirt ann.

Mar an gcéanna le nós na gcroiseanna Bríde — in áiteanna ba chleachtas a bhí scartha ó na nósanna eile é nós an ribín nó an bhrait ach in áiteanna eile ba chuid amháin den chleachtas foirmiúil é. Sa chleachtas foirmiúil seo ba ghnáthach ball éadaigh amháin nó ball le gach duine sa teaghlach a fhágáil taobh amuigh den doras in éineacht leis an luachair nó an tuí i gcomhair na gcroiseanna. In áiteanna bhíodh an t-éadach mórthimpeall na punainne tuí nó luachra agus in áiteanna eile bhíodh sé i gcliabh in éineacht le hábhar na gcroiseanna. Ansin ag am suipéir thógtaí isteach ábhar na gcroiseanna agus an t-éadach agus bheadh an t-éadach mar bhrat Bríde i gcaitheamh na bliana.

In áiteanna i gContae na Gaillimhe ba iad na cailíní a théadh ó theach go teach leis an mbrídeog agus do théadh na garsúin timpeall le Crios Bríde. Súgán tuí a bhíodh sa chrios de ghnáth. Bhí sé dúnta mar a bheadh fáinne nó ciorcal, agus de réir tuairiscí éagsúla bhíodh crois amháin nó a trí nó a ceathair de chroiseanna air. Chun a thairbhe a fháil b'éigean d'fhear nó do bhean an tí dul tríd an gcrios trí huaire. De réir roinnt tuairiscí ba chóir don teaghlach go léir an turas seo a thabhairt chun bheith faoi choimirce Bhríde i gcaitheamh na bliana a bhí le teacht. Tá cuntas ginearálta mar leanas i dtuairisc ar an nós ó Ros Muc, Contae na Gaillimhe:

Déantar crios Bríde freisin. Is é an chaoi a ndéantar é, faightear roinnt tuí agus déantar trilseán di. Ansin ceanglaítear a dhá cheann dá chéile agus ceanglaítear crois nó dhó nó níos mó déanta de luachair dhá bharr. Téann na gasúir thart lá Fhéile Bríde leis an gcrios seo agus faigheann siad pingin nó dhó in 'chuile theach. Nuair a thagann na gasúir ag teach téann 'chuile dhuine sa teach amach tríd an gcrios.[7]

Tá sonraí breise le fáil i dtuairisc ón Spidéal:

> Déantar an crios tráthnóna Lá Fhéile Bríde, san teach de ghnáth. Is é gnás na ndaoine é.
> Bíonn na buachaillí ar bís an oíche sin le seachtain roimhré, mar is iad a dhéanann í agus
> téann beirt acu thart léi. Uaireanta bíonn ceithre chúpla ag gabháil thart as an mbaile
> céanna. Tá trilseán sa gcrios agus é casta. Tá sé dúnta mar bheadh fáinne agus trí nó
> ceathair de chrosanna air.
>   Déantar an crios as tuí. Téann na buachaillí thart an bóthar léi ó theach go teach.
> Bíonn siad ó ocht mbliana go trí bliana déag d'aois. Bíonn an crios casta acu nó go
> dtéann siad isteach i dteach agus ansin osclaíonn siad í. Nuair a thagann siad isteach
> deireann siad:
>   'Seo í isteach an crios, crios na gceithre gcros,
>   Éirigh, a bhean an tí, agus téirigh trínár gcrios,
>   Agus pé 'bith caoi a bhfuil sibh anocht
>   Go mba seacht fearr a bheas sibh bliain ó anocht.'
> Téann bean an tí trí huaire tríd an gcrios agus coisríonn sí í féin leis na crosanna a bhíos
> uirthi. Tugann siad airgead dóibh ansin. Uaireanta gheibheann siad uibheacha. Roinneann
> siad an t-airgead eatarthu ina dhiaidh sin agus ceannaíonn siad milseáin ar chuid de.
>   Téann daoine eile sa teach tríd an gcrios freisin. Tugtar an crios ar ais go dtí an teach
> inar déanadh í. Ní coinnítear í ach go mbíonn Lá Fhéile Bríde thart.[8]

I dtuairiscí áirithe tá cur síos ar conas a dheintí an crios. De réir a bhformhór
ba as tuí, casta nó trilsithe mar shúgán, a dheintí é.[9] Act tá eisceachtaí ann. I
dtuairisc ó Mhaoras deirtear gur as luachair a dheintí é;[10] de réir tuairisce ón
Líonán d'úsáidtí tuí nó luachair[11] agus de réir tuairisce ó Inis Mór, Árainn, ba
féar a d'úsáidtí ann[12]. I dtuairisc a foilsíodh i 1889 tugtar le tuiscint nach n-úsáid-
tí tuí mura mbeadh ganntanas luachra ann.[13]
   Tá cuntas againn ón gCnoc ar mhodh déanta an chreasa:

> Bíonn an crios déanta de shúgán tuí. Castar an súgán i dtosach le rud nó deis a úsáid-
> tear le haghaidh na hócáide a dtugtar corr súgáin air. Déantar an súgán cúig nó sé slata
> ar fad, ansin é a dhúbailt agus é a fhíochán ar a chéile. Nuair atá sé fite cuirtear an dá
> cheann le céile sa gcaoi go mbeidh sé ina chiorcal. Cuirtear trí chroiseogaí air, in ainm an
> Athar agus an Mhic agus an Spioraid Naoimh.[14]

I dtuairisc ó Inis Mór, Árainn, deirtear:

> Is as súgán féir a bhíodh an crios Bríde déanta agus a dhá cheann ceangailte dho íochtar
> na croise. Bhí an crios dhá throigh déag nó mar sin. Ba gnás le cuid na daoinibh turas
> a thabhairt: is é sin dul isteach faoin gcrios trí huaire. Phógaidís an chrois agus is í an
> chos dheas a chuiridís amach ar dtús ag dul amach dóibh faoin gcrios. Bhí an chrois
> tuairim is dhá throigh ar airde agus troigh ar leithead. Bhíodh ribíní nó píosaí éadaigh
> deasa fuáilte don chrois.[15]

Sa chuntas atá luaite cheana a foilsíodh i 1889 deirtear:

> This is a rope made of green rushes, procured the day before, or if rushes be scarce, it
> is made of straw, with three green rushes plaited into it. The rope is made sufficiently
> long to allow a tall man to pass through the circle without difficulty when the ends are
> joined together to form the girdle.[16]

De réir tuairiscí éagsúla bhíodh crois amháin nó a trí nó a ceathair de chroiseanna ar an gcrios.[17] Ní deirtear ach i gcuntas amháin, an ceann ó Ros Muc atá
luaite cheana thuas (1ch. 245) go mb'fhéidir go n-úsáidfí dhá chrois ar an gcrios. I
gcónaí, beagnach, is as tuí a bhíodh na croiseanna déanta. I dtuairisc ó Charna,
áfach, cé nach bhfuil sé ráite cad as a dheintí an crios féin, tagraítear do chrois
bheag 'déanta de thuí nó de chipíní'.[18] Tá a fhios againn ón gcuntas as Ros Muc

atá luaite cheana (lch. 245) go ndeintí an crios ann as tuí agus go mbíodh croiseanna déanta de luachair air. Féar atá sa chrios ó Árainn atá léirithe ar lch. 243, agus adhmad atá sa chrois.

B'fhéidir gur féidir linn, uaireanta, glacadh leis an bhfianaise sa véarsa a bhíodh ag na garsúin maidir le líon na gcroiseanna ar an gcrios acu. Ach ní hamhlaidh don scéal i gcónaí, mar atá léirithe sa tuairisc ó Inis Mór, Árainn, atá luaite suas, ina ndeirtear go raibh crois amháin tuairim is dhá throigh ar airde agus troigh ar leithead ar an gcrios, ach luaitear 'crios na gceithre gcros' sa véarsa a d'úsáidtí.[19]

Garsúin a thógadh an crios mórthimpeall de ghnáth. Mar a chonaiceamar sa tuairisc ón Spidéal (lch. 246), ba ghnáthach beirt gharsún a bheith ann agus uaireanta bheadh ceithre bheirt nó cúig bheirt ón mbaile beag nó ón mbaile fearainn céanna ag dul thart. I dtuairisc amháin ó Indreabhán agus sa tuairisc dar dáta 1889 tugtar le tuiscint go mbíodh daoine fásta ag dul timpeall comh maith le garsúin.[20]

Tugann cuntas a foilsíodh san *Ireland's Own* i 1935 dearcadh maith ar an nós ó thaobh buachalla a bhí páirteach ann. Deirtear gur le dalta scoile as Sailearna, i bparóiste Chill Aithneann, an cuntas seo:

B'fhada mise ag fanacht le hOíche 'l Bríde. Sul má tháinig sé 'chor ar bith bhí 'chuile réiteach déanta agam féin agus ag an mbuachaill eile 'na comhair. Bhí crios déanta againn as tuí coirce. Crios breá láidir bhí inti, mar bhí trí duail inti agus fuinneadh breá fáiscthe. Bhí sí breá fairsing freisin i gcaoi is go bhféadfadh an tseanbhean ba mhó ar an mbaile dul isteach is amach inti. Oíche 'l Bríde, chomh luath agus thainic mé ón scoil chuaigh mé féin agus Colm Ó Gríofa ag baint brobh. Cheangail muid suas ina mbeairtín iad sa gcaoi go mbeidís go deas pointeáilte againn le scaipeadh ins na tithe agus nach mbeidís briste ná brúite. Le titim na hoíche d'éirigh mé féin agus Colm amach lenár gcrios agus lenár gceaintín agus lenár mbeairtín brobh. Le haghaidh uibheacha bhí an ceaintín againn. Is iomdha duine a mbeadh cúpla ubh aige nach mbeadh aon phighin rua aige agus sa gcaoi nach mbeadh aon leithscéal ag aon duine muid a leigean folamh ón doras is ea a thug muid an ceaintín — as teach an táilliúra — linn. Is é an chéad teach a d'fhág muid beannacht agus comharthaí an chreasa ann teach Mháirtín Pheaits.

B'é Colm fear an chreasa agus is aige a bhí dul isteach 'un tosaigh. Bhaineas féin mo chaipín díom agus shnámh mé isteach ina dhiaidh. Ach má bhíos-sa cúthail is beag an chúthaileacht a bhí ar Cholm ach é chomh teann le fear na ndeichniúr ag cur beannacht ar an teach.

'Seo í isteach mo chrios,
Crios na gceithre gcros;
Éirigh, a bhean an tí,
Agus téirigh thríd an gcrios —
Más fearr atá sibh anocht
Go mba seacht míle fearr
A bheas sibh bliain ó anocht!'

'Go mba hé dhuit, a dhriotháirín,' a deir Máirtín Pheaits agus a chomhluadar d'aon ghuth ón teallach. D'éirigh bean an tí agus choisric sí í féin le ceann de na crosóga agus chuaigh amach sa gcrios trí huaire. Ansin choisric sí na páistí leis an gcrios. Chuir Máirtín a lámh ina phóca agus thug sé trí pighne dhúinn. Ghlacamar buíochas leis agus thugas féin trí bhrobh do Mháire le crois a dhéanamh. 'Go mbeire muid beo ar an am seo arís,' a deir Máire. 'Amen' a deir muid féin, agus d'fhag muid slán acu.

Shiúl mé féin agus Colm an Baile Nua, an Baile Láir agus Baile an Logáin. Thugamar cuairt na crosóige ar bhunáite gach teach sna bailte sin agus d'fhágamar ábhar crosóige le déanamh ins gach teach dhá ndeachamar ann. Fuaireamar síneadh láimhe éigin ins beagnach 'chuile theach, cé gurb iomdha brobh a bhí fágtha romhainn i gcuid acu. Is iomdha beirt eile a choinnigh inár seasamh muid ag fiafraí dhínn cé mhéid a bhí déanta againn. Déarfainn féin go raibh an oiread de théagar faighte de bharr na hoíche againn agus a bhí ag beirt ar bith eile.

Nuair a chomhairigh muid tairbhe ár gcuid siúil i dtigh an táilliúra bhí toirtín deas airgid againn agus taoscán maith uibheacha. Ina cheann sin bhí oíche dheas thaithneamhach againn, agus muid tar éis croí óg a thabhairt arís do sheanchailleacha na mbailte seo! Dá mbeadh muid gan aon phighin a fháil ariamh air bheadh muid lán-tsásta tar réis a raibh de ghreann faighte againn ar na seanmhná ag dul isteach agus amach sa gcrios.[21]

Chun a thairbhe a fháil ba chóir do dhuine dul tríd an gcrios nó é a chur mórthimpeall air féin nó é a chorraí mórthimpeall ar a chorp. Mar a deirtear i dtuairisc ó Charna:

> . . . téitear tríd trí huaire. Cuireann sé seo an t-ádh ar an teach agus ar mhuintir an tí i gcaitheamh na bliana.[22]

De réir roinnt tuairiscí b'éigin don teaghlach go léir dul tríd an gcrios, ach de réir tuairiscí eile níor ghá ach amháin d'fhear an tí nó do bhean an tí dul tríd.[23] Sa tuairisc ó Inis Mór, Árainn, atá luaite cheana (lch. 246) agus sa cheann atá luaite díreach thuas ó Charna deirtear gur gnáthach dul tríd an gcrios trí huaire. Ina theannta sin ba ghnáthach in Inis Mór an chrois a phógadh. I dtuairisc eile ó Inis Mór tá breis sonraí le fáil faoi thuras a thabhairt tríd an gcrios:

> When houses were thus visited each of the parents used to gather up the rope. It would then be about two feet long. The rope and cross were then taken in the right hand and with the face of the cross inwards it was moved around the body three times — being changed from the right hand to the left as was necessary to complete the circle — saying at each round 'In the name of the Father and of the Son and of the Holy Ghost.' It was not folded around the waist as a belt would be.
>
> Next the parents went through the rope with the right foot foremost, the cross in the right hand, and the rope and cross passed over the head saying 'In the name of the Father and of the Son and of the Holy Ghost.' This was done three times.[24]

Ó pharóiste Chill Aithneann deirtear.

> Chaitheadh gach duine dul tríd an gcrios sin — é féin a choisreacan leis an gcrois ar dtús, ansin an chois dhead agus an lamh dheas i dtosach, agus dul trasna tríd ansin.[25]

De réir na tuairisce a foilsíodh i 1889:

> . . . the master of the house holding it doubled up in his right hand makes the sign of the cross with it in the name of the Trinity and passes it three times from right to left around his body. Then holding it out at arm's length in his right hand he lets one end drop so as to form a circle, through which he passes three times, putting the right foot through first each time. He then doubles up the rope and again passes it three times around his body as at first. He is followed in turn by every member of the family. In some cases the girdle is simply laid on the floor in the shape of a circle and each one passes through it by lifting up one side to step under, and then raising the other side to step out again.[26]

Tugann Caoimhín Ó Danachair cuntas dúinn ar an tslí cheart chun turas a thabhairt:

> The 'proper' way of going through the *crios* by men was, first the right leg, then right arm and shoulder, next the head, then left shoulder and arm, then left leg: Women put it down over head, shoulders and body and then stepped out of it.[27]

Tá leaganacha éagsúla ann den véarsa a d'úsáideadh na garsúin nuair a thugaidís cuairt ar theach leis an gcrios. Deir an chuid is mó acu ar dtús go mbeadh an crios ag na garsúin agus críochnaíonn siad le dea-ghuí. D'úsáidtí an leagan seo i Leitir Móir:

Crios Bríde mo chrios —
Crios na dtrí gcros —
Pé ar bith cé rachaidh trí mo chrios
Go mba seacht fearr a bheas sé bhliain ó inniu![28]

Tá leaganacha eile den véarsa níos faide agus i gcuid acu déantar tagairt do Chríost nó don Mhaighdean Mhuire, Naomh Pádraig, na hAspail, nó naoimh eile.

Seo leagan a foilsíodh i 1892:

Crios Bríde na gcros —
Crios na gceithre gcros,
Crios le ar gineadh Críost —
Críostaí a gineadh as.
Éirigh suas, a bhean an tí,
Agus gabh trí huaire amach
In ainm an Athar agus an Mhic agus
an Spioraid Naoimh. Amen.[29]

Foilsíodh dhá leagan ón gCeathrú Rua i 1942:

Crios, crios, crios na gceithre gcros,
Crios na gcineadh maithe,
Máire d'fhan istigh agus Bríd chuaigh amach,
Agus an té a chuirfeas pighin in mo phóca-sa,
Go ma seacht míle fearr a bheas sé bliain ó inniu![30]

Crios Bríde mo chrios —
Crios na gceithre gcros —
Bríd a chuaigh amach,
Máire a d'fhan istigh!
Pé an chaoi a bhfuil tú inniu,
Go mba seacht fearr a bheas tú bliain ó inniu![31]

I leagan ó Inis Mór, Árainn, déantar tagairt do Mhuire agus do Bhríd:

Crios, crios Bríde mo chrios —
Crios na gceithre gcros —
Muire a chuaigh ann,
Agus Bríd a tháinig as!
Más fearr atá sibh inniu,
Go mba seacht fearr a bheas sibh bliain ó inniu![32]

I leagan eile ó Inis Mór tá Bríd is Pádraig luaite in ionad Mhuire is Bhríde faoi mar atá sa leagan deireanach.[33]

Deineann leagan ó pharóiste Mhainistir Chnoc Muaidhe tagairt do naoimh is do na hAspail:

Crios Bríde mo chrios,
Crios na naomh deas,
Crios Aspal Chríosta
A dtáinig Bríd as.
Cé a chuireas comaoin ar mo chrios
Go mba seacht fearr a bheas sé bliain ó inniu![34]

I leaganacha éagsúla tá línte áirithe dírithe ar an bhean an tí — mar shampla, sa leagan atá luaite i gcuntas ó bhuachaill scoile (lch. 247). Tá an leagan sin an-chosúil leis an gceann seo ó timpeall na háite céanna:

Seo í isteach mo chrios —
Crios Bríde mo chrios,
Crios na dtrí gcros!
Éirigh suas, a bhean an tí,
Agus téirigh tríd an gcrios!
Más fearr atá sibh anocht
Go mba seacht bhfearr a bheas sibh bliain ó anocht![35]

I leagan ó pharóiste Chill Bheanáin, in ionad a rá le bean an tí turas a thabhairt tríd an gcrios, iarrtar uirthi ubh a thabhairt mar bhronntanas do na garsúin:

Éirigh suas a bhean an tí,
Tabhair dúinn ubh na circe buí
Atá thuas i dtóin an tí,
Is ná crádh Dia do chroí![36]

Lorgaítear pingin nó ubh mar bhronntanas i leagan as Órán Mór, agus moltar do bhean an tí a páiste a chur tríd an gcrios:

Crios, crios Bríde mo chrios —
Pingin as póca bhean an tí,
Nó ubh as tóin na circe buí
Atá thoir i dtóin an tí!
Éirigh suas, a bhean an tí,
Is cuir do pháiste faoin gcrios.
Más fearr ag gabháil ann é,
Go mba seacht bhfearr ag teacht as é![37]

De réir tuairisce ó Mhaigh Cuilinn d'úsáidtí an leagan seo ann:

Crios Bríde mo chrios —
Crios na gceithre gcros —
An té nach rachadh tríd an gcrios
Go mba seacht míle fearr a bheas sé bliain ó anocht![38]

Sa tuairisc seo leis deirtear go ndéarfadh siad 'go mba seacht míle measa a bheas sé bliain ó anocht' don duine ná rachadh tríd an gcrios.

Ó thaobh mallachta de arís tugtar an leagan seo i dtuairisc ó Ros Muc:

Crios Bríde mo chrios —
Crios na gceithre gcros —
An té nach dtabharfadh pingin dom
Go mbrise an diabhal a chos![39]

Luaitear an leagan seo i dtuairisc eile as Conamara:

Seo í isteach crios Bríde agaibh —
Crios na gceithre gcros —
An té nach rachadh tríd an gcrios
Ní móide go mbeidh sé beo bliain ó inniu![40]

Sa tuairisc leis an mbuachaill scoile atá luaite cheana (lch. 247) agus i dtuairisc ó Indreabhán[41] deirtear go raibh beart brobh comh maith leis an gcrios ag na garsúin ag dul thart agus gur fhág siad trí bhrobh as an mbeart i ngach teach ar thug siad cuairt air. I dtuairisc as Inis Mór, Árainn, deirtear go dtógadh na daoine soip as an gcrios agus go gcuiridís faoin díon iad.[42]

De réir roinnt mhaith tuairiscí ar an nós, d'fhaigheadh na garsúin rud éigin i ngach teach.[43] Mar shampla, i dtuairisc as Leitir Mór deirtear: 'D'fhaigheadh na buachaillí nó na stócaigh pingeacha nó uibheacha ar an gcuma chéanna agus a d'fhaigheadh na cailíní ar an mbrídeog.'[44] De ghnáth ba airgead nó uibheacha a d'fhaigheadh siad mar bhronntanas, ach i dtuairiscí ó Inis Mór, Árainn, deirtear gur prátaí nó airgead a d'fhaightí.[45]

De réir corrthuairisce dheintí crios mór in áiteanna agus thiomáintí na hainmhithe tríd an gcrios sin chun go mbeadh an rath orthu sa bhliain a bhí le teacht.[46] Mar shampla, i dtuairisc as Ros Muc deirtear:

> Bhíodh sé de nós fadó an crios seo a chur ar dhoras an sciobóil sula dtagadh na beithígh amach mar deirtí go mbeadh rath orthu go ceann bliana.[47]

Tá tagairt amháin do chrios i mBeathaí Bríde agus baineann sí le scéal faoi Bhríd ag tabhairt a creasa do bhean bhocht.[48] I gcuntas i mBeatha Bríde ó Leabhar an Leasa Mhóir deirtear gur tháinig bean áirithe chuig Bríde ag lorg déirce agus go raibh an bhean seo beo bocht i gcónaí. Thug Bríd a crios di (*go tard Brigit a criss di*) agus dúirt Bríd go leigheasfaí pé teidhm nó galar lena gcuirfí an crios. Sin a tharla, agus is mar sin a shaothraigh an bhean a beatha as sin amach.[49]

Tá bua seo an leighis a bhaineann leis an gcrios i scéal na mBeathaí níos cosúla le bua an leighis a bhaineann leis an Ribín nó leis an mBrat Bríde sa seanchas. Bua cosanta ar dhochair, ar aicíd nó ar mhí-ádh a bhaineann leis an gcrios féin sa seanchas.

SUMMARY

The custom known as the Brigid's Girdle is traditionally associated with the feast-day of St. Brigid in Ireland. The feast falls on the first day of February which, as the beginning of spring, was one of the four cardinal points in the calendar of the ancient Celts. The original name of the festival was 'Imbolc' or 'Oimelc', but it has become christianised as St. Brigid's Day. The general history and tradition of St. Brigid are outlined, with particular emphasis on those elements of her cult which have survived in folk life down to our own time. Such include the Brigid's Cross, the Brigid's Ribbon or Mantle, and the Brigid's Girdle. They also include the colourful custom called the *Brídeog,* which consisted of a group of people going from house to house on the eve of St. Brigid's feast carrying an effigy of the saint. The members of this group were usually disguised, wearing festive clothing and masks, and were given small presents in the houses they visited. In County Galway, it was often the girls only who went around with the *Brídeog,* whereas the boys travelled from house to house with the Brigid's Girdle. This Girdle usually consisted of a straw rope, closed in a circle, and decorated with crosses. It was believed that to pass through this rope three times gave protection from misfortune during the ensuing year. Various oral accounts of the making of this Girdle are cited, as well as of the custom of bringing it from house to house. It was customary, also, for the boys to recite a certain rhyme at each house they visited, and variants of this rhyme are cited and discussed. The writer ends by comparing the idea of Brigid's Girdle in folk tradition with the account in a mediaeval *Life* of the saint of how her girdle could cure all ailments to which it was applied.

NÓTAÍ AGUS TAGAIRTÍ

1. Mac Cana, Proinsias, *Celtic Mythology* (London, 1970), 34.
2. Ó Súilleabháin, Seán, Mason, T. H., 'St. Brigid's Crosses', *Journal of the Royal Society of Antiquaries of Ireland*, 75 (1945), 164.
3. Ó Danachair, Caoimhín, 'The Quarter Days in Irish Tradition', *Arv*, 15 (1969), 47-55; Buchanan, R. H., 'Calendar Customs', *Ulster Folklife*, 8 (1962) 15-34, 9 (1963), 61-79; Mac Neill, Máire, *The Festival of Lughnasa* (1962).
4. Cnuasach Bhéaloideas Éireann (CBÉ) i Roinn Bhéaloideas Éireann 904, 133-38.
5. O'Sullivan, John C., 'St. Brigid's Crosses', *Folk Life*, 11(1973), 60-81.
6. de Bhalraithe, Tomás, eag., *Cín Lae Amhlaoibh* (Baile Átha Cliath, 1970), 28; CBÉ S424, 232.
7. CBÉ 902, 32.
8. CBÉ 1010, 356-57.
9. CBÉ 65, 196; 303, 69; 902, 28, 32, 35, 69, 70, 81, 125; 969, 59; 970, 474; 1010, 356-57; 1135, 11; S1, 265; S6, 75; S7, 238; S21, 229; S30, 183; S61, 542; S71, 57, 253; S72, 247-48; Mooney, James, 'The Holiday Customs of Ireland', *Proceedings of the American Philosophical Society*, 26 (1889), 382.
10. CBÉ 236, 161.
11. CBÉ 1335, 592.
12. CBÉ 902, 4; S1, 268.
13. Mooney, J., op. cit., 382.
14. CBÉ 1135, 11.
15. CBÉ 902, 4-5.
16. Mooney, J., op. cit., 382.
17. CBÉ 65, 196; 303, 69; 902, 4, 28, 32, 35, 70, 81; 1010, 357; 1135, 11.
18. CBÉ 65, 196.
19. CBÉ 902, 4.
20. CBÉ 969, 59: Mooney, J., op. cit., 381.
21. *Ireland's Own*, 65 (2/3/1935), 274.
22. CBE 65, 196.
23. CBÉ 65, 196; 303, 69; 902, 5, 7, 8, 28, 35, 70, 82; 969, 59; 1010, 357; 1335, 592; S1, 265, 268; S6, 75; S7, 238; S21, 229; S61, 543; S71, 57, 253; *Ireland's Own*, 65 (2/3/1935), 274: Mooney, J., op. cit., 382-83.
24. CBÉ 902, 7, 8.
25. CBÉ 902, 28.
26. Mooney, J., op. cit., 382-83.
27. Danaher, Kevin, *The Year in Ireland* (Cork 1972), 35.
28. CBÉ 303, 69.
29. O'Fotharta, Domhnall, *Siamsa an Gheimhridh* (Baile Átha Cliath, 1892), 135.
30. *Ar Aghaidh*, Feabhra 1941, 6.
31. *Ibid.*
32. CBÉ 902, 4.
33. CBÉ 902, 9.
34. CBÉ 970, 474.
35. CBÉ 1135, 12.
36. CBÉ 39, 167-68.
37. CBÉ S30, 183.
38. CBÉ 902, 70.
39. CBÉ 902, 35.
40. CBÉ 101, 405.
41. CBÉ 969, 59.
42. CBÉ 902, 9.
43. CBÉ 902, 7, 28, 32, 48, 70, 82, 89; 969, 59; 1010, 357; 1135, 12.
44. CBÉ 902, 82.
45. CBÉ 902, 7; S1, 265, 270.

46. CBÉ 236, 161-62; 902, 32, 35-36, 90, 99, 103; 1335, 592: Mooney J., op. cit., 383.
47. CBE 902, 32.
48. Stokes, Whitley, (ed.), *Lives of the Saints from the Book of Lismore* (Oxford 1890), 44, 192; Colgan, John, (ed.), *Triadis Thaumaturgae*. . . (Louvain, 1647), 531.
49. Stokes, W., op. cit., 44, 192.

Printed by Mount Salus Press Ltd., Dublin 4.